American Diplomatic Relations
With the Middle East,
1784 - 1975:
A Survey

by

THOMAS A. BRYSON

The Scarecrow Press, Inc.

Metuchen, N.J.   1977

Library of Congress Cataloging in Publication Data

Bryson, Thomas A   1931-
    American diplomatic relations with the Middle East,
1784-1975.

    Bibliography: p.
    Includes index.
    1. Near East--Foreign relations--United States.
2. United States--Foreign relations--Near East.
I. Title.
DS63.2.U5B79   327.56'073   76-44344
ISBN 0-8108-0988-5

TABLE OF CONTENTS

iii

PREFACE

Since the conclusion of the fourth Arab-Israeli war, one has heard arguments on every hand that American foreign policy vis-à-vis the Middle East needs to be reexamined in terms of the American national interest. In order to abstract from this conflict some meaningful conclusions with a view to reassessment, it is first necessary to take a longer look at American diplomatic relations with the Middle East.

It has been said that the story of the American diplomatic experience in the Middle East is an almost forgotten saga frequently overlooked by historians. Yet the enunciation of the Monroe Doctrine and the Truman Doctrine are inextricably connected with the American diplomatic experience in the Middle East. Arab oil is now vital to American industrial needs. A number of historians who did address themselves to the story of American-Middle Eastern relations have claimed that the United States had no diplomatic policy governing its intercourse with Middle Eastern countries until the post-World War II era gave rise to the Truman Doctrine. But an examination of the diplomatic record discloses that a number of varied interest groups, namely, cultural, philanthropic, religious, and economic gained the support of American diplomats in the Middle East. These diplomats pursued the goals of these interest groups, and to that extent it can be said that the United States possessed a Middle Eastern policy. Accepting this premise, it should be noted that American diplomatists followed certain traditions or basic guiding principles in pursuit of their goals: non-involvement, the Open Door, freedom of the seas, and expatriation and naturalization. They also recognized that the right of self-determination of peoples related to the Ottoman minorities. Finally, American diplomats observed the concept of national interest in the conduct of their negotiations. For the purpose of this study I have chosen to use the definition of the term "national interest" that was given by Secretary of State Charles Evans Hughes in 1923. In an address given at Philadelphia on 30 November 1923, Hughes said:

v

Foreign policies are not built upon abstractions.
They are the result of practical conceptions of national interest arising from some immediate exigen-
cy or standing out vividly in historical perspective.
When long maintained, they express the hopes and
fears, the aims of <u>security and aggrandizement</u>,
which have become dominant in the national consciousness and thus transcend party divisions and
make negligible such opposition as may come from
particular groups. They inevitably control the machinery of international accord which works only
within the narrow field not closed by divergent national ambitions or as interest yields to apprehen-
sions or obtains compensation through give and take.
Statesmen who carry the burdens of empire do not
for a moment lose sight of imperial purpose and
requirements. 1*

As defined by Hughes the term "national interest" is
more specifically used to include activities and policies that
protect the national security and promote the prosperity of the
American people.   No American security interests were in
jeopardy in the Middle East until World War II and thereafter.
However, those Americans who engaged in economic activities
in the Middle East were involved in actions within the definition of this term, insofar as they promoted American economic aggrandizement.

But there were other interests that sought diplomatic
protection.   American Protestant missionaries and philanthropists became involved in activities related to many Middle Eastern peoples.   Moral considerations motivated their
activities.

At times there was conflict between the economic goals
of merchants, shippers, and investors and the aims of the
missionary-philanthropic element.   Whenever the interests of
the latter group clashed with those of the former, diplomatic
officials usually resolved the conflict in a manner consonant
with the national interest.

This study will illustrate several points.   First, that
U. S. diplomatic policy is based on the needs of interest
groups.   Second, that American diplomats pursued the goals

---

*Notes to the Preface and Chapters 1-19 are found beginning
on page 307.

of the various interest groups in a manner consonant with the
national interest and within the boundaries established by the
applicable guiding principles. Third, that when conflicts occurred between the interest groups, policy-makers resolved
them to serve the national interest.

This work will generally follow a chronological outline
and will be divided into three eras. During the period 1784-
1920 a number of American interests existed in the Middle
East, with the missionary-philanthropic interest being predominant. While economic interests did have the ear of the
State Department, it was the missionary lobby that asked for
and received the greatest attention from U.S. diplomats. The
period 1920 to 1945 witnessed an evolution in policy as economic elements vied with the missionary-philanthropist for a
greater voice in shaping American policy. In the decade of
the 1920s, U.S. diplomats employed the Open Door policy to
obtain for American oil men access to Middle Eastern petroleum resources, now considered vital to the national interest.
World War II was a watershed in American relations with the
Middle East, for national security interests emerged during
that conflict. In the period 1945-1975 questions of national
security conflicted with the emotional involvement on the side
of Israel in the nation's relations with the Middle East. Containment of Russia and preservation of access to the Middle
Eastern oil fields became uppermost in the minds of policy-
makers. But U.S. officials had handicaps. How could the
United States reconcile containment of Soviet Russia with the
necessity of associating with Britain and France, two powers
that had low esteem among the Arabs? How could the United
States retain the good will of the Arabs whom they tried to
protect from the Soviets and yet protect Israel, a state that
was anathema in the eyes of Arab nationalists?

Association with Israel and the former imperial states
of Europe was a liability during the 1940s and 1950s. In the
decade of the 1960s American policy-makers adopted a new
approach to the Middle East, one that employed a more even-
handed treatment of Arabs and Israelis. But the 1967 war
between Arabs and Israelis demonstrated that the Arab world
still viewed the United States as pro-Israel. The decade of
the 1970s made it apparent that the interminable Arab-Israeli
conflict might well involve the two super-powers. The year
1972 marked the beginning of détente between the United
States and the Soviet Union as the necessity of survival took
precedence over any other vital interests that the two nations
had in the Middle East or elsewhere.

But the decade of the 1970s also marked the beginning
of the energy crisis in the United States. How could the
American people continue to bear the emotional burden attached
to Israel and at the same time satisfy the growing energy
needs that demanded the importation of Middle Eastern oil?
The question requires an immediate answer. Hopefully, this
study will provide some understanding of the American problem and some means for finding a solution to a question that
vitally affects the future and economic well-being of the American people.

The writing of this book was originally prompted by
Professor John A. DeNovo's suggestion that there was no
single survey of the U. S. diplomatic experience in the Middle
East.[2] I am indebted to him for helping me to conceptualize
this work and for his critical reading of the manuscript. I
am also grateful to Dr. Harry N. Howard, one of the earliest diplomatic historians to address himself to the U. S. diplomatic role in the Middle East, for his reading and critical
commentary on this work. I am also obliged to Professor
Robert W. Sellen for his reading of the manuscript and for
his many suggestions and comments.

Thomas A. Bryson

West Georgia College
Carrollton

Chapter 1

MEDITERRANEAN TRADE AND
FRICTION WITH THE BARBARY STATES, 1784-1816

After the American War of Independence, the budding
American nation found that it faced a hostile world of large
empires that practiced mercantilism and did not agree with
the principle of free trade. American merchants and shippers then realized that they no longer enjoyed trading privileges taken for granted as an integral part of the British
Empire. James Madison wrote in 1785: "The Revolution
has robbed us of our trade with the West Indies, the only
one which yielded us a favorable balance, without reopening
any other channels to compensate for it."[1] Trade relations
with Spain and France left much to be desired. Foreign
commerce was necessary to the survival of the new republic.[2]
American merchants and shippers, faced with a depression of
growing magnitude, determined that new markets must be
found to stimulate a sagging economy and promote prosperity
so necessary to the well-being of the American people. They
decided that the Baltic, the Orient, and the Mediterranean
offered trading opportunities to make up for those lost with
Britain, France, and Spain. Consequently, the record of
American diplomacy in the Confederation era is almost wholly
commercial in nature as American diplomats aided the mer-
cantile community to acquire new markets.[3] Soon merchant
ships sailed between the U. S. and China and the northern
European ports. But access to the Mediterranean trade was
obstructed by the Barbary pirates of Morocco, Algiers, Tunis,
and Tripoli. Long accustomed to supporting bands of corsairs that raided the commerce of the Mediterranean, the
Barbary states were little disposed to overlook the rich Yankee merchantmen that plied the blue waters of the Mediterranean. No longer having the protection of British men-of-war,
these ships fell easy prey to the small, fast vessels of Barbary.

The merchant-shipping lobby pressured Congress to

1

negotiate treaties with the Barbary states to ensure freedom
of the seas for American commerce in the Mediterranean. [4]
The lobby recalled that prior to the Revolution the American
colonies had a considerable trade with Barbary which Thomas
Jefferson estimated at one-sixth of their export in wheat and
one-fourth of their export of dried and pickled fish, and which
occupied between eighty and one-hundred ships. [5]

*   *   *   *   *

The United States began its Middle Eastern diplomacy
in 1784 when Congress appointed in May a special commission, comprising Benjamin Franklin, John Adams, and Thomas
Jefferson, to negotiate treaties with the Barbary states.   In
the following year it appropriated $80,000 to facilitate the
treaty-making process.   Congress also authorized the commissioners to send delegates to Barbary, because it was not
deemed advisable for the commissioners to go in person.   In
the autumn of 1785, Adams, then minister to France, appointed Thomas Barclay to go to Morocco and John Lamb to
negotiate with Algiers. [6]

Barclay's mission to Morocco was fruitful.   He negotiated an agreement in July 1786.   The expense involved was
modest, amounting to only a few thousand dollars in presents
and no outlays for tribute.   It contained clauses that guaranteed neutral rights and it granted American commerce the
same rights as the most favored nation.   The Senate approved it promptly in July 1787, and passed a vote of thanks
to the Emperor of Morocco.   The conclusion of this treaty
was the commission's only success with the Barbary states,
because negotiations with Algiers and Tripoli were not successful. [7]

Algiers was the strongest of the Barbary states, and
the United States wished to negotiate a treaty as expeditiously
as possible.   John Lamb, the commission's agent, arrived
in Algiers in March 1786 and had three interviews with the
Dey, who expressed a desire to treat.   Instructed to first
ransom the captives, Lamb offered $4200.00, but the Dey
was asking $59,496.00.   Lamb could not meet his price.
The talks failed, and with them the negotiations for a treaty.
Negotiations with Tripoli were also barren of results.   A
lapse in negotiations occurred, and a new round of talks
would have to await the writing of a new constitution and the
adequate funds that would become available with the success
of Alexander Hamilton's financial plan.

Jefferson and Adams suggested radically different solutions to the Barbary question. Jefferson wanted to create a navy and use force to protect the country's commerce. Congress would appropriate no funds. Adams favored purchasing peace.[8] Both men were ultimately successful. In 1790 Jefferson, now Secretary of State, recommended to the new Congress a plan to build a navy to end the Barbary menace. In January 1791 the Senate committee on Mediterranean trade reported that a naval force was necessary to the protection of American trade, and when funds became available the government should found a navy to support the nation's commerce and diplomacy.[9] As Vice President, Adams continued to argue for peace by purchase, and in February 1791 the Senate agreed to set aside annual payments of $100,000 for peace and $40,000 for ransom.[10] Action on the diplomatic front soon followed.

David Humphreys received instructions in September 1793 to negotiate a treaty with Algiers. He proceeded to Gibraltar but got no further, for the Dey refused to see him and treaty talks did not go forward. Humphreys promptly sent dispatches to Secretary of State Jefferson, warning of the resumption of Algerine depredations on U.S. shipping and advising that the nation must use a naval force to convoy shipping and facilitate diplomacy.[11]

Jefferson's solution to the Barbary question, which called for a show of force, now received attention. Word of Algerine captures reached the United States in January 1794. War between France and England had commenced in 1793, and reports of British seizures of American ships soon followed. American public opinion called for force, and the shipping lobby pressured Congress to act.[12] Rising government revenues from Hamilton's financial plan provided the wherewithal for a navy. In March 1794 Congress authorized the procurement of six American ships for use against the Algerian pirates, thus founding the U.S. Navy.

The new Constitution and the recently created navy were in part the result of the American experience in the Middle East. The national interest required an expanded commerce, which in turn called for the negotiation of treaties. Commerce and diplomacy needed the support of the navy. Together, merchant-shipper, diplomat, and naval officer would enable the country to realize an expanded market place, a factor so necessary to the survival and development of the new republic.

Although making preparations for war with Barbary, the government was willing to treat. Secretary of State Edmund Randolph, who had replaced Jefferson, set up a fund of $800,000 to purchase peace and ransom captives from the Algerines. David Humphreys and Joseph Donaldson proceeded to Paris in April 1795. The former remained in the French capital, while the latter proceeded to Algiers where a treaty was approved on 28 November 1795. The treaty was costly, but liberal. For $642,500 and an annual payment of $21,600 the U.S. obtained a treaty and return of the captured sailors.[13] But there was a delay in raising the money, and the Dey threatened to repudiate the agreement. Timothy Pickering, Secretary of State since 10 December 1795, was a strong believer in the expansion of American commerce. He represented the commercial aristocracy of New England and was determined to make a treaty; he pressured Humphreys to proceed.[14] Humphreys sent Joel Barlow to assist Donaldson with the talks. Barlow successfully concluded negotiations in January 1797.[15] The total cost amounted to nearly one million dollars to meet the Dey's additional demands.

Tripoli was the third Barbary state to make a treaty with the United States. Joel Barlow, the newly appointed consul general at Algiers obtained the treaty with Tripoli on 4 November 1796 for a cost of $56,000. It guaranteed peace, required no tribute, contained a most favored nation clause, but failed to recognize the principle of exterritoriality.[16] Barlow, one of the "Connecticut wits," was not content. He employed Joseph S. Famin, a French merchant and chargé d'affaires for the United States in Tunis, to carry on the talks. Famin concluded the treaty with Tunis in August 1797 at a cost of $107,000. The Senate required certain revisions before finally approving in 1799.[17]

At the end of the century, a summary of the Federalist solution to the Barbary question indicates assets and liabilities. Peace was expensive, but in 1799 trade in the Mediterranean increased as eighty American ships passed the Straits of Gibraltar. Peace with Barbary was uncertain, and the pirates cast longing gazes on the Yankee ships, eagerly awaiting an opportunity to resume their forays.

It was not unexpected that war with Tripoli came in 1801, marking the first declaration of war by the American Republic. Newly elected President Thomas Jefferson's decision to use force had been anticipated by both Secretary of

State Pickering and William Eaton, the American consul at
Tunis.   Anxious to preserve and extend American commerce,
Pickering and Eaton firmly believed that force was necessary
to protect the nation's national interests in the Mediterranean.[18]   So Jefferson's decision to employ American naval
power was not unexpected.   In February 1801 the Pasha repudiated the American-Tripolitan treaty of 1797 and demanded
payment of $250,000 and an annual tribute of $20,000 as an
alternative to war.[19]   Anticipating that hostilities would be
resumed, the American government dispatched a squadron of
four ships to the Mediterranean.

   Commodore Richard Dale commanded the first American naval force in the Mediterranean.   He and the sailor-
diplomats who succeeded him were to write some of the
brightest pages of American diplomatic history with the Middle East.   Combining force with persuasion, these naval officers obtained agreements favorable to the American national interest.   They not only protected American commerce,
but extended American power to the Mediterranean world and
opened the door to the East.   Dale arrived off Tripoli on 24
July 1801.   Although he engaged in offensive operations, Dale
lacked the requisite force and necessary instructions to bring
about a solution.   He departed for continental shores in
March 1802.[20]

   Commodore Richard V. Morris arrived at Gibraltar in
May 1802 with the relieving squadron.   He commenced the
blockade of Tripoli in June, but problems with Morocco and
Tunis dictated that he use the ships of his command to preserve peace.   Difficulties were settled and Morris proceeded
to Algiers in March.   Failing to settle the dispute with the
Dey, Morris finally returned his force to Tripoli in May
1803, but was unable to negotiate a settlement.   He departed
in September.[21]

   Where Morris proved dilatory, Commodore Edward
Preble, Morris' successor, proved to be aggressive.   Preble
not only blockaded Tripoli, but made a show of force before
Tangier to preserve peace with Morocco.   It was off the
shores of Tripoli that Preble's force founded some of the
traditions still revered by American Naval and Marine Corps
personnel.   To assist, the American minister at Paris, Robert R. Livingston, persuaded the French to use their good
offices on behalf of the United States, and between August
and September Preble alternated attacks with talks in hopes
of bringing the war to an end.   His strategy was to no avail,

and on 10 September Preble turned over his command to
Commodore Samuel Barron.[22]

Barron was not as effective as his predecessor but he
brought with him William Eaton, the former American consul
at Tunis who had been authorized to undertake an overland
expedition against Tripoli. Eaton mounted his expedition and
reached Tripoli, following a long trek across desert waste-
land.[23] Threatened by Eaton's land force from behind and a
naval force before, the Pasha decided to negotiate with Barron. Plagued with ill health, Barron turned over command
to Commodore John Rodgers who immediately instituted negotiations aboard his flagship Constitution. Humiliated, the
Pasha agreed to make a treaty that was satisfactory to the
United States. Signed on 4 June 1805, it provided for the
restoration of peace, ransom and release for the prisoners,
the right to exchange consuls, and a most favored nation
clause.[24]

Commodore Rodgers moved his squadron to Tunis, determined to maintain peace with the Bey, who had threatened
war. Peace with Tripoli and the presence of an augmented
naval force in the Mediterranean caused Rodgers to take a
hard line. He offered the Bey the alternatives of peace or
war. The Bey ultimately agreed on 15 August to maintain
peace in accordance with the treaty of 1797.[25]

His mission successfully concluded, Rodgers returned
home in late 1806 with all but three of his ships. No relieving squadron arrived, for strained relations between the
United States and Britain required the use of all American
warships in home waters. American commerce in the Mediterranean between 1807 and 1815 was unguarded, and Yankee
ships were on their own.[26] The pirates took the opportunity
to renew their illicit practices against American shipping,
with Algiers and Tunis giving the most trouble. The War of
1812 with Britain prevented the dispatch of American war
ships to the Mediterranean, but the conclusion of peace at
Ghent in 1814 provided the opportunity to settle differences
with Algiers, the most obstinate of the Barbary states, and
later with Tunis and Tripoli.

In March 1815 the United States declared war on Algiers for the protection of American economic interests in the
Middle East. Two squadrons, one under Commodore Stephen
Decatur, and the other under Commodore William Bainbridge,
were fitted out with orders to proceed to the Mediterranean,

with William Shaler, consul general to the Barbary states,
along, to negotiate a treaty with Algiers. Decatur sailed
first and on reaching the Mediterranean, his force promptly
captured two Algerine ships. Decatur began talks and offered the Dey peace or war. The Algerines rejected the
draft treaty. Aware of the approach of an Algerine squadron,
Decatur insisted on acceptance, else he would destroy the
ships. The treaty negotiated by Shaler and Decatur was lib-
eral and provided peace, the cessation of tribute, exchange
of prisoners without ransom, recognition of the principle of
exterritoriality, acceptance of the most favored nation clause,
and indemnification for destruction of American property.
Negotiated at the mouth of the cannon, this treaty was the
envy of all Europe. 27

At the conclusion of peace with Algiers, Decatur
sailed to Tunis. He demanded settlement in the amount of
$46,000 to rectify Tunisian treaty violations resulting from
the handing over to Britain of two prizes of war taken by an
American ship. The Bey delayed, but Decatur insisted on
and obtained an agreement. Decatur then moved his force to
Tripoli, arriving on 5 August 1816. Here the British had also been permitted to retake two American prize ships. Decatur demanded payment of $30,000, but settled for $25,000.
Bainbridge anchored as Decatur was winding up activities
with Barbary, and in company the two sailed for home waters
in October 1816, leaving four warships in the Mediterranean
to protect American economic interests. The Barbary question was settled to American satisfaction. 28

*   *   *   *   *

To eliminate the Barbary menace from the Mediterranean in order that American merchant ships might enjoy
freedom of the seas to expand American commerce, the
United States had required the use of a naval force to support a diplomacy aimed at obtaining the treaties necessary
for the protection of an augmented trade. The employment
of naval power was a requisite adjunct to the diplomatic intercourse needed to attain desirable economic ends that were
in the national interest.

Coming as it did shortly after the conclusion of the
War of 1812 with Britain, the solution of the Barbary problem greatly enhanced the American reputation in Europe and
increased public confidence in the American government.
Patriotism gave way to a spirit of nationalism.

While a strong spirit of nationalism pervaded American society in 1815, there was also a strong feeling of republicanism sweeping the land.   The egalitarian doctrines so well enunciated in the Declaration of Independence and in the Constitution of 1787 were becoming a reality.   The aristocratic trappings of the coast were giving way to the tide of democracy that was emanating from the frontier.   With the establishment of manhood suffrage, men soon exuded an individualism that expressed itself in a desire to achieve a better way of life.

Americans turned from the pursuit of war to the business of peace, to the task of founding a territorial empire on the American continent, and to the expansion of the American market place abroad.   In the latter activity free men engaged in free trade in a crusading spirit to spread ideas of republicanism in the farther reaches of the Mediterranean.

An opportunity in the Middle East was soon forthcoming that would enable Americans to express their republican zeal.   Revolution broke out in Greece in 1821 as Greeks attempted to establish their independence from the Ottoman Empire.   The Greek Revolution threatened to involve the United States and the American response contributed to the issuance of an important state paper that enunciated a cardinal principle of American foreign policy.

Chapter 2

GREEK REVOLUTION AND THE APPLICATION OF THE
MONROE DOCTRINE TO THE MIDDLE EAST, 1821-28

The 1821 outbreak of revolution in Greece wherein
Greeks, emulating the American Revolution to gain freedom
from the Ottoman Empire, aroused American public opinion.
To the American, not long removed from the War of Independence and its association with the republican spirit of '76,
the ancient Athenians were progenitors of republicanism, and
their 19th-century Greek progeny should have U.S. support.
The American admiration for the classical Greek culture that
developed democratic ideas and laid the basis for western
culture manifested itself in the spirit of philhellenism that
swept America in the 1820s.   Republicanism and philhellenism caused many Americans to support the extension of aid
to the embattled Greeks.   Aware of American sentiment the
Greeks appealed to republicans across the sea for assistance.
This appeal led to debate in the cabinet and the halls of Congress, which caused the United States to define its policy toward the subject minorities of the Ottoman Empire and to
make an important foreign policy statement that became a
basic guiding principle of American diplomacy.

*   *   *   *   *

At the time of the Greek Revolution the United States
had various interests in the Middle East that included commercial operations, missionary activities, and the presence
of a naval force.[1]   The Turkish port of Smyrna was the
entrepôt of American commerce with the Middle East.   American trade in this port was larger than that of any other
country, with the exception of Britain.[2]   American merchants, motivated by considerations of self-interest, feared
that American support of the Greeks would endanger American property in Smyrna and jeopardize the successful negoti-

9

ation of a commercial treaty between Turkey and the United
States.[3] The work of the American missionaries was an important factor in arousing American public sentiment for the
cause of the Sultan's Greek Christian subjects.[4] While the
American naval squadron in the Mediterranean maintained a
discreet neutrality in the Greek revolt, it can be readily understood that American commercial and missionary interests
were in conflict. In spite of a growing public opinion favorable to the Greeks, the U.S. government gave priority to the
commercial interests, because their activities were of an
economic nature and consonant with the American national interest.

In May 1821 the Greek revolutionary government believed that aid might be forthcoming from the U.S. Accordingly, the Senate at Calamata appealed to the "fellow-citizens
of Penn, of Washington, and of Franklin" to abet the cause
of the Greeks.[5] Mathew Carey, the Irish immigrant and editor, and Edward Everett, professor of Greek at Harvard and
editor of the North American Review, were pro-Greek and
gave considerable effort to spread word of the plea.[6]

The Greek entreaty stimulated the diffusion of philhel-
lenism in America. Taking its roots in the city of Albany,
N.Y., in 1822, it surfaced in New York, Philadelphia, and
Boston, extended to the South where it appeared in Virginia,
South Carolina, and Georgia, and spread west to Cincinnati.
University and college students espoused the Greek cause at
Yale, Columbia, Andover Theological Seminary, Dickinson
College, Hampden-Sydney, Transylvania, and the University
of Georgia. "Greek balls" aroused the terpsichorean spirit
and the virtue of charity among dancers in Richmond,
Charleston, and Savannah who readily contributed to the
Greeks.[7]

The growth of philhellenic sentiment accompanied a na-
tionwide campaign to raise funds for the Greeks and to win
official support for their endeavor. In December 1822 a congressman from Massachusetts presented a memorial to the
House of Representatives on behalf of the Greeks. Sentiment
in the House opposed involvement and the memorial was allowed to lie on the table.[8]

The rise of public opinion sympathetic to the Greeks
compelled the U.S. government to formulate a policy with respect to the minorities in the Ottoman Empire. Although
Americans might make expressions of sympathy, send their

dollars to support the revolution, and even volunteer to aid that effort, the government was bound by the traditional policy of non-involvement in the affairs of foreign powers.[9] The United States had long adhered to the tradition of non-intervention in the affairs of the European Powers. It was the guiding hand of John Quincy Adams, President James Monroe's Secretary of State, that caused the United States to observe strictly the policy of non-interference in the affairs of the Turkish Empire, a policy precedent the nation would follow for more than a century in its dealings with Middle Eastern minorities. Influenced by Adams, Monroe's annual message to Congress in December 1822 expressed sympathy with the Greeks but did not promise aid.[10]

There the matter rested until February 1823 when Andreas Luriottis, a representative of the Greek revolutionary government, submitted to the American minister in London a request for American recognition of the provisional government, the formation of an alliance, and for the extension of aid to the Greeks.[11] On 15 August Monroe consulted with his advisers on the Greek question. William H. Crawford, Secretary of the Treasury, and John C. Calhoun, Secretary of War, favored extending recognition and aid to the Greeks. Calhoun was a rabid philhellene and his Turkophobe sentiments expressed the feelings of many Americans. John Quincy Adams, then trying to negotiate a treaty with the Turks, was not inclined to violate the principle of non-intervention. The cabinet decided that Adams would answer the Greek plea.[12]

On 18 August Adams dispatched his reply to Richard Rush, the American minister in London, saying that the President and people of the United States sympathize with the cause of freedom. Although empathetic with the Greek struggle, Adams continued, the United States was bound by the tradition of non-interference and could not abandon its position of neutrality.[13]

This was an important American statement on the Greek request for recognition, assistance, and an alliance, but when the time came to consider the 1823 presidential message to Congress, a further statement was desirable. On 21 November President Monroe issued a call for a cabinet meeting at which he intended to consider the Greek matter. He had already consulted Thomas Jefferson and James Madison. While Jefferson said nothing on the matter, Madison said the U.S. should invite the British to make a joint

declaration on behalf of the Greeks.[14] Albert Gallatin, minister to France, suggested the dispatch of a naval force to
help the Greeks.[15] When the cabinet met, Adams learned
that the first draft of the message contained an acknowledg-
ment of the Greeks as an independent country, and a suggestion that Congress appropriate funds to send a minister to
Greece. Adams said this line was not acceptable. He
wished to make a strong statement in the message against
European interference in the affairs of South America and to
assert non-interference on the U.S. part in the affairs of
Europe. Among certain circles in the cabinet this latter
statement applied to the Greeks and was not popular. Calhoun and Crawford still favored the use of force. But Adams'
view prevailed.[16]

     President Monroe's message to Congress on 2 Decem-
ber 1823 enunciated the Monroe Doctrine. A part of that
doctrine related to the Greek question and its application to
European affairs. Monroe observed that American citizens

>   cherish sentiments ... in favor of the liberty and
>   happiness of their fellowmen on that side of the At-
>   lantic. In the wars of the European powers in mat-
>   ters relating to themselves we have never taken any
>   part, nor does it comport with our policy to do so.
>   Our policy in regard to Europe which was
>   adopted at an early stage of the wars which
>   have so long agitated that quarter of the globe,
>   nevertheless remains the same, which is, not to
>   interfere in the internal concerns of any of its
>   powers....[17]

     The policy declared so clearly by Adams and Monroe
did not deter the vocal element of the American populace that
still supported the Greeks. The philhellenic movement continued to grow under the leadership of such Americans as
Nicholas Biddle, Governor DeWitt Clinton, General William
Henry Harrison, and of course Mathew Carey, and Edward
Everett. The wave of philhellenism appears to have reached
its height in 1824, and it was this sentiment that caused Daniel Webster, the orator from Massachusetts, to champion the
Greek struggle in Congress.[18] Influenced by Everett,[19] Webster introduced in the House of Representatives on 8 December 1823 a resolution calling for the appointment of an American agent or commissioner to Greece.[20] The ensuing debate
on the Webster resolution is important, for it helped to clar-
ify American policy with respect to the Christian minorities

of the Ottoman Empire and to focus attention on the conflict
between American economic and missionary-relief-cultural interests.   The debate demonstrated the conflict of interests
and the thought processes that determined the ultimate resolution of the conflict in the American national interest.

Webster's oration on behalf of the Greeks and in support of his resolution precipitated the debate on the Greek
question on 19 January 1824.   He disclaimed any concern
with the ancient Greek heritage but addressed himself to the
Greeks of the modern era whose revolution was in the cause
of freedom and Christianity.   He did not suggest that the
United States should become directly involved, but asserted
that the nation should exert its moral influence for the cause
of liberty, nationality, and freedom.[21]   Henry Clay spoke in
support of Webster's measure.   Since the American people
were sympathetic with the Greeks and supported the cause of
freedom and republicanism, he questioned whether the government could isolate itself from that public sentiment and do
nothing for the Greeks.[22]

But Webster's resolution did not pass, because the op-
position, led by men like John Randolph of Virginia and Joel
Poinsett of South Carolina, persuaded their colleagues in the
House that the resolution was not in the national interest and
should be set aside without a formal vote.   Randolph and
Poinsett received the support of Timothy Fuller of Massachusetts, Silas Wood of New York, Ichabod Bartlett of New
Hampshire, Alfred Cuthbert and George Cary of Georgia,
Christopher Rankin of Mississippi, and Samuel Breck of Pennsylvania.   In general these men argued that sending an agent
to Greece would depart from the American tradition of non-
involvement.   It would jeopardize American economic interests in the Ottoman Empire.   It could result in war, and it
might also set a precedent leading to incursion by a European
power into the affairs of a small nation in the Western Hemisphere.   At all events, policy in this instance must be separated from the will of the American public.[23]

More specifically, the opposition's argument was
couched in terms to protect the American national interest.
John Randolph of Roanoke argued that he and his fellow members of the House of Representatives were "delegated to this
house to guard the interests of the People of the United
States, not to guard the interests of other people."[24]   Wood
of New York pointed out that involvement in the Greek question risked complications with the Ottoman Empire and Holy

Alliance that might lead to war. Wood also observed that
recognition of the Greek revolutionary government violated the
American principle of recognition, because the Greeks had
not as yet established themselves as the de facto government.[25] Poinsett, a member of the House Committee on
Foreign Relations, asserted that the Sultan was perfectly capable of endangering American lives and property at Smyrna,
and in so doing, he could imperil the full range of American
interests in the Middle East. Involvement might produce hostilities with the Sultan, with whom the United States was trying to establish treaty relations.[26] Congressman Breck of
Pennsylvania requested the Secretary of the Treasury to furnish a statement of the extent of American trade in the Middle East. A report of American commercial operations in
Smyrna showed that the trade was substantial, amounting to
$2,300,000 for 1820-1822, with duties collected in excess of
$170,000. During 1823 the trade had exceeded $1.2 million.
The Smyrna trade was too important to be overlooked, and
congressmen, representing the interests of commercial men
like Boston merchant-prince Thomas H. Perkins and his associates, won the day. On 26 January the Webster motion
was indefinitely postponed.[27]

There was much criticism leveled at Webster on State
Street in Boston, where merchants dealt in Turkish figs, opium, and other products that came from the port of Smyrna
in American bottoms. These commercial men, led by Perkins, had refused to associate with the Boston Committee on
Greek Relief, for they believed that it was not in America's
interests to do so. While they believed in Greek independence, they felt Greeks should acquire freedom by their own
efforts.[28]

Responsible for the opposition to Webster's resolution
was John Quincy Adams, who supplied members of the House
many of the arguments opposing Webster's measure. Adams
saw the situation clearly. He realized that American intervention in the Greek question might supply the precedent for
the Holy Alliance to interfere in South America where Spain
hoped to regain her colonies. With Monroe's Doctrine having
only just been enunciated the previous December, Adams was
convinced that American non-intervention in European affairs
would set a clear precedent for Europe to abstain from involvement in the American hemisphere.[29]

Monroe had clearly stated the policy of non-intervention in the Greek question, and not even an 1827 congres-

sional resolution to appropriate $50,000 for the relief of
distressed Greeks could gain support. [30]   But the revolution
did have a strong appeal to Americans who had collected
funds to relieve the Greeks, thus inaugurating a philanthropic
venture that served as a prototype for later relief efforts.
Although in late 1826 Mathew Carey commenced the fund-
raising campaign to provide assistance to the Greeks, a New
York committee became the clearing house for contributions.
In 1827 Americans contributed in excess of $100,000, and it
required five merchant ships to carry the valuable cargoes
to Greece.   In the following year about $60,000 was real-
ized, requiring additional ships to dispatch the supplies to
hungry Greeks.   American relief was critical in late 1827,
for it provided the aid that enabled the Greeks to continue
until the destruction of the Turkish fleet at Navarino in October 1827 decided the issue. [31]

          In addition to making financial contributions, Ameri-
cans also volunteered for service with the revolutionaries.
This too was precedent-setting, for in later years Americans
would give their blood and treasure to assist Armenians,
Cretans, Bulgarians, and Jews to achieve the goal of independence. [32]

                    *   *   *   *   *

          The Greek Revolution and the American response to
it is important, because it gave the American government and
people an opportunity to react in ways that had a vital bearing on other American responses to later efforts of subject
peoples in the Ottoman Empire to achieve independence.   On
the one hand, the United States established its policy of non-
interference toward minorities in the Ottoman Empire, and
not once during the remainder of that empire's existence did
the United States sign a treaty that would guarantee the rights
of subject peoples.   While it did on occasion use its good offices, it did not attempt to use its official influence to alter
relations between subject peoples and the Sultan.   The government even refused to give material aid.   On the other
hand, American citizens, persuaded by reasons of morality,
did by their contributions to the Greeks establish precedents
for later fund-raising efforts on behalf of the Armenians and
Jews.   And so a two-fold response of public non-interference
and private largesse became the norm for the American reaction to the cause of Middle Eastern peoples to win self-
determination. [33]

So tradition-bound was the Department of State, that it delayed recognition of Greece until 1833, because it was in the American national interest to do so. The United States was negotiating with the Sublime Porte during the 1820s to establish relations with the Ottoman Empire. A treaty was needed to guarantee the growing trade in the empire. Early recognition of the Greeks would have jeopardized American property and the diplomatic intercourse. The national interest determined that recognition would come only when it was propitious. That time arrived after the negotiation of the Turkish treaty. [34]

Chapter 3

EARLY RELATIONS WITH THE OTTOMAN EMPIRE TO 1850

When in 1784 the Confederation Congress appointed
John Adams, Benjamin Franklin, and Thomas Jefferson to a
treaty commission, the Ottoman Empire was one of the lands
with which they were directed to seek treaty relations to expand American commerce. At that time the Ottoman Empire
was much larger and more populous than the United States,
for it included Anatolia, the present homeland of Turkey, Ru-
mania, Bulgaria, Albania, Yugoslavia, Greece, Syria, Egypt,
Arabia, and the Barbary states of Algiers, Tunis, and Tripoli. The United States considered the initiation of treaty negotiations with Turkey in 1786, but discontinued them because
the Confederation did not have sufficient funds to make a
treaty. Growing commercial relations with Turkey demanded
the negotiation of a treaty, but it required almost half a century to realize this goal.

*   *   *   *   *

Although American relations with Turkey would eventually encompass the activities of merchants, missionaries,
mechanics, and mariners, trade was the first link between
the United States and the Sultan.[1]   Between 1783 and 1820
commerce with Turkey increased, in spite of the Barbary ob-
stacle and the War of 1812 with Britain.[2]   But the absence
of a treaty with Turkey hurt commerce, and American ships
depended on the protection of the British consul. Although
they enjoyed the privileges of the Levant Company, holder of
a monopoly of British trade in the Middle East, Americans
paid the tariff that applied to British goods plus a special
protection fee to the British consul.[3]

Rufus King, American minister to England, initiated
efforts to obtain a treaty with Turkey, for he influenced

17

President John Adams to nominate William Smith on 8 February 1799 as diplomatic agent to the Sublime Porte, with orders to negotiate a treaty. The wars of the French Revolution and Napoleon caused complications that resulted in the abandonment of the mission. [4]

It is unfortunate that Smith did not carry out his mission, for the Sultan was disposed to treat with a representative from the United States. Captain William Bainbridge, U.S. Navy, had taken his frigate George Washington to Algiers in 1800 with the annual tribute. The Dey had then directed him to carry presents to the Sultan, to whom the Dey was liege man. While in Constantinople, Bainbridge learned from a Turkish official of the Sultan's willingness to negotiate. He so informed the Secretary of the Navy, who advised the President. [5]

The U.S. government made numerous efforts between 1802 and 1828 to strengthen commercial ties with Turkey and to negotiate a treaty. No treaty was forthcoming, for the efforts of William Stewart, David Offley, Luther Bradish, George B. English, and Commodore Rodgers were frustrated by events stemming from the Greek Revolution, by the British, or by chance. [6]

In 1829 President Andrew Jackson, anxious to expand American commerce, appointed Captain James Biddle of the Navy, David Offley and Charles Rhind, merchants, to negotiate a treaty. The Jacksonians, having opened trade with the West Indies and dispatched agents to the Far East to negotiate commercial treaties, wanted to conclude a treaty with Turkey. [7] Rhind sailed from New York on 14 September 1829 and joined Biddle and Offley at Port Mahon. The three commissioners proceeded to Smyrna. Rhind then went on alone to Constantinople where on 14 May he signed a treaty. The instrument contained the most favored nation clause, a provision for exterritoriality, and a secret article that required the American minister to help the Turks make ship-building agreements in the United States and to acquire ship timber. Biddle and Offley arrived at the capital and found the treaty completed and signed. [8] Jackson submitted the treaty to the Senate on 2 February 1831. It approved the treaty with the exception of the secret article. This it rejected because it violated the policy of neutrality and the concept of non-involvement. President Jackson appointed Commodore David Porter to be the American diplomatic representative to the Porte and he selected William Brown Hodgson, a career

officer with the State Department, to return the treaty to
Turkey. [9]

Hodgson and Porter, traveling in the American warship John Adams, arrived at Constantinople in August 1831.
After the usual delay of several months and the distribution
of presents, Porter and Hodgson made the exchange of ratification on 5 October 1831. [10]

Commodore Porter was a controversial diplomat. He
soon picked a quarrel with Hodgson, who had taken the ratified treaty to Washington and then returned to serve as the
Commodore's dragoman. [11] Porter avoided performing some
of the duties normally expected of a diplomat. For example,
he did not visit Syria, Palestine, or Egypt--areas in his
jurisdiction--during his twelve years at Constantinople. At
the Commodore's death in 1843, his nephew John P. Brown
took over the legation until Dabney S. Carr arrived in 1844.
Brown remained as dragoman, and during Carr's temporary
absence in 1845, the former approached British ambassador
Sir Stratford Canning with a view to stopping British vessels
from engaging in the slave trade in the Black Sea. [12] This
was a success for the diplomat, and it came at a time when
the United States found the slavery question onerous.

During the 1850s, with slavery threatening to rend the
republic, American diplomats resorted to a diplomatic strate-
gem to distract the attention of the American public from the
slavery question. An episode occurred in Turkey that needs
to be mentioned, for it shows the extent to which diplomats
would go to heal the sectional breach. Americans applauded
the republicans in the European revolution of 1848, and the
Hungarian rebels particularly appealed to Americans. With
the defeat of the Hungarian revolutionaries, rebel leader
Louis Kossuth and his associates, fled to Turkey where Austria and Russia demanded that the Sultan deliver the refugees. John P. Brown, then in charge of the American legation, interceded on behalf of the rebels, urging the Turks to
permit them sanctuary. Secretary of State Daniel Webster
wrote a stinging note of rebuke to Chevalier Hulsemann, the
Austrian chargé, in reply to the latter's protest that the
U.S. was interfering in the affairs of Austria. This communication appealed to the pride of nationhood among the divided American people whose attention was temporarily distracted from the worrisome question of slavery. [13]

At length, Senator Foote of Mississippi introduced in

February 1851 a resolution calling on the President to bring
Kossuth and his fellow rebels to America. With popular
sentiment growing, the Mississippi arrived at Constantinople
on 30 August and on 7 September departed with the rebels.
The Kossuth affair, which culminated in the revolutionary's
triumphal progress through the United States, served as a
temporary respite from the black cloud of sectionalism.

Two years later in 1853, another episode occurred
that also distracted Americans from their growing sectional
crisis.   Martin Koszta, a Hungarian revolutionary, had fled
to the United States, declared his intention of becoming an
American citizen, and then returned to the Levant. He was
subsequently seized on 21 June 1853 at Smyrna, and placed
on board an Austrian brig. American consul Edward S. Offley intervened when Koszta claimed protection.   Ultimately,
Commander Duncan N. Ingraham of the American warship
St. Louis took Koszta into custody, and he eventually reached
America in October.   Austrian Chargé Hulsemann lodged a
protest with William L. Marcy, the new Secretary of State.
Marcy, hoping to boost the sagging reputation of Franklin
Pierce's administration, sent a strong note of protest to
Hulsemann. [14]

The Koszta affair was clearly an example of domestic
politics influencing U.S. Middle Eastern policy--a novel situation indeed.   Generally, U.S. policy resulted from the initiative of Americans outside the government.   Mechanics,
merchants, missionaries, and mariners all claimed protection from American diplomats.

One of the early Americans who sought and acquired
diplomatic aid was Henry Eckford, an American shipbuilder
who had made a fortune building warships in the War of
1812.   Eckford proceeded to Constantinople, and there sold a
ship of his own design and construction to the Sultan for the
sum of $150,000.   He then remained to direct the construc-
tion of other Turkish vessels, an activity that was "entirely
a private and individual enterprise ... in which this [U.S.]
Government has no concern whatever...."[15]   Eckford enjoyed good repute in Turkey, and Commodore Porter who
made every effort to facilitate a smooth working relationship,
reported that American influence in Turkey was supreme because of the activities of Eckford.   This is not to say that
the United States used this influence to pursue political objectives.   Nevertheless, Eckford's efforts and those of his
successor resulted in the primacy of American prestige at
the Porte in the 1830s. [16]

But a most important link between the United States
and the Ottoman Empire was that based on commerce.   It
was the growth of American trade with Turkey that dictated
the negotiation of the treaty.   The Jacksonian hope to achieve
an expanded Middle Eastern commerce via the treaty of 1830
was not fulfilled.   The export trade that had been developed
with the Turks was lost by default to the British and French
and the "Tariff of Abominations" had levied an exorbitant rate
on raw wool, which made up the bulk of return cargoes to
the United States.[17]   In the twenty years following the negotiation of the treaty, there was a slow increase in exports to
Turkey, but mostly the trade fluctuated.   Imports also followed a cyclical pattern.   It was only after 1850 that a no-
ticeable increase in total trade occurred.   Even so, American commerce with the Ottoman Empire continued to be based
on the Smyrna trade.[18]   One might well expect that American trade would have increased as American missionaries expanded their activities in the years before mid-century.   Although the missionaries served as instruments of innovation
to introduce American products to the Middle Eastern peoples,
they were not agents of rank commercial imperialism.[19]
While European nations subsidized their missionaries as
agents of empire, American missionaries were on their own
and they frequently resorted to pressure on American diplomats to obtain protection.[20]

With these preliminary remarks on the relationship
between the missionary and merchant, it now becomes necessary to discuss in greater detail the role of the American
missionary in the Middle East in the years before mid-century.[21]   In the generation after the negotiation of the Turco-
American treaty in 1830, the American Board of Commissioners for Foreign Missions sent out some sixty missionaries to the Middle East.   They spread from Greece to Persia and from Constantinople to Syria-Palestine.   Finding the
Muslim population impervious to fervent missionary efforts,
the American Protestants turned their attention to the conver-
sion of Eastern Christians.   Soon the missionaries were not
only preaching to save souls, but they were also engaged in
the printing of books and the teaching of the young in order
to bring progress and modernity to the benighted people of
the Middle East.

The missionaries stimulated cultural nationalism among
the Armenians and the Arabs of Syria.   This cultural nationalism later led to political nationalism that resulted in the
efforts of the subject peoples of the Ottoman Empire to

achieve self-determination. But the missionaries did not engage in activities of a political nature to encourage the minorities to revolt. [22]

But what can be said of the relationship between the
Protestant missionary, the American diplomat, and the U.S.
Mediterranean squadron. Did the diplomat and the naval officer give the missionary the protection that had been given
to the American merchant and mariner? The answer to this
question requires a little explanation. In the early years,
American missionaries frequently relied on British diplomatic protection. [23] Commodore Porter was somewhat indiffer-
ent toward the missionaries. Although during the decade of
the 1830s he took steps to ensure that the American fleet
made frequent calls at Syrian ports to show the flag for the
protection of missionaries, he was sometimes hesitant to
take those steps necessary to safeguard their interests.
Shortly before his death in 1843, Porter was reprimanded by
Secretary of State Daniel Webster for not properly defending
the missionaries. [24] This move demonstrated the growing
strength of the missionary lobby in Washington, and shortly
thereafter in 1850 several missionaries were serving in the
Middle East in a consular capacity. [25] By mid-century missionary influence waxed, but trade remained important to
policy-makers. It now remains to examine American efforts
to expand commerce with Egypt in the 1830s when Mehemet
Ali, the Sultan's viceroy, exhibited an interest in commercial relations with the U.S.

In a long report in 1833, John Gliddon, the American
diplomatic agent at Alexandria, advised that there was little
chance of real commercial intercourse with Egypt since
American exports resembled those of Egypt.[26] However,
President Jackson's Department of State was not satisfied
with trade expansion. In early 1833 Commodore Daniel T.
Patterson of the American naval squadron advised the Secre-
tary of State that Mehemet Ali was now independent of the
Turkish Sultan and wanted a commercial treaty with the
United States. [27] Aware that William Brown Hodgson and
Commodore Porter were feuding, Secretary of State Louis
McLane advised Hodgson that he was withdrawn from the le-
gation at Constantinople and was to proceed with all haste to
Egypt as a "confidential agent." There he was to determine
if Mehemet Ali was free to make commercial treaties. [28]

Having a knowledge of Middle Eastern languages and
an awareness of political developments in that region, Hodg-

son readily accepted the appointment.[29] His reports disclosed that Mehemet Ali had captured Syria from the Sultan
and was still a potent political figure. He advised that the
Egyptian leader was de facto independent and de nomine subject to the Sublime Porte, paying no assessed tribute, and
yet making large voluntary presents. His reports devoted
considerable space to economic development in Egypt, suggesting that there was the possibility for the development of
a modest commerce between the two countries. His report
also contained a lengthy description of the esoteric diplomatic usage in the Middle East and an account of the British
consular organization in Alexandria. He noted that Mehemet
Ali had as yet made no commercial treaties. He recommended that the United States appoint a consul general at
Cairo to protect American interests. Hodgson departed
Egypt, arriving in the United States in early 1835.[30]

No American treaty with Egypt was forthcoming, and
American commerce with Egypt did not increase. The most
that can be said of Hodgson's mission was that the Department of State acquired a vast amount of information about
diplomatic, political, and commercial matters in the Middle
East. As a young nation, the U.S. vitally needed such information upon which to base its foreign policy.[31]

We must now turn our attention to American relations
with the Barbary states, three of which--Tripoli, Tunis, and
Algiers--were still fiefs of the Sultan. Algiers was the most
important, and its Dey was elected, subject to the approval
of the Sultan. Shortly after the conclusion of the treating
ending hostilities between the U.S. and Algiers in 1815, William Shaler took up his new position as consul general to the
Barbary States, with general responsibility for Algiers, and
oversight of the American consuls at Tripoli, Tunis, and
Morocco. Shaler took every opportunity to assert his influence and used various diplomatic stratagems to protect American shipping. He warned the Dey that if American commerce
were menaced, naval bombardment would surely follow.[32]
But even after the rough treatment that Commodore Decatur
had meted out to the Algerians, the Dey was reluctant to exchange ratifications of the treaty. Shaler approached the Dey
in the autumn of 1816 for the purpose of negotiating a second
treaty, containing slight modifications of the one negotiated
by Decatur. Following some obstinacy on the part of the Dey
and a threat of force by Shaler, the Dey agreed to negotiate
the second treaty, which was duly signed on Christmas,
1816.[33] Never again would an Algerine vessel take an

American merchantman or a Barbary prince attempt to blackmail an American diplomat.

For the remainder of his tenure at Algiers, Shaler
was for the most part occupied with routine tasks. He was
a well respected diplomat whose stature with the Dey was
very high.   In 1817 and again in 1823 he was able to use diplomacy, supported by force, to maintain peace. [34]   Shaler
also engaged in scholarly pursuits: assisted by William
Brown Hodgson, sent out by the State Department to study
Oriental languages, Shaler made a study of the Berber dia-
lects. Shaler later published Sketches of Algiers. [35]

As the United States had lost interest in Algiers following the conclusion of the Barbary question in 1816, so it
also had little interest in Morocco and Tripoli. The Barbary
diplomatic posts were dead ends for Americans who desired
a career in the foreign service. The quality of Americans
at these posts was very low. Americans were more interested in westward expansion. The forces of Manifest Destiny
proved more influential, and American business men were
little disposed to develop a trade with Morocco. British suspicion that the United States was secretly negotiating for a
Moroccan entrepôt were groundless. [36]

*   *   *   *   *

As the United States approached mid-century, there
was a growing interest in the Middle East, but as in the past,
the missionary predominated over any other American group
in the region. But American foreign policy pursued the traditional course of non-intervention. The United States business man continued to show little interest in developing trade
with the Middle East, for he looked elsewhere, principally
toward the markets of the Far East and Latin America where
the promise of profit was greater.

But in the years between 1850 and 1900 there would be
an increase in American activity in the Middle East, with the
missionaries leading the way. They founded a number of
schools and colleges during this era. The American government also took an interest in Egyptian affairs during the period but maintained its policy of non-intervention.

Chapter 4

TO THE END OF THE CENTURY

During the latter half of the nineteenth century Americans continued to exhibit little political interest in the Middle East, and the official policy of non-involvement, still obtained. But some Americans demonstrated a practical and idealistic interest in that region. Missionaries constituted the most important interest group in the Middle East as they continued to work among the Eastern Christian minorities. While the missionary work prospered, the commercial effort was not quite so fruitful.

*　　*　　*　　*　　*

The United States government did not interfere in matters between Turkey and the Christian minorities--the Armenians, the Cretans, and the Bulgarians--and the Monroe Doctrine played a part on three different occasions between 1850 and 1900 in the relations between Turkey and the United States.[1] In 1864-65 the U.S. applied Monroe's principle of non-interference to an incident growing out of the Turkish epidemic of 1864. The Ottoman government invited various nations to a conference to find a remedy to prevent the recurrence of the plague. The United States rejected an invitation on the grounds that it was not in harmony with the tradition of non-involvement. The United States was also bringing the Civil War to a close, but the primary reason for rejection was fear of involvement in a conference that might pursue political goals, thereby enmeshing the United States in the coils of the Eastern Question.[2]

In 1865 the Doctrine again came into play, for the United States protested to the Porte the dispatch of 900 Sudanese troops to Mexico to aid the Archduke Maximilian of Austria, then serving as Emperor of Mexico. The State Depart-

ment claimed that these African troops were slaves, in a
condition the United States had fought a four-year war to end.
But the principal reason for opposing the presence of Sudanese troops in Mexico was that it violated the Monroe Doctrine.   The Sublime Porte was conciliatory and no more
troops were sent.   The Sudanese soldiers departed with the
French in 1867. [3]

The third incident involving the Monroe Doctrine
stemmed from the 1875 effort of the Ottoman Government to
increase duties on imports from 8 to 11 per cent ad valorem.
To do so, it needed the consent of the powers with which it
had treaties.   Like the European powers, the United States
used this Turkish goal to achieve diplomatic demands.   The
United States acquired an understanding with the Turks in
matters of discrimination against American schools and missions, and it ultimately agreed to the increase in duties on
imports.   But in so doing it technically violated Monroe's
non-interference principle when the State Department agreed
to associate with the European Powers in pressing its diplomatic demands. [4]

The United States Government's consent to raise the
tariff on American goods to achieve goals for the missionary
interest was unique, for American commercial interests ante-
dated missionary operations and were ultimately to receive
greater diplomatic support since they were in the national interest.   Although American commerce with the Levant remained modest, it nevertheless enjoyed a steady growth to
the end of the century.   After 1850 the annual value of trade
with Turkey reached one million dollars, and on several occasions it exceeded two million dollars.   In 1897 it climbed
to seven million.   By and large the United States had a deficit in the balance of payments with Turkey; American exports
ran less than imports.   Strange to relate, one of the chief
American exports to the Middle East during the period 1850-
1900 was petroleum and related products, mainly kerosene. [5]
If exports increased little, Americans continued to import
Turkish goods such as figs, drugs, raw wool, rugs, tobacco,
and chemicals.

What is often overlooked are American diplomatic efforts to promote trade.   The U. S. Navy's influence in Turkey
was strong at mid-century, when Minister George P. Marsh
suggested to the State Department that the Capudan Pasha's
interest in the Navy might offer an opportunity to find a new
market for American naval technology.   Marsh proposed that

the Turkish Admiral send a naval officer to the United States
to tour docks, yards, and shops.   The State Department endorsed the plan.   Marsh also approached the Egyptians, hoping they would follow suit.   While nothing came of the latter
move, an officer of the Sultan's navy came to the United
States, but the tour brought no increase in American trade
because British diplomats frustrated the venture. [6]

Americans were unable to sell ships to the Sultan's
navy, but the conclusion of the Civil War left a surplus of
arms and munitions in American factories.   The Turks readily purchased large stocks of surplus rifles, revolvers,
sabers, and ammunition from American manufacturers.   The
years between 1865 and 1880 showed a marked increase in
American exports to Turkey, and no doubt the shipment of
arms and munitions, plus the continued sale of petroleum
products, accounted for this increase.   American petroleum
fueled the lamps in the mosques of the Holy Cities in Arabia,
and American rum was being imported at Constantinople. [7]

But even with the increase in trade between the United
States and Turkey, missionary pursuits continued as the predominant American interest in the Middle East.   By 1900 the
American Board maintained in Turkey some 29 stations with
162 missionaries and over 900 native assistants.   It operated
36 boarding schools and 398 primary schools, with 2700 students in the former, 15,000 in the latter.   Missionaries were
associated with numerous colleges, including Constantinople
Women's College, Robert College, and Syrian Protestant College, all of which operated under independent boards of
trustees.   Junior colleges were also functioning at Smyrna,
Marsovan, Aintab, Marash, Tarsus, and Harput.   In training
a new elite, the first three colleges had tremendous impact
on the Middle East. [8]

But although the number of missionaries grew in order
to staff the educational institutions, the missionaries complained that American diplomats were not effective in protecting their interests.   Prior to 1864 the Ottoman government
placed no obstacles in the way of the missionaries.   But
reasoning that missionary schools were related to the disrup-
tive nationalism among the subject peoples, the Turks made
life difficult for American missionaries in the years following
1864, and they were compelled frequently to seek British diplomatic protection. [9]   Lack of interest on the part of some
U.S. diplomats and failure to maintain an adequate naval
presence in Eastern Mediterranean waters accounted for some

of the difficulty. But there was more to it. The question of
exterritorial rights greatly harmed the missionary, for the
Sublime Porte did not interpret Article IV of the Turco-
American Treaty of 1830 as did the United States. The
Americans claimed that the article guaranteed full exterritorial rights. American complaints of Turkish violation were
frequent, and more often than not they involved missionaries. [10]

Another factor that irritated the missionaries was the
passage of Turkish laws in 1864 that banned Americans from
owning real estate. This affected the missionaries who
owned property in many parts of Anatolia and European Turkey. Even after President U. S. Grant concluded the 1874
Protocol--one that accepted for Americans the law of the Ottoman Empire that granted foreigners the right to own prop-
erty--missionaries continued to have trouble. [11]

By 1885 lack of diplomatic protection of the missionary
caused such difficulty that the American Board complained to
the President, requesting greater protection. By the end of
the century the Board was satisfied that missionaries were
receiving better protection by U. S. diplomats. [12]

But the Porte was suspicious of the missionary lobby
in Washington, for it maintained that American missionaries
were responsible for setting alight the flame of political nationalism among the subject nationalities of the Ottoman Empire. [13] Historians have debated the cause-and-effect relationship between missionaries and the secular nationalism
of the Christian peoples. It seems safe to say that the missionary contribution was mainly in the realm of cultural nationalism, but that this was a factor in the rise of political
nationalism among Armenians, Arabs, and Bulgarians. [14]
Such nationalism inspired revolutions in Crete and Bulgaria,
and revolutionary activities among the Armenians gave rise
to the terrible massacres of the 1890s. The reaction of the
American people and government to the cause of self-determination in the post-Appomattox era reveals the dual response of humanitarian concern on the part of private American citizens and traditional non-interference on the part of
the U. S. government.

American missionaries were not present on the island
of Crete at the time of the 1866 revolution during which the
islanders, mostly Greek, attempted to gain independence from
the Ottoman Empire. Even so, the islanders looked to the

American example and hoped that U.S. influence in the Mediterranean might aid their cause. At the outbreak of the revolt, the American consul William J. Stillman supported the Greeks against the Turks. In August 1866 Stillman forwarded an appeal from the revolutionaries to the President, requesting American aid for the Cretan liberation from Turkey and annexation by Greece. [15]

Not only did Consul Stillman support the insurrectionists, but E. Joy Morris, the American minister in Constantinople, also used his influence on their behalf. Morris requested the British and Russians to intervene, and he urged Washington to dispatch U.S. Navy ships to help evacuate civilian refugees, subject to the consent of the Porte. [16]

As in the case of the earlier Greek revolt in the 1820s, the latent spirit of philhellenism had broken out in the United States, and pro-Greeks, such as Dr. Samuel G. Howe who had served with the Greek revolutionaries in the 1820s, elicited assistance from other likeminded persons, such as Edward Everett Hale, to collect funds for relief on Crete. The response was gratifying, for $37,000 was soon gathered. But the Civil War had dulled American sympathies for rebellion, and beyond resolutions in the Maine legislature and the Congress, expressing sympathy for the Cretans, little was done. However, the Porte did not receive these expressions of sympathy well. It greatly feared American intervention in the Cretan episode, believing that the U.S. government was set on obtaining a naval base on the island of Crete to replace that lost at Port Mahon on Minorca some years earlier. [17]

Although the U.S. government followed a policy of non-inolvement, the Turks would not consent to the U.S. Navy evacuating refugees. The activities of Stillman and Dr. Howe created difficulties and efforts to help the Cretan refugees were fruitless. Thus the American response to the Cretan revolution followed past precedent. Private persons engaged in relief activities, and the government preserved a correct posture of non-intervention. In 1867 the Turks, in appreciation for the American position, increased diplomatic ties with the United States by establishing a legation in Washington.

American missionaries were not on Crete, but they were largely responsible for provoking the Bulgarian nationalism that led to revolt in the Balkans in the 1870s. [18] Teachers at the missionary-operated Robert College had stirred up the pride of young Bulgarian students. Too, missionaries had begun their work in Bulgaria at about the time of the American Civil War. They have been described as "very good men but ultra Bulgarians."[19] Not only did the missionaries work for the Bulgarian cause, but Eugene Schuyler, the U.S. consul general at Constantinople, was dispatched to Bulgaria to investigate the violent massacres that accompanied the Turkish repression of the rebellion. Not only did Schuyler draft a constitution for the rebels (Schuyler obtained one of the earliest Ph.D. degrees from Yale University), but he also investigated the Turkish atrocities and submitted his report to a London newspaper for publication. This act was highly irregular, and the Turks later called for and obtained Schuyler's recall.[20]

While the missionaries were sympathetic to the Bulgarian national cause, the U.S. government pursued a policy of non-interference as it had in the Greek and Cretan revolutions. The U.S. Navy showed no predisposition toward the rebels. Elements of the fleet were stationed at Constantinople, Smyrna, Salonica, and Beirut solely to protect American interests. If Turkish suspicions of U.S. intentions remained, they were removed in the following decade by the efforts of a new American minister.[21]

General Lew Wallace, the author of Ben Hur, was appointed American minister to Turkey in 1881. Wallace was a remarkable diplomat. The Sultan frequently called on him for advice. He was also effective in accomplishing diplomatic goals. While the Sultan admired Wallace's personal qualities and considered him a confidant, there can be little doubt that he appreciated American neutrality during the Bulgarian episode.[22]

But amicable relations between the Sublime Porte and the United States became strained during the decade following Wallace's departure from Turkey in 1885. The Armenian Question entered American-Turkish relations in 1894 and would be prominent in the diplomatic intercourse between the two nations for over a generation.

American missionaries were not responsible for having stimulated the Armenian political nationalism that led to Turkish reprisals against Armenians and the destruction of missionary property in the 1890s. Political nationalism among the Armenians was largely the result of Russian and French influence.[23] Armenian revolutionaries, emulating the example of the Bulgarian nationalists, increased their political activities in the 1890s, and in 1894-1895 the Turks perpetrated several Armenian massacres, believing these would dampen the revolutionary activity of nationalists who sought Armenian independence. The initial massacres occurred in the Sassoun district of Turkish Armenia in September 1894. American Minister Alexander W. Terrell reported on 28 September the occurrence of the bloody acts that would jar American sensibilities.[24]

At the time of the Armenian massacres--which strained American-Turkish relations--relations between the two countries were already uneasy due to the expatriation controversy. The United States had long been guided by the basic principle that people have the right to emigrate from their native lands and take up new citizenship by process of naturalization. Armenians had been accustomed to migrate to the United States, assume American citizenship, and then return to live in the Ottoman Empire as American citizens. Under the imperial edict of 19 January 1869, the Sublime Porte refused to accord these peoples their new legal status, claiming they were still Ottoman subjects. A naturalization treaty was signed by the two governments in 1874 to clear up the question but it was not ratified, and in subsequent years the status of naturalized Americans caused considerable friction. The matter was partially settled after the turn of the century, but in the decade of the 1890s it continued to cause bad feeling.[25]

It was in this strained atmosphere that Minister Terrell sent word on 30 November 1894 that the Sultan invited the U.S. to send a consul to join a commission to investigate the massacres in the Sassoun district.[26] President Grover Cleveland declined to comply.[27] A second request from Terrel caused the President to appoint a member to the special commission.[28] But the Turks now rejected the presence of an American on the commission. In his annual message of 1895 President Cleveland said that American action with regard to the commission was motivated by the desire to obtain information about conditions in the Ottoman Empire that would enable the government to afford better protection for American interests.[29]

In 1895 there were more disorders in the Ottoman Empire which led to loss of life and destruction of missionary property. On 15 November a number of Turks plundered three buildings and burned another at the mission station in

Marash.   At about the same time a mob looted two school
buildings and a missionary home at Harput.   Eight other
buildings were burned.   The total property damage was later
estimated to be just under $100,000.   Terrell demanded an
indemnity, but to no avail. [30]   Cleveland's annual message to
Congress on 2 December 1895 made it clear that he would
not violate the tradition of non-intervention, and he refused
to forward a Senate resolution, calling on the European
Powers to stop the massacres, to the respective powers. [31]
Terrell was effective in protecting the more than 500 missionaries and their property during the year 1896. [32]   He had
requested the presence of American naval vessels in Turkish
waters, and the cruisers Marblehead, San Francisco, and
Minneapolis cruised the Eastern Mediterranean, frequently
visiting Turkish ports. [33]   But there were problems on the
home front.

Complaints about the missionaries came from Mav-
royeni Bey, the Turkish Minister to the United States, for
the Minister claimed that the missionaries in Turkey and
their supporters in the United States were guilty of activities
that jeopardized the relations between the two governments.
He alleged that the missionaries inspired the Armenian revolutionaries and that missionary supporters in the U.S. slan-
dered the name of Turkey and projected a bad Turkish image
in the press. [34]   He threatened reprisals, and in early 1896
the Ottoman government issued a decree that required all
persons engaged in revolutionary activities to leave the country.   This was to include the missionaries who were then
disbursing supplies to the destitute.   Terrell remonstrated
with the Sublime Porte, and, with the full cooperation of the
British ambassador, got the order rescinded. [35]

The Sultan's officers had long felt that the mission
schools were hotbeds of nationalism, and this attitude in large
measure explains the crackdown on the mission institutions.
While the missionaries did arouse national pride by frequently referring to the so-called Armenian "nation" and by teaching about democratic institutions in the United States, there
is little cause to feel that they actively engaged in movements to provoke revolution.   In fact, several missionaries
publicly denounced Armenian revolutionary goals, and many
of the Armenian national revolutionary leaders disliked the
missionaries for their attitude. [36]

If American missionaries did not engage in the con-
spiratorial operations of the Armenian nationalists, what can

be said of the efforts of pro-Armenian Americans? A number of organizations came into being to express American interest in Armenian cultural life, namely the United Friends of
Armenia, founded in Boston in 1894, the Phil-Armenic Association, founded in Washington in 1895, and the National
Armenian Relief Committee, established in New York in December 1895 to coordinate the efforts of the smaller pro-
Armenian bodies in the United States and to collect relief
funds.   The work of the various pro-Armenian groups were
supported by Episcopalian, Congregationalist, and Presbyter-
ain clergymen, who joined business leaders in New York,
Chicago, and Boston to organize rallies for Armenian relief.
These men of the cloth added their voices to those of other
interested Americans to call for the use of naval force to
protect American interests and punish the Turk.   One Senate
resolution submitted by Senator Call of Florida echoed the
sentiments of many Americans.   It urged the use of force to
protect American interests and to help establish an Armenian state. [37]

Pro-Armenian Americans must have been gratified
when Joseph Chamberlain, British Colonial Secretary, suggested in September 1896 to British Prime Minister Lord
Salisbury that Britain and the United States initiate a joint
naval demonstration to influence the Sultan to halt the massacres and commence political reforms.   Salisbury consented
and on 19 September Chamberlain wrote Secretary of State
Richard Olney, asking if the United States cared to associate
with Britain in a joint naval effort to curb the Sultan's behavior.   Olney replied a week later, saying that the Monroe
Doctrine would not permit the United States to take part in
such a venture because it would amount to interference in the
political affairs of the Ottoman Empire.   Nothing came of
the proposal. [38]

Unable to bring about a naval demonstration in Turkish waters, the missionaries were successful in another
sphere.   They were responsible for distributing relief to the
Armenians, doling out over a half-million dollars in supplies
to the destitute Armenians. [39]

President Cleveland's last message to Congress on 7
December 1896 demonstrated that the American response to
efforts to enlist this country's support for the Armenians had
followed traditional policy guidelines.   While the Navy had
been employed to protect American interests, Cleveland said
that the Armenian Question was one for the Berlin Treaty

powers to decide and that the United States had maintained a correct posture of non-intervention. [40]

After President William McKinley came to the White House in 1897, American-Turkish relations continued to be strained, and it was not until September 1899 that the Sultan agreed to indemnify the missionaries. He agreed in the presence of American Minister Oscar Straus to include the payment for the indemnity for damages to missionary proper- ty as part of the purchase price of an American warship. [41] The Sultan wanted to handle the affair in this manner to avoid similar payments to the other powers. Even so, the Porte hesitated and it was not until 24 December 1900 that Lloyd Griscom obtained a final settlement. The matter was settled on 12 June 1901, when $83,600 was deposited in the imperi- al Ottoman Bank for the account of the American Board.

What can be said of the American response to the Armenian Question? The United States stretched the policy of non-intervention by dispatching a warship to Turkish waters in 1900 to enable Griscom to collect the indemnity. [42] But we can conclude that overall the American reaction was consistent with the past policy of non-interference in the Mid- dle Eastern question in that diplomats did not intervene in the domestic affairs of the Turks. This policy was realistic, and policy-makers did not bow to the moral indignation of American citizens who favored intervention. The response of private American citizens in giving relief to the Armenians was in keeping with the record of American philanthropic ef- forts in the Middle East during the nineteenth century.

No discussion of American relations with the Ottoman Empire in the period 1850 to 1900 would be complete unless mention were made of the diplomatic record between the United States and Egypt. Commerce with Egypt did not de- velop, and there was always, with few exceptions, an annual deficit in the trade balance. Exports to Egypt amounted to over $500,000 in only four years between mid-century and 1900, while imports from Egypt exceeded the million-dollar mark in only nine years during the same period. The two decades prior to the Civil War marked a low period in the commerce between the two countries. It was not until 1873 that there was a notable increase in American exports to and imports from Egypt. [43] The growth in American exports was due to the increase in petroleum shipments and the sale of arms and ammunition during the period when American offi- cers advised the Egyptian military forces. American trade

with Egypt was conducted on the most favored nation principle
in accordance with the 1830 Treaty with the Ottoman Empire.
But after the British occupation of 1882, the United States
negotiated with Egypt a commercial convention in 1884 that
also continued the most favored nation treatment. [44]

As American trade expansion proceeded slowly in
Egypt, so it was with the work with the missionaries.   The
first American missionaries arrived in 1854.   During the
early years of their tenure, their main concern was evangel-
ism and the distribution of religious literature.   The number
of conversions was small at first.   Even the Copts exhibited
antagonism toward the missionaries, and in 1863 American
Consul General William Thayer had to intervene with the Cop-
tic Patriarch on behalf of a missionary. [45]   On the whole,
the American consul general in Egypt gave adequate protection to the missionaries.   In fact, Daniel S. Mcauley and Edwin DeLeon, who served as consuls general from 1848 to
1854 and from 1853 to 1861, respectively, achieved promi-
nence.   Mcauley had a wider knowledge of diplomatic practice, but DeLeon exerted a greater amount of influence. [46]
Unfortunately, these men were hindered by a lack of money,
but in spite of this condition protection for the missionary
was fairy good. [47]   For example, there is the case of Walter
Dickson, an American missionary at Jaffa.   On 11 January
1858, a mob attacked Dickson's house, murdered his son-in-
law, raped his wife and daughter, and pillaged the house.
J. Warren Gorham, U.S. consul at Jerusalem, asked Edwin
DeLeon, consul general at Alexandria, to help.   DeLeon intervened, impressed the Turkish dignitaries when he threatened a naval demonstration off Jaffa, and eventually they punished the guilty. [48]   The consuls general were keenly aware
of the intrinsic value of the missionary in providing educational services to the people of Egypt.   In 1873 Consul General Richard Beardsley advised that a large number of Egyptian public servants in the railroad, telegraph, and post offices had received education at mission schools. [49]

But American missionaries were not the only people
from the United States to contribute to modernization among
Egyptians.   The American Civil War resulted in much closer
relations between Egypt and the United States.   Many American soldiers and naval officers, both Union and Confederate,
entered the Egyptian military after the war.   The Civil War
had profoundly affected Egypt.   Trade with the United States
all but disappeared.   The Confederacy embargoed cotton
shipments to Britain, and her supply of cotton virtually dis-

appeared.   The British turned to Egypt, and thus reserves
of Southern cotton, supplemented by long-staple Egyptian cotton, kept Lancashire mills in operation.   This eventuated in
the development of large-scale British interests in Egypt, a
fact that resulted in the British occupation in 1882.[50]   There
is an indication that the U.S. government acted to stimulate
Egyptian cotton culture.   The vigilant American Consul General William Thayer, aware of the relationship between
Egyptian cotton cultivation and American diplomacy, encouraged the Egyptians to grow more cotton.   On one occasion
he accompanied the Egyptian Viceroy to England to counter
the influence of Southern diplomats who might try to discourage Egyptian cotton culture.[51]

But cotton was not the only facet of American-Egyptian relations during the Civil War.   We have already exam-
ined the application of the Monroe Doctrine to the sending of
Sudanese troops to Mexico, an incident that temporarily
caused a strain between Turkey and Egypt and the United
States.   Otherwise relations with Turkey and Egypt were satisfactory.   Both countries observed strict neutrality.   Neither
fitted out Confederate privateers or permitted them to enter
port.   To ascertain Egyptian neutrality, Consul General
Thayer employed several secret officials to visit Egyptian
ports.[52]

The conclusion of the Civil War determined that Egypt
would suffer an economic decline, but otherwise she enjoyed
benefits from Americans who entered the Egyptian military
forces.[53]   Khedive Ismail Pasha urgently wanted to strengthen
his military forces in order to undercut the 1841 settlement
that left Egypt securely in the Ottoman Empire.   A stronger
army would give Ismail the leverage he so badly needed.
For his purpose he selected American naval and military officers to train his cadres, reorganize his army, and complete some vitally needed public works projects.   A number
of reasons dictated Ismail's selection of Americans.   Soldiers
and sailors in the Blue and Grey had only recently demonstrated military and nautical expertise of a high order.   But
the Viceroy had another reason.   Addressing the newly arrived soldiers, he said: "Your experience and the lack of
any selfish interest on the part of your country are the motives which suggested Americans for the proposed service."[54]

The U.S. government advised the Americans that they
in no way represented the government and that they did not
constitute an American mission.   While the British, French,

and Turks disapproved their presence, none lodged a protest
with the State Department, for all knew that these Americans
did not represent the U.S. government.[55]

The American military advisers were effective. They
reorganized the Egyptian army, instituted training programs,
effected programs of education to end illiteracy, ventured out
on scientific expeditions, improved Egyptian defenses, completed numerous public works projects and mapping tasks,
and made a number of other contributions of a technical nature. All the while the U.S. government remained an interested observer, refusing to capitalize on the presence of the
military advisers to acquire political advantages.[56] The only
benefit that accrued to the United States was the Egyptian
purchase of substantial quantities of surplus arms and ammunition from two American manufacturers.[57]

So disinterested was the U.S. government in Egypt
that no American representative took part even in the diplomatic activities associated with the building and opening of
the Suez Canal. The State Department reasoned that the U.S.
had "little direct interest" in the canal and that American
presence was of little consequence.[58]

Contrary to a lack of interest in the Suez, the U.S.
government exhibited a desire to participate in the development of the mixed courts in Egypt, because this involved the
capitulatory rights enjoyed by the United States. By virtue
of the capitulatory rights, the citizens of a foreign power
could sue an Egyptian in an Egyptian court. But with the
growing Egyptian indebtedness, it seemed necessary to arrive
at a more just method of deciding issues. In the past the
United States had opposed mixed courts, and Consul General
DeLeon had been outspoken against them. But in 1869 an
American delegate attended a conference at Alexandria for the
purpose of making judicial reforms. In March 1874 Congress
authorized President Grant to accept the jurisdiction of mixed
Egyptian tribunals in lieu of consular jurisdiction. The
Khedive instituted the mixed courts in June 1875. Although
the U.S. government manifested little interest in the operation of the courts, it did appoint two men to sit on the Court
of Appeals.[59]

During the period of the late 1870s and early 1880s
when European states were trying to solve the problem of
Egyptian indebtedness by fixing their control on the Khedive,
the United States remained aloof. The tradition of non-inter-

vention led to the absence of an American on the debt-liqui-
dation commission.   Ultimately, the Egyptian fiscal crisis
caused the Khedive to sell Egypt's shares in the Suez Canal
and to dismiss the American officers serving in the Egyptian
armed forces.

The Egyptians appreciated the American aloofness from
the debt controversy.   Literate Egyptians felt that the United
States was Egypt's friend, whereas the European states were
out to plunder.   The Egyptians admired missionary educational efforts that provided the Egyptian civil service with a supply of literate personnel.   The War Department's facilitation
of Egyptian arms procurement in the United States and the
Department of Agriculture's aid in controlling pests also added
to the Egyptian fund of goodwill toward Americans.   U.S.
diplomats could do no wrong in Egypt, for during the period
of the British differences with the Khedive that led to the occupation in 1882, the U.S. used its good offices to mediate
the dispute between Britain and Egypt.   Although the American effort was fruitless, nevertheless, it earned an additional deposit of goodwill in Egypt.

The chain of events that led to the British occupation
of Egypt was begun by the revolt by Colonel Ahmad Arabi, an
Egyptian army officer who intensely resented the growth of
European control in Egypt.   The extremely nationalistic Arabi gained control of the Egyptian government, an event the
British and French could not tolerate.   Tension between the
Egyptians and the British and French, whose squadrons were
drawn up off the Egyptian coast, grew.   A bloody riot broke
out in June 1882, leading to the deaths of many Europeans
but no Americans.   Despite this evidence of Egyptian friend-
liness toward Americans, the U.S. Navy had dispatched the
U.S.S. Galena to Alexandria.   The commanding officer then
proceeded to hire a merchant ship to remove all Americans
in Egypt.[60]   Tensions grew and finally on 4 July the Turkish
Sultan summoned Lew Wallace, the American minister at
Constantinople, and urged that the United States use its good
offices to settle the dispute between Egypt and Britain.   Wallace consented, and on 5 July cabled the Sultan's request to
Washington.   On the following day the Department urged Wallace to proceed.   The Minister went ahead with the mediation
effort.   On 9 July he advised that he had consulted Lord Duf-
ferin, the British Ambassador, and the Sultan, and was confident that he could bring the dispute to a peaceful conclusion.
This was not the case, for Britain commenced hostilities on
the 11th.   Wallace blamed the British government for thwart-

ing his mediation effort.   The British were aware of the American offer of good offices on 6 July, but made no real effort to be conciliatory.[61]

The naval bombardment of Alexandria commenced on 11 July, but on the preceding day the U.S. Navy had begun to evacuate some 50 missionaries and their families and about 250 Europeans.   The U.S. Navy landed 150 sailors and marines to help restore order, an action motivated by humanitarian considerations.   This act earned the plaudits of the Egyptians who realized that the American government had no political ambitions to fulfill during the episode.[62]

The U.S. government established no official policy with respect to the British occupation, and it continued to view the Sultan as the head of state in Egypt, with the Khedive as his viceroy.   American consuls general during the early period of British occupation were critical of the British attempt at reform.   However, in the 1890s they lauded the work of Lord Cromer in bringing reform and progress to Egypt, thus evincing growing goodwill toward the British.

Evidence of the Anglo-American rapprochement was manifest not only in Egypt but also in Persia, where the American Minister was attempting to associate with Britain in an effort to thwart the Russian effort to achieve hegemony. But good relations between the U.S. and Britain had not always obtained in Persia, because at mid-century Britain stood in the way of the establishment of U.S.-Persian relations.   In 1855 the United States sought the good offices of Russia to assist with the making of a treaty of friendship with Persia, and Russian support was necessary in view of British hindrance.[63]   But Carroll Spence, the American minister at Constantinople, reported that the Persians were interested not only in making a treaty but also in American naval intervention to offset European influence.   He advised the Persian chargé in Constantinople of the long-standing American policy of non-intervention.   Ultimately, the United States signed a treaty of friendship and commerce with Persia on 13 December 1856.[64]   But President James Buchanan's inaugural address served notice that the United States would continue its policy of non-intervention in the affairs of other nations but would pursue a policy of commercial expansion.   With a view to expanding the American market place, Buchanan advised Congress that an appropriation for the opening of a legation in Teheran would be most opportune.[65]   Congress did not go along with this advice, and it was not until 1883 that an American legation opened in Persia. The establishment of the legation resulted from the American desire to protect missionaries. On 14 February 1883 Secretary of State Frederick Frelinghuysen advised Samuel G. Benjamin of his appointment to the post as consul general at Teheran. Before departure, Benjamin received the title, Minister Resident.

Frelinghuysen did not inform Benjamin that the main reason for sending him to Persia was the protection of missionaries, and on arrival in Teheran, the new minister immediately began to seek out commercial opportunities for American merchants and investors. He reported that Persia would gladly offer the United States a political treaty in return for valuable commercial concessions that would extend to the exploitation of Persian coal, lead, copper, and petroleum. The State Department was not influenced by Benjamin's pleas for expanded commercial operations. Benjamin interviewed the Shah who admitted that economic advantages were being offered the United States to offset the political aims of the European Powers.[66] But the U.S. was not yet ready to pursue economic goals in the Middle East, a fact emphasized by President Chester Alan Arthur in his annual message to Congress on 1 December 1884.[67] Although Benjamin continued to press for expanded economic interests in Persia, the State Department would have none of it, a fact that tends to deny radical historians' assertion that the United States' pursuit of overseas markets was constant.[68] The State Department ultimately recalled Benjamin for engaging in an altercation with the German Minister. Although Benjamin looked after the interests of American missionaries, he never seemed to grasp that this was his primary purpose, and he continued to promote commercial expansion.

That the United States would not become embroiled in the political intrigues of the powers in Persia was emphasized in President Grover Cleveland's inaugural address in March 1885.[69] The President and his Secretary of State, Thomas F. Bayard, were determined to remain aloof from the machinations of the powers in Persia. That Persia played a small role in the American world view is borne out by F. H. Winston, Benjamin's replacement, who resigned shortly after assuming office. In his letter of resignation, Winston said that maintenance of an American legation in Persia was unwarranted. There were only twenty American missionaries in Persia and there was no American commerce with that country.[70]

Winston's successor was E. Spencer Pratt, who served at Teheran for five years.   Like Benjamin before him, Pratt worked unsparingly to improve Persian-American relations and to increase commercial opportunity in that country for American interests.   Secretary Bayard wrote to Pratt on 3 May 1887 that the U.S. government could not advise American companies or citizens how to invest their capital, although the Department could make known in American financial circles the Shah's readiness to use American capital in developing his country.   Two months later Bayard again told Pratt of the Department's opposition to diplomats acting as agents for any given manufacturer seeking commercial opportunity in Persia.   Pratt had been encouraging the Gatling Gun Company to seek markets for its arms in Persia.   At length Pratt advised the Department that the government should institute a program to use public funds to develop Persia.   On 10 February 1888 the Secretary replied, saying that Pratt's suggestion was a violation of the principle of nonintervention. [71]

It is ironic that the efforts of individual American diplomats to enhance American commerce in Persia were thwarted by the State Department.   With the decline of the American merchant marine in the post-Civil War years, the U.S. government seems to have been unwilling to seek new commercial opportunities in the Middle East.   Perhaps investment opportunity closer to home, the development of the American West, and the rapid growth of industry precluded the expansion of economic efforts in the Middle East.   Too, with the presidency of Benjamin Harrison, American overseas commercial efforts were directed at Latin America as Secretary of State James G. Blaine inaugurated a policy of aggressive diplomacy that aimed to capture new markets there.

During Harrison's term missionary problems, not trade expansion, were the order of the day.   Pratt's successors in Teheran tried to give protection to missionaries, but with growing frustration.   More often than not, American Protestants were compelled to turn to the British for protection.   Worthy of note, was the Shah's willingness to let the American missionaries own property in their own name.   American influence in Persia was so restricted that diplomatic agents thought it even futile to press claims against the Persian government for infringement on personal and property rights by Persians. [72]   While timidity and concern with missionary problems characterized American-Persian rela-

tions during the early part of the 1890s, the tone was more
positive in the post-Spanish-American War era.   Previous
U.S. ministers, with few exceptions, had accepted the State
Department's lack of concern with the growth of Russian power in Persia and were passive toward economic expansion.
Not so Herbert W. Bowen, who arrived at the American legation in Teheran in 1899.

Bowen was determined to contain the expansion of Russian influence in Persia by use of the Open Door, but in so
doing, he received a rebuke from the State Department.
Bowen viewed the avaricious Russian practice of levying heavy
transit duties on non-Russian goods traveling across Russian
territory to Persia as a violation of the Open Door policy.
He suggested to the Department that the U.S. employ the
Open Door in Persia as in China.   While acting Secretary
David J. Hill saw merit in Bowen's suggestion, he also realized that employment of the Open Door in Persia would involve the United States in the Great Power political struggle
in that country, a practice that would exceed the bounds of
the policy of non-intervention.   He so advised Bowen.[73]   But
this did not deter Bowen, who then suggested to Cecil Spring-
Rice, British chargé, that the U.S. and Britain join with
Germany to make an agreement to prevent Russian control
over Persia.[74]   Bowen's act had so involved the United States
in the international intrigue in Persia that Secretary of State
John Hay disavowed his activities and instructed him that application of the Open Door in Persia would be inexpedient at
this juncture, for it would make the U.S. a party to the intrigue of the Great Powers.[75]   Inasmuch as Britain was attempting to contain Russian advances in Persia, one is inclined to ask if Bowen's efforts to thwart Russia were not in
response to the plea of some British diplomat to use American influence on behalf of British imperial ambitions.

But it is probable that Bowen hoped to realize American economic benefits from the Open Door just as other
American diplomatic agents were doing in the Barbary states.
From the inception of the American Republic, trade with the
Barbary regencies had been an elusive goal, but there was
an effort to increase commercial opportunity in the late 19th
century.   Michel Vidal, the American Consul at Tripoli,
urged the State Department in the 1870s to follow an aggressive policy in the Mediterranean, where Britain was already
achieving hegemony.   To facilitate competition with Britain
in the commercial sphere, Vidal recommended that the U.S.
acquire a naval base in the Tripolitan province of Cyrenaica.

Nothing came of this recommendation and Vidal was ultimately recalled. His policy would have involved the U.S. with the Ottoman Empire, which still claimed sovereignty over Tripoli. [76]

Although plans for a naval station were shunted aside, President U. S. Grant's Secretary of State, Hamilton Fish, favored a forward commercial policy in the Middle East. In 1876 the Department instructed General Edward F. Noyes, the American minister to France, to begin a tour of the Middle East with a view to finding new commercial opportunities. Noyes set out in 1880 and visited Smyrna, Constantinople, Cyprus, Syria, Palestine, Egypt, Tunis, and Algeria. Although no concrete results came from Noyes' mission, it did demonstrate the Department's interest in new markets to alleviate the distresses caused by the depression of 1873. In fact, the European Powers viewed Vidal's activities, the Noyes mission, and the American participation in the Madrid Conference in 1880 as evidence of a new, more forward American posture in the Middle East. [77]

But a radical departure was not to be, for U. S. participation in the conference at Madrid to iron out Moroccan questions was based on a desire to enforce the American policy of expatriation and naturalization rather than to establish an aggressive position in Morocco leading to commercial expansion. Britain, desirous of reforming Morocco and preventing French hegemony in that country, had called the conference at Madrid for the purpose of making those reforms conducive to continued Moroccan territorial integrity and political sovereignty. The U.S. was represented by a delegate whose prime responsibility was to see that the conferees were willing to guarantee the right of expatriation and naturalization of Moroccan subjects. But in strict compliance with the tradition of non-intervention, the delegate did not attempt to force reform upon the Sultan of Morocco, which would have amounted to intervention in the domestic affairs of that country. It is worthy of note that President Rutherford B. Hayes advised the Congress that the U.S. had encouraged the Sultan to reform his house to end persecutions of non-Muslims. He said that the U.S. had been especially solicitous of the welfare of Jews resident in Tangier. [78]

Thus U.S. efforts to develop stronger economic ties with Barbary were sporadic. Opportunity for American merchants lay closer to home, and at century's end American commercial interests had not realized benefits anticipated by making commercial treaties.

*   *   *   *   *

Official U.S. relations with the Middle East during
the last half of the nineteenth century continued to be governed by the principle of non-intervention.   Aloofness dictated policy during political disturbances involving subject
peoples of the Ottoman Empire.   Although missionaries continued to dominate the nation's relations with the Middle
East, the forces of industrialization were at work and the
United States was rapidly becoming one of the world's leaders in the new age of machines.   There were interests at
home that demanded new markets, new outlets for American
capital investment, and new sources of raw materials.

The coming of the twentieth century would see American commercial interests begin to vie with the missionary
for a voice in the shaping of American Middle Eastern policy.   During the first decade of the new century, the U.S.
government gave precedence to commercial interests over
those of the missionary.   And so it was that the dawning of
the twentieth century resulted in the advent of new and larger
interests in the Middle East.   The efforts of Americans to
obtain concessions in the Ottoman Empire to build railroads
were but a harbinger of the coming of the American oil men
whose derricks would soon punctuate the sands of Arabia,
Kuwait, and Libya.

Chapter 5

PRE-WAR MIDDLE EAST: A TIME OF TRANSITION

The period prior to World War I was one of transition that saw the growth of national consciousness in the Ottoman and Persian empires. Armenians, Arabs, Turks, Zionist Jews, Egyptians, and Persians expressed a restiveness with the status quo. Indeed, so marked was the emergence of ethnic sentiment that revolution brought about changes in government in Constantinople and Teheran. Although the United States continued to respond to the upheavals in the Middle East with its policy of non-intervention, nevertheless the State Department's sponsorship of the Chester concession and dispatch of two delegates to the Algeciras conference constituted a new vigor in U.S. Middle Eastern policy. Support for the Chester project and participation at Algeciras amounted to brief deviations from the tradition of non-involvement. The Chester concession indicated that when necessary the U.S. government would give precedence to economic interests over missionary interests, and participation at Algeciras demonstrated a willingness to take part in an international conference whenever it was deemed that such action was in the national interest.

This is not to say that U.S. economic interests had begun to overshadow those of the missionaries or that the tradition of non-intervention had been discarded, for the work of the missionaries continued to eclipse that of other interest groups, and the policy of non-intervention remained a foundation of American foreign policy. Before discussing this policy toward the various components of the Middle East, a general overview is necessary to an understanding of the more specific.

*　　*　　*　　*　　*

45

Mission stations dotted Turkey, Syria, Persia, Egypt, and a few in the Persian Gulf area by the early twentieth century. The missionary work was educational and medical. Hospitals and schools, from primary to high school and junior college level, enabled the missionaries to reach all segments of Middle Eastern society. [1] While uplifting the people and bringing better health to them, the missionaries did not escape censure by the Turks, for the Sultan's government was convinced that the American Protestants abetted the revolutionary sentiments of the nationalist leaders of the minority elements. In spite of growing opposition to missionary work, the American good will investment in schools and hospitals outstripped that of American business. [2]

Although trade with the Middle East had maintained a steady growth in the nineteenth century, it remained primarily linked to the import of figs, rugs, raisins, licorice, tobacco, and opium from Smyrna, and a few agricultural items from Egypt. The main export was petroleum products, with industrial goods lagging far behind. Capital investment in the area was negligible. There was hope for an expanded export trade, for in 1911 the American Chamber of Commerce established an office at Constantinople and opened branches in larger cities. It published the Levant Trade Review, hoping to enhance commercial contacts and opportunity. But trade was handicapped by the lack of American shipping and banking interests in the region. [3]

In addition to the activities of the missionaries and entrepreneurs, there was a miscellany of American interests and problems. A growing number of tourists and archaeologists called upon the services of the American diplomatic network. At the same time, there was an increase of persons seeking to migrate from the Middle East to the United States. But perhaps the most onerous problem facing American diplomats was the growth of nationalism among the subject peoples of the Ottoman Empire, and Armenians, Zionists, and Arabs would soon express themselves in official circles. But that was sometime hence, and it now remains to examine American relations with the Ottoman Empire in the years prior to World War I.

Turkey assumed greater importance in official American eyes during this period, for the U.S. mission in Constantinople was raised to an embassy in 1906. Intercourse between Turkey and the U.S. in this era was marked by several themes. The diplomatic strain that developed in the

decade of the 1890s continued as the Turks maintained their
sanguinary treatment of the Armenians, discriminated against
American commerce, suspected missionaries of fomenting
revolution, and delayed the granting of exequaturs to American consular officials. A second theme is the tension between intervention and non-intervention that characterized
U. S. diplomacy with the Sublime Porte. On the one hand,
the U. S. government adamantly refused to be drawn into the
problems related to the Armenian question. On the other
hand, the State Department was willing to joust with the
Porte on behalf of American economic interests.

Toward the latter part of the pre-war era, Turkey became embroiled in two wars, and the State Department dusted
off the Monroe Doctrine and rejected Turkish requests for
mediation. During the Italo-Turkish War that broke out in
1911 as Italy attempted to annex the Ottoman province of
Libya, the U. S. issued a proclamation of neutrality. Considerable pressure was put on the administration to act as in-
tercessor, and President William H. Taft advised Secretary
of State Philander Chase Knox of his desire to settle the dispute. As the advocates of Dollar Diplomacy gave some
thought to mediation, Assistant Secretary of State Francis M.
Huntington Wilson suggested that American mediation should
be contingent upon Turkish willingness to grant Americans
economic concessions in the Ottoman Empire. But Alvey A.
Adee, the second assistant Secretary of State, argued that
mediation would violate the Monroe Doctrine and might serve
as a precedent for European intervention in the Western Hemisphere. In the end, his argument prevailed. Knox replied
to the Sublime Porte, saying that the problem was European
in nature and that the U. S. did not wish to become involved.[4] However, Ambassador William Rockhill and his
counterpart in Italy, Thomas J. O'Brien, did serve as a
means by which Italians and Turks could exchange views, and
this intercessory service helped to bring about peace.

During 1912 and 1913 the Turks were again at war,
trying to thwart the Balkan states from wresting more of the
Balkan peninsula from Ottoman rule. Once more, the Porte
asked for U. S. mediation. Secretary Knox instructed Ambassador Rockhill to reject the Turkish plea. Although the
U. S. dispatched naval forces to the Middle East to protect
American lives and property during the Balkan Wars, it
nevertheless pursued a course of non-intervention in refusing
to become mired in a European imbroglio.[5]

American policy-makers also withstood the requests
of American missionaries and others to proffer good offices
on behalf of the Armenians.   In 1906 a number of European
dignitaries urged President Theodore Roosevelt to use his
influence to prevent further Turkish massacres of the Armenians.   Elihu Root, Secretary of State, refused, citing the
century-long tradition of non-intervention. [6]   In the following
year, fifty prominent Americans petitioned the President in
January 1907 to use his personal influence to find a solution
to the Armenian question that would prevent further bloodshed.   Although Roosevelt was pro-Armenian and violently
anti-Turk, he took no action. [7]   But Armenians caused problems on another score, for the question of expatriation and
naturalization of Armenians continued to complicate Turkish-
American relations.   Armenians expatriated themselves from
the Ottoman Empire and sought naturalized American citizenship.   With a new status that guaranteed freedom from Turkish depredations, these naturalized Armenian-Americans returned to the Ottoman Empire.   But the Porte did not view
them as American citizens, denying that they could expatri-
ate.   The U.S. government, after lengthy negotiation, compromised in 1907 and advised all Americans who were formerly Turkish subjects that if they returned to Turkey and
remained there for a period in excess of two years they
would then forfeit their U.S. citizenship. [8]   Another Armen-
ian-related problem was the question of the continued operation of missionary schools.   In 1908 the Young Turks, a
group of Turkish nationalists who desired to westernize and
modernize Turkey, staged a coup d'état and gained control
of the Turkish government.   The Young Turks regarded the
missionaries as responsible for fomenting revolution, and
they passed the Law of Associations to restrict the function
of missionary educational institutions. [9]   Ambassador Oscar
Straus spent considerable time during the years 1909-1910
attempting to free the American schools from the restrictions imposed by the Law of Associations.   He was partially
successful. [10]

The operation of Armenian revolutionaries in the
United States also placed a strain on Ottoman-American relations.   In 1906 the State Department transmitted to the
Turkish minister in Washington a report that described the
organizational structure and activities of Armenian revolutionary societies in the United States.   The document de-
tailed the manner in which leaders beguiled their audiences
into supporting a program designed to free Armenians from
the Ottoman yoke.   The information so furnished was de-

signed to protect Armenian-Americans then resident in the
Ottoman Empire. [11]

But the Armenian question continued to perplex Turkish-American relations.   Following the Young Turk Revolution
in 1908, there occurred the counter-revolution led by Sultan
Abdul Hamid II.   Subsequently, the Turks massacred several
thousand Armenians in the Cilician city of Adana, where two
American missionaries also perished.   Turkish mobs also destroyed and damaged American property.   The U.S.   responded immediately, and in April 1909 the battleships North
Carolina and Montana were dispatched from Cuban to Turkish
waters where their presence had a calming effect on the dis-
traught Turkish populace.

The official American response to the Young Turks
was one of optimism and hope that many problems outstanding between the two governments would be resolved.   This
confidence manifested itself when the State Department replied to a member of Congress who had submitted a petition
for American action on the Armenian question, saying that
the new Turkish government was not wholly involved in the
massacres. [12]

The United States hoped for increased trade with Turkey now that a new regime was in power.   At the time the
U.S. government was involved with the Armenian question, an
American business group was seeking an economic concession
in Turkey known as the Chester Concession.   The question is
raised: Did the U.S. government turn aside missionary requests for protection and indemnity and the pleas for protection of the Armenians in order to further American economic
interests?   Ambassador Oscar Straus records that Secretary
of State Knox instructed him that the indemnity claim should
not be pressed, and that his influence should be used to further American commerce. [13]   The Taft administration was
clearly more interested in Dollar Diplomacy than in missionary work.   Secretary Knox advised Ambassador William W.
Rockhill in 1911 that he should pursue the "real and commercial rather than the academic interests of the United States
in the Near East."[14]   That economic interests were para-
mount in the Taft administration's list of priorities is evidenced by the dispatch of F. M. Huntington Wilson, Ambassador Extraordinary, in 1910 to Turkey to pursue an economic
concession, with no mention being made of the missionary
claims or the Armenians. [15]

Not only did commercial interests carry greater weight
with the Taft administration, but the advocates of Dollar Diplomacy were also quite willing to violate the tradition of
non-intervention in the quest for new commercial opportunity.
Two instances are cited.   The first involves the Turkish effort to raise the tariff on imports.   For a number of years
the Turks had attempted to revise upward their tariff on
goods from abroad.   The Turks wanted 11 per cent.   Opposed, the European Powers tied customs revision to concessions they desired from Turkey.   The U.S. followed suit,
and, in return for acquiescing to an increase in customs
duties, presented five demands to the Turks.   The first three
conditions aimed at securing better treatment for American
religious institutions.   The fourth was designed to prevent
further discrimination against American commerce.   The last
involved exterritorial jurisdiction.   In assocation with the
European Powers the U.S. made a technical transgression of
the commandment to avoid intervention.   The Turks readily
agreed to the first four provisions.   After more than a generation the Turks gained customs revision, and the U.S.
settled several outstanding issues.[16]

The second episode that saw American policy-makers
exceed the limits of non-intervention occurred in the negotiations related to the Chester Concession.   Not only was the
U.S. apparently willing to consider relating mediation in the
Italo-Turk War to furthering the Chester Concession,[17] but
the State Department was inclined to use its diplomatic machinery to abet the cause of the Chester group.[18]

In the years just prior to World War I a group of
men led by Rear Admiral Colby M. Chester, a retired American naval officer, attempted to obtain an economic concession from Turkey that would include the building of railroad
lines and the right to exploit mineral deposits.   The Chester
group's efforts to obtain diplomatic support coincided with the
Taft administration's pursuit of Dollar Diplomacy in both
Latin America and the Far East.   As originally conceived,
the Chester project called for the building of a railroad line
from Aleppo in Syria to the Mediterranean port of Alexan-
dretta. Admiral Chester began to negotiate with the Sultan
Abdul Hamid in 1908, and continued his efforts with the
Young Turks after the revolution.   Because the Young Turks
encouraged the Americans, who were devoid of political ambitions in Turkey, the Chester syndicate enlarged its project
considerably.   In 1909 it applied for an extended concession
that would include a railroad line from Sivas to Sulaimaniya

near the border of Persia, and the right to exploit mineral
deposits on the rights of way.   Compelled to compete temporarily with another American concern known as the J. G.
White Company, which was eliminated in the autumn of 1909,
the Chester syndicate organized the Ottoman-American Development Company.   Counting on adequate financial backing
from U. S. Steel and several large railroad interests, the
Chester associates proceeded with the initial quest for a concession.   Secretary of State Knox advised that the Department
would support the enterprise, but he refused to comply with
a request from the Turkish chargé in Washington to give the
Department's imprimatur on the Chester syndicate.[19]   In
early 1910 Chester representatives acquired a preliminary
agreement with the Turks and promptly made a deposit of
20,000 Turkish pounds.   Secretary Knox agreed to make several concessions, including the ending of a number of capitulatory rights, should the Turks agree to accept the project.[20]
But German interests opposed the Chester project, which
would interfere with the German-sponsored Berlin to Baghdad
Railroad, and in June 1910 the Turkish Parliament adjourned
before approving the concession.

Pessimism pervaded the ranks of company leaders, and
it required State Department encouragement for the syndicate
to continue efforts to acquire the concession.[21]   Although the
Department was optimistic, a number of diplomatic representatives were despondent, and their reports conveyed a gloomy
picture.   Ambassador Straus reported that much greater government support was necessary to acquire a concession in
Turkey.   Huntington Wilson, the special American emissary
sent to tout the Chester effort, advised from Turkey that the
Levant was not an American sphere and that Americans
should confine their efforts to Latin America and China.[22]
The company's continued feeling of despair was justified, for
in June 1911 the Parliament voted to postpone consideration
of the concession.

The Chester group girded for a final attempt and so
informed the State Department.   Delighted with this news,
Secretary Knox advised Ambassador Rockhill to devote himself to furthering the Chester plan to the exclusion of missionary interests.   But with the outbreak of the Italo-Turk
War, some company officials wanted to withdraw.   It was at
this juncture that the Department debated tying the Chester
Concession to the Turkish request for mediation.   The Chester board of directors withdrew its application in October
1911, much to the State Department's consternation.

Having temporarily exceeded the bounds of non-intervention in supporting the Chester Concession, it was an embarrassed Secretary Knox who drew in his horns and returned
to the tradition of non-interference in Middle Eastern affairs.
Although the Chester syndicate continued its efforts after Woodrow Wilson assumed the presidency, it did so without the
support of the new administration, which adhered to the tradition of not giving special governmental endorsement to any
one company's economic enterprises.

Official American support for the Chester Concession
did not mark the first instance of U.S. pursuit of a policy in
the pre-war period at variance with the tradition of non-intervention.   Earlier, President Roosevelt participated in the
Algeciras Conference through the presence of two delegates.
The Conference had come about in this manner.   France had
long sought to extend her control to Morocco, only to be
thwarted by the British.   But France and Britain concluded
the entente cordiale in 1904, allowing France hegemony over
Morocco in exchange for British supremacy in Egypt.   But
Germany, aware that France's ally Russia was involved in
war in the Far East, hoped to effect a diplomatic stratagem
that would destroy the Franco-Russian alliance, nullify the
entente cordiale, and establish German mastery in Europe.
First, Kaiser William II journeyed in March 1905 to the Moroccan port of Tangier where he delivered a provocative
speech in support of a free Morocco.   The Kaiser created the
first Moroccan crisis which could have led to a general European war, pitting France and Britain against Germany and
Austria-Hungary.   The Kaiser then solicited the assistance of
President Roosevelt to help maintain the Open Door in Morocco, thus obstructing French imperial ambitions and deliv-
ering a blow to the entente cordiale in the bid to achieve hegemony over Europe.[23]   The Kaiser called for an international conference to discuss the Moroccan question.   Roosevelt
was reluctant to participate, even though the United States was
signatory to the Madrid Convention and a staunch advocate of
the Open Door policy.   At first, he replied that the U.S. had
no vital interest in Morocco, but, as war clouds loomed on
the horizon, Roosevelt agreed to participate.   Historians have
debated the reasons for Roosevelt's change of heart.   His primary reason for departing from the tradition of non-involvement was that he wanted to preserve world peace.   War might
endanger American national security.   A violation of the tenets
of Monroe's doctrine seemed justified by considerations of the
national interest.   It is doubtful that Roosevelt's pro-French
sentiments influenced his decision, or that his concern for the

Open Door was a factor, for American trade with Morocco was negligible. [24]

The United States was represented at Algeciras by veteran diplomat Henry White and Samuel Gummere, minister to Morocco. The entente cordiale proved viable as Roosevelt supported France, [25] not because he was joining the entente as a de facto member, but because he supported world peace. On 7 April 1906 the American delegates signed the Convention of Algeciras, an instrument that guaranteed the territorial integrity of Morocco, ensured the Open Door, but awarded France and Spain a special position of authority with the Moroccan constabulary.

The U.S. Senate advised and consented to the convention, but with the reservation that it in no way compromised the tradition of non-intervention. While the press was critical of Roosevelt's departure from the age-old policy of non-interference, he seems to have been justified, for a general European war might have embroiled the United States.

Taken as a whole, the American participation at Algeciras and the pursuit of the Chester Concession marked two sharp compromises with the tradition of non-involvement. But this practice was not universally followed in the Middle East, for the U.S. continued to adhere to this policy guideline in Persia where the Shah offered commercial advantages as an inducement for political support against the European Powers.

With Roosevelt in the White House, a more positive American posture in Persia might have been expected. Lloyd C. Griscom, Bowen's successor, reported that the Persians hoped the U.S. would accept commercial advantages in return for diplomatic backing against the European states or for sending advisers to assist the Persian government. Although the State Department continued to abide by the dictates of non-intervention, some effort was made to increase Persian-American trade. To this end, Griscom made a two-month journey through Persia and submitted a brief report on commercial opportunity. In sum, he concluded that Russian domination in the North and British control in the South would debar any substantial American economic penetration of Persia. [26]

But American diplomatic agents continued their primary function of offering protection to American missionaries,

and steps were taken to vindicate the death of missionary
Benjamin W. Labaree, murdered by a Kurdish tribesman and
religious fanatic in March 1904. [27]   This incident set in motion a chain of events in which American missionaries caused
the United States to become involved in an international crisis
between Turkey and Persia.   Richmond Pearson, American
minister to Persia, looked into the Labaree murder and determined that the assassin's ancestral tie to Mohammed made
it difficult for the Persian government to arrest and punish
him.   But the missionary lobby in Persia demanded action.
Pearson consulted with the British ambassador, who did not
oppose sending U.S warships to the Persian Gulf.   Ultimately, the Shah announced that because of his ancestral background the chief culprit in Labaree's murder would not be ex-
ecuted, but would be imprisoned for life and the government
would award an adequate indemnity to Labaree's widow.   The
State Department considered the matter closed. [28]   But the
missionaries did not, maintaining that all of the murderers
must be punished by death, and it was at this juncture that
the Labaree murder assumed international proportions.
Since the other culprits had fled across the Persian border to
Turkey, a Persian expeditionary force was mounted to return
them for trial.   Missionaries insisted that American consul
William F. Doty leave his post at Tabriz and accompany the
force to explain to the Kurds that the matter could be settled
by surrendering the guilty parties.   The Labaree affair resulted in border skirmishes between Turkey and Persia, a
crisis from which the State Department wanted to disengage,
for it was generally held that the murder was directly responsible for the border incident.   Turks invaded Persia and
the Shah's government wanted the United States to make good
Persian losses in the amount of $100,000.   The Department
was aware that Persia had used the Labaree affair to rationalize its invasion of Turkey and refused to be drawn into the
matter.   The U.S. declined to accept any request for money.
But it was an embarrassed Department of State that learned
of Doty's claim that he had brought about the Persian action
against the Kurds.   The Department reprimanded Doty for
compromising the American tradition of non-intervention. [29]

Just as the United States remained aloof from the Labaree episode, so it also refrained from support of the Persian revolutionaries who established a constitutional government in the 1907 revolt that ousted the absolutist system of
government.   While the U.S. had expressed sympathy with the
Greek cause early in the nineteenth century, no such expression of concern was forthcoming from the State Department

during the Persian revolution. [30]   The Department enjoined
Minister John B. Jackson from encouraging the Shah to support the Constitutionalists, since such action would violate
the tradition of non-intervention. [31]   When the revolutionaries
tossed out the undemocratic Shah and set his son on the
throne, they took steps to punish supporters of the deposed
Shah.   The Department was irate when Charles W. Russell,
the new minister, acted to prevent the Constitutionalists from
persecuting the reactionaries.   Russell received word from
the Department that his activities were at odds with the policy of non-involvement. [32]   The Department also discouraged
diplomatic agents from awarding asylum to Persian refugees. [33]   American missionaries did not abide by the Department's injunction against granting asylum, and there was an
isolated instance of a missionary serving the cause of the
Constitutionalists.

     The policy of non-intervention was also strictly fol-
lowed during the time that the Shuster economic mission was
present in Persia.   Because the U. S. had no political ambitions in Persia, the Shah's government wanted the State Department to send economic advisers to Persia to rationalize
the Persian financial system.   After the signing of the Anglo-
Russian Convention in 1907, an instrument whereby Britain
and Russia divided Persia into economic spheres, Persian
Constitutionalists were insistent that American advisers
straighten out the Persian financial morass with a view to
strengthening Persia's hand against Britain and Russia.   The
State Department opposed sending government officials, but
when W. Morgan Shuster and a group of four assistants
agreed to go to Persia for a three-year period, the Department advised that they were employed by the Persian government and did not represent the U. S. government. [34]   Thus
Shuster, like other Americans who had gone to the Middle
East, as experts in the employ of a foreign government, was
on his own.

     The Persian government appointed Shuster Treasurer-
General of Persia, and the former Washington, D. C. lawyer
set about the task of reforming Persian finance.   Almost immediately Shuster and associates ran into opposition from
corrupt Persian politicians and from the Russians.   When
Shuster sought to obtain the services of a British army officer to head a police force to enforce treasury laws, Britain
added her opposition to that of Russia.   The Russians wanted
Shuster dismissed and supported their position with the dispatch of a military force into northern Persia.   Ultimately,

in December 1912, the Shah's government terminated Shuster's position. [35]

Russian motives were obvious, as the Persian Foreign Minister informed the State Department. A reformed Persian financial system would enable the Shah to exercise greater independence vis-à-vis Russia and Britain. The Russians, with British support, could not tolerate this condition. Although the British admired Shuster's work, they were obligated by the terms of the Anglo-Russian convention of 1907 to support Russian demands. [36]

Just as the United States government rejected involvement in the Shuster mission, so it also turned down Persian appeals for economic and diplomatic assistance. American public opinion, decidedly anti-Russian because of Tsarist persecution of Russian Jews, favored the offer of aid to Persia. Persian supplications and American public sentiment could not persuade the State Department to compromise with the tradition of non-intervention.

Shuster left a legacy of reform in Persia, and his devotion to his task, plus the American government's unwillingness to gain political or commercial advantages from his position, gained goodwill for the United States. With the visible evidence of the missionaries' good works and a knowledge of the pro-Persian sentiments of the American public, Persian government officials knew that the United States was a trusted friend. In years to come this fund of goodwill would work to the mutual advantage of both nations. The Shuster mission was not entirely inconsistent with American efforts to reform Middle Eastern peoples, and it might well be placed alongside efforts to reform the Barbary pirates, improve the Egyptian military, and educate the subject peoples of the Ottoman Empire. But the efforts of Shuster, the private citizen, like those of Henry Eckford before him, did not in any way compromise the American tradition of non-intervention.

One final topic needs to be discussed: the American relationship to Middle Eastern oil. While Great Britain became involved in the quest for Middle Eastern petroleum in the years before World War I, the same cannot be said of the United States. When the U.S. Navy decided to convert to oil to fuel its ships, there was concern about the adequacy of domestic sources of oil; even so, the State Department did not exert pressure in the pre-war years to support Americans

seeking oil concessions in the Middle East.   While U.S. petroleum interests were exporting oil to the Middle East, and
several American engineers had been retained by the Egyptian government to search for oil, no official U.S. support
for petroleum concessions was forthcoming in the pre-war
period. [37]

*   *   *   *   *

With the exceptions of State Department support of the
Chester concession and President Roosevelt's participation at
Algeciras, the United States continued to uphold its policy of
non-intervention in the Middle East.   American interests in
the Middle East during the years prior to World War I continued to be primarily of a religious and educational nature,
with missionaries outnumbering other Americans in the region.   However, the quest for the Chester concession, accompanied by a strong State Department endorsement, fore-
shadowed the day when other American businessmen would engage in the exploration for oil in the Middle East with the
backing of the State Department.

But the outbreak of World War I would set in motion
a chain of events that precipitated the fall of the Ottoman Empire.   This long-expected event caused the United States to
assume a larger role in the Middle East.   For a time it appeared as though President Woodrow Wilson would have a
large voice in the Middle Eastern settlement, but the U.S.
Senate thought otherwise as it caused the United States to return to the policy of non-intervention in Middle Eastern affairs.   In the aftermath of the war, which depleted American
domestic reserves of oil, American petroleum interests, with
the support of the U.S. government, engaged in the post-war
quest for the rich oil resources that lay under the sands of
Middle Eastern countries.

Chapter 6

WORLD WAR I AND THE AMERICAN RESPONSE
TO UPHEAVAL IN THE MIDDLE EAST, 1914-1920

World War I was a watershed in modern Middle Eastern history, for it set in motion a chain of events that led
to the fall of the Ottoman Empire and released forces of nationalism long brewing in the subject peoples who hoped to
achieve the goal of independence. In juxtaposition to the
hopes of the subject peoples were the ambitions of the European Powers, which had sat at the bedside of the "Sick Man
of Europe" waiting for his death that they might satisfy their
imperial aspirations. War, nationalism, and imperialism
made for an upheaval that drew the United States away from
non-involvement to assume a role in Middle Eastern affairs.
But this departure was only temporary, for the American
people and Congress determined that the U.S. would not become enmeshed in the political affairs of the Middle
East.

*   *   *   *   *

During the early years of World War I the U.S. adhered to the policy of non-intervention. American diplomatic
representatives did not even attempt to dissuade Turkey from
entering the war as the ally of Germany and Austria-Hungary.
But the war strained American-Turkish relations.[1] In October 1914, the U.S. protested the Sublime Porte's abrogation of the capitulations. Relations became more tense when
the State Department asked the Turkish ambassador to leave
the country because of his comparisons between Turkish
treatment of the subject minorities and the American handling of the Philippine insurrectionaries and Southern Ne-
groes.[2]

Although relations remained correct, Turkish repres-

sions of the minorities led the "man on the street" to regard
the Turk as an unspeakable fellow.   Before the U.S. entered
the European War, officials in the State Department began to
anticipate the demise of the Ottoman Empire. [3]

The war tested the normal intercourse between the
U.S. and Turkey.   Commercial relations diminished, but
American schools and colleges remained open.   Their continued operation was not without incident, for Turkish officials
wanted the schools to adhere to a prescribed curriculum, and
there were times when the schools were on the verge of closing.   There was also a feeling of uncertainty among Americans in the various cities in the empire, because there was
fear of mob violence.   Americans repeatedly begged diplomatic agents for the protection of U.S. warships.   Their pa-
tience must have been tested when Turkish coastal guns fired
blank shots at the gig of the commanding officer of the U.S.S.
Tennessee as she lay anchored at Smyrna. [4]

The primary interest that concerned the U.S. in the
Middle East during the war was the protection of the missionary institutions.   Wartime conditions imposed harsh conditions
tions on the missionaries in the field.   At the outbreak of
hostilities in 1914, the American Board employed some 150
missionaries in Turkey.   While they were determined to continue their work, the departure of American diplomats in 1917
dampened their ardor, and many soon followed.   Numerous
stations were closed, and only one-fifth of the missionaries
remained at their posts.   The missionaries were fortunate to
have Henry Morgenthau as American ambassador in Turkey,
for he zealously represented their interests in Constantinople.[5]
He enjoyed the friendship of missionary leaders Caleb Frank
Gates, the president of Robert College, Mary Mills Patrick,
the president of Constantinople Women's College, and William
W. Peet, treasurer of the American Board. [6]   At the beginning of the war, the missionaries faced a financial crisis that
was alleviated when Ambassador Morgenthau and the local
Standard Oil Company manager advanced funds to the missionaries from their personal accounts. [7]   The missionaries not
only counted on the services of Ambassador Morgenthau, but
they could also rely on President Woodrow Wilson, whose administration restored the Open Door to preeminence in American-Middle Eastern relations and once again gave priority to
the interests of the missionary. [8]   Missionary influence in the
Wilson administration assumed large proportions after 1915
when the Turks once again perpetrated a massacre upon the
Armenians.   The Turkish leaders hoped to destroy the pro-

Russian Armenians, who provided a threat.   The Young Turk triumvirate resorted to genocide in their Turkification plan and the Armenians paid the price.   Between the 1915 massacres and 1919, American missionaries played a predominant role in shaping the nation's Middle Eastern policy in response to the upheavals that accompanied the war.

The Turkish onslaught on the Armenians began in the spring of 1915 when the Turks attacked Van, a stronghold of Turkish Armenians whom Enver Pasha considered disloyal. The Turks failed to take Van, but this failure provoked the Ottoman leadership to seek a final solution to the Armenian problem.   The plan called for the extermination of all able-bodied men and the deportation of older men and women and children.   The deportation route from Turkish Armenia to Syria was a long trail of tears as Armenians perished by the thousands.   In spite of Turkish censorship, news of the horror filtered in to the American embassy as missionaries provided the initial reports.   Ambassador Morgenthau remonstrated with Djemal Pasha, Minister of Marine, with Enver, the Minister of War, and with Talaat Bey, Turkish Minister of the Interior, but to no avail.[9]   On 3 September 1915 Morgenthau cabled the State Department the grim news, and suggested that Cleveland Dodge, a wealthy American industrialist and philanthropist, organize a relief committee to save the Armenians.   In mid-September Dodge convened a group in his New York office, and there founded one of the most effective relief organizations in modern history.[10]

But in the Middle East the Turks subjected other minorities to hardships, and Zionist Jews, Greeks, Syrians, and others felt the force of Turkish repression.   Morgenthau protested these barbaric acts as did his successor, Abram Elkus. As news of Turkish atrocities appeared in the press, American public opinion rallied quickly to support the relief efforts to alleviate the distress in the Middle East.   Cleveland Dodge's committee became the American Committee for Armenian and Syrian Relief and was later incorporated by Congress in 1919 as Near East Relief.   With Dr. James L. Barton of the American Board as its chairman, and with the support of wealthy men like Cleveland Dodge and industrialist Charles R. Crane, the group had little difficulty in raising $100,000 to meet immediate relief needs of refugees.   Ultimately, the organization raised over $100 million in relief funds.[11]   Originally dominated by Protestant leaders, Armenian and Syrian relief expanded its base to include Roman Catholics and Jews.   President Wilson endorsed the organiza-

tion, and the State Department cooperated with it.   The distribution of relief was handled in the main by missionaries,
but diplomatic agents assisted in Constantinople, Beirut,
Cairo, Jerusalem, Tabriz, and Tiflis.   The U.S. Navy also
assisted by providing transport for supplies and relief workers.[12]

The influence of relief officials and missionaries at
the policy-making level increased during World War I.   The
missionary-relief lobby was effective in pressuring the State
Department to persuade the Turks to allow American relief
to enter the Ottoman Empire.[13]   Finally, James L. Barton,
the Secretary of the American Committee for Armenian and
Syrian Relief, regularly communicated to officials at the
Near East desk at the State Department the missionary position on the Armenian question.[14]

The Zionist issue also intruded into American foreign
policy considerations.   Since its inception in 1897 the World
Zionist Organization aspired to the creation of a Jewish national home in Palestine.   In 1914 the population of Palestine
was largely Arab.   There were approximately 600,000 Arabs,
while the Jewish population was less than 85,000.   At that
time there were some 20,000 Jews in Zionist organizations
in the United States, but with a total Jewish population of
over 3,000,000, this was a small percentage.   Zionism did
not expand in the American Jewish community until after the
outbreak of war.   Notable converts to Zionism were Louis
Brandeis who became in 1916 a Supreme Court Justice, Judge
Julian W. Mack, Rabbi Stephen S. Wise, and Felix Frankfurter,[15] also later to become an associate justice of the Supreme Court.   Brandeis became an ardent Zionist in 1912,
and he cultivated Wilson's interest in the aspirations of
World Zionism.[16]   Later Frankfurter and Rabbi Wise also
exercised considerable influence on the President.   It was behind Wilson's leadership that the American diplomatic machinery responded to the plea of American Zionists for aid to
the hard-pressed Jewish community in Palestine.   Shortly after the outbreak of war, American Consul Otis Glazebrook at
Jerusalem advised Ambassador Morgenthau that Jews in Palestine were destitute.   He appealed for food and financial
aid.   Since the European Powers had removed their diplomats
from the Ottoman Empire, Germany and Austria-Hungary excepted, American diplomats were the sole advocates for Jews
in Palestine.   Ambassador Morgenthau, an assimilationist not
sympathetic with Zionist goals, was their chief hope, and he
responded to their call for help.[17]

The initial Jewish problem centered about the fate of
some 50,000 Russian Jews in Palestine.   With Russia at war
with Turkey, the Turks determined to expel these Jews.
Morgenthau advised the State Department of their plight on 25
December 1914, and the U.S. Navy made the cruiser Tennessee available to lift some 6000 Jewish refugees to Alexandria.
Most of the remaining Russian Jews agreed to accept naturalization as Ottoman subjects to avoid expulsion. [18]   To make
matters worse for the Jews, the commanding officer of the
Tennessee filed a report that Turkish nationalists were determined to destroy the Zionist movement in Palestine.   An official proclamation was issued to that effect in January 1915.
The influence of Ambassador Morgenthau and the diplomatic
agents of the Central Powers was responsible for Djemal
Pasha's calling off Turkish persecutions of Jews by March.
Further, American Jews proffered the economic aid to Palestinian Jews that made the difference between survival and ex-
tinction. [19]

The American Joint Distribution Committee, a Jewish
philanthropic organization, cared for Jews in the Ottoman Empire.   The State Department obtained the necessary permission from the Turks and from the British and the French for
the dispatch of relief shipments to Palestine Jews.   Secretary
of the Navy Josephus Daniels provided space on the U.S.S.
Vulcan, a U.S. Navy collier, to carry some 700 tons of food
to Palestine.   But these Jews needed additional help, [20] for
they had turned to agriculture, and their orange crops were
in danger.   In 1915 Zionists asked the State Department to
use its good offices with the Turks and the Allies to permit
shipments of petroleum so necessary for the operation of irrigation pumps in the orange groves.   The British and French
refused, saying the Turks might confiscate the fuel for their
war effort. [21]

But U.S. government officials aided the Palestinian
Jews in other ways.   Ambassador Morgenthau facilitated the
transfer of money to them when the war brought a halt to the
normal movement of funds.   The State and Navy Departments
aided the channeling of medical supplies and food. [22]

Thus, prior to American entry into World War I, the
Protestant missionary lobby and American Zionists had exerted sufficient pressure on official government circles to obtain a more active American role in Middle Eastern affairs.
But the high points of Protestant and Zionist utilization of political pressure came after the United States declared war on

Germany in April 1917. Although in his annual message to
Congress in December 1917 he urged a declaration of war on
Austria, Wilson elected not to ask for a declaration on Turkey, even though British, French, and Italian officials would
have welcomed such a move.[23] Why did Wilson omit Turkey?
It seems that he was primarily motivated by two basic considerations. First, American military advisers opposed entry into the conflict in the Middle East, because it would
drain off forces needed on the Western Front.[24] Wilson also
considered the arguments of the Protestant lobby, which
claimed that war with Turkey would end all relief efforts and
cause the closing of missionary institutions.[25] It has even
been suggested that hope of revival of the Chester Concession
was a factor underlying Wilson's decision.[26] It appears safe
to assume that considerations of a humanitarian and strategic
nature dictated Wilson's decision. We can conclude that missionary interests coincided with the national interest, which
opposed diversion of U.S. forces from the Western Front
where the war was eventually won.

But Zionist influence on Wilson was also important, as
demonstrated by the abortive 1917 Morgenthau mission to seek
a separate peace with Turkey and by President Wilson's consent to endorse a Jewish national home in Palestine. The
former ambassador to Turkey suggested to Secretary of State
Lansing in May 1917 that he believed Turkey wanted a separate peace. Such a move would, on the surface at least,
benefit hard-pressed Palestinian Jews.[27] Lansing broached
Morgenthau's idea to Wilson who was interested. The State
Department arranged for Morgenthau to travel to Switzerland
to contact Turkish diplomats. But American Zionists opposed
this move. Justice Brandeis knew of its purpose, and he advised Dr. Chaim Weizmann, the leading Zionist in Britain,
who promptly told British Foreign Secretary Arthur J. Balfour.
The two agreed that the Morgenthau mission should be
scotched, for an anticipated British offensive against the Turks
in Palestine would do far more to assure the future of a Jewish national home. Brandeis arranged for Felix Frankfurter
to accompany Morgenthau to ascertain that the latter would not
make an agreement, compromising the Zionist goal. Acting
through Balfour, the Zionists arranged for Morgenthau and
Frankfurter to meet Dr. Weizmann at Gibraltar where he de-
terred Morgenthau from his task.[28]

American Zionists also influenced Wilson's approval of
the promise to create a Jewish national home in Palestine.
Following the Russian Revolution of March 1917, the English

Zionist leadership persuaded the British Foreign office that
a declaration supporting the realization of a Jewish national
home in Palestine would earn the acclaim of Russian Jews
and keep them from joining forces with the Bolsheviks, and
also win the allegiance of American Jews.   Whitehall obtained the French and Italian consent, and it only remained
to gain Wilson's approval.   The President turned down an initial British request for such an endorsement on 3 September
1917, but on 13 October he secretly affirmed to Colonel Edward House his endorsement.   With Wilson's consent, Balfour wrote Lord Rothschild on 2 November, and in what has
become known as the Balfour Declaration he declared that
Britain would support the creation of a Jewish national home
in Palestine.   What caused Wilson to change his mind in
such a short period of time to make a decision so totally at
odds with the concept of self-determination and with the tradition of non-involvement?   Historians disagree, but it seems
safe to assume that Justice Brandeis was the chief influence
on Wilson's reversal. [29]   Apparently the President would not
give consent in September, for to do so would place undue
strains on American-Turkish relations and possibly jeopardize
the missionary operation in the Middle East.   Wilson ultimately decided to give a secret endorsement in October, but
his public endorsement did not come until some ten months
later when Turkey was on the verge of defeat.   It is reasonable to infer that the missionary-relief lobby was responsible
for this delay. [30]

Other than missionary institutions, the United States
had no major interests in the Middle East, but in December
1917 Wilson decided the time had come to make a comprehensive statement of U.S. peace aims covering the Middle
East and elsewhere.   He had been prompted by the Bolshevik
publication of the secret wartime treaties negotiated by the
Allies.   These treaties branded the Allies as imperialists.
Wilson had instructed Colonel House to organize in September
1917 a fact-finding body that would provide the information on
which to base a just peace.   The Inquiry, as it was called,
produced a memorandum on 22 December.   With respect to
the Middle East, the document called for "strong allied control" over the various parts of the Ottoman Empire. [31]   Officials in Washington were aware that the drafting of peace
aims in the Middle East would be complicated by the British,
French, Russian, and Italian secret treaties partitioning the
Ottoman Empire, and by the nationalistic aspirations of Armenians, Jews, Arabs, and Greeks.   Wilson would not accept the aims of the Allies, even though he knew the contents

of the secret agreements. In January 1918 Wilson laid out
the American peace aims in the Fourteen Points.   Point XII
provided that the "Turkish portions of the Ottoman Empire
should be assured a secure sovereignty, " but that the national minorities under Ottoman rule should be assured the right
of self-determination. [32]

Wilson went to the Paris Peace Conference determined
that the Middle Eastern settlement would be based on the
broad principle of sovereignty as expressed in Point XII of
Fourteen Points.   But he had not reckoned with the Allied
Powers' determination to partition the Ottoman Empire in accordance with the wartime pacts.   Thus, the President broke
with the American tradition of non-involvement and injected
the United States into negotiations over the Eastern Question.
At Paris Wilson learned officially of the imperial aims of the
Powers.   Russia was to have taken Constantinople and the
Turkish Straits.   Britain was to have Mesopotamia and Palestine, while France would take Syria and a portion of Anatolia.
Italy was to have a slice of western Anatolia.   Matters were
complicated by British commitments to Zionists and Arabs.
Britain had agreed that an Arab state would be formed at the
conclusion of the war, in return for Arab support during hostilities.   She had also promised that a Jewish homeland would
be established in Palestine, a goal that conflicted with Arab
hopes.   Wilson had of course endorsed the pledge to the Zionists, and the missionaries had predisposed him to work for
an independent Armenia.

In January 1919 at Paris the Council of Ten took up
the question of the Ottoman Empire.   The Powers wanted outright annexation of the territories awarded them by the wartime pacts.   Wilson opposed annexation, saying this would
discredit the proposed League of Nations.   At length, Prime
Minister Jan Smuts of South Africa produced the mandate concept, a compromise between imperial annexation and Wilsonian self-determination.   The Smuts solution was acceptable,
and on 30 January the Council of Ten accepted a draft resolution by which Armenia, Syria, Mesopotamia, Arabia, and
Palestine would be separated from the Ottoman Empire and
placed under individual mandates. [33]   It was at the 30 January
meeting that the Council considered the Armenian mandate.
The British hoped the United States would accept the mandate.
They were aware that the Protestant missionary lobby had
nurtured in Wilson the idea of an American protectorate for
Armenia.   They hoped to translate American humanitarian
concern for the Armenians into a mandate that would serve

British imperial aspirations. An American mandate for Armenia would serve as a buffer between British oil in Persia and potential reserves in Mesopotamia and the Bolsheviks in Russia; would counter French influence in the Middle East; would halt a Pan-Turanian movement that might sweep through the Middle East jeopardizing the British position in India; and finally would mean that American participation would give the Turkish settlement added prestige. [34] But Wilson warned that Congress and the American people would not accept responsibility in the Middle East lightly and that his acceptance of the mandate was subject to Congressional approval. [35]

The subject peoples of the Ottoman Empire were anxious to have their day in court, and during the month of February they had ample time to present their cases. On 6 February the Emir Feisal of the Hejaz asked for the creation of an Arab confederation. Another group of Arabs desired that Syria be set aside as a monarchy under French mandate. In late February the Armenians appeared and requested an integral Armenian state, consisting of Turkish and Russian Armenia, under the aegis of a Great Power. Zionists urged that the Balfour Declaration be carried out, with Britain acting as mandatory. In addition, the Greeks presented a case for a portion of western Anatolia, claiming that a large Greek population entitled Greece to annex this territory.

With such a welter of counter-claims the situation reached an impasse, at which point a letter from President Howard Bliss of the American University of Beirut suggested to President Wilson the possibility of sending a commission of inquiry to Syria to determine the wishes of the people. [36] This suggestion was harmonious with Wilson's concept of self-determination, and, at the President's insistence, the Supreme Allied Council agreed on 20 March to send such a commission to Syria. Initially known as the Inter-Allied Commission on Mandates in Turkey, the fact-finding body ultimately became an American venture, because the British and French elected not to participate. The President appointed Dr. Henry C. King, president of Oberlin College, and Charles R. Crane of New York. The King-Crane Commission, as the mandate commission became known, consisted also of advisers such as Dr. Albert H. Lybyer, Dr. George R. Montgomery, and Captain William Yale. In spite of opposition on all sides, the group set out on its mission in late spring of 1919 just as President Wilson became involved in another controversy that ultimately changed the political complexion of the Middle East. [37]

In late April 1919 the Italians landed a force at Smyrna.   Lloyd George proposed to the Supreme Allied Council
that the Greeks land a force at Smyrna to counter the Italians.
Ignoring the advice of his advisers, Wilson agreed.[38] Subsequently the Greeks launched an aggressive campaign in Western Anatolia that aroused Turkish nationalism.

On 14 May, while the Greeks were proceeding with
plans in Turkey, the Council of Four accepted a resolution
providing for cession of the Smyrna district to the Greeks.
In addition to setting aside Turkish territory in Anatolia, the
Council awarded territory to Italy and France, and provided
that the United States be assigned mandates for Constantinople
and Armenia.[39] Wilson warned that his acceptance of the
Turkish mandates was subject to approval by Congress, but
it appeared that the Allies had at last drawn the U.S. into
the Eastern Question.   Not only had Wilson ignored his staff
in making the decision to send Greek forces to Smyrna, but
his acceptance of the mandates also ran counter to the thinking of the other commissioners.   Admiral Mark L. Bristol,
the American High Commissioner at Constantinople, had bom-
barded the American Peace Commission with dispatches pointing up the dangers of being implicated in the disposition of the
Ottoman Empire.   He influenced Henry White, Robert Lansing, and General Tasker Bliss who agreed that U.S. acceptance of mandates for Armenia or portions of Anatolia was
fraught with dangerous consequences.[40]

Discussion of the Middle Eastern question continued in
June at which time an Ottoman delegation appeared and requested the continuation of the Ottoman Empire as an integrated whole.   The Council rejected this plea.   On 25 June
Lloyd George suggested that peace with Turkey should be concluded while the Turks were in Paris, but Wilson demurred.
It was decided that further discussion of the Turkish question
was impossible until President Wilson could determine if Congress would permit American acceptance of mandates.[41]

The treaty with Germany having been signed on 28
June, Wilson returned to the United States where he promptly
presented the Versailles Treaty to the U.S. Senate.   A prolonged Senate hearing and growing public resentment over various features of the treaty disclosed an unmistakable tide of
opinion against both it and acceptance of the mandates.

With Wilson's hands tied by a reluctant Senate, events
in the Middle East deteriorated.   Greek aggression in Turkey

aroused a national sentiment that opposed Allied partition of
Anarolia. The Council of Four learned that the plight of the
Armenians was dire, for unless additional relief shipments
were sent to the Transcaucasus, the Armenians would starve.
The Council appointed a director for relief in the Caucasus,
and gave Herbert Hoover's American Relief Administration
jurisdiction over the region. The situation worsened with
the British withdrawal of an expeditionary force from the
Caucasus, leaving the Armenians to their fate. [42] Finally,
the British and French could not agree on a disposition of
Syria that would satisfy both Arabs and French imperialists.

The turn of events in the Middle East and the growing
isolationist sentiment in the United States boded ill for a
Middle Eastern senttlement to the liking of the Powers. The
British blamed Woodrow Wilson, alleging that he misled the
Allies about American acceptance of Middle Eastern mandates. Furthermore, the British claimed that Wilson deliberately delayed making a decision on mandates and that this
delay brought on the complete disruption of the Middle Eastern settlement. [43] These accusations could not be further
from the truth. The President at no time led the Allied delegation at Paris to believe that acceptance of the mandates
would be final until Congress consented. As for the charge
that Wilson delayed the settlement, it must be recalled that
Senator Henry Cabot Lodge, chairman of the Senate Foreign
Relations Committee, was responsible for the dilatory tactics
that held up the treaty during the summer. Too, the President was aware of the onerous burdens of assuming a mandate, and he did not consider them as selling points for the
League of Nations. His list of priorities called first for
Senate acceptance of the Treaty of Versailles with its League
Covenant. After the Senate had consented to the treaty he
would ask for Senate permission to accept the mandates. [44]

The United States continued to play an interested role
in the Middle East by its participation on fact-finding bodies.
The King-Crane Commission collected data that Wilson hoped
would serve as the basis for a settlement in keeping with his
principles. It completed its report on 21 August, and it recommended a British or American mandate for Syria, with
Palestine included in a state ruled by Feisal. Zionist plans
could not be realized, for a Zionist state of 10 per cent Jews
in Palestine could violate the principle of self-determination.
Britain was to hold a mandate for Mesopotamia, while a
small Armenian state, an internationalized Constantinopolitan
state, and a Turkish state in Anatolia would be placed under

separate mandates. Greek claims for an Anatolian enclave
were rejected. Non-Arabic portions of the Ottoman Empire
were to be placed under one mandate, with the U.S. as mandatory. The report reached the White House in September
while Wilson was on his speaking tour in behalf of the League
of Nations. He never saw the report, and French and Zionist influence prevented its use in making the Middle Eastern
settlement. [45]

The United States also participated in a second commission in the Middle East. On 18 July the Council of the
Heads of Delegations appointed an investigating body to determine the cause of the violence that accompanied the Greek operation at Smyrna. The fact-finding team consisted of British, French, Italian, and American members. The American
commissioner was Rear Admiral Mark L. Bristol, soon to be
appointed high commissioner at Constantinople. The Interallied Commission of Inquiry on the Greek Occupation of Smyrna and Adjacent Districts held over 40 meetings between mid-
August and mid-October and interviewed about 200 witnesses.
At length it submitted its report which described the Greek
landing as an unjustified mistake. While the Turks were not
blameless, the Greeks bore the burden of guilt for the violence. It recommended that the Greeks be withdrawn and replaced by an Allied force. The Council allowed the Greeks
to remain and suppressed the report. Ultimately, the Turks
emerged at the end of a three-year war with Greece as an
independent state, and the fiasco resulted in the fall of premiers Venezelos and Lloyd George. [46]

The U.S. government also sponsored the American
Military Mission to Armenia, known as the Harbord Mission.
Walter George Smith, a member of the American Committee
for Relief in the Near East, came to Paris in the summer of
1919, bringing news of the declining situation that he found on
his tour of the Armenian Republic earlier in the year. On
25 June he met with Herbert Hoover, Henry Morgenthau, William L. Westermann, the U.S. adviser on Near Eastern affairs, and others. The conferees agreed that Morgenthau
would request the President to appoint General J. H. Harbord,
U.S. Army, to make a fact-finding tour of Armenia to determine the situation there and the feasibility of an American
mandate. The President appointed Harbord on 1 August. [47]

Harbord collected a team of experts and advisers and
proceeded to the Middle East. [48] The Mission left Constantinople in early September and returned in mid-October, having

toured a number of cities in Armenia and the Transcaucasus.
It reported on the Armenian situation and appended information relative to an American mandate in Armenia. While he
made no recommendation on the matter, his report contained
positive and negative data on the latter subject. The General
did stress some points in favor of an American mandate, but
he cautioned that a mandatary for Armenia should also have
mandates for Asiatic and European Turkey. Harbord submitted his finding to the American Mission at Paris. Ultimately,
his report played an important part in the Senate's rejection
of the Armenian mandate. [49]

While Harbord collected data, President Wilson toured
the United States to build up support for the League of Nations. His tour covered some 8000 miles in 22 days. His
speeches reflected a desire for the U.S. to take part in the
new world order. He mentioned the mandate on three occasions, and only once did he ask for support of an Armenian
mandate. A reading of the speeches indicates Wilson's priorities. Senate approval of the treaty must precede a request for a mandate. [50] The President was stricken in late
September in Pueblo, Colorado. With Wilson unable to function, European leaders despaired of American participation
in the Middle Eastern settlement. Evidence of a withdrawal
is found in U.S. reluctance to be drawn into the British-
Arab-French controversy over Syria. [51] A second indication
of withdrawal came with the Senate's November rejection of
the Treaty of Versailles. The President felt compelled to
withdraw Frank Polk, head of the American Delegation at
Paris, from his post in December, and the United States
ceased to have a representative at the conference.

The Allies moved ahead on the Armenian matter in
1920. Pressure from the Turkish nationalist forces of Mustapha Kemal and from the Bolsheviks spurred them on. The
Peace Conference accorded the Armenian Republic de facto
recognition in January, but the U.S. did not do so until April,
in spite of the growing pressure by pro-Armenian Americans
to do so.

The most articulate pressure group was the American
Committee for the Independence of Armenia, led by James
W. Gerard, former American ambassador to Germany, and
Vahan Cardashian, an immigrant Armenian attorney. [52] Equal-
ly effective in applying pressure on the White House was the
American Committee for Relief in the Near East (formerly
the American Committee for Armenia and Syrian Relief),

later incorporated by Congress as Near East Relief. This
organization, while chiefly concerned with relief, was an important pressure group for the Armenians as demonstrated
by the effectiveness of its chairman, Dr. James L. Barton.[53]
Of growing importance to the Armenian cause was the newly
formed Armenia-America Society, led by Walter George
Smith, the attorney, who served as president, and George
Montgomery, a former member of the King-Crane Commission, as secretary.[54] But the various groups differed on
aims. Barton of Near East Relief envisaged an American
mandate over a large portion of the Turkish Empire, while
Gerard favored large-scale American assistance to the Armen-
ian Republic and the extension of de facto recognition.
Smith's group tended to go along with the goals set by the
Barton organization.[55]

Aware that Wilson was ill and could no longer press
for an Armenian mandate, the Allies decided to resume negotiations on the Turkish treaty. Accordingly, they opened
the London Conference on 12 February 1920. Although special interest groups in the United States urged the sending of
an American delegation, the U.S. was not represented except
by an observer who took no part in the proceedings.[56] By
February the United States had retreated from the position of
full-involvement in the Middle Eastern settlement assumed by
Wilson at Paris to the normal, traditional stance of non-intervention. At London the Allied premiers agreed to allow the
Sultan to remain in Constantinople and to establish an international commission to govern the Straits. Greece was to have
an enclave at Smyrna, while Armenia was to be recognized as
an independent state. Turkey would renounce claims to Mesopotamia, Arabia, Palestine, Syria, and the Aegean Islands.
Lloyd George announced that President Wilson retained his interest in Armenia, and since the conference leaders had received hundreds of telegrams from the United States asking
that some measures be taken to ensure the viability of the
Armenian Republic, the Allied leaders decided to ask the U.S.
to participate.[57] On 12 March Jusserand, the French ambassador to the United States, asked Frank Polk, acting Secretary of State, if the U.S. would take part in negotiations.[58]
The Versailles Treaty was again before the Senate, and on 19
March senators voted a second time to reject. Wilson's reply to the Allied premiers came on 20 March, advising that
the Turks be removed from Constantinople, that Armenia be
accorded fair treatment, and that no final settlement be made
with respect to the Straits unless Russia were consulted. Wilson further advised that the U.S. would not participate in the

treaty with Turkey, but would retain a voice in the settlement
to protect American interests. He asked that the Open Door
be maintained and urged the Powers not to discriminate
against non-signatories to the pact.[59]

Lloyd George took Wilson to task for presuming to advise on the Turkish question, while at the same time refusing to respond affirmatively to the Allied appeal. He believed that the United States was leaving the Allies "in the
lurch." But Wilson's hands were tied by the second Senate
rejection of the treaty. The Senate's negative action, coupled
with Wilson's refusal to participate, gave the Council little
hope that the U.S. would take part in the Middle Eastern
settlement. The Allies proceeded without U.S. participation.[60]

The Allied premiers repaired to the Italian town of
San Remo in April where they continued discussion of the
Turkish question. The U.S. was represented unofficially by
Robert U. Johnson, the American ambassador to Italy, who
served as an observer. The Allied leaders agreed that the
Arabian peninsula was to receive full independence, that
Syria was to be assigned to France as a mandate, that Britain would serve as mandatory for Mesopotamia (Iraq), Palestine, and Transjordan. The Armenian question received
much attention. The League of Nations turned down a mandate for Armenia just prior to convening the San Remo Conference. On 23 April the U.S. recognized the Armenian Republic, and perhaps it was this news that led the Allied premiers on 27 April to request the United States to accept a
mandate for Armenia. The premiers also asked Wilson to
arbitrate the boundary between Armenia and Turkey, leaving
the boundary to the north to be settled by direct negotiations
between Armenia, Georgia, and Azerbaijan.[61] In addition to
the question of Armenia and the mandates, the Allied leaders
drafted a tripartite agreement, providing for the partition of
Anatolia into spheres of influence over which the French,
Italians, and Greeks would have jurisdiction. The British and
French also signed an oil agreement by which France would
receive 25 per cent of the crude oil output from the Mesopotamian oil fields in return for which the British received the
right to run a pipeline from Mosul across Syria to the sea.[62]

Secretary of State Bainbridge Colby, successor to Robert Lansing, advised the American ambassador at Paris on
17 May to notify the Allies that President Wilson would arbitrate the Armeno-Turkish boundary.[63] Nothing was said
about accepting the mandate for Armenia, but on 24 May

President Wilson submitted his request to the Senate, calling for permission to accept the mandate.[64] Undoubtedly, Wilson believed that he had made a moral contract with the Allies at Paris to take up the international responsibility for Armenia. At all events, an American mandate for Armenia would inject the U.S. once again into the Middle Eastern imbroglio. If moral imperatives, legalistic bargains, and theories of international world order underlay Wilson's motives, what can be said of the Senate's rejection of Wilson's request in June 1920? Was the Senate's rejection of the mandate more in tune with the tradition of non-involvement, or was the President's willingness to accept a mandate consonant with the national interest? The portion of the Senate debate in late May 1920 that opposed the mandate would certainly find favor with the realist historians who view American foreign policy in terms of the national interest. But it would dismay those traditional historians who see moral considerations and legal contracts as the foundation stone of American foreign policy.

Many senators opposed the mandate because it violated the Monroe Doctrine, arguring that U.S. intervention in Armenia would set a precedent for European intrusion into the affairs of the Western Hemisphere. Responsibility for Armenia might involve the U.S. in a war with Turkey, Bolshevik Russia, or the peoples of the Transcaucasus. Many senators were suspicious of British motives in urging the U.S. to accept a mandate, for they viewed the League of Nations as an imperialistic scheme to give Britain hegemony in the Middle East--a condition that would award Britain the plums and send Uncle Sam to the poor house. Others based their opposition to the mandate on the Harbord Report, a document that contained many reasons for nonacceptance of responsibility to Armenia. Senate repudiation of Wilson's request came on 1 June 1920.[65] This action was in keeping with the tradition of non-intervention in the Middle East.

But the Senate vote did not deter Wilson. Even though the U.S. was not a signatory to the Treaty of Sèvres, signed in August 1920 by the Powers and Turkey, Wilson's interest in Armenia remained firm. He urged the Democrats to place a strong Armenian plank in the party's platform for the 1920 election.[66] In November he delineated the Armeno-Turkish boundary and offered his good offices to settle the war between Turkey and the Armenian Republic. His boundary award and his offer to mediate came too late, for in December 1920 the Turks defeated the forces of the Armenian

Republic.   By agreement with Russia, the districts of Kars
and Ardahan were placed under Turkish control, while the
remainder of the Republic fell to the Bolshevik control.[67]

*   *   *   *   *

For many Americans, Senate defeat of the mandate request and the Turco-Russian partition of the Armenian Republic relegated the Armenian question to the pages of history.
However, many Americans retained a strong interest in the
Armenian cause, and their continued pursuit of an alternative
solution to the partition of the Republic during the 1920s was
an important factor in American-Turkish relations.   But,
what is more important, the Senate rejection of the mandate
was symptomatic of the reversion of U.S. Middle Eastern
policy to its tradition of non-intervention.   American policy
in the Middle East in the inter-war years was rooted in this
tradition, as American policy-makers stood aloof from the
Palestine question, responded maturely to the forces of nationalism among Middle Eastern peoples, and avidly assisted
several American petroleum interests to acquire oil concessions.

Chapter 7

THE INTER-WAR YEARS
AND AMERICAN RESPONSE TO NATIONALISM
IN THE MIDDLE EAST, 1920-1939

The United States withdrew from the political dynamics
of the post-war Middle East in 1920, but the missionary-relief element continued to operate schools, hospitals, orphanages, and technical-vocational programs.   It also sustained a
movement in behalf of the Armenians which influenced American-Turkish relations until 1927.   Commercial interests increasingly entered the Middle East, seeking new markets, new
targets for investment, and new sources of raw materials.
Frequently the missionary-relief lobby was in conflict with the
commercial men.   The State Department acted as a broker to
reconcile the differences.   In shaping a Middle Eastern policy,
policy-makers had to consider the rising force of nationalism
that emerged in post-war Turkey, Iran, and the Arab lands.
Peoples of the Middle East looked to the U.S., for Americans
had made an illustrious example in breaking the bonds of colonialism a century and a half before.   Perhaps the best example of American accommodation to Middle Eastern nationalism occurred in Turkey.

*   *   *   *   *

Prior to the signing of the Turco-American Treaty of
August 1923, U.S.-Turkish relations can be characterized as
a struggle between the missionary-relief lobby and the mer-
chant-investor-petroleum lobby that sought new commercial
opportunity for American capital.   After the negotiation of the
pact, the American Board, an important segment of the missionary lobby, joined forces with the business interests in supporting approval of the treaty and accommodation with Turkey.
U.S. diplomats had to consider the imperatives imposed by
Turkish nationalism in defining policy objectives consistent

with the national interest.   But running through the diplomatic
intercourse between the U.S. and Turkey is the Armenian
question which continued to complicate matters until late in
the decade.   Irrespective of U.S. national interests, one element of the missionary-relief lobby continued to exert pressure on the policy-making machinery as it pursued objectives
for the Armenians.   Unfortunately for the Armenians, this
lobby did not coordinate its efforts. [1]

     The Armenia-America Society continued to work close-
ly with Near East Relief.   Growing to approximately sixty
chapters, it affiliated with the International Philarmenia League,
with headquarters in Geneva.   During the summer of 1920 it
urged President Wilson to send food to the Armenians and to
equip the small Armenian army.   But after the London Conference failed to create the Armenian state provided by the
Treaty of Sèvres, the society's officials beseeched the assembled premiers to create an Armenian homeland in Cilicia,
a province of Anatolia.   This solution the premiers rejected.
Society leaders then asked Secretary of State Charles Evans
Hughes on 14 April 1921 to use his influence to support a national home solution.   Hughes refused.   The society's leaders
flooded the country with propaganda, calling attention to the
"Terrible Turk" and urging support for an Armenian homeland. [2] The society's secretary, George Montgomery, attended
the Lausanne Conference, the international meeting called by
the Powers for November 1922 to revise the inoperative
Treaty of Sèvres.   He pressed the assembled diplomats to
create an Armenian homeland but failed.   The Turco-American Treaty negotiated at Lausanne contained no provision for
a national home. [3]   The Armenia-America Society claimed
that the U.S. delegation traded the national home in return
for economic concessions from the Turks, a charge that the
State Department adamantly denied. [4]

     The Turkish treaty was submitted to the Senate in May
1924, but the pro-Armenia lobby, less the American Board,
built up strong opposition to the treaty which became a controversial political issue between Democrats and Republicans.
That the treaty was defeated in January 1927 indicates the
success of the pro-Armenia lobby in creating a "Terrible
Turk" image in the United States to influence the course of
Turkish-American relations. [5]   While the Armenia-America
Society and Near East Relief now endorsed passage of the
treaty, the Gerard-Cardashian element formed the American
Committee Opposed to the Lausanne Treaty, and used the
services of Senator William King, a Utah Democrat, to lead

the opposition in the Senate.   The Committee also asked the
Democratic Party to place an Armenian plank in the party
platform of 1924.   The January 1927 Senate vote was six
votes short of the needed two-thirds majority.[6] So successful was the pro-Armenia lobby in shaping the course of U.S.-
Turkish relations by holding up the treaty that the U.S. high
commissioner in Constantinople was compelled to negotiate
with the Turkish government in 1926 a commercial modus
vivendi to continue commercial intercourse between the two
countries.   This was renewed in 1927, when normal U.S.-
Turkish relations were once again restored.[7]

        Thus the missionary-relief lobby left a dual legacy to
U.S. diplomacy in the 1920s.   On the one hand, it created
the "Terrible Turk" image in the United States that was
largely responsible for blocking resumption of normal Turkish-American relations.   On the other hand, it left a fund of
goodwill in Turkey because of its acts of charity and relief
in its educational activities.   The goodwill investment in Turkey far exceeded the investment in commercial enterprises.[8]
In over one hundred years of operation in Turkey, the American Board had expended approximately $13 million while the
American Bible Society spent about $3 million.   The three
American colleges in Turkey spent in the neighborhood of
$10 million.   Near East Relief expended about $40 million
in maintaining hospitals, orphanages, and clinics for the Armenian refugees.   In the course of a century American missionary-relief organizations had expended a total of some
$80 million.

        But the operation of missionary institutions was not
without difficulty during the post-war decade, for the Turks
viewed the missionaries as being responsible for anti-Turkish sentiment in the United States.   Because of the rapid
growth of national sentiment in Turkey, Turkish officials imposed restrictions on the missionary schools.   No religious
instruction would be tolerated, and the curriculum was subjected to close inspection by the Minister of Public Instruction.   The missionaries had two alternatives: conform to
the forces of nationalism or move out.   Most chose the former, but some schools did close.   But in those that remained open, many missionaries practiced "unnamed Christianity."[9] To meet the demands of the growing seculariza-
tion in Turkey, missionaries curtailed the teaching of the
Christian religion and ethics, but expressed Christian principles in their daily lives, hoping thereby to impress the
students by their model behavior.   While American diplomats

continued to protect the missionaries and their property interests, they also demanded that the missionaries comply
with the forces of nationalism and secularism. The missionaries made the adjustment and continued to supply trained
personnel for the new Turkish regime.

Near East Relief also adopted a new approach to comply with new conditions. The initial relief task of NER was
accomplished and by the mid-1920s its leadership turned to
vocational education and rural development. This endeavor
anticipated the later Point Four program and built up a fund
of goodwill for the United States in Turkey. [10]

But what of the relationship of the missionary to the
diplomat? Did U.S. diplomats continue to protect the missionary or did they give sole protection to commercial interests? Elements of the missionary group claimed that diplomats sold them out at the Lausanne Conference. They leveled charges at Admiral Bristol, asserting that he failed to
protect their interests, while using his office to advance those
of merchants, industrialists, and investors. [11] This could not
be further from the truth. While Bristol championed the
cause of commercial men, he safeguarded missionaries and
their property, albeit he requested them to comply with the
forces of nationalism. [12] With respect to the allegation that
economic interests took precedence at Lausanne, there is
sound evidence to show that the Turks granted economic privileges to enlist American diplomatic support against the European Powers and to sweeten the pill for the surrender of the
capitulations. [13] Richard Washburn Child, the leading American delegate at the Lausanne Conference, claimed that the
delegation did not even see the oil promoters who supposedly
lobbied at Lausanne--this in answer to the charge that diplomats sought oil rights in return for surrender of the Armenian national home. [14] The diplomatic record also indicates
that the American diplomats did not use the missionary to win
economic benefits, but that missionaries and philanthropists
did have a salutary effect on the Turkish populace, and that
commerce tended to follow the tract.

While the missionary-relief element created a deposit
of goodwill in Turkey, it also left a legacy of ill feeling carried over from the creation of the "Terrible Turk" image
that accompanied its efforts for the Armenians. Turkish resentment of this image complicated Turkish-American relations, and this image was probably a factor in the rise of
xenophobic nationalism in post-Ottoman Turkey. [15] Numerous

American missionaries and diplomats, notably Dr. Barton of
the American Board, Admiral Bristol, and Ambassador Joseph Grew, Bristol's successor, worked continuously to dis-
pel this image.   Grew urged the Turkish government to undertake an educational program in the United States.   Bristol
was vigilant in ensuring that American journalists presented
a proper view of the Turks so as not to reinforce the "Terrible Turk" image.   But it was the American Friends of
Turkey, an organization founded by Asa Jennings of the
Y. M. C. A. , that did much to eradicate the myopic American
view of the Turk.   The work of Jennings, Barton, and the
enlightened missionaries, and American diplomats to correct
the poor Turkish image in the United States was a factor in
American commercial relations with Turkey during the
1920s. [16]

In the initial years following the war there was evidence that American economic investment and trade with Turkey might grow rapidly.   Exports increased from $25 million
in 1919 to $42 million in 1920.   This was an abnormal
growth, easily explained by the lack of competition from Europe, the impoverished condition of the Turks, the outpouring
of American relief, and the employment of American Shipping
Board vessels in peacetime trade.   A decline set in in 1921
as European competition reclaimed pre-war markets.   The
paucity of shipping and cable facilities, the absence of banking outlets, the impossibility of collecting credit information,
the lack of interest on the part of American merchants, and
restrictive Turkish banking and labor legislation proved to be
obstacles to economic development and increased trade between the United States and Turkey in the 1920s.[17]

Nevertheless, Admiral Bristol worked to reduce Allied
control over Turkey and to expand commerce in that country.
He embarked on a six-point program to utilize the Open Door
policy for American economic aggrandizement.   First, he
built a climate of goodwill in Turkey conducive to commercial growth.   His opposition to the Armenian mandate, anathema to the Kemalist Turks, and his careful coaching of
the missionaries to observe the demands of Turkish nationalism gained him credibility with the new Turkish regime.
Second, the Admiral tried to achieve a measure of economic
reform in Turkey that would induce Americans to invest.
Third, he worked to neutralize Allied control in Turkey so
that American business interests might achieve a foothold.
Fourth, he created an infrastructure to facilitate American
economic penetration.   He used naval personnel, Chamber of

Commerce officials, missionaries, business men, and news-
men to gather information about commercial opportunity.
Fifth, Bristol realized that only an integrated American economic effort would achieve success against the well-organized
efforts of the Europeans.   He advocated the association of
the various factors of American industry--banking, trading,
shipping, and others--to meet the European competition.
Finally, the Admiral encouraged American business representatives to enter the field for Turkish markets that would take
the surplus from American factories, thus maintaining a high
level of economic prosperity in the post-war era. [18]

Bristol assisted the effort of Admiral Colby M. Chester to obtain a concession from the Turks to build railroads,
exploit mineral resources, construct ports, and sell agricultural equipment.   In May 1920 Admiral Chester advised the
State Department of his intention to obtain a concession in
Turkey and asked for the Department's support.   The Admiral even solicited the endorsement of the Navy Department,
suggesting that the concession contained oil-bearing territory
that might be to the Navy's advantage. [19]   While the Navy Department was enthusiastic, Secretary of State Hughes was of
the opinion that Chester's claim was as superficial as that of
the British-controlled Turkish Petroleum Company. [20]   During
1922 the Chester group dispatched two representatives from
the Ottoman-American Development Company, as it was then
known, to Turkey to pursue the concession.   At length, in
April 1923, the Ankara government granted the concession
for the construction of railroads and for the exploitation of
mineral resources along the right of way. [21]   But the Ottoman-American Company was unable to raise adequate financial resources to commence construction, and the Turks canceled the concession in December 1923. [22]

The failure of the Chester syndicate was simply symptomatic of the general inability of American investiment capital to find employment in Turkey during the 1920s.   Although
he devoted much time to aiding American entrepreneurs,
Bristol's efforts did not lead to heightened commercial intercourse between Turkey and the United States because of factors already mentioned.   But he did lay the groundwork for
better political relations between the two countries, and his
activities provided the basis for the increased trade that came
in the following decade.   Finally, Bristol alerted American
interests to the necessity of conforming to the demands of
Turkish nationalism. [23]

The emergence of the irrepressible force of Turkish national sentiment in response to the repressive Allied policies was the single most important factor in post-war Turkey. It was apparent to informed observers in the State Department as early as the autumn of 1921 that Turkish victories over the Greeks would compel the Allies to revise the Treaty of Sèvres.   American interests in Turkey required protection, and Admiral Bristol urged the Department to participate in the revised settlement that was soon to come.[24] He was not alone in suggesting this course of action.

The American Board, with its multi-million dollar investment in Turkey, also clamored for U.S. participation in the conference.   Equally anxious for American participation was the Armenia-America Society, one of the champions of the Armenian cause.   Society spokesmen also hoped the State Department would use its influence in the forthcoming conference to achieve a national home for the Armenians.[25]   Although convinced by Admiral Bristol's arguments that U.S. attendance at a future conference was necessary, Secretary Hughes would not accept the arguments of the Armenia-America Society that the U.S. should intervene in the making of the settlement.   While the United States utilized the Open Door policy to protect American commercial interests in the postwar Middle East, the policy of non-intervention still held.

The British desired the United States to attend the conference, as Lord Curzon, British Foreign Secretary, made plain to Ambassador George Harvey on 12 October 1922.   The State Department prepared a position paper on American interests, and on 27 October Hughes sent an aide mémoire to London, Paris, and Rome to be handed to the respective foreign offices, advising that U.S. interests were divided into seven groups: capitulations, educational and philanthropic activities, commerce, claims, the Turkish Straits, the minorities question, and finances.   Hughes concluded that the United States would not be a party to the settlement but would send a delegation to safeguard American interests.   The Powers welcomed American attendance.[26]

The State Department appointed career diplomats Joseph C. Grew and Richard Washburn Child and Admiral Bristol to represent the U.S. at the Lausanne Conference convened on 20 November 1922 to revise the Treaty of Sèvres made obsolete with the Turkish victory over the Greeks.   The British hoped that the Powers would present a united front to the Turks, but the U.S. delegation remained detached, the

better to represent American aims.   Along this line, Richard
W. Child, the American ambassador to Italy and the spokesman for the delegation, opposed the Turkish Petroleum Company's concession in Mesopotamia, claiming that it was in-
valid and a violation of the Open Door.   American support
for the capitulations and for the Armenian national home
early ran into difficulties, for the Turks were adamantly opposed to restoring the capitulations and to awarding the Armenians a national home.[27]   While the Americans were not
concerned with certain financial and military problems between the Europeans and Turkey, they favored the establishment of an international regime to govern the Straits.

Special American interest groups were present at
Lausanne.   The pro-Armenian lobby was well represented,
with Dr. Barton, Dr. Peet, and George Montgomery in attendance lobbying for the national home.[28]   Representatives
of American oil interests were present, and their role will
be treated in the next chapter.

A rupture between the Turks and the Powers occurred
in early February 1923, when the former rejected Allied
terms on financial and economic questions.   The Conference
adjourned on 4 February and during a three-month recess
some interesting developments transpired.   First, the Allies
snubbed the American delegation, refusing to keep it posted
on the exchange of proposals between the European foreign
ministers and the Turks.   Second, the Turks granted the
Chester Concession, an act that separated the U.S. from the
Powers.

The Conference resumed on 23 April, with the U.S.
having a strong position as evidenced by the granting of the
Chester Concession.   Joseph Grew, now head of the delegation, frequently acted as mediary between the Turks and the
Powers.[29]   At length, the Turks and the Powers signed the
Treaty of Lausanne on 24 July 1923.   The treaty was a victory for Turkish nationalism, because it replaced the Treaty
of Sèvres that left Turkey in bondage to the Powers.   The
Lausanne Treaty abolished capitulations, established protection for minorities, provided for the continuation of philanthropic and educational insitutions, and created an international regime to govern the Straits.   Turkey gave up the non-
Turkish portions of the Empire and was not required to pay
reparations.

The completion of the treaty with the Allies paved the

way for an American-Turkish treaty that would restore relations broken during the war.   Formal talks between Grew
and Ismet Inönü, head of the Turkish delegation, commenced
during April and continued into the summer of 1923.   Ismet
Inönü proved an able negotiator.   At length a treaty was
signed on 6 August.   The capitulations were abolished.
American merchant vessels and warships could enjoy freedom of passage of the Turkish Straits on a most favored nation basis.   American philanthropic and educational institutions in Turkey were protected. [30]   Inasmuch as the treaty
contained no clause with respect to claims and naturalization
and made no provision for an Armenian national home, Grew
readily understood that it would meet tough opposition in the
Senate.   A group of over one hundred Episcopal bishops petitioned the Senate to oppose the treaty.   The American Committee for the Independence of Armenia formed the American
Committee Against the Lausanne Treaty and launched a propaganda campaign against it, with James Gerard leading the
way.   Senators Claude Swanson, a Virginia Democrat, and
William King, a Utah Democrat, took up the standard against
the treaty in the Senate.   They and other opponents of the
treaty claimed the U.S. delegation had bartered the national
Armenian home in exchange for economic concessions. [31]
Numerous Democratic senators opposed the treaty for partisan reasons.   The Democrats placed a strong anti-treaty
plank in their 1924 platform, claiming the treaty traded
"American rights, and betrays Armenia for the Chester Oil
Concession." [32]   So strong was the opposition to the treaty in
the Senate that the 18 January 1927 vote on it was six votes
short of the necessary two-thirds majority. [33]   Opponents of
the treaty had voted against it for reasons that ran contrary
to the national interest.

Relations between the U.S. and Turkey were normal-
ized by an exchange of notes between Admiral Bristol and a
Turkish official in Constantinople.   The notes agreed that
diplomatic relations were restored, and that the modus vivendi
negotiated by Bristol the year previously would be extended
so as to permit the continuation of commercial relations.
The Senate approved the exchange of notes and also confirmed Joseph C. Grew as the first ambassador to the new
Turkish state. [34]

By the late 1920s the "Terrible Turk" image had
eroded sufficiently to allow for the negotiation of a new commercial treaty between the U.S. and Turkey.   Ambassador
Grew obtained in the spring of 1928 an extension of the com-

mercial modus vivendi for another year.   In October 1929
the U.S. and Turkey could celebrate the signing of the Treaty
of Ankara which provided for most favored nation treatment.
The Senate approved the treaty immediately, having been
warned that the modus vivendi would expire and leave the nation without means to continue commerce with Turkey. 35

Although the United States had been anxious to expand
commerce with Turkey in the 1920s, the same did not hold
true in the following decade.   During the depression the
State Department did not seem to encourage American diplomats in Turkey to extend the boundary of the American marketplace. 36   But in spite of the Department's hesitancy,
there was an expansion of American exports to Turkey by
mid-decade.   The Turks purchased automobiles, sewing machines, and electric household appliances.   The 1930s also
saw the increase of investment capital in Turkey.   Several
companies established branches there, and soon the products
of the Ford Motor Company and the Curtis Wright Corporation were seen on Turkish roads and in Turkish skies. 37
The last effort to expand commerce with Turkey during the
inter-war years was the reciprocal trade agreement of 1939.
Based on the Reciprocal Trade Agreements Act of 1934, this
1939 measure was a New Deal nostrum for increasing exports to stimulate a depressed economy.   The Turks were
agreeable, and there was no domestic opposition.   This executive agreement was not productive, because German efforts undercut the measure in Turkey.   Although the at-
tempts to improve commercial intercourse were not fruitful,
they nevertheless indicated the mutual willingness of the two
nations to enjoy better diplomatic relations. 38

Another development that made for better Turkish-
American relations was the dispatch of American technical
advisers to Turkey in the 1930s in answer to the Turkish
Five Year Plan of self-improvement.   They gave advice in
education, cotton cultivation, minerals, public works, public
health, communication, and economic development.   Although
accomplished by private persons who did not represent any
government agency, the efforts of these individuals were precursory to the Point-Four program of technical assistance
that followed World War II.   Their accomplishments also contributed to better Turco-American relations and were indicative of the American willingness to adjust to Turkish nationalism. 39

During the decade of the 1930s American missionary

institutions continued to function, albeit under Turkish restrictions. Turkish nationalism and secularism remained a
constant hindrance to the missionaries, and their continued
operation was a monument to their ability to accommodate
Turkish nationalism and to their tenacity.   Some schools
were closed, and the curricula of schools at all levels were
subjected to inspection. As no religious instruction was permitted, the missionaries continued the practice of "unnamed
Christianity."[40] In spite of gift and building taxes on them,
the schools continued to function. When the school at Bursa
was closed down for converting three Muslims to Christianity, Ambassador Grew was able to show the Turks that news
of this closing could have substantially bad effects on Turkish-American relations.   While the school at Bursa remained
closed, Grew persuaded the Turks to open another school.[41]
By personal tact and astute diplomacy Grew induced the Turks
to exempt American schools from the building and gift
taxes.[42]

Missionaries and diplomats were able to heal the
breach between the U.S. and Turkey, and the relationship
between the countries might well be characterized as a rapprochement.   Because of the growing good feeling, American
diplomats were able to accomplish a number of diplomatic
chores that might not otherwise have been possible.[43] For
example, there was the Treaty of Establishment and Sojourn
signed on 28 October 1931 that provided for the residence of
Americans in Turkey on the basis of the most favored nation.[44] There was the settlement of claims arising out of
damage to American property during the 1914-1922 period.
An agreement provided for a mixed-claims commission that
awarded some $900,000 to cover 33 business and missionary
claims.[45] The United States also played a major role in
pressuring Turkey to shut down the illicit opium traffic.[46]
Unresolved at the opening of World War II was the nationality
issue, which could not be settled because the Turks would not
permit the temporary visit of ex-Turkish citizens.

In concluding, it can be said that the U.S. government
did not permit the missionary-philanthropic lobby to force the
pursuit of goals at variance with the national interest.   It
continued to adhere to the policy of non-intervention and to
follow a course leading to better relations between the two
countries.   The chief reason for the growing rapprochement
was the willingness of American missionaries, educators,
diplomats, businessmen, and relief workers to accommodate
themselves to the force of Turkish nationalism.[47]

The United States employed the same formula used in
Turkey to maintain and improve relations with Iran during
the period between the two world wars.   Americans made a
realistic response to Iranian nationalism, a force that erupted
in the post-war years as Iranians sought to free themselves
of Russian and British hegemony.   In so doing, they turned
to the United States, hoping to find a makeweight against the
Europeans.   The United States response was within the con-
fines of the tradition of non-intervention.   Iranians held out
the lure of economic concessions to induce the U.S. government to send economic and political advisers to Iran.   They
also hoped that American petroleum companies would take oil
concessions in return for loans to the Iranian government.
In many respects the history of Iran followed that of Turkey,
for Reza Shah, the new ruler of Iran, emulated Mustapha
Kemal Atatürk, the Turkish dictator-president.   Nationalism,
westernization, and xenophobia seem to have been main
themes of both countries in the interwar era.   It was to the
credit of the United States that accommodation characterized
the American reaction in both nations.

Wilsonian concepts of internationalism and self-determination appealed strongly to the Iranians, who were trying
to shake off the domination of Germany, Russia, and Britain.
With the war concluded, Britain had no rival in Iran, and
British Foreign Minister Lord Curzon tried to establish a
protectorate over Iran to enhance British imperial aspirations
in the Persian Gulf region.   At the Paris Peace Conference
the Iranians unsuccessfully requested U.S. aid to hinder British aims.   On 19 August 1919 Britain and Iran signed the
treaty, making the latter a client of the former.   The American response was one of dismay, for the British position
violated the Wilsonian principle of national sovereignty and
ran contrary to the interests of American oil men who wanted
a concession in northern Iran.   During interchanges with
Britain and Iran, Secretary of State Robert Lansing assured
the British of American disapproval of the treaty which violated the Wilsonian principle of open covenants, openly arrived at, and he made clear to the Iranians that the U.S.
disapproved the agreement.[48]   Although American efforts to
acquire a petroleum concession in Iran will be treated in a
later chapter, suffice it to say here that the question of oil
was in part related to the U.S. opposition to the Anglo-Persian treaty of 1919.   Ratification of that treaty by the Iranian Majlis would have been prejudicial to the advancement of
American oil interests in northern Iran.[49]   In June 1921 the
Iranian Majlis rejected the Anglo-Iranian treaty.   There can

be little doubt that U. S. opposition was a factor in Iranian repudiation.[50]

Simultaneous with the British intrusion into Iran was the Soviet effort to penetrate that country. Whereas the U. S. used its influence to block the British, the State Department rejected the Iranian plea for advisers, arms, and a loan to contain the Russians, maintaining that this would amount to acceptance of a virtual protectorate over Iran.[51]

The Iranian government required technical assistance to strengthen the state and to replace the British experts who departed the country with the defeat of the treaty. Its request for American advisers was linked to the granting of an oil concession and to the hope that the advisers would arrange loans from American investors. The Iranians recalled the excellent work of W. Morgan Shuster in the pre-war years, but efforts to enlist him proved of no avail.[52] Iranians required an adviser to strengthen finances in order to remove the threat of foreign domination, and they sought assistance elsewhere. At length the State Department recommended Arthur C. Millspaugh to lead a new financial mission to Iran, with the stipulation that Iran understand he was a private citizen in no way connected with the U. S. government.[53] The appointment of Millspaugh, a former economic specialist in the Department, was both disappointing and gratifying to the Iranians, who had hoped for a government official with the attendant implication of U. S. endorsement of the mission.

Iranians gave Millspaugh and his small staff a five-year contract. Employees of the Iranian government, the Americans arrived in Teheran in the autumn of 1922. They remained until 1927. Millspaugh held the title Director-General of Iranian Finances, a position that gave him a voice in economic planning. He enacted an impressive number of reforms, which included the centralization of revenues, the rationalization of tax collections, the enactment of tighter budget controls, the use of national funds for civil works, and an increase in commerce and industry.[54] But bureaucrats protested the rapidity of change, and aristocrats opposed the paying of higher taxes. At the outset the Shah gave his cooperation to Millspaugh, but eventually he turned against the director-general. In the face of royal opposition, protests from bureaucrats and aristocrats, Millspaugh resigned in 1927.[55] He had accomplished reforms that benefitted Iran. In addition to improved fiscal and administrative procedures,

an array of transportation, irrigation, and industrial projects
could be attributed to Millspaugh's efforts.   As testimony to
his success, the Iranians would request Millspaugh's services
again during World War II.   Not only did the United States
gain a measure of prestige by Millspaugh's work, but there
was another reward that was not then appreciated.   The
Americans so improved revenue collection procedures that the
Shah was able to embark on the building of the Iranian State
Railroad, a line that would be of inestimable service to the
United States in supplying Lend-Lease to the Russians in
World War II.   Too, the building of this railroad employed
the services of American engineers.[56]

     Between 1928 and 1930, American interests partici-
pated in construction of the trans-Iranian railroad from the
Caspian Sea to the Persian Gulf.   As early as 1926 the
Shah's government hired William B. Poland and ten other
American assistants to help with the survey of the projected
railroad route.   Two years later Henry Ulen and Company,
an American firm, signed an agreement with the Iranian government to cooperate with three German concerns to build the
railroad line.   Organized as the Syndicate for Railroads in
Persia, it eventually extended its organization when Ulen and
Company brought in French and British companies.   Work
proceeded, but unforeseeable floods and other difficulties led
the Shah's government to cancel the contract and assume control over construction in 1930.   The international combine
was disbanded.   The American company lost out, and the
State Department remained aloof from the difficulties that accompanied the 1930 debacle.   While the venture proved disastrous for the American company, the completion of the line
in 1938 was important in American-Soviet relations during
World War II.[57]

     Another facet of Iranian nationalism was the growing
restrictions placed on American missionary schools by the
Ministry of Education, which issued new regulations on 10
May 1927 to compel the missionaries to conform to the educational aims established by the Ministry.   In 1932 a government decree declared that Iranian children could not attend
foreign schools at the elementary level.   The final blow came
in August 1939 when the government announced the assumption of control of all foreign schools in the nation.   American
diplomatic assistance was necessary to handle the financial
details involved in the takeover of property.[58]   Iranian nationalism grew to a fine edge in the mid 1930s, and American-Iranian relations became somewhat tense.   Iranian gov-

ernment officials created difficulties for American archaeologists, closed down American missionary schools, and created
a diplomatic incident out of all proportion to the seriousness
of an event involving the arrest of the Iranian minister in
Maryland in 1935. Although commercial contact between the
two countries continued, and the Shah's government granted
an oil concession to an American firm, nevertheless relations
were not wholly satisfactory. While the breach might well
be attributed to incidents that exacerbated an over-zealous
Iranian nationalism, it is possible that German influence
might have been at the bottom of the diplomatic impasse.
Large numbers of German experts had been brought into Iran
in the 1930s to counter British and Russian influence. [59] In
spite of the diplomatic difficulties, the U. S. still retained
a large deposit of goodwill in Iran, largely as a result of the
work of Morgan Shuster, Arthur Millspaugh, the missionaries,
and diplomats who had not manifested national political ambitions in a country over-burdened with the international intrigue of the European Powers. At the outset of hostilities
in 1939 American-Iranian tension had eased. American
prestige in Iran was high and this proved a valuable asset
during the war years. [60]

    American prestige was also high in the Arab coun-
tries where Zionism had not yet complicated relations with
the Arab peoples. Not only did Arabs respect Americans for
their philanthropic activities in education, relief, medicine,
and technical assistance, but they recalled that the United
States stood for self-determination of peoples, which was contrary to the colonialism enforced upon them by the European
Powers. American interests in the Arab lands had long been
of an educational and philanthropic nature, but during the
years between the wars American economic interests increased as oil men developed new sources of petroleum. Now
the complex of American interests was compelled to take
note of the increase in nationalism that pervaded the Arab
region. Although many Arabs were the charges of Britain
and France--Iraq and Palestine were under British mandate,
while Syria and Lebanon were under French tutelage and
Egypt was a British protectorate--there was a growing restiveness as the forces of nationalism continued to simmer.
While American relations with the Arabs were generally conducted through the diplomatic machinery that normally handled
intercourse with Britain and France, the U. S. remained aloof
from the political unrest that emerged. Its primary concern
was the protection of the rights and interests of American
citizens, and State Department officials demanded the drafting of treaties to protect their rights in mandated lands. [61]

On 4 April 1924 the United States and France signed
a convention by which the U.S. assented to the French mandate and obtained rights for its citizens equal to those granted the citizens of League of Nations members. These included the rights to operate schools and to conduct business.
The State Department was vigilant to guarantee equal treatment for American missionaries and business men.[62] During the time the Druze Rebellion spread to all parts of Syria
and Lebanon in the mid-1920s, the U.S. Navy stationed two
destroyers off the Lebanese coast to embark Americans if
the French failed to contain the rioting. The uprising in
Damascus resulted in damage to three American business
concerns, for which the State Department demanded indemnification.[63] The Department also represented the missionaries who continued to function under the mandate. On occasion it cautioned them against the pursuit of evangelical
activities that might inflame Muslims. While isolated missionary acts did arouse the people, the American University
of Beirut continued to win for the United States goodwill
among Arabs. With the help of a Rockefeller Foundation
grant, the University expanded during the inter-war years,
and its influence pervaded the Middle East, where graduates
served as pharmacists, physicians, dentists, accountants,
and in vocational positions. On balance, the missions and
the University performed a necessary function in providing
personnel to do the tasks needed by a rapidly modernizing
people. They created a legacy of goodwill among the Arabs.
Unfortunately, the force of Zionism was beginning to grow in
the United States with a view to establishing a Jewish national home in the British mandate of Palestine.[64]

During the inter-war years, American Zionists urged
the U.S. government to use its good offices to influence
Britain to implement the Balfour Declaration that a Jewish
national home might be created. This pressure was accompanied by British pleas for assistance in handling the growing Zionist problem in Palestine. But the State Department
remained detached from the Zionist problem, adhering to the
position that its main concern was the protection of American interests in Palestine.[65] At the conclusion of World War
I, British forces occupied Palestine, and the Supreme Allied
Council awarded Britain a mandate for that country at the
San Remo Conference in April 1920. The League of Nations
approved the mandate in July 1922, but with the stipulation
that Britain should create a Jewish national home. This
provision also presumed that Britain would facilitate Jewish
immigration to Palestine. As a balm to the disappointed

Arabs, Transjordan was created in 1928, with the Emir Abdullah as reigning monarch.   U. S. concern for Palestine did
not extend to the implementation of the Balfour pledge, but
merely to the protection of American rights.   In spite of a
1922 Congressional resolution calling on the U. S. to support
the realization of a Jewish national home, the State Department remained impervious to Congressional pressure and
Zionist importunities.   It was only at British insistence that
the Anglo-American Convention of 1924, protecting U. S. rights
in Palestine, included the preamble of the Palestine mandate,
which pledged Britain to create a national home for Jews. [66]

    But American Zionists did not give up the fight.
Zionism was not yet a strong political force in America in
the 1920s, for it was plagued with factionalism.   It was not
until the Arab riots of 1929 that American Jews began to
show a greater interest in the Zionist cause. [67]   Numerous
Jewish organizations in the United States asserted that it was
imperative to create a Jewish homeland in which Jews would
be safe from additional violence.   But even after the 1929
Arab riots, Zionist pressure on Secretary of State Henry L.
Stimson produced little more than a repetition of Hughes'
declaration that the U. S. had no cause to take up the Zionist
program. [68]   During the 1920s the State Department adhered
to the tradition of non-involvement and continued to protect
American rights.   But the following decade would see the
Palestine question loom larger in American-Middle Eastern
problems, because of the turn of events both in Europe and
in the Levant.

    By 1930 Arabs had ceased to fear that Jewish immi-
gration would overrun Palestine, but the persecution that accompanied Adolf Hitler's rise to power in Germany was to
change all that.   Jewish migration to the United States and
Britain was paralleled by a rapid rise in the migration of
Jews to Palestine.   This movement resulted in the violent
Arab uprising of 1936.   Britain appointed an official commission, known as the Peel Commission, to investigate the causes
of unrest.   It recommended in 1937 the partition of Palestine
into two states: one Jewish, the other Arab. [69]   This solution found favor with neither Jews nor Arabs.   The outbreak
of Arab disturbance in 1938 required British forces to restore
peace and led to an official reassessment of the British position in Palestine.   In 1939 the Foreign Office issued the
White Paper, a document designed to appease the Arabs.   It
repudiated the British pledge to implement the Balfour Declaration and announced that Jewish immigration to Palestine

would be limited to 75,000 over the next five years.   It also
limited Jewish acquisition of farmland.[70]

American Zionists had not been idle, and in 1938 they
inundated the State Department with telegrams, urging the
Roosevelt administration to use its influence to realize the
Balfour pledge.   In October 1938 a delegation of Jewish dignitaries called on Secretary of State Cordell Hull, asking
that the U.S. government act to fulfill Zionist goals.[71]   Zionists also flooded the country with propaganda in an effort to
whip up public support for their program.   American Arabs
protested, but their effort was minuscule compared to that of
the Zionists.   American missionaries voiced the opinion that
a change in the status quo would alter their work with the
Arabs, and they were unalterably opposed to the creation of
a Jewish homeland.   American oil interests, then adding to
their holdings in Arab lands, asserted that U.S. support for
the Zionist program would run counter to American petroleum needs.   In spite of the various pressures, both pro and
con, U.S. Middle Eastern policy remained steadfastly non-
interventionist.   The Roosevelt Administration regarded Palestine as an issue to be decided by Britain.[72]   There the matter rested at the outbreak of World War II.[73]

U.S. acceptance of British primacy in Palestine also
applied in Egypt where the British protectorate continued to
hold force.   But nationalism in Egypt after World War I was
strong, and in 1922 Britain recognized the nominal independence of Egypt.   American interests in that land were chiefly
cultural, with missionary schools, the American University
of Cairo, a few archaeological expeditions, and tourists constituting the main concerns.   But with the establishment of
independence in 1922, the missionary lobby requested the
State Department to create legal safeguards to protect their
operations.   Working through the British Foreign Office, the
Department complied with missionary wishes.   The rapid
growth of nationalism in Egypt during the inter-war years
was steady, and it manifested itself in several ways, felt especially by missionaries and archaeologists.   On the whole
American interests did not feel the full force of nationalism,
for the U.S. was not identified with the colonial powers.
But American diplomatic agents in Egypt remained aloof from
Egyptian efforts to shake off the shackles of British imperialism, and they were content merely to protect American interests.[74]   In 1937 the United States, in company with the
European Powers assembled at the Montreux Conference,
agreed to the abolition of the capitulatory rights in Egypt.

Shortly thereafter Egypt was admitted to full membership in the League of Nations.

While American interests in Egypt were mainly of a cultural nature, those in Iraq were chiefly related to petroleum. The American search for oil in Iraq will be related in a sequential chapter. In addition to oil, there were some American educational and business interests. But Iraq, like Egypt, was mainly a British problem. Iraq not only contained rich oil fields, but also provided a buffer to British interests in Iran and served to protect the approaches to India, the gem of the British Empire. American treaty relations with Iraq not only safeguarded American educational and missionary interests, but also secured American rights to participate in the oil lands then opening up. The State Department initiated talks with the British Foreign Office in 1925 with a view to establishing a convention similar to the Anglo-American convention in Palestine and the Franco-American convention in Syria-Lebanon. The Anglo-American convention on Iraq was signed in January 1930.[75] It recognized the British mandate and provided for the guarantee of American philanthropic and property rights. Subsequent to Britain's granting independence to Iraq in 1930, the U.S. negotiated a new set of diplomatic instruments with Iraq, guaranteeing traditional rights. But as was the case in Egypt and in Palestine, the United States deferred to the superior British position. While British interest in these Arab lands was strategic, American relations were based on the aims of the missionaries, oil companies, and archaeologists. Because American missionaries and business men accommodated to the nationalism so prevalent in Iraq as in other Arab lands, Americans did not feel the full brunt of xenophobia that was the lot of the British and French.

Unlike the other Arab lands, the Arabian peninsula was not placed under a mandate after the breakup of the Ottoman Empire. The strong forces of nationalism and westernization were slower to kindle in this country. The initial American contact in the Arabian peninsula resulted from the activities of missionaries in the 1890s with the building of hospitals, schools, and clinics. Their good work laid the foundation of goodwill that met American oil men who came later.[76] Although Americans were not responsible for locating the petroleum resources in Iraq and Iran, it was the genius of two Americans that discovered oil in Saudi Arabia. While the American quest for Saudi Arabian oil will be told in a later chapter, suffice it to say that it was Charles R.

Crane, American diplomat and philanthropist, who persuaded
King Ibn Saud to permit Karl S. Twitchell to make a geological survey in Arabia. Twitchell's finds alerted American
oil interests to the potential in Arabia, and American petroleum companies entered the field in the mid-1930s.[77] They
persuaded the State Department to recognize Saudi Arabia,
the better to protect petroleum interests. By the middle of
the decade, Standard Oil of California and the Texas Company
were exploring for oil, having received valuable concessions
without diplomatic assistance. Shortly thereafter the United
States recognized Saudi Arabia and accredited its first minister to that country in 1939. The need to secure American
oil interests and the necessity of dampening the growing
Arab displeasure at the increase of Zionism in the United
States seem to have been the chief reasons for extending recognition.[78]

At the outbreak of World War II, U. S. government officials and petroleum experts began to realize the importance
of the oil fields of Saudi Arabia to the United States. The
development of petroleum interests in Saudi Arabia in the
late 1930s marked the turning point of American relations
with the Middle East. Henceforth, oil would play an increasingly vital role in the American attitude toward the region. Saudi Arabia would loom large in considerations of
the American national interest in the years to come.

*   *   *   *   *

The American diplomatic experience in the Middle
East during the period between the wars can be described as
one of continued non-involvement in both the political intrigue that surrounded the settlement of the Eastern Question
immediately after the war and in the political activities of
Armenians, Arabs, and Jews who sought to achieve the goals
of self-determination. The response of Americans--diplo-
mats, missionaries, technical advisers, archaeologists, relief workers, naval personnel, and business men--to the
growth of nationalism in Turkey, Iran, Iraq, and Egypt was
one of rational accommodation. This response and the continued activities of American missionary and technical personnel left a legacy of goodwill for the United States in the
minds of the Middle Eastern peoples. American economic
interests developed steadily during the inter-war period and
assumed a large position in the spectrum of American interests in the Middle East. While the goodwill investment

continued large, it now held a lesser position in the totality
of American interests.   But as the period ended, there appeared on the horizon a conflict of interests.   The rapid
growth of Zionist sentiment in the United States during the
1930s was contrary to the aims of those Americans investing
in oil development in the Middle East.   This conflict of interests would present American policy-makers with a dilemma
that would plague U.S.-Middle Eastern diplomatic policy for
many years to come.   Inasmuch as some treatment has been
given to the rise of Zionism in America in the inter-war
period, it now remains to discuss the development of American interest in Middle Eastern oil during the same era.

Chapter 8

THE OPEN DOOR AND THE AMERICAN QUEST
FOR MIDDLE EASTERN OIL, 1919-1939

Although U.S. diplomats frequently deferred to the British position of supremacy in the Middle East, during the inter-war era the United States engaged in a keen competition with Britain for access to Middle Eastern oil fields. The State Department employed the Open Door policy to aid American petroleum companies to obtain concessionary rights in the British mandate of Iraq, where the Turkish Petroleum Company had exclusive right to Mesopotamian oil fields. With the rapid growth of American oil interests in the Middle East, economic considerations assumed a higher position in the hierarchy of American interests in the Middle East. Between 1919 and 1939 the record of oil development and ownership in the Middle East changed remarkably, because American petroleum interests had successfully challenged British control of the region's oil. On the eve of World War II American oil interests controlled substantial holdings in the Middle East, owning about one-fourth of the Iraq Petroleum Company (Turkish Petroleum Company's new name), a monopoly of production in Saudi Arabia and Bahrain, and holdings in Kuwait.

*   *   *   *   *

World War I wrought a revolution in the way nations fight wars, for not only did a number of new weapons appear on battlefields, but man also began to employ petroleum products to power his ships and other conveyances of war. Prior to the war Britain pioneered the use of oil to power ships of the Royal Navy, and British geologists began to seek new sources of petroleum in the Middle East. During the pre-war years when American officialdom refused to consider the quest for overseas oil sources, the British government purchased a controlling interest in the Anglo-Persian Oil Company. In World War I the United States used vast quantities of petroleum and petroleum products to fuel its engines of war. So rapidly did the American war effort deplete domestic reserves that government officials expressed concern that domestic oil would not suffice to meet future U.S. needs. At the same time, leaders feared that other industrial nations were acquiring exclusive control over known sources of petroleum in the four corners of the world. In 1919 and 1920 members of the U.S. Senate demanded that the State Department take steps to remove all restrictions placed by foreign governments on oil exploration.[1] Wilson's administration, followed by those of Harding and Coolidge, utilized the Open Door for American interests to gain access to Middle Eastern oil fields.

In the immediate post-war era the United States embarked on an aggressive search for oil in Iraq, the Dutch East Indies, Mexico, Venezuela, Colombia, and Peru in response to warnings by government officials and American oil executives. The State Department sustained the efforts of American oil men to gain access to the fields in Mesopotamia, a British-held mandate that Whitehall hoped to reserve for exclusive exploitation by a consortium owned by British, Dutch, and French interests.[2] But, first, the Department had to render assistance elsewhere, because in March 1919 officials of the Standard Oil Company of New York (SOCONY) complained that the British were obstructing oil exploration in Palestine where SOCONY had acquired concessionary rights. SOCONY leaders urged the State Department to question this opposition. But the Foreign Office maintained that Palestine was still under military occupation and that no oil exploratory activities would be permitted.[3]

By late summer of 1919 SOCONY executives complained again to the Department, asserting that British authorities had refused SOCONY geologists permission to explore for oil in Mesopotamia. Exploration rights thus linked the American quest for Middle Eastern oil to the mandate question.[4] To make matters worse, the Allied Powers met at San Remo, Italy in the spring of 1920. In addition to partitioning the Ottoman Empire, Britain and France negotiated an oil agreement whereby France obtained a portion of Mesopotamian oil in return for granting Britain permission to construct an oil pipeline across Syria to the Mediterranean. The State Department received unofficial copies of the agreement, and protested it in notes in May and July 1920,

arguing that the Anglo-French oil accord violated the principle
of the Open Door and the equal opportunity concept established by the Paris Peace Conference.   Further, it claimed
that it discriminated against the United States which had contributed greatly to the Allied victory.   Finally, the Department questioned the validity of the claim of the British-controlled Turkish Petroleum Company.[5]   The Department declared that the Ottoman government had not granted a concession to the TPC prior to the outbreak of hostilities, but had
merely promised a concession, which held no weight in international law.   Lord Curzon, British Foreign Secretary, replied in August, asserting that the TPC had a valid claim in
Mesopotamia and denying that the San Remo oil agreement ex-
cluded other petroleum interests.[6]   Secretary of State Bainbridge Colby responded in November, saying the United States
had the right to discuss issues related to the mandates and
repeating the allegation that the TPC's claim was not legal.[7]
The British ignored the American charges, and submitted
their draft for mandates for Mesopotamia and Palestine to the
League of Nations on 6 December 1920.[8]   Colby advised the
League that the United States had the right to approve mandate plans.

In the following year, Warren G. Harding became
President and Charles Evans Hughes, his Secretary of State,
was equal to the task of advancing American claims to entry
into the Middle Eastern oil fields.   He continued to base the
American case on the Open Door policy and on the principle
of equal commercial opportunity in the mandates, while denying the validity of the British claim.   Hughes urged the British to settle the claim question by arbitration, which the Foreign Office refused to do.   The Harding administration also
worked closely with the oil men, who by this time included
officials of both SOCONY and the Standard Oil Company of
New Jersey.   In supporting American interests, Hughes was
joined by Herbert Hoover, the Secretary of Commerce.   Always an advocate of government aid to business, Hoover took
the lead in calling the executives of large American oil companies to Washington in May 1921 to boost the possibilities of
entry into the potentially rich Mesopotamian oil fields.[9]   Van
H. Manning, the erudite director of research for the American Petroleum Institute, had suggested that the American oil
companies form a consortium to present a united front against
the intransigent British.[10]   Hoover and Hughes advised the
oil executives at the conference that they had good reason to
believe that Britain would admit an American syndicate to
minority interest in the TPC.   They wanted assurance from

the officials, affirming their willingness to form a consortium and to commence operations once concessionary rights
were obtained.   The oil executives agreed.[11]   In November
1921 W. C. Teagle, president of Jersey Standard, acting as
spokesman for the oil men, advised the State Department that
a syndicate of seven companies (Jersey Standard, SOCONY,
Sinclair, Texas, Gulf, Mexican, and Atlantic) had taken form
and wished to explore the Mesopotamian area.[12]   The Department advised the group that Britain would not give the green
light on exploration because military occupation precluded it.

   With the consortium well organized and determined to
move ahead, Jersey Standard's A. C. Bedford advised the
State Department that it was prepared to commence private
negotiations with the British.   Teagle of Jersey Standard proceeded to London in July 1922 to begin the conversations that
ultimately led to American success.   The State Department
continued to adhere to the principle of equal opportunity and
to deny the validity of the TPC claim, but, as Department
officials advised Bedford, the Department would not let theo-
retical considerations stand in the way of meaningful negotiations.   This implied that any qualified American company
that wished to enter the Mesopotamian arena would be permitted to do so.[13]   The British and American officials opened
talks in July, with much discussion given to the State Department formula concerning the Open Door.   At length Teagle
drew up an agreement that would meet the Department's cri-
teria.   Called Exhibit "A," the document specified that TPC
would select for itself up to twelve parcels of land, each par-
cel not to exceed 16 square miles.   Oil rights for the remainder of the concession--some 15,000 square miles--would
be opened to qualified companies.   This agreement met the
State Department's specifications, but the negotiators were unable to agree on a percentage arrangement.   TPC officials
were willing to offer the Americans 12 per cent, a figure the
latter deemed far too low.   Teagle was convinced the Americans could get as much as 20 per cent and a voice in the
company's direction.[14]   There matters stood as the Lausanne
Conference opened.

   At Lausanne the Americans were encouraged to believe
that problems could be resolved to the satisfaction of all parties.   The outstanding issues between the consortium and the
TPC were the percentage question and the status of the TPC
claim.   Also complicating the oil negotiations was the question of Mosul.   Turkish nationalists claimed that oil-bearing
area, which the British asserted to be part of Mesopotamia.

Another factor to be considered by the State Department was
the presence of two other American groups seeking oil concessions.   One was the Chester syndicate, and the other was
associated with the heirs of ex-Sultan Abdul Hamid.   Faced
with three competing American concerns, the Department adhered to the principle of impartiality. [15]   The U.S. government remained neutral in the conflict between Turkey and
Britain over the status of Mosul, but the American consortium continued to negotiate with TPC.   An agreement was
reached on 12 December 1922 whereby the Americans would
participate in the joint venture and receive 24 per cent of the
shares.   The Anglo-Persian Oil Company, the French company and the Royal-Dutch Shell interests would each receive
a like amount.   Calouste Gulbenkian, the wily Armenian oil
speculator who held rights in the TPC, would receive 4 per
cent.   Since Anglo-Persian reduced its share, the other par-
ticipants agreed to deliver 10 per cent of the crude from
TPC production to Anglo-Persian.   But the agreement stipu-
lated that the State Department must recognize the validity of
the TPC title and that it must encourage its delegates at
Lausanne to support the agreement, irrespective of other
American oil interests. [16]   Secretary Hughes objected, declaring that the TPC did not have a clear title and that the U.S.
could not support one group to the exclusion of all others, for
this would violate the Open Door principle.   Hughes advised
Teagle that if the government of Iraq confirmed TPC's title,
the Department would consider it valid. [17]   In January 1923
the American consortium rejected the British invitation to
join the Mesopotamian oil venture on the December terms,
stating that the 10 per cent donation of oil to Anglo-Persian
was excessive.

        The first phase of the Lausanne Conference broke up
in February 1923 over differences between the European Powers and the Turks.   During the second phase of the conference, which opened in April 1923, the Mosul question and the
issue of the TPC claim was before the conferees.   The Mosul
question was settled by independent negotiations between Britain and Turkey.   The British acquiesced to U.S. pressure
and applied for a new title from the Iraqi government. [18]   Another interesting development was the Turkish government's
granting to the Chester group an extensive concession during
the interim period.   Chester's syndicate defaulted through
lack of financial backing, and since Abdul Hamid's heirs soon
withdrew, the American consortium was the only serious con-
tender for participation in Mesopotamian oil development. [19]
That the British had agreed to negotiate with Iraqi officials

for a new title was a victory for the Open Door policy, because at State Department insistence the Open Door principle was to be included in the agreement.   Further evidence of the Department's adherence to the Open Door was its unwillingness to support one American oil group to the exclusion of all others.

While the State Department has been criticized for utilizing its influence on behalf of American oil companies in a manner that transcended the tradition of non-involvement, it must be recalled that in the immediate post-World War I era American government and business leaders believed it imperative that the U.S. acquire new sources of petroleum. Granted the Department's activities departed from the policy of non-interference, but inasmuch as oil was necessary to the economic well-being of the American people, such activities can be justified as serving the national interest.   In spite of State Department assistance, the consortium's Lausanne negotiations were disappointing, for it had not gained access to the Mesopotamian oil.

After the Lausanne Conference ended in 1923, there were five more years of negotiations between the Americans and the TPC.   Developments moved along at a steady pace. In November 1924 the consortium arrived at a new agreement with TPC which gave it a 23.75 per cent share in the company.   A like equity was awarded Anglo-Persian, Royal-Dutch Shell, and the French Petroleum Company.   Gulbenkian, hereafter known as "Mr. Five Percent," would receive 5 per cent.   The new agreement called for TPC to choose two dozen parcels of land, eight square miles each, within a period of two years following a new agreement with the Iraqi government.   Other areas would then be opened to sublessees.[20]

Britain and Iraq negotiated an agreement in March 1925 that confirmed the TPC concession.   In compliance with State Department wishes, the treaty included the Open Door principle, but since TPC retained power over the competitive bidding of companies seeking subleases, the Open Door was but a myth.[21]   In 1926 Turkey and Britain settled the complicated Mosul question, with the rich oil-bearing area being left within the boundaries of British-mandated Iraq and the Turks receiving a financial equivalent.

But even with the Mosul question resolved and with the Anglo-Iraqi agreement a reality, it was several more years before the Americans gained full membership in TPC.   The delay in reaching a final settlement was due to the intransigence of Gulbenkian, who expected TPC to refine and market the oil, from which he would then obtain a 5 per cent profit. But the TPC partners anticipated the production of crude oil and its allocation according to the percentage agreements laid down in the 1924 draft. The question hinged on the matter of profits. Eventually, the year 1928 witnessed a final settlement. The American consortium incorporated in 1928 as the Near East Development Corporation, shares in which were held as follows: Atlantic Refining Company 16.66 per cent; Gulf Oil Corporation 16.66 per cent; Pan American Petroleum and Transport Company 16.66 per cent; Standard Oil Company of New Jersey 25 per cent; and Standard Oil Company of New York 25 per cent. Near East Development Corporation signed an agreement with TPC on 21 July 1928. It contained the famous "Red Line Agreement," a self-denying clause that prohibited all TPC members from independently exploring for oil beyond an area marked on the map by a red line. The area encompassed by the red line included virtually the whole of the old Ottoman Empire. The American group received a 23.75 per cent share. The French company agreed to purchase Gulbenkian's share; Anglo-Persian, Royal-Dutch Shell, and the French Company each received a 23.75 per cent share. [22] By 1929, when TPC changed its name to Iraq Petroleum Company, its wells were producing, and oil from Iraq began to flow into world markets shortly after the completion of the pipeline from the Mosul fields to the Mediterranean in 1934.

American entry into the TPC raises a question: What caused the British to retreat from their original position denying U.S. participation? John DeNovo concluded that the efforts of U.S. oil men, aided by the State Department, resulted in success. [23] George Stocking attributed success to the genius of A. C. Bedford, the Jersey Standard official. [24] George Gibb and Evelyn Knowlton maintained that British oil men needed American capital and engineering expertise. They also say that Calouste S. Gulbenkian urged the British to admit the Americans on restrictive terms rather than let them compete freely. [25] All of these explanations seem to be necessary to an understanding of the American association with IPC.

But one final word needs to be said about the Open Door. While that principle was an important tool used by the State Department to enable the American consortium to gain membership in TPC, in later years it was rarely observed.

Members of IPC considered the Open Door principle at variance with good business practice. Inasmuch as IPC placed numerous restrictions on the subletting of concessions, the Open Door became a chimera, not a verity.[26] No new American oil competitors had a chance of entering Mesopotamian oil fields, and IPC had a monopoly. But the Open Door had served its purpose, for when the 1928 agreement was signed, five American companies participated: Atlantic, Gulf, Pan-American, Jersey Standard, and SOCONY. Subsequent merger developments left only two American companies in the IPC-- Jersey Standard, (now called Exxon) and Socony-Vacuum (Mobil Oil).

        The American quest for oil also ran into obstructionist tactics in Persia (Iran), but the endeavor in that country must be understood in terms of the surge of Iranian nationalism in the post-World War I era.   Soviet Russia had withdrawn her dominating influence in northern Iran and the Iranians elected to offer American oil companies concessions in the five northern provinces, in exchange for which they wanted the concessionaire to grant Iran a loan, enabling her to assert independence from Britain--then seeking to make Iran a protectorate.[27] But Iranian oil was enmeshed in international politics, because the Persian cabinet had issued in 1916 to Akakie Khostaria, a Russian subject, an oil concession in four of the five northern provinces. In 1919 Anglo-Persian, which held a large concession in the south of Iran, hoped to acquire access to the northern region as well. But anti-British sentiment was rife in post-war Iran, which sought American help. The Iranian government employed Morgan Shuster to locate an American oil company that would grant Iran a loan in exchange for concessionary rights in the northern provinces, thereby offsetting British influence. Shuster was successful in approaching Jersey Standard, which in 1919 exhibited a desire to bid for rights in the North.[28] Pro-American feeling ran high in Iran, for knowledgeable Iranians knew that the U.S. government had no political ambitions in their country. It was not surprising that the Iranian government offered to Jersey Standard a definite proposition in September 1921 that would grant a 55-year concession in the five northern provinces. In return, Jersey Standard would lend Iran $5 million, make royalty payments of 10 per cent a year, and within two years of operation retrocede to the government one-half the area leased.[29] Although the State Department had supported Jersey Standard's efforts, the oil company's problems were not solved with the Persian offer of a concession. Anglo-Persian had purchased one-half of the Khostaria con-

cession and wanted the concession in the North. Since it had
the only feasible outlets for crude oil in the south of Iran it
held a commanding position with Jersey Standard. Ultimately, on 6 February 1922 Jersey Standard and Anglo-Persian
reached an accord whereby Jersey Standard acquired a half
interest in the Khostaria concession of some £178,000 and
Anglo-Persian agreed to provide one-half of the $5 million
loan to Iran. The two companies consented to share costs
and profits from the undertaking. This was a sensible move
on Jersey's part, for State Department official John Bassett
More advised that British control of pipelines through Iran's
southern provinces blocked other outlets to the Persian Gulf.
Too, the Bolsheviks controlled outlets through the Black Sea,
and with their unstable, hostile attitude toward private enterprise, they were seen as not likely to cooperate with Jersey
Standard. [30]

But Jersey Standard's agreement with Anglo-Persian
ran counter to the anti-British sentiment of the hyper-nation-
alistic Iranians. On 28 February 1922 the Iranian Prime
Minister rejected out of hand the offer made earlier by Jersey Standard, because Iran would not tolerate British involvement in the North. Herbert Hoover, who facilitated the arrangement between Jersey Standard and Anglo-Persian, was
unaware of the link between nationalism and oil in Iran.
While the Persians wanted an American concessionaire in the
North, they also desired American financial backing and
hoped for a makeweight against the British. [31]

To complicate matters further, Jersey officials learned
that the Sinclair Exploration Company, an American concern,
had submitted a bid in Teheran for the northern provinces, in
return for a loan of $7 million. Although the State Depart-
ment had aided Jersey Standard, it assumed a neutral position. Jersey Standard officials were on the horns of a dilemma. To back down would allow Sinclair, an arch competitor,
a fair field. To divorce Jersey entirely from Anglo-Persian
would be unwise, since Anglo-Persian was a major partner
in the TPC, an organization that Jersey Standard wanted to
join. In working alone Jersey would certainly be able to obtain a new concession, but since Anglo-Persian controlled
pipeline and port facilities, there would be the added problem
of transporting the crude oil to a refinery. Jersey executives
agreed to go it alone. On 30 June 1922 they assured Iranian
leaders that it would own, operate, and control the venture in
the North. On 22 August 1922 a revised contract was drawn
up, Jersey covering its relationship with Anglo-Persian by a

subcontractural arrangement by which Anglo-Persian would
function as a silent, but non-secret partner.[32] It now remained for the Iranian Majlis to decide between Jersey Standard and Sinclair.   A number of factors entered the decision-
making process.   Arthur Millspaugh, director-general of finance, urged the government to award Jersey the concession.
But Iranian officials found the relationship between Jersey and
Anglo-Persian unsatisfactory.   On 21 September the Iranian
government advised E. J. Sadler of Jersey Standard that the
Iranians would not tolerate the accord between Jersey and
Anglo-Persian.   This statement placed Jersey Standard in an
untenable position, and on 28 September Jersey's board of directors voted to withdraw from the field.[33]

        Jersey Standard's retreat left the field open to Sin-
clair.   Morgan Shuster had also arranged for the contract between Sinclair and the Iranian government.   Sinclair obtained
a concession with Iran on 20 December 1923, providing for a
50-year lease in four of the five northern provinces, with
Sinclair giving the government 20 per cent of the profits, and
a promise to arrange a $10 million loan.[34]   Sinclair officials
hoped to use outlets through Soviet Russia.   Harry Sinclair
had obtained transit rights from the Russians, provided he
could arrange for U.S. recognition of the Soviet Union.   But
in 1924 the Teapot Dome scandal embroiled Sinclair, and the
failure of American recognition of Russia to materialize negated his understanding with the Soviet Union.   With no assured outlets through Russia and with an oil glut on the American market, Sinclair withdrew from Iran in 1925.[35]

        The Sinclair retreat did not end American interest in
Iranian oil during the inter-war years.   Jersey Standard continued to work for an arrangement, but after a fruitless pursuit determined to pull out in 1927.   Another American concern, the Amiranian Oil Company, evinced an interest in the
northern provinces in the following decade.   Although Amiranian and the Shah's government negotiated two concessions in
January 1937, the company elected in 1938 not to commence
operations and to surrender the concessions.[36]

        Success came to Standard Oil of California in 1930 when
Standard Oil of California (SOCAL) officials acquired exclusive
rights in the Bahrain Islands.   The Sheikhdom of Bahrain consisted of a group of islands in the Persian Gulf some fifteen
miles off the coast of Saudi Arabia.   Since December 1880 the
sheikhdom had been a part of a complex of protectorates dependent on Britain.   The Foreign Office had signed treaties in

1880 and 1892 with the Sheikh, who agreed in 1914 not to grant oil rights or to develop his own petroleum resources without British permission.   In the mid-1920s, Major Frank Holmes, an official of the British-flag organization, Eastern and General Syndicate, signed a pact with the Sheikh of Bahrain, providing a concession of about 100,000 acres.   Holmes failed to interest British oil interests in taking up his option, and he turned to the Gulf Oil Company.   But the Red Line Agreement prevented Gulf, a member of TPC, from exploring in Bahrain.   On 21 December 1928 Gulf sold its rights in the Bahrain concession to Standard Oil of California.   The British posed obstacles to SOCAL, for there was a nationality clause in the Bahrain treaty requiring that a majority of the directors of a concession-holding company must be British and that the company must be British-registered.   SOCAL called upon the services of the State Department, which on 28 March 1929 queried the Foreign Office about the status of the concession.   Whitehall replied on 30 May, advising that it had no objection to SOCAL's concession, but that it must be British-directed.[37]   The Eastern and General Syndicate negotiated with the Colonial Office and the Sheikh and transferred its title to the Bahrain Petroleum Company, a Canadian subsidiary of SOCAL.   State Department efforts were necessary to arrange a contractural agreement whereby SOCAL gained its concession in Bahrain through Bahrain Petroleum Company (BAPCO), Canadian-incorporated, British-directed, and American-owned.   SOCAL geologists went to work immediately, and the first well was spudded in in May 1932. By 1935 there were sixteen producing oil wells, and SOCAL needed new markets.   It therefore sold one-half of its concession in Bahrain to the Texas Oil Company in order to acquire the use of the company's marketing complex in the Eastern Hemisphere.[38]

Gulf Oil Company also utilized the services of the State Department in winning a concession in Kuwait.   The Sheikhdom of Kuwait is located on the northwestern shore of the Persian Gulf.   In 1899 Britain brought it into the British Persian Gulf complex by a treaty in which the Sheikh agreed to seek British approval prior to making any bargain with a foreign government.   In 1913 the Sheikh showed British officials the location of possible oil reserves and promised to permit only British-approved persons the right to explore for oil.   The story of American oil activities in Kuwait is a replica of that in Bahrain.   Major Holmes of the Eastern and General Syndicate obtained a concession from the Sheikh in 1925, but, unable to sell it to Anglo-Persian, he turned to the

Gulf Oil Company.   Gulf wanted a concession, for Kuwait
was not within the Red Line area.   The Sheikh was willing
to accommodate Gulf, but not the British Colonial Office,
which again required the inclusion of a nationality clause.
The State Department protested in 1931, but during the following year negotiations between the United States and Great
Britain went forward simultaneously with the Colonial Office's
granting to Anglo-Persian a concession in Kuwait.   It was
apparent to Secretary of State Henry L. Stimson that the
British were determined to bar the Americans from the potentially valuable Kuwait oil fields.   Following negotiations
in 1932, the British relaxed the nationality clause, but continued to delay a settlement.   In November 1932 American
Ambassador Andrew Mellon delivered a stinging note to the
Foreign Office, asserting that the delay in settling the Kuwait matter was "exasperating."[39]   At length the British
backed down and forwarded the draft concession applications
of Gulf Oil and Anglo-Persian to the Sheikh in January 1933.
The Sheikh promptly rejected both of them.   In December
1933 Gulf and Anglo-Persian made a pact that provided for
joint exercise of the Kuwait concession, which would be
owned equally by the two companies.   In 1934 the Kuwait Oil
Company came into being as a British-registered, jointly-
owned enterprise with an exclusive concession to explore for
oil in the Sheikhdom of Kuwait.   Drilling operations commenced in 1936, but with negative results.   Success was
achieved two years later and by 1942 there were nine producing wells.   In July 1942 the British Army suspended all operations, which did not resume until after the war.   Kuwait
became one of the largest producers of crude oil in the world
in the years after World War II.[40]

Eventually, the world's largest proven oil reserves
would be found in Saudi Arabia.   Great Britain had signed an
agreement with Ibn Saud in 1915 that made his country a
British protectorate.   The treaty also contained a clause that
gave Britain the right of approval of prospective oil conces-
sionaires.   But this relation soon changed.   In 1926 Ibn Saud
defeated Sherif Hussein and became King of the Hejaz, and
the new status was recognized by a 1927 treaty between Britain and the King.   Britain no longer had the right to veto
prospective oil men.   By this time the concession acquired
by Major Holmes for the Eastern and General Syndicate had
lapsed, the field was open, and the Americans entered the
scene.   In 1931 Charles Crane, the American who had participated on the King-Crane Commission, visited Arabia.
Crane had a profound admiration and respect for the Arabs,

and the American philanthropist provided the King with the
services of a mining engineer to survey the mineral resources of Saudi Arabia. Accordingly, Karl S. Twitchell
commenced a geological survey of the land and reported that
it was potentially rich in petroleum. [41]   The King trusted
Americans in general and Twitchell in particular, and he
hoped that the American would locate adequate capital and
technical skills necessary for Saudi Arabia to develop her own
oil resources.   Twitchell claimed that he was no financier,
but agreed to promote Arabian oil concessions in the United
States.   He arrived in New York in the summer of 1932 and
interested officials of Standard Oil of California in applying
for a concession in Saudi Arabia. [42]   Twitchell received the
power of attorney to act for SOCAL, but on his return to
Jidda he learned to his dismay that the Iraq Petroleum Company and the Eastern and General Syndicate were also competing for the concession.   However, Eastern and General
soon dropped out of the race and, IPC geologists having reported negatively on the oil potential of Saudi Arabia, then
IPC withdrew from the competition, leaving SOCAL as the
sole applicant for a concession.   The King awarded the prize
to SOCAL on 29 May 1933, basing his decision on the superior financial terms offered by the Americans and by a profound distrust for the British who had sponsored the Hashemite dynasty. [43]   In August the company made the requisite
loan payment and the concession was awarded to the California-Arabian Standard Oil Company, the SOCAL subsidiary.
Exploration was begun immediately and in 1936 CASOC brought
the Texas Company into the operation in order to acquire that
company's marketing facilities. [44]   Oil was soon produced in
commercial quantities, but World War II greatly hindered
production, thus reducing the King's royalties and producing
a financial crisis in Saudi Arabia that had important consequences for the United States.

                    *   *   *   *   *

        By 1939 the United States interest in Middle Eastern
oil was considerable.   In that year approximately 15 per cent
of the oil produced in Middle Eastern oil fields was for the
account of American companies.   Jersey Standard and SOCONY
had a 23.75 per cent interest in the IPC, which produced
30.7 million barrels of oil in 1939.   SOCAL and the Texas
Company had an exclusive concession in Bahrain where production reached 7.5 million barrels per year.   In Kuwait,
Gulf Oil and Anglo Persian operated jointly.   Although pro-

duction began only in 1938 and was soon closed down, the American participation promised enormous profits in the post-war years that would see the United States come to depend on imports of Middle Eastern oil.   In Saudi Arabia, CASOC and the Texas Company enjoyed an exclusive concession in which the first commercial field was discovered in early 1938.   Production in 1939 was negligible, but the potential was great.

The ability of American petroleum interests to gain access to Middle Eastern oil resources was due to the efforts of the State Department.   In every instance, Saudi Arabia being the sole exception, State Department assistance was necessary to facilitate American entry.   While the Open Door was not strictly adhered to in later years, it proved valuable at the outset in assisting the Americans to participate in IPC.

At the outbreak of World War II American oil interests faced new problems in the Middle East.   With American entry into the conflict in 1941, United States petroleum interests in the Middle East assumed great import and became part of the national interest as American forces sought to achieve a military victory and to protect vital petroleum sources.

Chapter 9

WORLD WAR II: A WATERSHED IN
MIDDLE EASTERN DIPLOMACY

Between the two world wars American economic and cultural interests in the Middle East expanded, but political aims remained restricted, and at the onset of hostilities in 1939 the United States continued to view Britain as the major power in the region. Some historians have claimed that the U.S. deferred to British dominance in the region during the entire period of World War II and formed no regional foreign policy.[1] American policy-makers, they asserted, were motivated by a single-minded desire to win the war. An examination of the record indicates that U.S. leaders followed the British lead prior to Pearl Harbor, but that they then became independent of British direction. Evidence of the autonomy of American policy was manifested by the anti-imperial stance expressed by the State Department's aggressive oil policy in Saudi Arabi and Iran and by an independent policy in Iran, Palestine, Turkey, and Syria.[2] The United States pursued an anti-imperial policy in order to expand its own interests that were economic in nature,[3] but this policy was also based on the idealistic considerations of the Atlantic Charter. The United States did defer to British leadership in some instances. It was the British War Office that determined to launch a joint Anglo-American military operation in North Africa in 1942 instead of in Europe to prevent a juncture of German and Japanese forces in the Middle East.[4] The U.S. and Britain also functioned harmoniously in Iran, the better to supply the Russians through the vital "Persian Corridor,"[5] albeit the U.S. pursued an independent policy in that country in other respects.

World War II was a watershed in American-Middle Eastern relations. Considerations of the national interest surpassed the importance of cultural interests, and national security demanded an effective diplomatic policy to sustain

the military effort. Protection of the sources of petroleum
called for a vigorous diplomacy to offset those forces that
might deny the Allies access to Middle Eastern oil fields.
The conclusion of World War II found the United States deeply involved in the Middle East. British dominance receded
as the United States gradually assumed the British role of
policing the region and containing the expansion of the historical Russian push toward the Mediterranean. But to complicate the formulation of American wartime Middle Eastern
policy, there was the growth of Zionist sentiment in the
United States--a sentiment based on moral considerations
that ran counter to the realization of the nation's vital interests.

                    *   *   *   *   *

     A number of historians have claimed that President
Roosevelt's anti-imperialism was not wholly altruistic, asserting that opposition to Britain was motivated by an aggressive quest for oil and by the necessity of protecting existing
American oil holdings. This is certainly true, and this facet
of American-Middle Eastern policy is consistent with the historical American record of acquiring new commercial opportunity. That the U. S. pursued a vigorous policy in Saudi
Arabia to protect American oil interests is good evidence of
the independence of U. S. policy from the dictates of Whitehall.[6] It will be recalled that Saudi Arabia's diplomatic intercourse with the U. S. was largely due to the needs of
American oil interests. In 1933 the U.S. signed with King
Ibn Saud's representatives an agreement for diplomatic and
commercial relations. In the same year the Standard Oil
Company of California obtained a concession to develop Saudi
Arabian oil, and the company established in 1933 as a result
of these negotiations was called California-Arabian Standard
Oil (CASOC), and it was wholly owned by Standard Oil of
California. In 1936 the Texas Company became a half-part-
ner. CASOC changed to Arabian-American Oil Company
(ARAMCO) in 1944. The King preferred to deal directly with
American oil officials, but the U. S. thought it advisable to
accredit Bert Fish, minister to Egypt, as the new U. S. min-
ister to Arabia.[7]

     The outbreak of war resulted in the curtailment of
American oil production and a decline in the number of pil-
grims visiting the holy city of Mecca. These two events
caused a marked reduction in King Ibn Saud's revenues. The

King required financial aid, and in 1940 the British government advanced him a sizable sum. CASOC officials did like-
wise, turning over almost $3 million in excess of royalties
due the King. In the following year the King demanded that
CASOC pay $6 million annually for a period of six years.
CASOC could not sustain these high payments and in the
spring of 1941 sought the assistance of the U. S. government.[8]
The Lend-Lease Act passed Congress and was signed by President Roosevelt in March 1941. CASOC saw this measure as
a possible solution to its financial problems with King Ibn
Saud. James A. Moffett, representing CASOC, wrote the
President on 16 April 1941, asking for assistance to preserve
the financial stability of Saudi Arabia. He advised that CASOC
had invested $27.5 million in the country, advanced $6.8
million in future royalties, and could not afford to provide
additional funds to the King. He explained that the company
feared Britain's growing influence in the country.[9] The President declared that the U. S. could do nothing directly for
Saudi Arabia, but he advised the Reconstruction Finance Corporation to grant Britain a loan, a portion of which could be
set aside to meet the King's fiscal needs. CASOC succeeded
in making arrangements with Britain to take care of the company's obligations to the King,[10] but CASOC officials realized
that the agreement with Britain carried mixed blessings. Although it did reduce the company's advances to the King, it
meant that American money was enabling Britain to gain influence in Saudi Arabia where the company had a large investment. Officials feared that British influence would supplant
that of the United States and that the King might cancel the
concession and award it to Britain. Britain had long been a
supporter of King Ibn Saud, and the recent British financial
gambit in Arabia caused company leaders to resume their efforts to obtain direct assistance from the U. S. government to
block the British.[11]

In early 1943 Harry D. Collier, president of Standard
Oil of California, and W. S. Rodgers, chairman of the Texas
Company, approached Harold L. Ickes, the Secretary of the
Interior and the newly appointed petroleum administrator.
They advised Ickes of the need to extend American Lend-Lease
to King Ibn Saud to preserve the American position in Saudi
Arabia and to protect the oil concession.[12] Collier and
Rodgers also carried their plea to the secretaries of Army,
Navy, and State.[13] Even before the oil company executives
requested the extension of Lend-Lease aid to Saudi Arabia,
the Near East Division at the State Department had already
so recommended, and when Ickes saw the President on 18

February 1943, he found him favorably disposed to help the
Saudis. Roosevelt advised Edward Stettinius, Lend-Lease Ad-
ministrator, that the defense of Saudi Arabia was vital to the
United States and should be accorded funds. This marked a
turning point in U.S. diplomacy in the Middle East. The
President's action committed the U.S. to support Saudi Arab-
ia to protect vital U.S. economic interests and to counter
British threats to these interests. The aid greatly enhanced
American prestige in Saudi Arabia, convinced the King of
American goodwill, and ensured stability in Saudi Arabia.[14]

The extension of Lend-Lease was but one manifestation of the growing good relations between the U.S. and
Saudi Arabia. An American Legation opened at Jidda in May
1942, and in that same month Karl S. Twitchell returned to
Saudi Arabia as head of a mission of technical experts. The
President invited King Ibn Saud to visit the United States in
1943, and the King graciously accepted, delegating his two
sons to represent him. In early 1944 the U.S. dispatched a
mission to advise the King's military forces. Rivalry with
the British continued and Secretary of State Cordell Hull advised the President that the U.S. should increase financial
assistance to Saudi Arabia. In the summer of 1944 the United
States responded to the King's plea for additional aid by making a joint agreement with Britain to meet his needs.[15]

But even with a joint Anglo-American agreement, there
was still a climate of suspicion between American oil men and
the British. The State Department received complaints that
S. R. Jordan, British minister at Jidda, was working to undermine the American position in Saudi Arabia.[16] Continued
fear of British activities in Saudi Arabia and a report by Dr.
Herbert Feis, State Department petroleum expert, that American domestic oil reserves were being diminished by the war
caused Americans to take a new approach to the oil situation
in Saudi Arabia.[17] Officials in the State, War, Navy and Interior departments began to think in terms of acquiring ownership of the oil concession in Saudi Arabia to ensure an adequate supply of petroleum to meet further U.S. military and
domestic needs. Harold Ickes was the leader of this movement, and he suggested that a government-formed Petroleum
Reserves Corporation acquire ownership of the American concession to offset the British and maintain a reserve for American needs. Ickes was not alone in suggesting government entry into the oil business, for the Joint Chiefs of Staff and
members of the President's cabinet shared the same opinion.
In June 1943 a cabinet committee proposed the formation of

the Petroleum Reserves Corporation to obtain an interest or
outright ownership of petroleum reserves beyond the continental limits.[18] The President agreed, and in June 1943 he
authorized the Reconstruction Finance Corporation to organize the Petroleum Reserves Corporation and appointed Harold
Ickes president.[19] Ickes began negotiations with CASOC officials to purchase the company's concession in Saudi Arabia.
They were shocked at this invasion of private enterprise and
refused to sell 100 per cent.   They would consider selling
one-third, and talks continued through the autumn of 1943 but
eventually broke down, because company executives opposed
government ownership.[20]

Although Ickes failed to acquire the CASOC concession,
he soon turned to another expedient.   Officials of PRC and
CASOC considered government construction and operation of
a refinery in Saudi Arabia to process some 100 to 150,000
barrels per day to meet military needs.   This scheme proved
impractical.   The oil men announced that they would build a
smaller refinery in Saudi Arabia with private capital.[21]   At
that juncture, Admiral Andrew Carter, petroleum administrator of the U.S. Navy, proposed construction of a government-
owned pipeline from the Persian Gulf to the Mediterranean
coast to serve American needs.   Ickes agreed and on 6 February 1944 he announced that PRC was authorized to build a
pipeline to ensure an adequate supply of oil for the armed
forces.[22]   Ickes' announcement created dissent, for opponents
of the proposal--for example, the Petroleum War Industry
Council (PWIC) that consisted of representatives of fifty-five
American oil companies--asserted that the government proposal to invade the private sector of the economy was unacceptable.   Instead, it should continue to adhere to the Open Door
policy to enable private enterprise to develop the oil resources of Saudi Arabia.[23]   Faced with opposition from American oil producers and from the British government, PRC
gave up the idea.   In the early spring of 1945 ARAMCO began construction of the pipeline, a venture that required some
five years to build.[24]

Even though PWIC opposed government invasion of pri-
vate industry, it favored an international agreement enabling
American oil companies to explore for new sources of petrol-
eum in various parts of the world.   Accordingly, the Presi-
dent abolished PRC in 1944 and initiated steps to commence
Anglo-American talks to negotiate an international agreement.
Conversations commenced, and the resulting Anglo-American
Oil Agreement, published in August 1944, provided for col-

laboration between American and British oil interests. The President submitted the agreement in late August to the Senate, where it aroused a storm of resentment. [25] Business leaders advised senators that it smacked of a European-type cartel, and that it was but the first step toward nationalization. Domestic oil men claimed that the vast influx of Middle Eastern oil would flood the American market and depress domestic prices. The agreement was reported out of the Foreign Relations Committee in July 1947, and the Senate withheld consent, for it did not meet the approval of the domestic oil industry. [26]

In retrospect, the record of American "oleaginous diplomacy" in Saudi Arabia during World War II was marked by tradition and innovation. On the one hand, the U.S. government continued to support oil interests as in the past. While the government considered entering directly into the business of oil production it drew back at the behest of oil men who appealed to the sanctity of private enterprise and urged the government to continue to pursue the Open Door, which had worked so well in the past. On the other hand, the government embarked on a new departure, for in rendering direct aid to Saudi Arabia it made that government more stable internally. The U.S. had sent missions to that country to further insure its stability, and these acts of financial and technical assistance transcended the tradition of non-intervention. American aid enhanced the prestige of CASOC, protected its concession, and prevented a possible British encroachment. Government intervention can be justified on the grounds that the national interest demanded new sources of energy be supplied by American oil companies, which required State Department assistance.

American and British policy differed not only on Saudi Arabia but also on military strategy in the Middle East. Following American entry into World War II, Prime Minister Winston Churchill traveled to Washington and met with President Roosevelt in the ARCADIA Conference in December 1941 and January 1942. The two leaders divided the world into military spheres, both nations taking co-responsibility for Europe, the U.S. assuming responsibility for the Western Hemisphere, the Pacific, and China, and Britain accepting the leading role in Africa, the Middle East, India, and South East Asia. They agreed on a Europe-first policy that called for the two powers to mount an all-out offensive on Germany, but remain on the defensive against Japan. The British leader also persuaded Roosevelt to postpone plans to launch an

invasion of Europe and instead to join with Britain in an offensive operation in North Africa. [27]

After the conference American planners began to develop a strategy that differed from that called for at the
ARCADIA Conference. General Dwight D. Eisenhower, working directly under Chief of Staff George C. Marshall, drafted
a comprehensive plan for an Anglo-American invasion of Europe by the spring of 1943. Eisenhower deemed this operation to be the most effective way to defeat Germany, but the
plan viewed the proposed invasion of North Africa as periph-
eral to the main task and not as strategically sound as the
cross-channel operation in northern France. [28] President
Roosevelt accepted the American strategic concept and sent
Harry Hopkins to Britain to gain the endorsement of Churchill and the War Office. The British accepted reluctantly but
did not give the plan their wholehearted support. The British proved so unenthusiastic that General Marshall briefly
considered a reversal of strategy that placed major emphasis
on the Pacific war. Americans believed the British approved
the North African operation to preserve the British Empire,
the center of which lay in the Middle East. In fact, in 1942
the Germans did pose a threat to the British position in
North Africa. [29] Although the British strategic conceptualiza-
tion was based in part on imperial aspirations, British leaders
also recalled the bloody stalemate of trench warfare in France
between 1914 and 1918, and they did not want to repeat that
performance in an invasion of France that held no promise of
a sure victory. Churchill returned to Washington in June
1942, still opposed to an early invasion of Europe and equally
disposed toward an Anglo-American landing in North Africa.
While Roosevelt and Churchill held their talks, news of the
fall of Tobruk arrived. This spelled possible disaster, because the Germans' desert army threatened the British position in Egypt. But instead of agreeing to the proposed invasion of North Africa, the Americans consented to dispatch additional guns and tanks to the British forces in Africa. And
in the following month, the British learned that the Americans
were planning an offensive operation against the Japanese in
the Solomon Islands, where American forces would strike at
Guadalcanal in August 1942. [30] Undismayed, the British continued to push for the North African landing. At length, the
President decided on 24 July 1942 that the British proposal
held merit and that the North African landings should take
place in the autumn. [31]

Another area in which Anglo-American cooperation was

accompanied by differences of opinion was Iran, where Britain and Russia had long competed for political and economic control. British oil holdings in the southern portion of Iran constituted a major interest that Britain had to protect. The Russians had for many years exercised influence in the northern section. During the 1930s Shah Reza Pahlavi introduced many German technicians into the country to offset British and Russian influence. At the outbreak of war, Iran was falling into the German sphere of influence. After the German invasion of Russia in June 1941, the British and Russians determined to remove the Germans from Iran because they constituted a potentially dangerous fifth column in the rear of the Russians and a possible threat to the Iranian oil so vital to the British war effort.[32] The British and Russians invaded Iran in August 1941, with the Soviet Union assuming responsibility in the sector north of Teheran and Britain taking over the southern region. The Shah cabled President Roosevelt, urgently requesting his good offices to terminate the Anglo-Russian occupation. The President replied on 2 September that the U.S. had ascertained that the two powers did not have selfish ambitions. He added that he had urged the British and Russians to make public statements guaranteeing the territorial integrity of Iran. The United States did not become involved in the three-way diplomatic imbroglio, and Secretary of State Cordell Hull advised the Iranian minister that U.S. sentiments were pro-Allied, that Iran should avoid giving aid to the Axis, and that she should cooperate with the Allies. But even with a pro-Allied posture in Iran, Hull refused to support an Anglo-Soviet request that Iran expel the Germans. Hull did warn the Iranian minister that Iran should take all necessary measures to curtail Nazi activities.[33] The British and Russians expelled the Germans, and the pro-German Reza Shah abdicated on 16 September in favor of his pro-Allied son, Muhammed Reza.[34]

The British, Russians, and Iranians signed the Tripartite Pact in January 1942, a move that revealed Cordell Hull's influence on the course of events in Iran. Hull had called upon the Allies the previous September to make a treaty setting forth the terms of the joint occupation. They agreed to respect the territorial integrity of Iran and to withdraw all military forces within six months of the cessation of hostilities. Iran agreed to remain neutral and to support the Allied logistical operations.[35] The main purpose of the Anglo-Soviet operation in Iran was to secure the Russian rear and maintain a firm hold on Iranian oil, but the Allies soon established a supply route over which Lend-Lease material could be transported to the Russians.

The Persian Corridor was one of five routes by which
some 19.3 million tons of Lend-Lease supplies were delivered to the Soviet Union.   A total of 8.85 million tons of
equipment was discharged at Persian Gulf ports, and of this
amount 5.7 million tons were delivered to the Russians.
This amount of equipment and supplies was sufficient to maintain about sixty Russian divisions.   Of the five avenues of
supply, the corridor in late 1942 assumed second place in the
total amount of tonnage shipped to the Soviets.[36]   The Allies
wanted the U.S. to assist in the Persian Corridor, and the
American Army served in that region for a little more than
four years.   In November Colonel Raymond Wheeler, an expert in railroad and truck transport affairs, arrived in Iran
at the head of an American military mission.   By December
1942 the size of the U.S. contingent in Iran had grown considerably, for in that month alone some 5000 American service troops landed.[37]   The Shah's government wanted American adherence to the Tripartite Pact, and it entered into a
long exchange with the State Department.   The U.S. refused
to adhere to the pact, and there was no more agreement between the two countries than an unwritten understanding.[38]
Perhaps American reluctance to adhere to the pact can be explained by the lack of any comprehensive regional policy.[39]

American involvement in Iran was at first subordinate
to the British, and U.S. Army forces served in an auxiliary
status.[40]   In September 1942 the U.S. accepted primary responsibility for operating transportation facilities through the
Persian Corridor to the Soviet Union.   In October 1942 Major
General Donald H. Connolly took command of the Persian
Gulf Service Command, as the U.S. force was called, and
gradually PGSC assumed a coordinate role when the British
turned over the task of operating the Iranian State Railway
from Teheran to the Gulf.[41]

In the early days of the war the United States possessed no long-range policy in Iran beyond the traditional adherence to the Open Door, non-intervention, and respect for
the integrity and sovereignty of the country.[42]   But at length
the U.S. began to formulate an Iranian policy.[43]   It cannot
be said, as some radical historians have claimed, that American wartime policy in Iran was motivated solely by political
considerations, stemming from the need to find new sources
of petroleum.[44]   Clearly, in the early days of the conflict
the United States directed its efforts in Iran toward waging
war against the Germans by supplying Russia with Lend-
Lease.   But the memoirs of Cordell Hull make it clear that

U.S. policy considerations toward Iran encompassed more
than traditional objectives as officials initiated a policy to
maintain Iranian territorial integrity from possible British or
Russian abridgment.   To that end, Hull recalled that the
U.S. had initiated Lend-Lease shipments to Iran and that
American technical and military advisers had been sent to
that country to strengthen the government.   Thinking in terms
of the Atlantic Charter, which provided for signatories to abstain from territorial ambitions, Hull began in mid-1943 to
conceive of a three-power declaration by which the U.S.,
Britain, and Russia would agree to guarantee the sovereignty
of Iran.   (Hull later suggested this expedient at the October
1943 Moscow Conference.)   But the Secretary was frank to
admit that the U.S. did not have an intention of adhering to
a treaty of alliance with Iran.[45]   The dispatch of several
economic and military advisory missions was another aspect
of the transition of U.S. policy vis-à-vis Iran.

Shortly after the Anglo-Russian occupation of Iran, the
Shah's government invited Dr. Arthur C. Millspaugh to organize a mission to reorder Iranian public finances.   Millspaugh organized the U.S. Financial Mission, comprising some
thirty-five economic experts.   This was not an official U.S.
government mission, but the State Department advised Millspaugh that it had high expectations for this mission's primary
purpose to stiffen the government that it might better aid the
Allies.[46]   The Iranians appointed Millspaugh as administrator-
general of finances in January 1943, giving him broader authority than he had received at the time of his earlier mission.   Vested by the Majlis with executive and advisory powers, Millspaugh hoped to achieve sweeping reforms.   He was
genuinely interested in accomplishing goals that would benefit
the government, but his Iranian supporters hoped that his
presence would result in greater American financial assistance and political support against the British and Russians.
The tragedy of his mission was that he wanted to accomplish
more reform than the Iranians had bargained for.   Millspaugh's accomplishments and failures must be viewed against
a background of political intrigue and numerous obstacles.
He did make progress in fiscal control, food supply, and internal transport, but he incurred opposition from cabinet ministers, wealthy landowners and merchants whose vested interests were jeopardized by reform, and Iranian Communists
who viewed Millspaugh as a dupe of the capitalists.[47]   His
accomplishments might have been greater, but he blamed the
State Department for failure to give him adequate support.
But Department officials viewed his mission as unofficial and

regarded the administrator-general as an employee of the Iranians. [48]

While Millspaugh's mission was the most important one in Iran, there were two other American advisory groups. In 1942 a U.S. military mission led by Major General C. S. Ridley arrived to advise the Iranian Army on matters of logistics. A former governor of the Panama Canal Zone, Ridley's mission was successful and he was able to accomplish the motorization of the Shah's Army. [49] A second mission, headed by Colonel H. Norman Schwarzkopf, arrived in Iran to reform the gendarmerie. A former police chief, Schwarzkopf proved to be the most successful of the American advisers in wartime Iran. The Shah had good cause to be pleased with Schwarzkopf, for he quickly brought wild tribesmen under control along the supply route, but in the Soviet sector he could do little, for the Russians restricted Iranian activity there. Iranian Communists, supporters of the Soviet-backed Tudeh Party, criticized the work of Schwarzkopf and his staff who were bent on restoring law and order to the country. [50] The two American military missions were supportive of the greater work of the Persian Gulf Service Command whose major responsibility was to continue the flow of supplies through the Persian Corridor.

The PGSC, consisting of 30,000 American service troops, built harbors, docking facilities, roads, highways, and warehouses. It operated that portion of the Iranian State Railroad from the Persian Gulf to Teheran. Over the line traveled three out of every five tons of aid sent to Russia through the Persian Corridor. After the PGSC took over its portion of the line, it hauled 3,397 tons per day. PGSC also operated a Motor Transport Service which by 1944 maintained a fleet of 2500 trucks to haul supplies over roads improved by U.S. service personnel. PGSC also organized truck and airplane assembly plants. When PGSC terminated its activities in 1945 it turned over to Iran a long stretch of the IRS in good running order. The two ports of Khorramshahr and Bandar Shahpur, operated by the Americans, were also handed over and proved of great service to Iran in the post-war era. [51]

American policy toward Iran developed gradually during the war. It was both pragmatic and idealistic. At the outset, the U.S. viewed Iran as a vital adjunct to the war effort, but it was also interested in maintaining a stable Iranian government. Cordell Hull desired to see the Atlantic

Charter provisions, denying member nations the right to annex territory, applied to Iran.   With that in mind, he approached British Foreign Secretary Anthony Eden and Russian
Foreign Minister V. I. Molotov at the October 1943 Moscow
Conference with a view to issuing a three-power declaration
guaranteeing the territorial integrity of Iran.[52]   At the summit conference held at Teheran in November-December 1943,
the Big Three--Roosevelt, Churchill, and Stalin--issued the
Teheran Declaration, a document that expressed gratitude to
Iran for her wartime assistance, asserted an interest in rendering economic assistance, and guaranteed the independence
and sovereignty of Iran.[53]   U.S. interest in Iran continued to
develop in the latter stages of the conflict, and the President's visit to Teheran sharpened his concern for the welfare
of that country.   He had sent General Patrick Hurley on a
fact-finding mission to the Middle East, scrutinized Hurley's
reports on Iran carefully and also read numerous State Department dispatches and memoranda on the state of affairs in
that country.[54]

On 12 January 1944 Roosevelt wrote Hull that Iran
was a poverty-stricken country and he believed that American technical assistance and financial aid could raise the
level of living of the people.[55]   It seems reasonable to believe that General Hurley's reports influenced the President,
who began to shape a more definite policy toward Iran.   By
extending aid the U.S. could uplift the Iranians and secure
that country for private enterprise.   A stronger Iran could
withstand the external pressures of Britain and the Soviet
Union as well as the internal forces of dissident political
elements.   Hull reports that U.S. assistance to Iran greatly
increased in 1944, and during the month of July the State Department prepared a position paper on Iran.   The paper declared that the President desired to use Iran as a "testing
ground" for social, political, and economic improvement.
The U.S. must also bolster that country, the better to protect its own national interests, which included extended commercial relations, access to air bases, and access to the
nation's oil fields.[56]   Although the U.S. had not come to the
point of making a hard and fast statement that it would guarantee the territorial integrity of Iran, it had come a long
way in formulating a policy toward that country.   While much
of U.S. Iranian policy--Roosevelt's social schemes, for ex-
ample--appear wholly idealistic, there is more to it than
meets the eye.   Iran was one of the great oil-producing re-
gions of the world, and one aspect of U.S.-Middle Eastern
diplomacy was to help stabilize nations with rich petroleum de-

posits to which American oil interests desired access.

Arthur C. Millspaugh was critical of the manner in
which the Department of State supported two American oil
companies in their pursuit of Iranian oil concessions.   In
view of the Atlantic Charter provisions on economic development, and in view of the cooperation of the three powers in
Iran, Millspaugh suggests that the Department blundered in
not obtaining a prior understanding with the Russians and
British. [57]   But Cordell Hull's memoirs justify U.S. action,
for the nation needed petroleum sources in the Middle East
to replenish domestic reserves. [58]   Thus when officials of
Socony-Vacuum Oil Company approached the State Department
in the fall of 1943, the Secretary replied on 15 November
that the U.S. had no objections to the company's initiative in
Iran, adding that there was no agreement with Britain that
would bar Americans from acquiring concessions in Iran. [59]
In early 1944 the international scramble for oil concessions
complicated the picture in wartime Iran.   In addition to
Socony-Vacuum, the Sinclair Consolidated Oil Company also
applied for a concession.   British interests sought further
rights in Iran, and in February the Soviet Embassy advised
that Russia had preempted the right to explore for oil in the
northern sector.   British and American companies negotiated
for concessions in the southeast but to no avail.   The Iranian government then decided to postpone further negotiations
on concessions until the conclusion of the war.   On learning
this decision, Hull reported that the U.S. accepted the ver-
dict, but he urged the U.S. ambassador in Teheran to tell
the Iranians he hoped American companies would be given
treatment equal to that accorded other foreign concerns in
the post-war era when applications were received.   While
the Americans and British accepted the Iranian decision, the
Russians continued their quest, an action that was partially
responsible for the international crisis in Iran in 1946. [60]

The conduct of U.S. policy in Iran during World War
II has aroused considerable controversy.   Some critics claim
that in the absence of a policy the U.S. followed the British
lead. [61]   Others assert that U.S. policy was marked by weak-
ness and lack of coordination and that this negative character encouraged the Russians who tried to establish hegemony
in Iran after the war. [62]   Some observers maintain that policy
in Iran followed traditional guidelines, and this failure to act
positively encouraged the Soviet Union. [63]   Others claim the
U.S. gradually developed a policy in Iran, and, in addition
to winning the war, the U.S. gave technical and financial

assistance and secured the Teheran Declaration to preserve
Iranian independence, [64] a condition that would permit American petroleum interests to seek concessions in the post-war
era.   What seems clear is that traditional U.S. policies toward Iran were supplemented during the war with measures
that had military motives, economic overtones, and altruistic-
pragmatic bases.   Policy considerations rested on the primary need to prosecute the war and to maintain the wartime
coalition with Britain and Russia.   In addition, the U.S.
hoped to sustain Iranian integrity and to improve the level of
living of the people.   At times policy toward Britain was
tense, because U.S. strategists had suspcions about a British
intent to abridge Iranian independence.

       At the outset the U.S. followed the British lead, but
it soon became a co-partner, and acted independently of
Whitehall.   That the U.S. did not take a stronger line toward
Russia is explained by Roosevelt's desire to build a bond of
mutual trust between the U.S. and the Soviet Union so that
the latter would cooperate with the West in the post-war
world, one based on democratic and capitalistic institutions.
Initially, the U.S. policy toward Iran followed past precedents, but with the passage of time, it would appear that policy-makers transcended traditional guidelines to serve American national interests.   Technical, military, and economic
assistance, coupled with the Teheran Declaration, indicate the
willingness of U.S. leaders to bolster the internal political
and economic structures of Iran so that it might remain a nation free and independent, a condition necessary to the satisfaction of future U.S. goals.   At all events, U.S. wartime
policies and activities in Iran yielded goodwill for the United
States and confirmed the Iranians in their view that the U.S.
was a disinterested power that might serve to check the aggressive tendencies of Britain and Russia at war's end.

       United States reaction to the Palestine question has al-
so raised questions.   Did President Roosevelt act independently of Britain in Palestine and work to create a Jewish
homeland or did he oppose such a measure?   Was American
wartime policy on Palestine influenced by domestic politics?
Was the national interest considered?   Although the U.S. government regarded Palestine as a British problem, after the
outbreak of war American Zionists and members of Congress
forced government officials to reconsider the question.   Cordell Hull characterized the issue as "delicate" and one that
posed a dilemma for policy-makers. [65]   Zionist Jews threatened to disrupt the Middle East and hinder the Allied war

effort, because creation of a Jewish homeland in Palestine
ran counter to Arab feelings. American Zionists, having assumed the leadership of world Zionism, hoped the U.S. government would use its good offices to establish a Jewish national home--a goal at variance with the advice of oil men
and State Department experts who warned that endorsement of
the Zionist cause would alienate the Arabs whose cooperation
was vitally needed. Like his predecessors, President Roosevelt did not view Palestine as a vital American interest, but
American Zionists soon propelled the Palestine question to
stage center.[66] In 1941 Emanuel Neumann, director of the
public relations program of the American Emergency Council
for Zionist Affairs, formed the American Palestine Committee, a prestigious organization of members of Congress and
high-level government officials, headed by Senator Robert F.
Wagner of New York. In 1942 on the 25th anniversary of the
issuance of the Balfour Declaration, this group, which now
included 68 senators and 200 members of the House of Representatives, issued a statement in opposition to the British
White Paper of 1939.[67] In May 1942 a meeting of American
Zionists in New York passed a proposal, commonly known as
the Biltmore Program, that called for the implementation of
the Balfour pledge.[68] To enlist the backing of American Jews
for this program, Henry Monsky, an ardent Zionist, called
upon thirty-four national Jewish organizations representing
some one million American Jews to send delegates to a conference at Pittsburgh in January 1943 to form an American
Jewish Assembly to marshall Jewish support for a common
program on Palestine. Known as the American Jewish Conference, it constructed a nation-wide network of Jewish
groups to raise funds, organize support for the Biltmore plan,
and stir up American public opinion for conference goals.[69]
The AJC utilized professional public opinion-propaganda techniques to win congressional and public support for the Biltmore Program. It used the media, mass meetings, and writ-
ten petitions to build up pressure for Zionist aims.[70] The
AJC's leadership was almost the same as that of the American Zionist Emergency Council. Under the direction of
Emanuel Neumann, the Council educated the American public
to support Zionist aims. It too used professional tactics to
sway public opinion and formed local emergency committees
to write congressmen about Zionist plans. It organized pressure on state legislatures, arranged for public rallies, and
obtained the endorsement of various groups such as university
professors.[71]

The rapid acceleration of Zionist activities in the

United States evoked a sharp reaction from Arab leaders.
Diplomatic agents in the Middle East advised the State Department late in 1942 and early in 1943 that Arab officials were
annoyed by pro-Zionist sentiment in the United States. King
Ibn Saud wrote Roosevelt in April and May 1943, urging him
to consult him before acting on Palestine. The Joint Chiefs
of Staff sent Lieutenant Colonel Harold B. Hoskins, a Middle
East expert, to the region on a mission, and he reported
early in 1943 that unless steps were taken to reduce Arab-
Jewish tensions over the Palestine question there might be a
violent outbreak that would throw the Middle East into chaos. [72] President Roosevelt could only conciliate. He advised
King Ibn Saud on 26 May 1943 that the U.S. would take no
steps on Palestine without consulting with him. But the President said that it would be valuable if Arab and Jewish leaders
could meet and come to a mutual understanding on the issue. [73] The President's efforts to reconcile the Arab-Jewish
conflict proved abortive. He tried to arrange a meeting between King Ibn Saud and some Zionist leader such as Chaim
Weizmann, but the King refused to oblige, saying that he
could not speak for the Arab world. [74] During the summer of
1943, American and British leaders considered issuing a joint
declaration that no final decision would be taken to settle the
Palestine question until after the war ended. The idea was
laid aside when the War Department advised against such a
proposal. [75]

In spite of the imperatives of the American national interest and the tradition of non-involvement, the U.S. was becoming a party to the Palestine problem. That Roosevelt had
advised King Ibn Saud that the question would not be decided
without prior consultation indicates that the U.S. would assume
a major role in reaching a final decision. That the U.S.
made numerous efforts to persuade the British to alter the
1939 White Paper provision for termination of Jewish immigration to Palestine after 1944 is evidence of further American
involvement. [76] But the U.S. was not yet ready to go full measure on the Palestine question as evidenced by official reaction
to two proposed 1944 congressional resolutions calling on the
U.S. government to use its good offices to create a Jewish
commonwealth. [77] The two resolutions, introduced in January
1944 and assigned to appropriate House and Senate committees,
immediately produced a furor in the State and War departments. Cordell Hull recorded that State Department officials
were then negotiating with King Ibn Saud to build a pipeline
across Saudi Arabia, and that passage of the resolutions might
disrupt these talks. Secretary of War Henry L. Stimson ad-

vised the chairman of the Senate Foreign Relations Committee that the resolutions could endanger the U.S. military interests in the Middle East, a reality reaffirmed by General George Marshall's testimony before the Senate Foreign Relations Committee.[78]

The President was alarmed over the consequences of the two resolutions, but he had to placate Zionists. In March 1944 he authorized Zionist leaders to issue a statement that when "future decisions are reached, full justice will be done to those who seek a Jewish National home...." Later in that election year, the Democratic platform carried a plank that favored "unrestricted Jewish immigration" to Palestine and the "establishment there of a free and democratic commonwealth."[79] The Palestine question placed Roosevelt on the horns of a dilemma. If the President and the State Department had encouraged the passage of the congressional resolutions and acted to implement them, they would have also brought on a disruption in the Middle East that would have hindered the war effort. Too, such action would have alienated the Arabs and might have caused King Ibn Saud to withdraw the important oil concessions held by Americans in Saudi Arabia. Representatives of the American oil companies urged officials in the State, War, and Navy departments to realize the importance of Middle Eastern oil to the war effort and the post-war well-being of the American people and to use their influence to oppose the resolutions.[80] But Roosevelt needed the Jewish vote in the 1944 election. Domestic politics demanded that the Palestine question receive sympathetic consideration, and to that end the President made a number of conciliatory statements to American Zionist leaders. But he avoided giving any hard commitment to them.[81] After the November election, Roosevelt advised Senator Wagner against passage of the resolutions.[82] Cordell Hull continued to dissuade senators and congressmen from affirming them. In the end, considerations of the national interest prevailed, and the resolutions were not reported out of committee. Roosevelt's policy vis-à-vis Palestine continued to be one of concerned non-interference. Although the State Department had persuaded the British to relax the White Paper prohibition of Jewish immigration after the March 1944 deadline, the Roosevelt administration did little else to implement the Biltmore Program.

The question arises: What was Roosevelt's intention toward the issue of Palestine? His ultimate purpose has aroused considerable debate, and there seems to be no con-

sensus on his final decision on the problem. One thing is
certain. During the course of the war, the President realized that Arab-Jewish tension over the Palestine question was
approaching the boiling point. To attempt a final solution
satisfactory to both parties during the war would court possible violence that would have disastrous consequences for the
Allied war effort. As he so often did when faced with insurmountable obstacles, Roosevelt postponed the issue. But how
would he have resolved it? Cordell Hull claims that the
President "talked both ways to Zionists and Arabs" but that
at least he did not permit the problem to embroil "the whole
of the Near East" which "continued to furnish the British and
ourselves with much needed oil and to serve as the southern
gateway for supplies to Russia...."[83] Under-Secretary of
State Sumner Welles has maintained that the President never
swerved from his intention to facilitate the creation of a Jewish national home, hoping to use economic assistance as an
inducement to win Arab support.[84] There seems to be some
truth in this interpretation, for the President did meet King
Ibn Saud briefly after the Yalta Conference and reputedly tried
to reconcile him to the creation of a Jewish homeland.[85] The
King would not consent. One of the President's close advisors, David K. Niles, remarked that had the President
lived there were serious doubts in his (Niles') mind that an
independent state of Israel would have come into being.[86]
But the whole matter is still open to speculation. Having
failed to reconcile Jews and Arabs, he might have opted for
a federal solution--one that would establish a multi-national
state under the administration of Jewish, Muslim, and Christian leaders, and placed in trusteeship status.[87]

The United States also pursued a policy independent of
Britain and in keeping with national interests in shaping a
wartime policy toward Syria and Lebanon.[88] France, holding
Syria and Lebanon as League of Nations mandates, had in
1936 promised them independence but had not carried out her
agreement. British and Free French forces occupied Syria
in June 1941 to counter the Germans, and in October the
British recognized Syrian independence. Whitehall asked the
State Department to follow suit, but received a negative reply, because U.S. recognition would jeopardize American
rights under the 1924 Franco-American convention and American relations with Vichy France.[89] U.S. relations with Syria
and Lebanon after the United States entered the war were
complicated by a number of factors. First, the State Department felt pressure to accord recognition, because the U.S.
had long enjoyed a reputation of anti-imperialism. Second,

the Department was conducting negotiations with the Vichy
regime, which still claimed de jure rights in Syria and Lebanon, to facilitate the forthcoming Allied invasion of North
Africa.   To extend recognition at that juncture would have
been premature and not in the country's best interests.   The
Syrian-Lebanese problem loomed larger in U.S. affairs in
the spring of 1942 when an Anglo-French conflict erupted,
because the British insisted that elections be held to select
popular governments to replace those installed by the French.
General Charles de Gaulle, head of the Free French, delayed
holding elections, claiming the British were merely trying to
oust the French from the Middle East and that the time was
not yet ripe for granting full independence.   Cordell Hull
took issue with de Gaulle's position and advised the French
that delay was hardly consistent with earlier promises of independence.   At length, in 1943 the French acquiesced and
agreed to hold elections in the summer.   The voters elected
nationalist regimes, but the French precipitated a crisis
when they refused to allow the newly elected representatives
to assume the powers necessary to govern.   In November
French reluctance to follow through on their agreements
prompted the U.S. to urge France to grant independence to
Syria and Lebanon.   Riots broke out and the French took repressive measures.   This action evoked an American threat
to denounce the French and caused Secretary Hull to recommend to the President that the U.S. support the British position on recognition.   In December the French gave in and
negotiated a number of agreements, effecting the transfer of
power to the duly elected national officials.   The U.S. extended recognition to Syria and Lebanon in September 1944.[90]

American opposition to imperialism contributed to
bringing about the independence of Syria and Lebanon.   That
the U.S. delayed recognition is readily understood when considerations of the national interest are brought into the picture.   The U.S. encouraged the two Arab nations to declare
war on the Axis and their leaders to assert their newly acquired independence.   In supporting Syria and Lebanon to
make a break with French colonialism, the U.S. assumed a
position that ran counter to the interests of the British, who
hoped the French would maintain a quasi-colonial position in
the Middle Eastern states not unlike the British position of
dominance in Iraq.

The United States also pursued in an anti-imperial
policy in Morocco, Algiers, and Tunisia that ran counter to
British and French interests.   The 1904 entente cordiale

required British support of the French position in Morocco. But following the North African landings of November 1942, the U.S. strongly supported the independence of Morocco in accordance with the principles of the Atlantic Charter. During the Casablanca Conference in January 1943, President Roosevelt dined with Sultan Muhammad Ibn Yusuf V of Morocco and led him to believe that the U.S. would help to bring an end to the French protectorate in the post-war era. [91]

The President remained firm in his opposition to colonialism, but not at the risk of breaking up the wartime coalition with Britain whose imperial interests in the Middle East exceeded those of any other country. For example, he agreed to support British imperial acts in Egypt and Iraq. Egypt, a British protectorate since 1882, was the pivot of the British Empire. A position of dominance in Egypt meant control of the vital Suez Canal and the vast military complex that Britain had built on the Suez. The British maintained in Cairo their headquarters for all Middle Eastern operations, both military and economic. In early 1942 an Axis victory in the Middle East seemed likely, and Egyptian nationalism erupted. King Farouk, pressured by unruly students and other dissident nationalists, considered installing an anti-British prime minister. On 4 February the British issued an ultimatum, supported by the U.S. diplomatic representative, that the King appoint Nahas Pasha, an appointee acceptable to the British. The King refused, and that evening the British ambassador, supported by British tanks, offered the King the alternative of appointing Nashas Pasha or being deported for the duration of the war. The King elected to remain in Egypt, and Egypt remained "loyal" to the British. This British action provoked a controversy in American policy-making circles. On the one hand, a number of State Department officials agreed that the U.S. should object to British high-handed treatment of the Egyptians. On the other hand, a group led by Under Secretary of State Sumner Welles believed that the U.S. should go along with the British act. No complaint was filed with the Foreign Office. [92]

The demands of war also caused the U.S. to support the British imperial position in Iraq. Britain had awarded this mandate its independence in 1932, but it remained a nominal client state. Nationalism ran strong in wartime Iraq. Anti-British nationalists followed Rashid Ali al-Gailani who hoped to use German and Italian aid to reduce the British position, a plan that resulted in the Iraqi Parliament's voting no confidence in his leadership. But Rashid organized a coup

d'état on 1 April 1941 and resumed power.   He held talks
with the British Ambassador, but reached no agreement.
Hostilities broke out when the Iraqi army attacked the British air base at Habbaniyah.   British and Jordanian troops relieved the besieged forces and routed the Iraqi in May.   The
British permitted Nuri al-Said, a pro-western leader, to assume power.   U.S. policy-makers approved of the British
action, rationalizing these imperial tactics by the imperatives
of war. [93]

But U.S. wartime support of British imperial policies
in Iraq and Egypt does not imply that the U.S. wholly departed from its adherence to anti-colonialism.   In the closing years of the war, there developed a pan-Arab movement
in the Middle East that aimed at a greater Arab unity.   In
1944 representatives of the Arab states met and drafted the
Alexandria Protocol which was not unlike the charter of the
Arab League.   Officials of Iraq, Syria, Lebanon, Transjordan, Saudi Arabia, and Egypt signed on 22 March 1945 the
Arab League pact. [94]   This momentous act had the support of
the U.S. and Britain.   Cordell Hull replied to a Saudi query
about U.S. reaction to the pact, saying the U.S. endorsed the
aspirations of the Arabs to govern themselves and favored
the concept of a viable Arab federation.   Inasmuch as the
formation of the Arab League meant opposition to the partition of Palestine and the birth of a Zionist state, Hull addressed himself to that problem, declaring the U.S. would
stand by its March 1944 decision not to participate in a solution of the Palestine question without full consultation with the
Arab leaders.   Hull added that the U.S. believed that the
Palestine problem would have to be solved before any Arab
unity could be realized. [95]

While the U.S. and Britain supported the Arab League,
they were miles apart on another issue.   The U.S. opposed
the continuation of the Middle East Supply Center (MESC), a
British-organized agency for formulating wartime economic
policies in the Middle East.   This Cairo-based adjunct of the
British Middle East Command successfully rationalized the
economies of the Middle East countries to provide the neces-
sities of life for the peoples of the region and for the Allied
military forces.   The U.S. joined MESC in 1942 and aided
Britain's effort at regional coordination. [96]   But in the closing
days of the war Americans interested in Middle Eastern markets began to pressure Washington to close down the MESC
at the conclusion of hostilities, for they viewed MESC as a
British tool for maintaining a position of economic superiority

in the Middle East. Although MESC would have been a valuable implement for aiding the Arab states in the post-war
era, U.S. economic interests called for the restoration of
the free marketplace and a return to the Open Door. Since
MESC did impose limits on imports, American policy-makers,
sensitive to U.S. post-war economic aims, agreed to withdraw from MESC in 1945 and the Center closed in November.[97]

The record of U.S. association with MESC had a
parallel in American wartime relations with the Turks. As
the United States supported Britain in MESC in the early days
of the war and then opposed her, so the U.S. supported and
followed the British diplomatic initiative in Turkey but then
in the latter years of the war opted for a course independent
of Britain. President Roosevelt and Prime Minister Churchill agreed at the Casablanca Conference in January 1943 that
the U.S. would follow Britain in matters related to Turkey.
Although General Marshall opposed Churchill, the Prime
Minister persuaded Roosevelt of the necessity of building up
Turkey militarily that she might play a role in the war.[98]
At the conclusion of the Casablanca Conference, Churchill
held the Adana conversations with President Ismet İnönü of
Turkey. Knowing that he had U.S. backing, Churchill obtained from İnönü a two-point agreement on 31 January: first,
Britain consented to build up the Turkish army; second, Brit-
ain agreed that the RAF would protect the Turks. While the
British made an agreement to send equipment to the Turks,
the latter made no commitment to enter the war. İnönü
warned Churchill that the Soviet Union had aspirations in the
Balkans. While he feared a possible German attack, he advised the Prime Minister that premature Turkish entry into
the war could result in German invasion of Anatolia, a possibility that would lead to Russian intervention and probable
Soviet territorial encroachment on Turkey. Russian post-war
aspirations in the direction of the Turkish Straits confirm the
wartime fears of İnönü. While he made no commitment to
enter the war, it does seem highly probable that he told
Churchill that Turkish entry would be predicated upon Anglo-
American support of a Turkish military operation in the Balkans, a venture that would strike a blow at the Germans and
thwart Russian territorial aspirations in the peninsula.[99]

At all events, Churchill cabled Roosevelt on 2 February 1943, advising that the two powers should give high priority to the Turks, and he suggested the possibility of Turkey's entering the war and cooperating with Anglo-American

forces in the Balkan peninsula.[100]   It is possible that Churchill's famous "underbelly" strategy, calling for an Allied
strike at the Balkans, originated with the Turks at Adana.[101]
Some Americans questioned Churchill's military policies toward Turkey, and they also queried Roosevelt's Casablanca
commitment to Churchill.   In March 1943 Cordell Hull asked
the President if the agreement extended to political and economic affairs as well as the military sphere.   Hull records
that he had the President's approval to advise the British
that the Casablanca military agreement in no way limited
American "independence of action" in Turkey "in either the
political or the economic sphere, either during the war or after."   At length, in July Admiral William Leahy, Roosevelt's
personal chief of staff, sent Hull minutes of the Casablanca
meeting which showed that the agreement did not go beyond the
military sphere.[102]

But British dominance in the realm of military affairs
--a condition that required American Lend-Lease aid to go to
Turkey via Britain--did not completely satisfy the Turks, because Inönü preferred to deal directly with the United States.
With their fear of Soviet Balkan aims, the Turks hoped the
U.S. and Britain would participate with them in a campaign
in Southeastern Europe that would block the Russians.   But
the Turks despaired of America's taking more than a passing
interest in the affairs of that region.[103]   They were not
wrong, for even after the Allies decided to invade Italy, the
Americans continued to drag their feet in the matter of logistical support of Turkey.   U.S. heavy bombers were needed to
bomb German targets in Italy far more than they were needed
by neutral Turkey.[104]   At the Quebec Conference in August
1943, Americans persuaded the British that the time was not
yet ripe for the Turks to enter the war.[105]   At the Teheran
Conference in November-December 1943, U.S. leaders continued their opposition to the British "soft underbelly" strategy.[106]   Churchill touted the plan, maintaining that an Anglo-
American military venture in the Balkans, with Turkish cooperation, would utilize armed forces available in the Mediterranean theater.   But the Prime Minister met stern opposition from Roosevelt and Stalin, neither of whom were at all
influenced by Churchill's arguments.   The Big Three did agree
that the Allied coalition should urge Turkey to enter the war
by February 1944.[107]   After the Teheran Conference, Churchill and Roosevelt met with Inönü at Cairo and informed him of
Allied hopes that Turkey would declare war in 1944.   The
Turks had strong reservations, believing that premature Turkish entry could result in a German onslaught that would lead

to Russian assistance and aggrandizement at the expense of
the Turks.   He did not try to warn the Western leaders of
Russian intentions, but argued that Turkey was not prepared
militarily to enter the war, a view that aroused Roosevelt's
sympathy. [108]

　　　　Anglo-Turkish military talks bogged down in 1944.
The delaying tactics caused the British to cool off toward the
Turks and Whitehall urged the State Department to follow
suit.   Hull advised the American Embassy in Ankara that the
U.S. would comply with British wishes and that there was
an embargo on arms shipments to Turkey. [109]   Isolated from
the Western Allies, Turkey tried unsuccessfully to reach an
understanding with the Russians.   But Ankara obtained no
clear agreement with Moscow.   Turkey had but two alternatives: she must modify her internal policy and bring her
foreign policy more closely into line with the Allies or remain isolated. [110]   To appease the U.S., Turkey made internal domestic reforms and modified her foreign policy.   At
the behest of the U.S. and British, the Turks agreed to
cease the export of chromite to Germany, to close the Sraits
to German warships, to dismiss Turgut Menemencioglu, the
pro-German Foreign Minister, and to sever diplomatic and
economic relations with Germany. [111]   In order to participate
in the conference of the United Nations at San Francisco,
Turkey agreed to declare war in February 1945, with the
provision that the Allies shore up the Turkish economy.
Turkish entry was also based on fear of the Russians whose
armies were then active in the Balkans.   Turkish fears were
not far-fetched, for in the following months the Russians
launched their diplomatic offensive on Turkey--a move that
would ultimately result in the enunciation of the Truman Doctrine in 1947. [112]

　　　　　　*　　　*　　　*　　　*　　　*

　　　　World War II brought the United States into the Middle
East to a degree theretofore unknown.   While American policy-makers viewed the region as a British sphere, the record
of U.S. diplomacy in the wartime Middle East is marked by
a definite rivalry with Britain.   The U.S. cooperated with
Britain in numerous areas but opposed her in others.   The
war also caused a reshaping of American priorities in the
Middle East.   No longer would the missionary-philanthropic
element dominate U.S. policy in the region, but oil interests
and American Zionists would assume an increasingly larger
role in the making of policy.

The American future in the post-war Middle East was being determined by many conflicting forces. The Soviet Union had clearly indicated aggressive tendencies toward the Middle East in both Turkey and Iran. American Zionists were poised to launch a campaign to realize the creation of a Jewish national home. Oil officials and members of various branches of the U.S. government were vitally interested in acquiring Middle Eastern petroleum to replenish domestic reserves depleted by the war.

The U.S. had no clear-cut, well-defined policy for the Middle East at the conclusion of hostilities beyond traditional policy guidelines. But the realignment of the power configuration in the Middle East--the decline of Britain and the rise of Soviet Union--and the redefinition of American policy objectives in the region would require the new U.S. President to develop a comprehensive Middle Eastern policy in the years after World War II.

Chapter 10

CONTAINMENT I: THE TRUMAN DOCTRINE

In early 1947 President Harry S Truman enunciated
the Truman Doctrine, a policy statement that committed the
United States to assume responsibilities in the Middle East
beyond traditional foreign policy guidelines. The United
States would accept the Western position of leadership slowly
being relinquished by Britain. Some attention must be given
the "swift movement of events" that marked this new departure in U.S.-Middle Eastern policy. A complex chain of
events developed in Iran, Greece, and Turkey that caused the
United States to respond to Soviet aggression. U.S. policy
was defensive in nature and designed to contain the outward
Russian thrust. While it is true that national security considerations demanded access to the sources of petroleum in
the region, it cannot be said, as the radical historians would
have us believe, that U.S.-Middle Eastern policy was designed solely to effect economic penetration of the region.
That is a simplistic interpretation that fails to give an adequate explanation of the development of post-war policy.

In a sense, the U.S. had leadership thrust upon it, because Britain's Middle Eastern power declined steadily. Accompanying this decline was the Soviet move into the Middle
East to realize historic goals--domination of the Balkans,
control of the Turkish Straits, and hegemony over Iran. U.S.
policy-makers concluded that the national interest demanded
a new role in the Middle East. In defending that region
policy-makers realized that American interests went far beyond the cultural sphere. First, officials in government and
industry urged that Middle Eastern oil was necessary to supplement domestic reserves. Second, policy planners realized
that should the Soviets dominate the Middle East, communication routes would be interrupted. Not only was the Suez Canal an important artery through which oil flowed from the
Persian Gulf to Europe, but American air lines hoped to de-

velop international routes through the region.   Third, American commercial interests desired to penetrate Middle Eastern
markets, an impossibility should the Soviets gain ascendancy
in the region.   In formulating a defensive policy, officials in
Washington experienced several major problems.   First, how
was it possible for the United States and Britain to make common cause to contain the Soviets without alienating the Arabs
whose rising nationalism was largely based on Anglophobia?
Second, how could the United States meet the demands imposed by the emotional burden of Israel and yet maintain regional stability in the face of a growing Arab hostility to the
State of Israel?

At the conclusion of World War II the United States
had no comprehensive policy to govern its response to the
Russian gambits toward Iran, Greece, and Turkey.   To understand the rapid transition in the U. S. -Middle Eastern posture between 1945 and 1947 an examination of the record of
American policy vis-à-vis Iran, Turkey, and Greece during
these crucial years is necessary.[1]

*   *   *   *   *

During World War II the U. S. and Britain coordinated
their efforts to ensure a continued flow of Lend-Lease to Russia via the Persian Corridor.   Although the Iranians were
certain that the United States entertained no political aspirations in their country, they were not sure of British and Russian intentions.   After the defeat of the Germans in May
1945, the Shah's government requested the Allies to evacuate
their troops pursuant to the provisions of the Tripartite Pact.
In June the State Department advised Iran of an immediate
reduction of U. S. troops.   In September the Foreign Office
declared its intention to remove British forces by December,
with the exception of those in the southern sector.   The Soviets insisted on keeping military units in Iran until March
1946 in accordance with the Tripartite Pact provision that
permitted a six-month extension beyond the cessation of hostilities.

In the summer of 1945 events in Soviet-occupied Iran
developed in a direction that drew the United States directly
into the Iranian question.   In the northern province of Azerbaijan, Iranian Communists (the Tudeh Party), with the aid
of Red Army soldiers, made a concerted effort to create an
autonomous state.   The Russians sent in additional military

units and distributed arms to the Tudeh Party membership,
and when the Shah dispatched government troops to put down
the rebellion, Russian forces barred the way and sealed off
the province from Iranian control.   To make matters worse,
the Kurdish Communists in western Azerbaijan staged an effort to establish the Mehabad Republic.   Thus the entire
northern sector of Iran was in the hands of Communists who
sought to establish autonomous states outside the control of
the Shah.

In the meantime the United States grew alarmed at
British and Russian reluctance to evacuate their forces in
keeping with the Tripartite Pact, and in November the State
Department addressed identical notes to Whitehall and the
Kremlin, urging the withdrawal of all Allied forces.   At the
Moscow Conference of Foreign Ministers in December, Secre-
tary of State James F. Byrnes lodged a second protest with
the Soviet Union, warning that if it did not comply with the
Tripartite Pact, the U.S. would support the Iranian position.
The Russians maintained they would retain forces in Iran to
protect Soviet interests.[2]

While the British were willing to reach a compromise
solution with the Russians over Azerbaijan, the United States
was not.[3] Supported by the United States, the Iranians determined to carry its problem to the United Nations Security
Council.   On 19 January 1946 Iran, with U.S. backing, won
a procedural fight to air her problem before the Security
Council.[4] In the face of a Soviet move to sidestep the issue,
the Iranian delegate asked the Council to inquire about Russian
violations of Iranian territorial integrity.   The delegate accused the Soviets of encroaching upon Iranian political sovereignty in the province of Azerbaijan.   The Council referred
the matter to direct negotiation between the parties to the dispute.   In February the Iranian Prime Minister traveled to
Moscow to reach a negotiated settlement with the Soviets, but
his efforts proved fruitless.   Inasmuch as the Soviets retained
their troops in Iran beyond the March deadline, the U.S. registered a protest with the Kremlin, and the Russians agreed
to a settlement.[5] An exchange of notes between the Soviet
ambassador and Prime Minister Ahmad Qavam defined the
terms.   The Russians agreed to withdraw all troops, but in
exchange they pressured the Iranians to consent to the formation of a Russo-Iranian oil company in which Russia held 51
per cent of the stock.   The company would hold a fifty-year
exclusive concession in the five northern provinces of Iran.
The last Russian soldier departed Iran in early May 1946,

and the Soviet diplomats urged the Iranians to ratify the
April treaty, providing for the troop evacuation and the oil
deal.   But the United States remained firm in its support of
Iran.

In January 1946 President Truman advised his Secretary of State that the United States must take a strong line
in Iran to compel the Soviets to comply with her international obligations.   He had decided on a get-tough policy.   Truman sent a stiff note to Stalin in March. [6]   That he faced the
Soviet leader with the threat of a U.S. military move to enforce Soviet withdrawal as Truman later claimed is open to
speculation. [7]   The U.S. had far too few troops to use force.
What seems apparent is that a positive diplomatic stance accomplished policy ends.   At all events, the United States
moved beyond the diplomatic tradition of non-intervention in
Iran in the spring of 1946.   Of the firm stand toward the
Russians, John Lewis Gaddis suggests that Secretary of State
Byrnes wanted to spell out to his domestic critics that the
United States would no longer appease the Soviet Union, that
henceforth they could expect a firmer response. [8] Domestic
politics became a factor in the American determination to
stand fast in the Middle East, and following the Soviet withdrawal from Azerbaijan, the Iranian gendarmerie, led by
Colonel Schwarzkopf, the American military adviser, entered
the disputed area, restored order, and reestablished Iranian
political authority.   Major General Robert W. Grow, U.S.
Army, advised the Shah's military forces as they effected a
reoccupation of Azerbaijan during the latter part of the year.
By December both of the autonomous republics in the north
had collapsed and were again under Iranian control--this with
the support of American advisers and diplomatic backing. [9]
What is even more striking is the support that U.S. Ambassador George V. Allen gave Iran in 1947.

The Soviet Union had continued that year to entreat the
Iranian government to ratify the April 1946 treaty, a course
the United States opposed.   Ambassador Allen issued a strong
public statement in September 1947, during which time the
Iranian Majlis was considering the 1946 Russo-Iranian Treaty,
advising that the U.S. government believed that Iran was free
to accept or reject the treaty.   In the event that she elected
to reject, Iran could count on U.S. support against further
Soviet coercion.   This speech was greeted by Iranians as
tantamount to an American guarantee of Iranian political sovereignty. [10] In October 1947 the Majlis rejected the treaty by
a resounding vote of 102 to 2.

During the years 1945 to 1947 U.S. policy-makers
gradually formulated a post-war policy for Iran. They considered American national interests and were motivated by
the overriding belief that defense of Iranian territorial integrity was vital to United States security. The crucial decision to defend Iran against Soviet moves was a part of the
U.S. decision to contain the Russians on a global basis.[11]
While oil came to play an important part in American foreign
policy vis-à-vis Iran during the following decade, there is
little doubt but that strategic considerations largely determined the American policy toward Iran during the crucial
days following World War II. While it is true that the British oil interests in southern Iran were enormous and that
Britain had the greatest stake in Iranian territorial integrity
and political sovereignty, the British were half-hearted in
their support of the Iranian government's stand against the
Soviets. In fact, Whitehall was willing to compromise with
the Soviets on the question of Azerbaijan. The British claim
that the U.S. followed the British lead in defending Iran
against the Soviet menace does not hold water. American
strategists had worked independently of the British to formulate a response to the Soviet thrust.[12]

U.S. diplomatic support of Iran was responsible for
the Soviet withdrawal. That the Russia retreat was due to
the efforts of the United Nations--an interpretation proffered
by revisionist historians--is not supported by the evidence.[13]
While it is true that the Security Council facilitated an agreement between the Soviets and the Iranians, the record is
clear that it was only with U.S. support that the Iranians obtained a hearing before the Security Council.[14] But it is
necessary to note that American domestic politics played a
role in determining policy-makers to adopt a hard line toward the Soviets to satisfy critics on the home front.

Equally erroneous is the radical claim that the Soviet
move into Azerbaijan was in response to aggressive thrusts
by the U.S. and British.[15] With the British firmly en-
trenched in the southern oil fields around Abadan, and faced
with an American effort to tie down a concession in the northern provinces, the revisionists claim, the Russians had little
alternative but to detach Azerbaijan and make their own oil
arrangements. This is a far-fetched assumption. The efforts of American petroleum interests to obtain a concession
in the north did not imply the extension of American political influence to that sector, nor did it carry with it a threat
to the Soviet Union.[16]

The development of a positive U.S. policy toward Iran
in the years 1945 to 1947 must be viewed within the larger
context of the American response to Soviet expansion that
gave rise to the Truman Doctrine. In a sense the Truman
Doctrine resulted, in small part at least, from the American
determination to uphold Iranian territorial integrity.[17] Support of Iran has a parallel in the American assumption of the
British obligation to back Greece and Turkey against the Sov-
iets--a move that led directly to the enunciation of the Truman Doctrine in March 1947.

The USSR's effort to enforce its will in Iran was accompanied by a similar Russian move to reduce Turkey to
the level of a client state, a move that provoked an American response to take up the British burden to defend Turkish
sovereignty. U.S. support for Turkey was welcome, for the
United States enjoyed a fund of goodwill in that country due
to the efforts of missionaries, merchants, philanthropists,
technicians, naval officers and diplomats.[18] The Soviet attempt to subjugate Turkey found the U.S. with no definite
Turkish policy beyond traditional guidelines.[19] In the closing
days of the war neither Britain nor the United States gave the
Russians any indication of a firm commitment to the Turks.[20]
While Churchill had made a definite agreement with Stalin
establishing British dominance in Greece, he had said nothing
about Turkey. Stalin's efforts to feel out the British and
Americans at Yalta about their feelings toward Turkey obtained a response of uncertainty. He was clearly trying to
obtain a revision of the Montreux Convention that governed
the Straits.

The initial indication of Russia's aggressive intent toward Turkey came in March 1945 when the USSR announced
its plan to end the 1925 Treaty of Friendship and Nonaggression with the Turks. While this Soviet move did not arouse
any real feelings in Washington or London, it sounded a harsh
note to the Turks who had long feared that Russia would manifest aggressive designs on Turkey. They were right, for in
June the Kremlin advised Ankara that to obtain a renewal of
the nonaggression pact the Turks would need to grant Russia
a base in the region of the Straits and to return Kars and
Ardahan to Russia. Alarmed at the Soviet demands, the
Turks consulted the British who protested the Russian move,
but Washington not only failed to join the British in register-
ing the protest, but attempted to conciliate the Turks. In
June 1945 President Truman was preparing to attend the Potsdam Conference with the British and Russians, and State De-

partment officials were reluctant to become involved in the
Soviet-Turkish affair, because to do so might jeopardize the
forthcoming talks.[21] The Department opposed Turkish efforts to accuse the Russians of violating the Atlantic Charter,
and Joseph Grew, acting Secretary of State, whose record of
friendship for Turkey was impeccable, advised the Turks
that he hoped they would conclude their differences with Russia in a spirit of amity, giving due consideration to the aims
of both countries.[22] In August 1945 the Turkish ambassador
in Washington accused the State Department of disinterest in
the Turkish-Soviet dispute, a charge that the Department
quickly rebutted.[23]

     Turkish efforts to achieve U.S. diplomatic support
were eventually successful, because in the autumn W. Aver-
ell Harriman, the U.S. ambassador to Russia, questioned a
Soviet troop build-up in the Balkans and in the Caucasus.
The Russians replied that there was no troop concentration
but merely an attempt to relieve troops long in the field. A
second American reassurance came in December when acting
Secretary of State Dean Acheson advised the Turks that the
U.S. took a dim view of Soviet territorial demands on Turkey, demands which Acheson described as jeopardizing world
peace.[24] The Turks regarded this affirmation as the initial
indication that the U.S. would support them.[25] By the spring
of 1946 U.S. concern for Turkey had grown considerably, for
in March Ankara received word that the U.S. would endorse
a $25 million loan from the Export-Import Bank. By April
President Truman, despairing of cooperation with the Russians in Europe and the Middle East, decided to make a public statement concerning the American reaction. On 6 April
he warned that subjugation and coercion of the Middle Eastern
states was intolerable. As evidence of the President's real
interest in Turkey, the American battleship Missouri arrived
on 5 April, bearing the remains of Turkish ambassador Erte-
gun who had died in the United States during the course of
World War II. Truman's public statement and the arrival of
the Missouri gave Ankara reasons to believe that it could expect U.S. diplomatic assistance.[26]

     The Turks could not yet count on large-scale American
aid, but they could depend on diplomatic support--as indicated
by American willingness to back Turkey when the Russians
launched in August a diplomatic move to revise the Montreux
Convention. On the 7th Moscow advised Ankara of the necessity of sharing control of the Straits with the Soviet Union, a
representation accompanied by Russian military maneuvers in

the Black Sea and Caucasus.   In response to the Soviet action Truman convened a high-level gathering at the White
House that included Secretary of the Navy James V. Forrestal, Under Secretary of War Kenneth C. Royall, and acting
Secretary of State Dean Acheson.   Acheson advised those assembled that the Russian note indicated a Soviet intention to
dominate Turkey, a condition not in the U.S. national interest.   Royall, Forrestal, and Acheson all asserted that the
President should support the Turks, and on 19 August the
State Department sent a reply to the Soviet Union.   It
stressed that Washington backed the Turks, asserting that
Turkey should remain the sole guardian of the Straits.   It
rebutted the Soviet suggestion that the Black Sea Powers
should share control over that strategic waterway.   Finally,
it advised that attacks against Turkey would promptly be
brought before the United Nations Security Council. [27]   The
U.S. protest arrived in Moscow simultaneously with protests
from London and Ankara.   The coordinated diplomatic effort
was followed in September by joint Anglo-American naval
maneuvers in the Mediterranean.

        The Turks were successful in enlisting effective Anglo-
American support, for in October the Kremlin advised the
British that revision of the Straits regime was an objective
that could be postponed.   The Soviet announcement coupled
with evacuation of Red Army troops from northern Iran, led
the Turks to feel relieved of the possibility of a Russian attack.   By the end of 1946 Soviet pressure on Turkey was reduced, but the Turks still had no assurance of American economic aid.   Although the U.S. was reluctant to advance assistance of this nature to the Turks, because it had counted
on Britain to continue to aid that country, the coming year
would see a marked change in Anglo-American power relationships in the Middle East.   By January 1947, the British economy was at near depression level because of a harsh winter
and the failure of the British industrial complex to revive.
This untoward turn of events meant that continued British support of Turkey was doubtful.   The decline in British ability
to uphold the Turks was accompanied by a similar British inability to continue aid to the Greek government, then faced
with a Soviet-backed guerrilla offensive.   Thus, the United
States faced a similar challenge in Greece.

        Greece, like Turkey, had been in the British sphere
for many years.   Churchill had negotiated the percentages
agreement with Joseph Stalin in 1944 whereby Britain would
maintain control over Greece as the Red Army entered the

Balkans to establish Soviet rule over much of that region.
British troops entered Greece in October in company with the
Greek government-in-exile and set about restoring order.
But the Communist-backed National Liberation Front (EAM),
refused to go along with the British effort, and many of its
elements retired to the countryside or beyond Greek borders,
there to maintain hostile pressure on the Greek government.
Supported by Yugoslavian arms, these rebels paid no attention to the role of the United States as a Middle Eastern
power in the autumn of 1945.   The revolt tied down 60,000
British troops, and Secretary of State Edward R. Stettinius
maintained a neutral attitude toward the rebellion, viewing it
as a British problem.   Just prior to his resignation, the Department replied on 16 June to a British query about American participation in supervising Greek elections pursuant to
the Yalta Agreement.   The Department advised Whitehall that
it regarded Greece as in the British sphere and that it traditionally maintained a posture of non-involvement in Greek
internal affairs.   Nevertheless, the U.S. would comply with
the Yalta agreement and help supervise the Greek elections,
which occurred in September 1946.[28]

During the autumn of 1945 the Greeks faced enormous
difficulties as the Communist-backed guerrillas stepped up
their activities.   Too, the government had pressing economic
problems and required immediate economic aid.   The British
promised a non-interest-bearing credit of £10 million, and
the U.S. endorsed an Export-Import Bank loan of $25 million.
But the U.S. government was chary of doing more, because
officials believed that additional aid would be of little effect
unless the Greeks made sweeping economic reforms.[29]   But
the U.S. gradually began to reassess its view of Greek problems.   Presidential adviser Mark F. Ethridge toured the
Balkans in the autumn of 1945 and submitted a gloomy report
to the President.   Russia, he said, intended to dominate
Eastern and Central Europe, and Britain was "through" as a
world power and could no longer be expected to help hold the
line against the Soviet Union, which was just as intent on controlling Greece and Turkey.[30]   This report gave the President food for thought in developing a tougher line toward the
Russians.   Secretary of the Navy Forrestal advised Truman
that American national security interests demanded a harder
line toward the Soviet Union, and he urged the presence of
the U.S. Navy in Eastern Mediterranean waters.[31]

In December 1945 the Providence, a 10,000-ton
cruiser, visited the Greek port of Piraeus.   The Greeks wel-

comed the arrival of the warship, seeing it as evidence of
growing American interest in Greek affairs.   But they were
ecstatic when the Missouri arrived in April 1946, following
its visit to Istanbul.   Of the Missouri's Mediterranean cruise,
Walter Lippmann wrote that the ship's presence in the Middle
East was designed to show that the United States maintained
a real interest in the affairs of the nations in that region. [32]
While the Greek government could express joy at the American naval presence, it could only react pessimistically to the
declining ability of Britain to provide economic and military
support.   In August the Greeks learned of the British intention to reduce their forces in Greece after the first of the
year, because the Treasury could no longer bear the financial
burden.   At the same time Whitehall was advising the Greeks
that Britain would have no objection to their seeking economic
aid from the United States.

As the British prepared to retrench their obligations
in Greece and Turkey, the United States commenced in August
to assume a greater role in the Eastern Mediterranean.   In
mid-August 1946 the State Department sent a note to the Soviet Union about the Russian intention to revise the Straits
agreement. [33]   To demonstrate a parallel interest in the
Greeks, the U.S. Navy dispatched the Franklin D. Roosevelt,
a large aircraft carrier, the light cruiser Little Rock, and
five destroyers to visit Piraeus in early September.   Admiral William "Bull" Halsey, the commander of this task force,
gave an interview to the press.   Reporters said the Russians
were critical of the U.S. naval presence in the Mediterranean, and they asked for Halsey's opinion.   He replied that the
U.S. had long adhered to the policy of the freedom of the
seas and "We demand the right to go anywhere at any time.
It is nobody's damned business where we go.   We can go anywhere we please."[34]

The Greeks welcomed the American show of naval
force in early September just following the 1 September plebis-
cite, which returned King George II to the throne and ensured
a pro-western government.   Although the election, overseen
by American and British observers, was a victory for democracy, the Greek government had little to gloat about during the
autumn of 1946.   Greek Communists stepped up their attacks
against the government in mid-September.   At this time the
British announced cutbacks on economic aid, advising the
Greeks that the United States would assume responsibilities in
this area.   Meanwhile in the United Nations the Russians
launched a verbal attack on the British presence in Greece.

The British then announced the reduction of military forces in Greece. [35] But the situation was not all black, for in November the Greeks learned that the United States intended to stand behind Greece. Aid would be extended following the investigation by an American economic mission. [36]

The U. S. economic mission to Greece, under Paul Porter, initiated its investigation in late January 1947. It urged that the United States extend economic aid to Greece to avert a fiscal crisis. At about the same time the Porter Mission was collecting data, American Ambassador Lincoln MacVeagh advised Secretary of State George C. Marshall that it was necessary to extend immediate economic assistance to the Greeks to avoid a crisis. Porter's findings substantiated this need in his March report. [37] The warnings of Mac-Veagh and Etheridge, soon to be supplemented by Porter, carried evil portents for the Greeks and indicated that the United States would need to render immediate economic aid to avert disaster. The United States would soon act on these recommendations. [38]

On 24 February 1947 Sir Archibald Clark Kerr, British ambassador in Washington, advised Secretary Marshall that, because of its pressing economic situation, the British government would no longer maintain its financial and military support of Greece and Turkey. [39] This meant that the British position in the Middle East was being relinquished and the United States would assume the lead in that region with the enunciation of the Truman Doctrine in March 1947.

The immediate cause of Truman's epochal speech in March was the impending economic crisis in Greece, but in reality his willingness to extend American aid to nations threatened by the Communist specter was based on the threats to Iran and Turkey. While pressures on these two countries had eased somewhat, they were both part of the picture that included the Truman Doctrine, a policy statement that had its origins in the State Department. With Dean Acheson leading the way, the Department began drafting a policy-planning paper on 21 February in response to the British notes of 24 February. The paper urged immediate transfer of military supplies to Greece and Turkey and suggested that Congress be approached for legislation to supply long-term economic aid. Secretary Marshall, along with Acheson, presented the Department's views to the President on 27 February 1947 at a high-level White House meeting. [40] Acheson proffered an able argument that called attention to the Soviet threat to Greece,

Turkey, and Iran, emphasizing that it was the Soviet intention to dominate the Middle East. Britain could no longer
assume the burden of defending that region. He said that
U.S. aid to Greece and Turkey would not simply be "pulling
British chestnuts out of the fire," but it would be acting to
protect the national security of the United States. If the Russians succeeded in dominating the Middle East and Europe
there could be no security for the United States. Acheson's
advocacy was successful, and the gathering of government officials agreed with the President that immediate aid to Greece
and Turkey was mandatory because of the imperatives of national security. Senator Arthur H. Vandenberg, the isolation-
ist-turned-internationalist, advised the President that his message to the Congress should be couched in frank terms that
would shock congressional leaders into the realization of the
enormity of the situation. [41]

     Events moved swiftly. On 1 March Acheson told the
British ambassador that the United States would undertake to
guarantee the territorial integrity of Greece and Turkey and
would take immediate steps to seek congressional approval.[42]
After consulting congressional leaders, the President in a 12
March message to Congress declared a new departure in
American foreign policy--one that carried global implications.
He said the United States must support "free peoples" every-
where who resist external forces of aggression. Citing the
needs of American national security, he asked Congress to
appropriate $400 million for immediate assistance to Greece
and Turkey, and for permission to send the necessary civil
and military authorities to supervise the use of this American aid. [43] In this speech the President was abandoning the
tradition of non-involvement, a move that caused considerable
controversy in the nation and in the Congress. There reaction was mixed, and many congressmen expressed misgivings
about the sweep of the new policy. Senate hearings in the
Foreign Relations Committee opened on 24 March and continued through the end of the month. Acheson testified on the
first day that the President intended a policy that was global
in scope and not confined to Greece and Turkey. He declared that U.S. national security interests were at stake in
this effort to contain the spread of Communism. [44] After the
hearings in the Foreign Relations Committee and a two-week
debate in the Senate, the bill that implemented the Truman
Doctrine passed the upper house 67 to 23, and House approval followed two days later. The President signed the bill into law on 22 May, and the Truman Doctrine marked the beginning of American assumption of global responsibility to

contain the force of Communism.   But it had specific applications for the Middle East.

  The United States was now committed to defend not
only Greece and Turkey but also the other nations of the
Middle East.   Acheson made it clear in his testimony to the
Foreign Relations Committee that should the Soviets dominate
Greece and Turkey, the other states of the region would
surely fall.   The United States would lose access to the strategic communication-transportation routes and to the petroleum so vital to the recovery of Europe. [45] While the justifi-
cation of this new policy was based on national security interests, it did not mean that the United States would assume
at one blow full responsibility for the Middle East, for Britain was still a power, albeit a diminished one, in that region.   But it did inaugurate a step-by-step movement that
would see the United States take greater responsibility for the
defense of the Middle East.   The Truman Doctrine initiated
the American policy to defend the region, a policy that would
continue through 1959.

  The declaration of the Truman Doctrine provoked considerable controversy in the scholarly community.   Many historians, commonly referred to as nationalists or traditional-
ists, view the American commitment to contain Communism
as a defensive response to the Russians' aggressive determination to dominate the Eurasian land mass, the realization
of which would endanger U. S. national security.   They ap-
plaud the rapidity with which the U. S. responded to the Soviet
menace, discounting the charge that the policy was aimed
solely at effecting economic penetration of the region to acquire new markets and sources of oil. [46]   They dismiss the
claim that American defense of the Middle East was a British-
instituted policy. [47]   They have suggested that the crisis in
the Middle East was easing by the time Truman made his
speech, and that the reason for the declaration to Congress
and the American people was to shock the nation into the
realization that Communism did pose a worldwide threat.
This tactic was deemed necessary to arouse a people noted
for its past isolationism. [48]   Realists view the Truman Doctrine with dismay, claiming that the crisis in Greece and Turkey was limited and did not require a policy-making statement
that carried worldwide implications and obligations.   George
F. Kennan, a State Department official largely responsible for
the policy of containment, questioned the grandiose nature of
the policy.   He asked the question: Was it in American national interests to provide aid and comfort to all nations

around the globe that might feel threatened by Communism?
He frankly admitted that the nation might not find it within
its economic means to implement a policy of such scope. [49]
Historians on the left have spilled much ink in their discussion of the motives behind the Truman Doctrine.   They are
in general agreement that the policy was not based on national security interests, that is, a need to contain Communism.
Rather, they view the policy as one tied mainly to economic
motives--the need to acquire new markets and gain access
to the rich oil fields of the Middle East.   Thus it sought to
supplant British colonial imperialism with American economic
imperialism. [50]   While there is a measure of validity to this
interpretation, it offers only half of the picture, failing to
answer one question: Was the Soviet Union motivated by an
aggressive design to dominate a geographical-political area
by imposing an ideology alien to the American democratic-
capitalistic system?   But there is little doubt that American
oil interests favored the implementation of an aggressive oil
policy in the post-war era.

*   *   *   *   *

        American national interests in the post-war era de-
manded the rapid development of Middle Eastern petroleum resources.   The flow of Middle Eastern oil was necessary to
the early recovery of Europe, a first line of defense against
the Soviet effort to dominate the Eurasian land mass.   Too,
both high-level policy-makers in government and industrialists
believed that Middle Eastern oil was required to replenish
American domestic reserves depleted during the war.   A major
consideration of American Middle Eastern policy in the world
after World War II was the implementation of policies guaranteed to ensure American oil companies equal access to Middle
Eastern oil fields.

Chapter 11

THE POST-WAR QUEST FOR OIL

That the United States would pursue an aggressive Middle Eastern oil policy in the post-war era was determined during World War II. As early as 1943 officials in government and industry realized the need to acquire additional sources of oil in overseas areas to replenish diminishing domestic reserves.[1] While there was a basic agreement that the Middle East held a rich potential in petroleum reserves, leaders in government and the oil industry could not agree on a strategy to develop the oil.[2] Some top-level government officials believed that the national security warranted government entry into the business of oil production, while oil officials firmly believed that it was the responsibility of private enterprise, backed by government, to develop and refine the petroleum. It was not until the closing years of the war that the conflict was reconciled. Basically, the U.S. strategy was based on government utilization of the Open Door policy to ensure American oil interests equal access to Middle East oil. As events turned out in the post-war years, Middle Eastern oil was not immediately necessary to the American domestic economy, but it was expedient for the U.S. to guarantee a steady flow of oil from the region to Europe where recovery was in the American national interest. The bulk of the oil produced for American accounts in the Middle East went to Europe and Japan.

American oil companies wanted government support for their activities in developing Middle Eastern sources of petroleum, and were also anxious that it pursue policies that would ensure regional stability. But the U.S. government was on the horns of a dilemma. On the one hand, American petroleum interests were actively pursuing the development of new sources of oil in the Middle East and were in need of government support which was forthcoming. On the other hand, the Zionist movement grew rapidly in the United States

and its advocates urged upon the government a policy supportive of the creation of a Jewish national state. In complying
with Zionist wishes the U.S. government incurred the wrath
of the Arabs and helped to create Arab-Israeli hostility, a
development that made for instability in the Middle East.

     Prior to World War II Britain dominated the develop-
ment of new sources of oil in the Middle East. In 1936
American oil interests received only 12 per cent of the oil
produced in that region. But since World War II the U.S.
has become the dominant factor in the development of the
region's oil. In 1946, American accounts received 30 per
cent of Middle Eastern oil production; by 1956 that figure had
reached 60 per cent.[3] Ten years later American investment
in Middle Eastern oil had risen to $4.35 billion. Inasmuch
as the Middle East held between 60 and 70 per cent of the
world's proven oil reserves, and given the rising American
domestic demand for imported oil, it was not difficult to project, in the late 1960s, that American need for Middle Eastern oil would increase.[4]

     In spite of the growing national dependence on Middle
Eastern oil, the American oil companies operating in that region are private concerns and not the property of the government. Even so, the Arabs see the companies as creatures
of the U.S. government--a government that has given support
to the State of Israel.[5] This has created problems for the
oil companies. Loss of their assets would directly hurt
American investors, but this loss becomes all the more real
when it is realized that the United States consumes approximately one-third of the world's production of oil, and will by
the end of the 1970s become increasingly dependent upon imports of Middle Eastern oil.[6]

*   *   *   *   *

     The first country in which Americans sought new
sources of oil in the post-war Middle East was Saudi Arabia.
In 1945 President Roosevelt conferred with King Ibn Saud, the
recipient of wartime Lend-Lease aid, in a meeting that has
been characterized as an effort to consolidate U.S.-Saudi
Arabian diplomatic relations for the benefit of American oil
interests.[7] ARAMCO increased its operations in Saudi Arabia in the closing years of World War II. Ultimately, the
U.S. government and ARAMCO officials agreed that the company would assume full responsibility for the development of

the oil fields and the task would receive full government support.   ARAMCO planned a large refinery at Ras Tanura, an
undersea pipeline from Dhahran to the refinery on the island
of Bahrain, and the construction of a pipeline from the Arabian oil fields to the Mediterranean Sea.   To achieve these objectives, ARAMCO required new sources of capital, the necessary allocations of steel, and diplomatic assistance from
the State Department for a pipeline that would cross several
Middle Eastern countries.   In 1944 the company began negotiations with Standard Oil of New Jersey and Socony-Vacuum
Oil Company to supply the necessary capital, in return for
which Jersey and SOCONY would receive new sources of oil
for their European markets.   Before the merger could be accomplished, one problem had to be solved.   Both Jersey
Standard and SOCONY were members of the Iraq Petroleum
Company, which bound member companies by the Red Line
Agreement prohibiting them from individual exploration for
oil in the region beyond the Red Line.   Saudi Arabia was in
the off-limits area.   Calouste Gulbenkian and the Compagnie
Française des Pétroles, both partners to the IPC pact,
brought suit against the proposed merger, and it required
several years of negotiations to arrange for Jersey Standard
and SOCONY to erase the Red Line and join with ARAMCO.
The State Department gave its support to the companies and
assured them it opposed agreements that restricted the rights
of entrepreneurs, thereby violating the Open Door.   While
Jersey and SOCONY officials were able to arrive at satisfactory arrangements with Anglo-Iranian and Royal Dutch Shell,
signatories to the Red Line Agreement, negotiations with the
French and Gulbenkian were protracted.

In the meantime construction had been started on the
pipeline, for the U. S. government had guaranteed the 20,000
tons of steel necessary to complete the job, and the State Department had assisted with the necessary diplomatic dealings
to build the projected 1040-mile line.   The Trans-Arabian
Pipeline Company (TAPLINE) had been organized by ARAMCO
in 1945 to build the pipeline with its terminus in Palestine.
The State Department opposed this plan because of the uncertainty surrounding the Palestine question.   The company then
decided to run the pipeline from Dhahran to Sidon on the Mediterranean coast of Lebanon.   While the company came to
early agreement with Transjordan and Lebanon for the rights
of way, talks with Syria bogged down.   At length the company
made a satisfactory agreement with the assistance of the State
Department, but the initial Arab-Israeli war interrupted construction and delayed Syrian approval of the agreement.

While the war was in progress, the company gave some
thought to terminating the pipeline in Palestine, only to meet
State Department opposition. When hostilities ceased, the
Syrian government, faced with the possibility of losing the
pipeline terminus to Palestine, gave in, and in May 1949 it
signed the pact with TAPLINE.

While negotiations were underway to build the pipeline,
Jersey Standard and SOCONY made their arrangements with
the French and Gulbenkian. Although the latter had driven a
hard bargain, the four parties had finally come to terms in
a Lisbon hotel in November 1948, freeing Jersey Standard
and SOCONY of the Red Line restrictions to merge with
ARAMCO. So certain of victory were Jersey and SOCONY
officials that they had given financial aid to ARAMCO to help
with the completion of TAPLINE. In December 1950 the
1040-mile pipeline was completed. Construction had cost
close to half a billion dollars, but the pipeline facilitated the
flow of oil to America's NATO allies in Europe. [8] The completion of TAPLINE enabled ARAMCO to increase production
from 580,000 barrels in 1938 to 277,963,000 barrels per
year in 1951. By the 1950s production reached one million
barrels per day, and Saudi Arabia became the world's fourth-
ranking oil producer, behind the United States, the Soviet
Union, and Venezuela.

With the rapid increase in production, Saudi officials
requested higher royalties. That American oil companies
agreed to a 50-50 profit-sharing agreement with Venezuela
was a large factor in King Ibn Saud's asking ARAMCO to negotiate a new concession in 1950. In December of that year
ARAMCO made a new pact with the King whereby the government would receive royalties on a 50-50 basis.

Thus the presence of the oil industry in Saudi Arabia
has conferred mixed blessings on the people. [9] On the one
hand, ARAMCO has paid out an increasing amount of royalties, and these funds have enabled the government to undertake programs for the improvement of Saudi Arabia. For
example, King Ibn Saud instituted a four-year program in
1947 that envisioned the outlay of some $270 million to con-
struct railroads, roads, port facilities, schools, hospitals,
and irrigation systems. Company employees have assisted in
a number of these projects. ARAMCO has also enriched the
country by giving employment to growing numbers of Arabs.
By 1953 the company had 22,345 on the payrolls. Not only
did these jobs improve the standard of living for a larger

number of people, but the company also maintained various
training programs. But on the other hand, by raising the
expectations of the peoples, the oil industry has created a
problem for itself. As the standard of living has risen, so
the expectations of the populace have increased. Given the
rise of personal aspirations, there is little wonder that the
Saudi leadership has demanded a larger share of the profits
and a role in the management of the company's affairs.

While Arab nationalists have often claimed that the
American oil companies were in league with the U.S. government, these claims could not be further from the truth. The
companies engaged in the oil business in Saudi Arabia are
private enterprises, and their relations with the government
are subject to change.[10] Oil is not the sole factor contribut-
ing to the making of an American Middle Eastern policy.
This reality is demonstrated by U.S. support for Israel during the various Arab-Israeli crises that are a constant source
of instability in the Middle East, and hence a threat to the
oil companies. Although the latter can frequently count on
government support, this is not always the case, as is demonstrated by two examples. In the 1950 dispute between
ARAMCO officials and Saudi leaders, an impasse developed
in the talks leading to the 50-50 profit-sharing plan. At
length the company requested and received the assistance of
a Treasury Department official who aided the parties to the
dispute to find a solution. George A. Eddy conferred with
Saudi officials and demonstrated that they could receive greater revenues from the company by inaugurating an income tax
system, requiring the company to pay an annual tax. This
solution satisfied the Saudis and the company executives.
While ARAMCO received government assistance in the 1950
concession talks, the company could not bank on government
support during the crisis involving the Buraimi oasis. ARAM-
CO officials provided the Saudi government with maps that
showed the Buraimi region as being part of Saudi Arabia.
Claimed as well by Abu Dhabi and Oman, it was rich in oil,
and the Sheikh of Abu Dhabi had granted concessions to the
IPC, one of ARAMCO's rivals. Company leaders sought
State Department support, while IPC officials obtained the
backing of Whitehall. The State Department adopted a neutral
role in the dispute and urged that the matter be submitted to
arbitration. ARAMCO did not receive the expected assistance
from Washington, and the arbitration proceeding proved a fiasco with the result that Saudi Arabia could not make good its
claim to the oasis and ARAMCO was the loser, for IPC got
the concession.[11]

The importance of the American investment in Saudi
Arabia is paralleled by the American oil development in Kuwait.   Since the early 1930s the Gulf Oil Company, in conjunction with what is today British Petroleum, Ltd., had
operated as the Kuwait Oil Company that produces 90 per
cent of Kuwaiti oil.   Inasmuch as Kuwait has proven reserves
only slightly less than those of Saudi Arabia (88 billion barrels for Saudi Arabia and 74.5 billion barrels for Kuwait),
and in view of Kuwait's current oil production falling only
slightly below that of Saudi Arabia (in 1972, Saudi Arabia
produced 5.6 million barrels per day and Kuwait, 3.7 million), it can be readily appreciated that the American investment in Kuwait is important and extensive. [12]   In the Neutral
Zone lying between Saudi Arabia and Kuwait two American
oil companies secured concessions.   In July 1948 Sheikh
Ahmad of Kuwait awarded to the American Independent Oil
Company (AMINOIL) a 60-year concession that called for a
50 per cent share in the zone's potential oil.   The company
paid $7.5 million for the concession.   But since AMINOIL
held only the Kuwaiti half of the zone, it remained for Saudi
Arabia to award a concession in its part of the zone before
work could begin.   In February 1949 King Ibn Saud awarded
a concession to J. Paul Getty's Pacific Western Oil Corporation.   Getty's 60-year concession cost an initial payment of
$9.5 million.   By 1971 AMINOIL and Getty, under a work-
ing agreement, were each receiving 94,000 barrels per
day. [13]

American oil companies also enjoyed success in other
Arab lands.   In Iraq, a country with proven reserves of 32
billion barrels and a daily production of some 1.9 million
barrels, two American companies, Jersey Standard and Mobil Oil (formerly Socony Vacuum) each enjoyed 23.75 per
cent participation in IPC, which produced 55 per cent of
Iraq's oil.   This company was nationalized in 1972 when the
state-operated Iraq Company for Oil Operations assumed ownership.   American interests are also to be found in Abu
Dhabi, Oman, Dubai, and Bahrain. [14]   But perhaps the most
important country into which American oil interests gained
access in the post-World War II era is Iran.

Of the Middle Eastern oil-producing countries, Iran
ranks second behind Saudi Arabia, with proven reserves of
80 billion barrels and a daily production of about 4.7 million
barrels.   American interests had been trying to gain access
to Iranian oil fields since the 1920s.   Participation in the
rich plum that is Iranian oil required the assistance of the

U.S. government and resulted from the abrupt 1951 nationalization of the British-owned Anglo-Iranian Oil Company. The
Iranian decision to nationalize Anglo-Iranian was based on a
number of factors. First, the 1943 Venezuelan petroleum
law gave Venezuela a larger share of oil revenues, a fact
that influenced Iranians who beseeched AIOC in 1948 to re-
negotiate the 1933 agreement. Second, the Iranian government had drawn up a seven-year Plan of Development, and
it requested the U.S. government to grant a loan of $250
million necessary to implement this plan. The U.S. rejected
the request, because the Iranian government did not demonstrate the will to carry out those reforms required by Washington. The failure to obtain the U.S. loan is directly tied
to nationalization, [15] for Iranians believed that state ownership would provide the capital necessary to fund a program
of development. Third, during the time that Iran was talk-
ing with officials of AIOC, members of the Saudi government
were obtaining from ARAMCO the 50-50 profit-sharing plan,
a major advance in the financial relations between company
and country in the Middle East. This new plan offered the
Iranians an incentive to obtain a similar concession from the
British. Fourth, IPC officials and the Iraqi government
were also engaged in talks aimed at giving Iraq a higher percentage of profits. Finally, the decision to nationalize must
also be seen in terms of the growth of nationalism in post-
war Iran, where opposition ran deep against foreign control.
Although AIOC officials and Iranian leaders had negotiated an
agreement in 1949, the Majlis rejected it in 1951, and on
15 March it passed a law to implement state ownership,
which became effective on 1 May 1951. By degrees, the
government of Premier Mohammed Mossadegh relieved AIOC
of its assets in Iran, valued in excess of one-half billion
dollars.

Following nationalization, the British in September ordered a boycott of Iranian oil. In what amounted to an embargo, AIOC officials asked its competitors not to take oil
from the Abadan Refinery, the world's largest. With the departure of British technical personnel and the imposition of
the oil embargo, the flow of Iranian oil dried up and with it
the revenue needed to nourish the Iranian economy. In October Britain and Iran severed relations. This dispute directly affected the United States, for during the Korean War
American forces required Middle Eastern oil, and the loss of
Iranian oil also endangered European recovery through the
Marshall Plan. Economic dislocation resulted in Iran, which
became a target for the Communist Tudeh Party.

Historians have debated the role of the United States
in this affair involving the loan request and nationalization.
Scholars on the left and British critics of U.S. foreign policy
claim the U.S. encouraged Mossadegh to take over AIOC in
order that American oil interests might enter the field.[16]
Non-revisionist historians are not in agreement about the
U.S. role.   M. K. Sheehan has asserted that United States
reluctance to grant the loan led to the oil crisis in 1951,
but he adds that this negative reaction was based on Iranian
unwillingness to reform government institutions and was not
due to any wish to oust Britain.[17] Stephen M. Longrigg declared that American public feeling was hostile to nationalization because it violated contractual relationships.[18] Benjamin Shwadran suggests that the Americans played the role of
a "disinterested third party vitally concerned with finding a
speedy solution, satisfactory to both parties to the dispute,"
but George Stocking's interpretation seems closest to the
truth.   The United States, he claims, acted as mediator in
the Anglo-Iranian dispute, "not unmindful of American interests."[19] It seems reasonable to suggest that at the outset
the U.S. had no prearranged plan of action, and that it acted
as an "honest broker" seeking to bring about an equitable
solution with due attention to American interests.

The American posture was that of an interested neutral.[20] However, both Iran and Britain sought to enlist
American support.   Mossadegh, representing the Iranian nationalists, wanted to fulfill the goal held by Iranian diplomats
for years: to gain U.S. assistance to counter British influence.   Whitehall wanted American aid, claiming that the
American stake in Saudi Arabia might be adversely affected
if Mossadegh were successful.   The State Department asked
both parties to make concessions, urging the British to accept the principle of nationalization and the Iranians to make
a just compensatory arrangement with the British.   But Mossadegh held out for U.S. support, believing that American access to Iranian oil would be an incentive to render large-scale
economic aid to Iran.   He also knew that Americans were
aware than an economic depression in Iran might turn the
country toward the Soviet Union.   American foreign policy
planners were in a dilemma, for to encourage Mossadegh
would also increase the possibility of wide-scale nationalization, which could be disastrous to American oil holdings elsewhere in the Middle East.   To reject Iranian overtures would
leave Mossadegh little alternative but to turn to the Russians.
But to step into the crisis could compromise the American
position with Britain and with oil-producing countries in which

the U.S. had interests, and this reality lead Washington to
maintain an impartial position, one that newly elected President Dwight D. Eisenhower made clear to Mossadegh.[21] But
Mossadegh's intransigence on the compensation issue began
to alienate Americans in 1953, and his hope of unilateral U.S.
support faded.   American oil companies did not need Iranian
oil, for there was a glut on the world market and they enjoyed high profits with Abadan shut down.   President Eisenhower advised Premier Mossadegh on 29 June 1953 that the
U.S. would not extend aid to Iran "so long as Iran could have
access to funds derived from the sale of its oil and oil products if a reasonable agreement were reached with regard to
compensation whereby the large-scale marketing of Iranian
oil would be resumed." He also advised that the U.S. would
not purchase Iranian oil in the "absence of an oil settlement...."[22]

Without assurance of revenue from American oil purchases and the possibility of an American loan, Mossadegh
turned to the Tudeh Party for support, thereby setting in motion a chain of events that led to his fall from power.   The
Shah dismissed Mossadegh and appointed General Fazlollah
Zahedi as the new prime minister.   Mossadegh did not leave
office.   He instituted what appeared to be a revolution.   The
Tudeh Party's cadres poured onto the streets of Teheran on
18 August.   On the following day the Shah's forces arrived
in the capital, and in the ensuing clash Mossadegh was forced
from power.   Zahedi assumed office and the Shah remained
on the throne.

Historians have debated the role of the United States
in the events leading to the fall of Mossadegh.   A growing
consensus seems to be emerging in the historical community
that the Central Intelligence Agency played a dominant role
in ousting Mossadegh.   Historians on the left claim that the
CIA plotted the coup in order that American oil companies
might achieve access to Iran's oil resources.[23]   The more
balanced view is that American policy at the time of the coup
was designed to prevent a Communist take-over, an event
that seemed possible when Mossadegh sought Tudeh Party support.   Thus the American goal in the transfer of power was
based on the need to contain Communist expansion and to prevent Iranian oil from falling to the Soviet bloc.[24]   R. W. Cottam a former foreign service officer in the U.S. Embassy
in Teheran, has discounted the charge that the U.S. was in
any way responsible for the ouster of Mossadegh.[25]   But it
now seems clear that the CIA was active, and President

Eisenhower had maintained that throughout the crisis the U.S.
government "had done everything it possibly could to back up
the Shah."[26]   This statement would tend to indicate that the
U.S. role was not passive.

But the fact remains that American petroleum companies, both major and independent, did gain access to Iranian oil following the ouster of Mossadegh.   This resulted
from official action on the part of the U.S. government and
not from lobbying on the part of the oil interests.[27]   Herbert
Hoover, Jr., President Eisenhower's adviser on petroleum
affairs and later Under Secretary of State, visited Teheran
following the ouster of Mossadegh.   He learned that the
Iranians would not accept the British resumption of ownership
of AIOC.   He conceived of the formation of an international
consortium consisting of American, British, French, and
Dutch oil interests to take over the operation of AIOC.   The
Iranians would not feel that any one country dominated Iran's
oil resources.   Hoover had to compel American oil concerns
to participate in the consortium, for, with the oil glut on the
market, they had no wish to see petroleum products pouring
out of the Abadan refinery to compete with them.[28]   He also
had to obtain assurances from the Justice Department that
their participation would not violate American anti-trust laws.
The consortium was acceptable to the Iranians   provided that
all parties recognized that the oil and the Abadan facilities
were the property of the Iranian people.   At length Hoover
won British acceptance of the idea, and in September 1954
the eight oil companies signed the consortium pact with Iran.
It provided that the member companies would extract, refine,
and market the oil for the National Iranian Oil Company,
which would receive a 50-50 share in the profits.   The remainder would go to the members of the consortium, with
Anglo-Iranian receiving 40 per cent, Royal-Dutch Shell, 14;
the Compagnie Française des Pétroles, 6; and five American
companies, 8 per cent each.   The latter included Jersey Standard, Mobil, Standard of California, the Texas Company, and
the   Gulf Oil Company.   The agreement between the nation
and the consortium was approved by the Majlis in August and
formally ratified in October 1954.

The U.S. government played a leading role in this arrangement.   By sustaining the Shah's government during the
trouble with Mossadegh, by extending a $45 million loan in
September 1953, and by bringing together the consortium,
American policy-makers intervened in the affairs of Iran to
prevent that country from falling into the Soviet sphere.   De-

fense of Iran, clearly in the American national interest, and
not acquisition of new sources of oil, was the motive.[29] But
inasmuch as the consortium, known as the Iranian Oil Exploration and Producing Company, produces 80 per cent of
Iran's oil (which amounted to 4.7 million barrels per day in
1972), the American interest in Iran is not inconsiderable.
American oil companies enjoy a 40 per cent interest in a
syndicate that produces the great majority of the oil in the
second largest producer of oil in the Middle East.

American success in acquiring access to new oil
sources in Iran was matched by equal success in Libya, the
newest of the oil producing giants.   In 1968 Libyan oil production reached the astounding figure of some 2.5 million
barrels per day.   Since American oil concerns control 90
per cent of this production, the American investment in
Libya is considerable.   The accomplishment in Libya is all
the more remarkable, given the reality that oil was only discovered in Cyrenaica in the mid-1950s.   At that time it was
determined that Libyan oil was of a high quality because of
its low sulphur content.   (American East Coast cities use
Libyan oil to cut down pollution.)   Following the writing of
the Libyan Petroleum Law of 1955, the oil rush commenced.
Within a few months a number of American companies, Esso
International (a subsidiary of Jersey Standard), Standard Oil
of California, Mobil, and Texaco, had acquired concessions
in Libya.   In 1965 the Libyan government opened up new
areas in Tripolitania, and the Occidental Petroleum Corporation, headed by the astute American entrepreneur Dr. Armand
Hammer, acquired a choice sector.   Occidental went into production in 1968 and soon reached 478,400 barrels per day.

*   *   *   *   *

The Middle East holds roughly three-fifths of the
world's proven oil reserves.   The United States is the largest
single oil-consuming nation.   While much of the oil produced
for American companies in the past has been shipped to Europe or the Far East, it is becoming more and more evident
that the U.S. will in the future require greater imports of
petroleum from the Middle East to meet the growing demand
of domestic consumers.   Unfortunately, the growing American
dependence on Middle Eastern oil has been accompanied by the
growth of nationalism among the peoples of that region, a
phenomenon largely due to the increase of Zionism, a secular
nationalism that produced Israel.   The American role in the

Chapter 12

AMERICAN SUPPORT FOR THE CREATION OF ISRAEL
ANOTHER "GREAT ABERRATION"

Given the tradition of political non-involvement in the
Middle East and the imperatives of the national interest,
American support for the creation of Israel in the years following World War II was a great aberration in the Middle
Eastern policy of the United States--one comparable to the
acquisition of the Philippines, which historian Samuel Flagg
Bemis described as a "great national aberration." The Palestinian Jews who formed the nucleus around which Israel was
founded were like the other minorities of the Ottoman Em-
pire--Greeks, Cretans, Bulgarians, Arabs, and Armenians--
in that all had elicited U.S. support for their quest for independence from the Ottoman Empire. The U.S. policy toward
Ottoman minorities had been well defined by John Quincy
Adams and James Monroe. The United States wished them
well but would not become involved in championing their
cause. That the U.S. became involved in the creation of Israel was a deviation from the tradition established by Adams
and Monroe. Moreover, while the U.S. had always espoused
support for the principle of self-determination of peoples, in
the case of Palestine, American endorsement for the Jews
was at variance with this high principle because the Arabs
were the majority population.

By the conclusion of World War II the United States had
important interests in the Middle East. American oil companies had assumed a large role in the development of Middle
Eastern petroleum. This resource was located in the land of
the Arabs, a people who greatly respected the United States,
but who were opposed to the creation of Israel. Given the
reality that America's European allies in the Cold War era depended on Middle Eastern oil, and given the current energy
needs of the United States, it can readily be understood that
American intervention in the Palestine question was a gross
miscalculation of the best interests of the United States.

*   *   *   *   *

To the time of his death President Franklin D. Roosevelt was still adhering to the principle of "full consultation"
--one that required the U.S. to consult both Arabs and Jews
in seeking a solution to the Palestine question.[1] But within
a few short years Washington departed from that policy and
supported the founding of Israel.   How did this radical change
in U.S. policy come about?

As World War II drew to a close and Harry S Truman
assumed the Presidency, American Zionists placed enormous
pressure on the new President, Congress, and the American
people in order to realize the establishment of a Jewish national state.[2] On 20 April 1945 Rabbi Stephen S. Wise, prominent among American Zionists, called on the President and
urged that he support unlimited Jewish immigration into Palestine.   This goal the Zionists considered necessary to the
realization of a Jewish national home.[3] The President was
aware of Zionist aims, for Secretary of State Stettinius had
briefed him on Zionist goals and on the Arab reaction to them.
Truman was sympathetic and he seems to have felt bound by
President Wilson's endorsement of the Balfour Declaration to
help bring about a Jewish state.[4] Unfortunately, the President was willing to apply Wilson's principle of self-determination to the Jews but not to the Arabs who predominated in
Palestine.   Although Truman endorsed the Zionist plan of unlimited immigration to Palestine,[5] the State Department urged
adherence to the precedent of "full consultation," and requested the President to permit the United Nations to handle the
Palestine problem.[6]

Swayed by David K. Niles, his adviser on minority
problems, and Eddie Jacobson, his former business partner,
the President chose to ignore the State Department's advice
and that of other high-level members of government.[7] At the
Potsdam Conference Truman wrote Prime Minister Winston
Churchill of the interest of the American people in the Jewish
question, and he urged that Britain lift the restrictions imposed by the 1939 White Paper to allow the immediate entry
of 100,000 Jewish immigrants.   At one stroke, Truman departed from his predecessor's policy of "full consultation" and
urged unilaterally that British permit Jewish immigration.[8]
Clement Attlee soon replaced Churchill, and he requested Truman to dispatch U.S. military forces to Palestine to help
carry out those measures necessary to maintain peace, but
Truman refused.[9]

    In the meantime the President received a report from
Earl G. Harrison, an adviser on refugee affairs, that profoundly influenced his views on the Palestine problem. A
former dean of the University of Pennsylvania Law School,
Harrison reported in late August that most Jewish displaced
persons wanted to migrate to Palestine. He suggested that
100,000 certificates of immigration be issued for this purpose, as recommended by the Jewish Agency, the quasi-offi-
cial Zionist governing body in Palestine.[10] In compliance
with Harrison's recommendation the President on 31 August
1945 wrote Attlee, urging Britain to permit entry of the Jewish refugees. Attlee's reply was not immediately forthcoming, but in the interim there was a debate in cabinet circles
in Washington,[11] where State, Navy and War departments
and the Joint Chiefs all concurred that U.S. support for the
realization of a Jewish state was at odds with American national interests. George F. Kennan, a high-level official at
State, urged that the American endorsement of Zionist goals
would permit Soviet Russia to establish a position of influence
in the Arab world.[12] Secretary Forrestal, aware of the
need to protect American access to Middle Eastern oil, urged
caution, recommending that the region's petroleum might be
necessary to replenish domestic reserves.[13] Secretary of
State James F. Byrnes was also concerned lest the United
States move too fast and warned that backing Israel was not
in the American national interest.[14]

    In the autumn Attlee replied to Truman's letter, pro-
posing that the United States should join Britain to find a solution to the Palestine issue. To that end, Attlee proposed
the formation of an Anglo-American Committee of Inquiry to
examine the condition of Jews in Europe. Truman agreed
and in November the two governments reached an accord on
the nature of the committee.[15] The Americans appointed to
the committee in December included Judge Joseph C. Hutche-
son, Frank Aydelotte, Frank W. Buxton, Bartley Crum,
James G. McDonald, and William Phillips.[16] Two of the
Americans, Crum and McDonald, were pro-Zionist, while
William Phillips maintained a more balanced view and opposed
his pro-Zionist colleagues.

    In the autumn of 1945 Zionists implored Congress to
pass resolutions endorsing formation of a Jewish national
home. In early October eleven senators, five Republicans
and six Democrats, called for an end to the White Paper restrictions on Jewish immigration. The Senate passed the
Wagner-Taft resolution on 17 December 1945 and the House

followed on the 19th.   This measure called for free and open
migration of all Jews to Palestine and urged the United States
to use its good offices that Palestine might be constituted as
a Jewish commonwealth. [17]   Zionists also employed sophisti-
cated public opinion and propaganda techniques to win the
support of the American Jewish community.   By publications,
radio, rallies, newspaper endorsements and letter-writing
campaigns, Zionist groups gained the backing of American
Jewry and contrived a climate of American public opinion
conducive to the achievement of Zionist ends. [18]   The American public, appalled by Hitler's treatment of Jews, was
readily susceptible to Zionist propaganda.

While Zionists continued to cajole Congress and the
American public, there was a high-level conflict in Washington over the Palestine issue. [19]   The Navy and State departments and the Joint Chiefs cautioned the President about proceeding too far.[20]   That the President disregarded this advice
and continued to make policy vis-à-vis Palestine is indicated
by his reception of the Anglo-American Committee of Inquiry
report in the spring of 1946.   The Committee completed its
report on 20 April and released it for publication on the 30th.
It called for the creation of a bi-national state and recommended the immediate admission of 100,000 Jewish refugees
to Palestine. [21]   Zionists opposed the bi-national solution, for
it ran counter to their goal of a Jewish commonwealth.   The
American Zionist Emergency Council urged the President to
reject the recommendation and to accept the part of the report calling for immediate migration. [22]   He complied, and
his action indicated the new course that American policy toward Palestine would take.   All the while, the U.S. and
British governments were attempting to find some means of
implementing the report of the Committee of Inquiry.   Loy
Henderson, director of the Office of Near Eastern Affairs in
the State Department, suggested that the President appoint a
cabinet committee on Palestine, consisting of the secretaries
of War, State, and Treasury.   This group, Henderson advised, would be designated to implement the Anglo-American
Committee report.   Truman complied and the appointment of
this high-level group was announced on 11 June.   The committee met once or twice in June, but its work was delegated
to surrogates, headed by Henry M. Grady, former Assistant
Secretary of State. [23]

During that summer of 1946 as the U.S. was girding
for the mid-term elections, Zionist terror groups continued
massive guerrilla tactics in Palestine to coerce the British

to open the gates to immigration of Jewish refugees. That
the President was leaning further toward Zionism is evident
from his reply to Attlee on 2 July that Jewish terrorists
should be released from captivity.[24]

   In light of the growing Zionist terror, it was imperative that the British and American governments find a solution to the thorny problem of Palestine. The alternates of
the American Cabinet Committee on Palestine journeyed to
London to meet a British group led by Herbert Morrison,
then Lord President of the Council. After a number of meetings, the committee issued the Morrison-Grady Report.
Leaked to the press on 25 July, it called for a federal solution that envisioned the founding of two Jewish and Arab autonomous states with a strong central government under British tutelage. Further, it recommended that the admission of
100,000 Jewish immigrants would be contingent upon acceptance of the federal solution.[25]

   Zionist influence in Washington was powerful, for on
12 August the President advised Attlee of his rejection of the
Morrison-Grady Report, and he urged upon the British Prime
Minister the acceptance of a plan of partition. This plan had
been proffered by the Jewish Agency, which had agreed that
it was an acceptable compromise with the Biltmore Program's
aim to create a Jewish state in the whole of Palestine. The
President's rejection went against the wishes of the State Department, which favored the federal solution.[26] On 4 October
1946, which happened to be Yom Kippur, President Truman
announced his rejection of the Morrison-Grady Plan, called
for the immediate admission of 100,000 Jewish immigrants,
and recommended the partition of Palestine as suggested by
the Jewish Agency.[27]

   That Truman made his announcement in the fall of 1946
at election time leaves room for speculation on his motives.
There is a growing consensus among historians that the President was motivated by political considerations when he rejected the Morrison-Grady Plan and opted for partition.[28]
But Evan Wilson, a retired foreign service officer, suggested
that Truman was motivated by humanitarian ideals that stemmed
from his Biblical background and that he felt bound by President Wilson's 1918 endorsement of the Balfour Declaration.[29]
Ian J. Bickerton has advanced the view that Truman did in
fact pursue a balanced policy that steered a mid-course between Zionism and realism.[30] It would appear that the President's true motives lay in a mixture of humanitarian and po-

litical considerations, but his unwillingness to follow the advice of his State, War, and Navy department heads and the Joint Chiefs--all of whom advised that support for partition was contrary to American national interests--is subject to criticism whatever his ultimate motivation.

Frustrated by Truman's October statement, Ernest Bevin, British Foreign Secretary, announced in 1947 that Britain would take the Palestine question to the United Nations. Bevin chided the President for giving in to the expediency of New York politics.[31] Tired of the bloodshed of the Jewish terror in Palestine, Bevin requested the United Nations to assume responsibility for Palestine.[32] Pursuant to the British request of 2 April 1947, the General Assembly placed the knotty Palestine issue on its agenda for discussion at the second regular session.[33] Zionists stepped up their pressure on the U.S. government to support partition to realize the Biltmore Program by means of U.N. action.[34] On 15 May 1947 the U.N. Special Committee on Palestine (UNSCOP) was designated to make recommendations on the ultimate disposition of Palestine.[35] After holding numerous meetings at Lake Success, Jerusalem, Beirut, and Geneva, UNSCOP was unable to make a unanimous recommendation. Seven of the nations, Canada, Czechoslovakia, Guatemala, Netherlands, Peru, Sweden, and Uruguay suggested partition, but India, Yugoslavia, and Iran proposed a federal solution. Australia supported neither the majority nor the minority report.[36] With no clear mandate to act on Palestine, the General Assembly appointed an ad hoc Committee on Palestine, consisting of all member states of the United Nations.[37] Between 25 September and 25 November 1947 the Committee held 34 meetings. On Saturday, 11 October, Herschel V. Johnson, the U.S. representative, asserted that the U.S. was bound by President Wilson's endorsement of the Balfour Declaration to give its full support to partition.[38] The United Nations voted on Saturday, 29 November in favor of the resolution for partition. The vote was 33 to 10, with 10 abstentions and one absentee.[39] The plan awarded Jews jurisdiction over 56 per cent of the Palestinian mandate, in spite of the fact that they constituted only one-third of the population and held less than 7 per cent of the land. The vote was a patent violation of the concept of self-determination so well enunciated by Woodrow Wilson's Fourteen Points and reaffirmed by President Roosevelt in the Atlantic Charter. In view of this violation, the vote raises the question that has intrigued historians for two decades. What role, if any, did the United States play in bringing about a vote in favor of partition that discrimi-

nated against the Palestinians?   While the President denied
the use of political pressure, there is a consensus in support
of Sumner Welles' conclusion that "by direct order of the
White House every form of pressure, direct and indirect, was
brought to bear by American officials upon those countries
outside the Moslem world that were known to be either uncertain or opposed to partition. "[40]

   Increasing violence between Jews and Arabs made
peaceful partition out of the question, and U.S. military and
diplomatic officials warned that the U.S. would be compelled
to dispatch U.S. forces to Palestine to implement the U.N.
decision on partition.   The military suggested that the employment of U.S. forces would bring about Soviet entry into
the Middle East, an eventuality that could result in a thrust
at the Suez Canal or at American oil holdings in Saudi Arabia.[41]   Military and diplomatic pressure, supported by the
plea of the oil interests, resulted in a temporary reversal of
American policy on the partition of Palestine.   Faced with a
new reality, American policy-makers elected to form a trusteeship for Palestine under the auspices of the United Nations.
Zionists organized a massive, nation-wide program to counter-
act the government's drift away from partition, and they bom-
barded Washington with telegrams and letters to support partition.   On the personal level, Chaim Weizmann tried to see
President Truman.   Rebuffed, he obtained the services of Eddie Jacobson, the President's old business partner, and persuaded him to visit the White House to present the Zionist
case for partition.   Jacobson's plea, coupled with that of
David K. Niles, was designed to ensure that there would be
no retreat from the partition solution.[42]

   In spite of enormous Zionist pressure, Warren Austin,
the U.S. delegate to the United Nations, asserted in the Security Council on 19 March that the U.N. should consider constituting Palestine as a temporary trusteeship under the auspices of the Trusteeship Council of the United Nations.   Austin advised that this measure would in no way compromise the
eventual partition, but it would provide the time necessary to
tone down Arab-Jewish hostility with a view to achieving a
peaceful settlement.[43]   Zionists reacted immediately, claiming the President deceived Weizmann.[44]   In rebuttal Truman
declared on 25 March that trusteeship was a temporary measure designed to fill the gap between the 15 May termination of
the British mandate and the time when partition could be implemented peacefully.[45]   Of course what the President did not
say is that the United States did not have sufficient military

forces to use in a peacekeeping mission. General Alfred
Gruenther and Secretary of Defense Forrestal advised the
President that an American police force to placate Arabs and
Jews would require between 80,000 and 160,000 men, while
the U.S. had only 53,000 troops available.[46] They also advised that an outbreak of fighting would endanger American
oil resources in the Middle East.[47] What is more, the trusteeship proposal was actually the product of the fertile mind
of Loy Henderson. Convinced that partition was not in the
nation's best interests, he suggested that the Palestine issue
should be recommitted to the General Assembly, where Palestine would be placed under a trusteeship and ultimately created as a federal state in compliance with the Morrison-
Grady Plan.[48] While Truman would not accept that portion
of Henderson's proposal calling for reversion to the Morrison-Grady Plan, he was willing to move toward a trusteeship.
On 30 March the United States delegate introduced in the Security Council two resolutions. The first urged the Arabs
and Jews to arrange a truce in conjunction with the Security
Council and the second called for the Security Council to convene a special session of the General Assembly to discuss the
Palestine question further. The Council accepted both resolutions. In the General Assembly the U.S. urged members
to accept a trusteeship solution, but this effort was to no
avail. The Palestine question was ultimately settled in Palestine and not at Lake Success.

But the question must be raised: Was Truman's acceptance of the trusteeship solution a complete reversal of
policy or merely a temporary expedient? Most historians are
in agreement that the President's resort to the trusteeship
was a temporary alternative to be used until such time as
partition could be effected peacefully. But they do score the
President, claiming that American policy vacillated and hurt
U.S. prestige at that stage of the game. Too, they suggest
that this policy of indecision was responsible for permitting
the situation to get out of hand, which resulted in the outbreak of war.[49] But given the nature of things--the growing
violence in the Middle East between Jews and Arabs, the
readiness of Russia to intervene to implement partition, and
the lack of U.S. military forces to keep the peace--Truman
seems to have had little alternative but to alter course. It
appears that Truman's guilt lies in his determination to direct
U.S. policy vis-à-vis Palestine, irrespective of the best advice from the State, War, and Navy departments. Not only
did he have little respect for the experts in the Near East
Division at the State Department, but he seems not to have

been conversant with the realities of the situation in the Middle East.

With the U.S.-sponsored trusteeship proposal tied up in the General Assembly and with the approaching termination of the British mandate on 15 May, the Jewish Agency decided to act.   It requested Weizmann to advise Truman on 9 April that the Jewish position in a trusteeship would be precarious.   They had little alternative but to achieve statehood or face "extermination."[50]   In the following month Weizmann wrote the President that at midnight on 14 May the Jewish state of Israel would become a reality.   With the end of the British mandate, a provisional government would assume control.   The Zionists urged Truman to accept the proposed fait accompli and be the first member of the international community to accord Israel recognition.[51]

At the time the United States remained committed to the dual policy of achieving a truce and establishing a trusteeship.   But if the President had reservations about following Weizmann's advice, he reckoned without the influence of David K. Niles and Clark Clifford.   Niles was a link between the Zionists and the White House, and his influence on the President's decision to accord recognition to Israel is important.[52] Clark Clifford, a Washington attorney with a superb sense of timing, was one of Truman's closest political advisers.   In contact with heads of the Democratic Party, Clifford assured the President that approval of the trusteeship solution in the U.N. would result in the President's defeat in the 1948 election.   On the same morning that Truman received Niles' and Clifford's advice, Elihu Epstein, the Jewish Agency's Washington representative, called on the President and advised that the state of Israel would join the world community as a sovereign state at 6:01 P.M. Washington time that day.[53] Without first informing the American delegation at the U.N. and without seeking the State Department's advice, Truman made his own decision to accord Israel de facto recognition. Although he conferred with top-level advisers, Marshall, Lovett, Niles, Clifford, and others, it was to tell them of his decision to extend recognition to Israel that afternoon.   Later in the day a press release from the White House revealed the President's action.

What can be said of Truman's decision?   Here again there is some disagreement.   A number of writers criticize the President for permitting domestic politics to influence him on the Palestine issue, pointing out that he took matters into

his own hands and permitted political advisers to determine
his course of action.[54]   Other historians claimed the President failed to take into account considerations of the national
interest.   That Truman saw Palestine in terms of the Jewish
question alone suggests that the President had a narrow view
of the Middle East that did not extend to the wide scope of
American national interests or the aspirations of the Palestinian Arabs.[55]   One of the few writers ascribing other than
political motives to Truman's actions was Ian Bickerton, who
maintains that the President followed a middle course Zionist
demands and State Department advice.[56]

While the American delegation at the U.N. was sur-
prised by the President's precipitate action, it was not sur-
prised when full-scale war broke out in the Middle East in
reaction to the Israeli declaration of independence.   With the
outbreak of hostilities the U.S. assumed the responsibility for
bringing the Palestine question to temporary settlement.
American policy-makers followed a three-fold scheme to
bring about peace: to establish an armistice, to organize relief for displaced Arab refugees who fled Israel, and to bring
the parties in the dispute to the council table.[57]   But they
had their hands full, for the conflict included numerous Arab
countries.   On 17 May, just three days after forces of Egypt,
Iraq, Lebanon, Syria, and Transjordan, with token forces
from Saudi Arabia, launched an uncoordinated attack on Israel, the U.S. submitted to the Security Council a cease-fire
resolution.   It did not pass, but a similar British resolution
did carry on 29 May.   The Swedish Count Folke Bernadotte,
appointed U.N. mediator in accordance with a General Assembly resolution of 14 May, had the responsibility to bring
all parties to the truce table.   After arranging a four-week
truce from 11 June to 8 July 1948, Bernadotte proposed a
novel solution.   He suggested that Palestine and Transjordan
form an economic unit in which Arabs and Jews might regu-
late their own affairs by virtue of a federal council.   He advised certain territorial adjustments that placed the city of
Jerusalem in Arab territory, with provision for an autonomous Jewish community.   Before a solution could be reached,
hostilities were resumed on 8 July and lasted for ten days.
At the end of July an indefinite truce was arranged, but it
was punctuated with intermittent violence until an armistice
was agreed upon in early 1949.   Bernadotte was assassinated,
but his successor, Ralph Bunche, brought the belligerents to
the council table shortly after the first of the year and negotiated armistice agreements between Israel and her four
Arab neighbors.[58]   The U.S. played no small part in the

talks on the island of Rhodes, where Bunche and the belligerents met between February and July 1949. Ultimately a solution was agreed upon. But was it satisfactory? The armistice line of 1949 was a cause of future problems, because it gave to Jordan (the new name of Transjordan after April 1949) the Old City of Jerusalem, leaving the other sector of the city to Israel. Although the General Assembly tried to internationalize Jerusalem, this effort proved fruitless, for neither Jordan nor Israel would agree to surrender its portion of the city. The agreement also left the West Bank of the Jordan River in the hands of Jordan, while it permitted Egypt to retain the Gaza Strip. This agreement, while it did provide for a cessation of hostilities, was fraught with bad features that would cause future warfare.

Both Bernadotte and Bunche tried to settle the refugee problem. The traumatic birth of Israel resulted in the ruthless displacement of 750,000 Palestinian Arabs. Many fled before the outbreak of hostilities to avoid the reprisals that had accompanied Arab-Jewish tensions in the previous decade. But to ensure a Jewish majority in the newly borne state, the Jewish Army, assisted by Jewish terror groups such as the Stern Gang and the Irgun, forced the Palestinians to flee their homes.[59] This act violated the principles of the United Nations Charter, but the Israelis camouflaged their act by claiming that the Palestinians voluntarily exiled themselves from Israel and sought domicile in neighboring Arab countries. But the Israeli government has never been able to substantiate this claim, and recent evidence has arisen to puncture this myth and to demonstrate conclusively that the Israelis employed terror to expel the unwanted Palestinians.[60] Ultimately, the General Assembly adopted the suggestion of Bernadotte and Bunche for the creation of the U.N. agency to assist the refugees, and the United Nations Relief for Palestinian Refugees came into being under the directorship of Stanton Griffis, the U.S. ambassador to Egypt.

Unfortunately, the refugee problem continued to plague those delegated to find peace. In December 1948 the General Assembly constituted the United Nations Conciliation Commission for Palestine, with the United States, Turkey, and France given the task for achieving a final settlement. Failure to make a formal peace was due to Israeli and Arab inability to agree on the refugee problem.

Real peace was impossible, for the region continued to experience border incidents. The Arab League inaugurated

an economic boycott against Israel, and Egypt forbade transit through the Suez Canal of any ship bound for an Israeli
port.   Iraq forced the Iraq Petroleum Company to discontinue
pumping oil to the Israeli port of Haifa, and compelled many
Jewish residents to flee to Iraq.   (Today however several
thousand Jews remain in Iraq.)

        The United States had assumed a commanding role in
an effort to find a solution to the Arab-Israeli question.   To
its credit, the U.S. prevented the advent of the Soviet Union
into the region.   By working through the United Nations,
U.S. officials succeeded in keeping the problem at the international level, but by 1950 American policy-makers realized
that the U.N. could provide no real solution.   At that point
the United States decided to adopt a new tack by seeking to
facilitate the U.N.'s task by negotiation of an Anglo-French-
American tripartite declaration to limit arms purchases in
the region.   In the spring of 1950 this declaration embargoed
the shipment of offensive weapons into the region.

                *   *   *   *   *

        That the United States supported the creation of Israel
was an aberration in the nation's foreign policy.   This departure violated the principle of non-intervention and the doctrine
of self-determination.   Too, it was not in the American national interest, because the nation's Middle Eastern oil companies dealt with Arabs to whom Israel was anathema.   Finally, the pro-Israel course complicated regional defense.

        But there is this to be said for Truman's endorsement
of and assistance to the Zionist program.   He was rightly
convinced that the American people supported partition of Palestine and the establishment of a Jewish homeland.[61]   In a
democratic polity the making of foreign policy should to a degree reflect public opinion.

        While the Palestine question was on the world stage in
1948, that year saw the Cold War in Europe take a turn for
the worse.   Not only did the Communists take over Czechoslovakia, but also the Russians blockaded Berlin.   These
events demonstrated the need for a better system of defense
and implementation of the Marshall Plan to deter a Communist advance in Europe.   U.S. policy-makers took a leaf
from the Cold War strategy in Europe, "applied it to the
Middle East, and thus began to search for a more compre-

hensive foreign aid program and for a more concrete structure to contain a possible Russian thrust. "62

Chapter 13

CONTAINMENT II: FOREIGN AID AND FROM
M E C O M TO THE BAGHDAD PACT, 1947 to 1955

The years between 1947 and 1959, a crucial period in
U.S.-Middle Eastern diplomacy, can be characterized by the
perceived need to defend the area from Soviet incursion. But
the creation of Israel introduced an unstable factor into the
region, and so it was necessary for the United States to take
on the added responsibility of dampening Arab-Israeli hostility. In so doing, the U.S. tried to create a climate of stability, necessary to the defense of the region and to the realization of economic goals, namely the extraction of oil. Britain
had traditionally dominated the region economically and defensive-
ly, maintaining a system of bilateral pacts with regional
countries for her purposes. But the growth of Arab nationalism, the decline of the British Middle East defense posture,
and the growth of Russian aggressive tendencies toward the
Middle East caused the U.S. to assume a position of leadership in the area. It extended military aid to regional nations
to further collective security and to strengthen pro-Western
regimes. It inaugurated Point Four, an aid program to extend technical assistance. Between 1951 and 1955 the U.S.
worked with Britain to erect structures for the defense of the
Middle East.

*   *   *   *   *

From 1947, when the United States initiated military
aid to Greece and Turkey pursuant to the Truman Doctrine,
to 1959 the U.S. extended $2.94 billion in military equipment
to Middle Eastern nations other than Greece. Turkey received $1.87 billion; Iran $464 million; Iraq $50 million;
Jordan $12.7 million; Lebanon $7.8 million; Libya $1.8 mil-
lion. Some $536.7 million was divided between Pakistan and
Saudi Arabia with the former receiving the lion's share.[1]

The primary purpose of this aid program was to foster collective security and to maintain order in the face of restive internal elements. It was hoped this aid would encourage the target countries to ally with the West in the Cold War struggle with the Soviet bloc. But President Truman anticipated that this aid would have other effects that would prove beneficial. First, aid would encourage regional leaders to initiate reform programs that would ensure orderly change to better the lives of the people. Modernity, progress, and hope constituted important aims. Second, foreign aid would dampen intra-regional hostilities caused by Arab hostility toward Israel. Thus the major aims of U.S. foreign aid were defense, reform, and stability.[2]

However, other motives have been imputed to the extension of American aid to the Middle Eastern countries. Some historians have viewed the aid programs as a means of economic penetration and political domination.[3] That the U.S. utilized foreign aid as a means of extending political power and achieving economic preferment at the expense of the older imperial powers was a charge that Radio Moscow leveled at American Point Four aid to Iran.[4] On occasion, leaders of Middle Eastern countries, both left wing and moderate, looked askance at U.S. assistance. For example, radical elements in Turkey viewed American aid as a means of making Turkey an American colony.[5] In Egypt and Syria, as well as other Arab lands, officials were skeptical about Point Four, claiming that there was probably some political motive attached.[6] While it is true, as President Truman admitted, that Point Four would encourage the investment of American capital, the primary purpose remained to furnish the target countries with technical assistance.[7] Total American investment in the Middle East was slight, but American petroleum interests invested heavily in the region, conferring benefits on the people.

While ARAMCO and other American oil concerns operating in the Middle East have contributed greatly to the social and economic well-being of the people of the host countries, these projects have not necessarily related to the overall U.S. program of defense. Given the increase of nationalism in Arab countries in the post-war era and the accompanying intra-regional tensions, aid projects emanating from private enterprise have contributed to toning down the Arab-Israeli hostility, a constant cause of concern to U.S. foreign policy-makers and to oil interests. Suspicion of the Western powers grew sharper in the wake of the creation of

Israel, for many Arabs viewed that land as the result of
Western imperialism. So concerned was the State Department in the aftermath of the 1948 Arab-Israeli conflict that
resulted in the displacement of almost one million Palestinian Arabs that it urged the United Nations Conciliation Commission for Palestine to dispatch an economic survey mission to the Middle East to find ways of reducing the poverty
of the refugees. Under the direction of Gordon R. Clapp,
chairman of the Tennessee Valley Authority, this mission
toured the area and recommended the establishment of the
United Nations Relief and Works Agency (UNRWA) to carry
out an economic development scheme to reintegrate the refugees into the regional economy. UNRWA instituted a number
of public works projects and expended some $59.9 million
during an eighteen-month period. Of this amount $37.7 mil-
lion was used for relief. Of the total pledged by the U.N.,
the United States paid in excess of 60 per cent. Unfortunately, the efforts of UNRWA did not remove the Palestinians
from relief, for of 878,000 refugees, only a small percentage
were employed, [8] and the refugee problem remained a cause
of tension.

Not only did the U.S. exhibit concern for the displaced
Palestinians, but it also demonstrated the need to help the
peoples of underdeveloped countries assist themselves. [9] It
was with this objective in mind that Truman instituted the
Point Four Program in 1950. "Point Four," wrote Truman
later, "was conceived as a worldwide, continuing program of
helping underdeveloped nations to help themselves through the
sharing of technical information already tested and proved in
the United States."[10] Truman pointed out that the program
was entirely "consistent with our policies of preventing the
expansion of Communism in the free world by helping to insure the proper development of those countries with adequate
food, clothing, and living facilities."[11] It would enable the
peoples of the Middle East to lift themselves from colonialism
to a level of self-support. Truman envisioned that Point Four
would require the output of the American industrial plant in
such a manner as to confer mutual benefits on the U.S. and
countries such as Iran, Iraq, Syria, Lebanon, and Morocco.
The United States became the first nation to employ economic
aid as a diplomatic tool in the Cold War, though such aid was
a revival of the wartime Lend-Lease program and the Marshall Plan. It was designed mainly to contain Communism but
also to quiet intraregional political disputes, promote economic and social stability, and ensure an orderly process of
change. The program was based on long years of experience

gained by American philanthropic ventures in the Middle East.[12] It provided that bilateral agreements would be drawn up between the U.S. and host countries to complete projects in agriculture, mineral development, road building, health and sanitation, education, and water conservation. Point Four became law with Truman's signature on the Act for International Development in September 1950. Congress appropriated $26.9 million for the first year's operation. The Technical Cooperation Administration, established to implement Point Four, emphasized the sending of American technical experts abroad to complete projects in designated countries. Arab League states, Iran, and Israel received $2.1 million of the initial year's allocation, and of this amount, Iran's share was two-thirds.[13] Point Four helped to construct schools and health centers, drilled wells, treated animals and poultry, and completed numerous public works projects in Iran.[14] A Point Four program in Jordan called for the construction of a grain elevator and an irrigation project. In Iraq Point Four personnel organized an agricultural experiment station. In Saudi Arabia TCA personnel worked in public finance, banking, and fiscal control. The TCA made arrangements whereby the American University of Beirut agreed to set up a regional center for training Arabs in agriculture and engineering, preventive medicine, economics, and public administration. A Point Four project in Egypt explored the possibilities of developing grasses for Egypt's western desert in order to increase the acreage available for foraging and grazing.[15]

The policy of containment, closely linked to technical assistance and economic aid, was expanded by the Mutual Security Program in 1951. As recommended by President Truman to Congress on 24 May 1951, the U.S. extended economic and military assistance to Middle Eastern countries to offset Soviet influence. Of the $540 million set aside for 1953 for the Middle East, some $415 million was allocated for military aid, mainly for Greece, Turkey, and Iran.[16] Limited military equipment was also extended to Iraq, Jordan, Lebanon, Syria, Saudi Arabia, and Israel. Between 1947 and 1959 the United States supplied $2.9 billion in military aid to facilitate collective security and to help maintain internal stability. But foreign aid and technical assistance were not adequate to contain the expansion of the Soviets in the Middle East, and the United States in 1951 began to search for a more effective means of defending the Middle East.

The Cold War sharpened in the late 1940s with the

Communist coup d'état in Czechoslovakia and the Berlin
blockade. The West was faced with a Soviet thrust in Europe, a reality that led to the formation of the North Atlantic
Treaty Alliance in 1949 for the defense of Europe. Although
the Soviet Union had become an atomic power by 1949, U.S.
military planners still thought in terms of trying to contain
the expansion of Soviet land armies into the Middle East. It
seemed logical to planners in the Defense Department that a
Western defense of the Middle East should be founded on the
British military base at Suez. But by 1951 the British position at Suez was uncertain, because Egyptian nationalists were
determined Britain should evacuate all forces from that base.
Since 1945 nationalists had been urging the British to renego-
tiate the 1936 treaty that regulated the British presence in
Egypt. They wanted Britain to terminate the protectorate.
In the post-war years there were numerous anti-British riots
and demonstrations. Ultimately, the British and Egyptians
agreed that the War Office would complete the troop withdrawal from Cairo and Alexandria by 31 March 1947. The
British kept their word but retained troops in the Suez Canal
Zone. [17] In April 1951 the British proposed to evacuate all
forces by 1956, suggesting that the Suez base be operated by
British civilians and that an integrated Anglo-Egyptian force
be retained on the base. The Egyptians rejected the proposal in July 1951.

     The United States was an interested spectator to these
talks, because the growing American position in Saudi Arabia
heightened interest in the Suez Canal and Egypt. American
oil flowed through the Suez to European markets. In 1946
Egypt and the United States signed a bilaterial air agreement
whereby American-owned Trans-World Airline was authorized
to operate out of Cairo. [18] In that year the U.S. turned over
Payne Field to the Egyptians for use as an international air-
port, and the U.S. Army agreed to train Egyptian civilians
in the operation of the field's navigational equipment. In
1946 the U.S. and Egypt raised their respective legations to
embassy status. In 1947 the Export-Import Bank granted to
Egypt a loan of $5.6 million for reconstruction and repair of
fertilizer and chemical facilities. In that year imports from
the United States increased to 11.3 per cent of Egypt's total,
making the United States Egypt's second greatest supplier.
Despite the more prominent position of the U.S. in Egypt,
Washington officials continued to view Egypt as a British
charge. In March 1947, when the Egyptians terminated the
services of a British military mission and requested the U.S.
to replace it, the Defense Department refused.

Even so, Washington believed that the rapid growth of American petroleum interests in Saudi Arabia, with increased American use of the Suez, demanded a larger American role in the defense of Egypt and the Middle East. Given the rise in U.S. interests, the growing tendency of the Soviets to move toward the Mediterranean, and the decline of the British defense posture, Secretary of State Dean Acheson requested Secretary of Defense George C. Marshall to assist with the drafting of a plan of defense for the Middle East. The latter proposed that the U.S. and Britain jointly coordinate a regional collective security system against possible aggressive Soviet acts. Acheson hoped that Greece, Turkey, and Iran would join the Western allies, and he anticipated that Turkey and Greece would function as members of NATO, which they eventually joined.[19] But in 1951 conditions in the region grew steadily worse, because Egyptian nationalists were determined to oust Britain from Suez, and Iranians had expropriated the British-owned Anglo-Iranian Oil Company. Too, the British were not keen to accept an American officer as NATO commander in the Mediterranean and were also reluctant to accept the U.S. as a joint partner in strategic planning in the Middle East. But when in June 1951 Anglo-Egyptian talks reached an impasse--a NATO-type organization did not seem feasible in the region--the Americans envisioned the establishment of a military structure similar to the British Middle East Command that functioned so well in World War II. After a period of conversations, U.S. and British leaders agreed on 8 September to form a Middle East Command, consisting of a Supreme Allied Commander, with headquarters at Cairo, who would be assisted by a staff committee made up of U.S., British, French, and Turkish advisers. It was anticipated that this multi-national force would be augmented by the Egyptians, who having assumed control of the Suez base from the British, would allow the MECOM force to be stationed on that base to protect the Suez.[20] Anglo-American military strategists hoped that the MECOM proposal would permit continued use of the Suez base facility to ensure passage of the Suez, provide for regional defense, and serve to dampen the intra-regional Arab-Israeli strife. On 13 October 1951 the British, American, French, and Turkish ambassadors jointly presented the proposal to the Egyptians.[21] Western planners believed that the success of MECOM depended upon Egyptian membership for two reasons. First, the Suez base was the key to the structure. Second, Egypt was a member of the Arab League and was considered the most important of the Arab states. If Egypt joined MECOM, the other Arab states were likely to follow her lead.[22] But the presentation

of the four-power proposal was badly timed, and the 15th of
October the Egyptian Prime Minister rejected the proposal,
advising the sponsors that this government "could not consider these proposals or any other proposal concerning the outstanding differences between the United Kingdom and Egypt,
while there are British forces of occupation in Egypt and the
Sudan."[23]   To Egyptian nationalists the MECOM plan appeared
to be a "cloak" under which the British would remain in a
position of power in the Suez base, a condition that smacked
of nineteenth-century imperialism.[24]   Too, the Egyptians did
not perceive the need to be defended from the Soviets during
the 1950s.   The Egyptian rejection was accompanied by the
unilateral abrogation of the 1936 Anglo-Egyptian Treaty and
the 1899 treaty, providing for the Anglo-Egyptian condomini-
um in the Sudan.   Before the end of the month an undeclared
war broke out between British and Egyptian forces.   In January riots broke out in Cairo and numerous business estab-
lishments were looted.

The MECOM idea failed because Western timing was
poor, and because no account was taken of the forces of nationalism that were so evident in the Middle East.   Too, the
planning was bad.   On 25 October, for example, Egyptian
Ambassador Kamil Abdul Rahim revealed in Washington that
Egypt was not consulted before the proposal was presented
and was not invited to take part in the planning talks.   Indicative of the spirit of nationalism that existed in Egypt, the
ambassador said further that Egypt regarded the proposal as
one that would perpetuate the type of occupation that Egyptians
had opposed for many years.[25]

The reaction in the other Arab states was mixed.
Some, like Iraq and Lebanon, were favorably disposed toward
the multinational proposal.   Others, like Syria, were opposed.
But in the face of Egypt's outright rejection, none of them
would go along with the plan.   On 8 November 1951 Abdul
Rehman Azzam Pasha, Secretary General of the Arab League,
declared that "the Arab world was unanimously opposed to the
Middle East Defense Pact suggested by the Western
Powers."[26]   The Arab states were far more concerned with
Israeli aggression than with the threat of Soviet aggression.

With Egypt out, the Western leaders had no alternative but to seek another solution.   In spite of the negative
Arab attitude, British service chiefs were prepared to try to
establish a defense organization based on the island of Cyprus.   Cyprus was close enough to Suez so that Allied forces

might influence the use of that waterway, but it lacked adequate fresh water and the single port of Famagusta was not equal to supporting the level of forces anticipated.[27] With Cyprus offering no good alternative, the British tried another approach. Winston Churchill returned to power, and on 17 January 1952 he suggested to a joint session of the U.S. Congress that the United States offer "token forces" to be located in the Suez Canal Zone as "a symbol of [the] unity of purpose" that had "inspired" the two nations to seek a solution for the defense of the Middle East.[28] The United States had already given this proposal "a cold reception."[29]

In the meantime, the United States had assumed the role of mediator in the Anglo-Egyptian dispute. American Ambassador Jefferson Caffery tried to mediate and restore order. He pointed out to King Farouk that the Western Powers were not trying to take advantage of Egypt. At the same time that Caffery was reassuring the King, Secretary Acheson urged Anthony Eden, British Foreign Secretary, to make some conciliatory gesture in the House of Commons, which Eden did. But American efforts on both counts were futile, and by March U.S. fortunes in the Middle East had reached a lob ebb.[30]

By August 1952 Western military chiefs had discarded the MECOM plan and decided to establish a Middle East Defense Organization. This arrangement would include Britain, France, the U.S., Turkey, Australia, New Zealand, and the Union of South Africa. It would consist mainly of a committee of military advisers who would plan for regional defense. The plan was drafted by the British and submitted in September to the interested powers.[31] General Mohammed Naguib, successor to King Farouk following the 1951 coup d'état, even intimated to the United States a desire to join in return for military and economic aid. While the U.S. government explored the possibilities of such an eventuality as Egyptian membership in a Middle East Defense Organization, nothing came of the plan.[32] Egyptian nationalism prohibited adherence to a Western military pact.

With the close of 1952 and the end of the Truman administration, the United States had not only failed to ameliorate Anglo-Egyptian antagonism arising out of the British presence in Suez, but had also failed to organize any sort of regional defense organization. U.S. fortunes in the Middle East were at an all-time low. Association with the imperial British in Egypt and in Iran won no plaudits among the Arab

people. In spite of expanded assistance to the Arab states
through Point Four and Mutual Assistance pacts, the United
States was able to win little Arab support for a defense pact.
American defense of the Middle East foundered on the reefs
of U.S. association with Britain and with Israel. A new approach to Middle East defense would have to await a change
of administrations.

In early January 1953, shortly after President Dwight
D. Eisenhower took office, Prime Minister Churchill came to
Washington urging the United States to support the British in
their talks with the Egyptians relative to continued British
military occupation of the Suez. [33] Eisenhower affirmed his
backing of the British attempt, maintaining that the "enlightened self-interest of the United States" demanded this endorsement, because Europe depended on the Suez Canal for
the vital flow of oil. [34] In the early spring British Foreign
Minister Eden came to Washington to discuss a renewed defense plan based on Suez, one that would provide for a British military presence at Suez. [35] Eisenhower advised Eden
that he thought it necessary for the British to maintain the
base and not to evacuate before making an agreement with
the Egyptians to join the defense plan.   Otherwise Britain
would be exposed to Egyptian blackmail. [36] In essence, Eisenhower pursued the policy initiated by Truman and Acheson,
but he was reluctant to join in a tripartite conference that
would include Britain, the United States, and Egypt.   He believed that American participation in such a conference could
follow only if General Naguib invited the United States to attend. [37] The President did try to influence the General to
extend an invitation, but this was to no avail, for the Egyptians had determined to reject the British proposition. [38]

Anglo-Egyptian talks opened on 27 April 1953, but
they soon broke down, for the Egyptians insisted that Britain
evacuate her troops from Suez before Egypt would consider
joining any Middle East defense organization.   Not only did
the talks prove fruitless, but the Egyptians also rejected outright Eisenhower's willingness to participate.   While his letter to the President was cordial, General Naguib insisted
that Britain must remove her troops before meaningful negotiations could take place. [39]   The British were disappointed
that the U.S. did not join the conversations, but Eden did not
seem to appreciate the United States position, for without formal invitation from Naguib an American attempt to enter the
talks could be construed as "gate crashing. "[40]

With Britain and Egypt at an impasse, Secretary of
State John Foster Dulles decided that a new approach must
be taken to the defense of the Middle East. He was convinced the Russians posed a real threat to the region, and
he elected to take a first-hand look at the situation to determine an alternative solution. Between 9 and 29 May
Dulles toured the Middle East. His first stop was Cairo
where the Anglo-Egyptian talks were breaking down. In conversations with General Naguib on 11 May Dulles learned
that the Egyptians were determined to effect a British withdrawal and operate the Suez base complex themselves without relying on British service personnel. The Egyptians
distrusted the British far more than they did the Russians.
Naguib advised Dulles that Egypt could not take part in any
pact with the Western Powers, but that Egypt would cooperate with them once the British had pulled out. [41] Leaving
Egypt, Dulles stopped briefly at Tel Aviv, and moved on to
Jordan, Syria, Lebanon, Iraq, and Saudi Arabia. He
learned of the hatred that the Arabs bore the Israelis, and
began to realize Arab apprehension of the pro-Zionist sentiment in the United States. On every hand he found strong
anti-British feeling and a lack of concern about the Soviet
Union. Dulles concluded his tour with brief visits to India,
Pakistan, Turkey, Greece, and Libya. [42] He returned home
in late May with some very definite impressions of conditions in the Middle East. The Secretary realized that a regional plan must accord with the desires of the peoples of
the area and that any attempt to impose such an organization upon them would be futile. He believed that there was
a strong tide of anti-western feeling in the region that kept
most of the states from associating in a defense arrangement with the Western Powers. Finally, he did learn that
the nations of the so-called "northern tier," Turkey, Iran,
Iraq, and Pakistan, were the most likely to join a regional
defense organization. He found that anti-British sentiment
was strong and that the Arab's fear of Israeli aggression
paralleled the American fears of Soviet aggression. He observed that the American association with Israel and with
the British and French was not an asset among the countries
of the region. It was apparent to the Secretary that the people were anxious to rid themselves of poverty, and he was
quite willing to recommend an immediate assistance program
to raise the level of living and to resettle the Palestinian
refugees. He concluded that any sort of military arrangement would have to emanate from within the region, and he
believed that Turkey, Iraq, and Pakistan were the most likely to cooperate. Iran was not yet ready, because she was

still under the leadership of the anti-British Mossadegh.[43]
On the whole, Dulles' survey was thorough, but he neglected
to take into account one important factor, the force of Arab
nationalism, which suspected Western pacts.

While the United States was considering ways and
means to implement Dulles' new approach, the British and
Egyptians were working out their differences.   On 28 July
1954 British and Egyptian leaders signed an agreement whereby Britain consented to withdraw all military personnel from
the Canal Zone, leaving civilian personnel to carry out maintenance operations.   British troops would be permitted to
return to the Canal Zone in the event of an attack on one of
the Arab states or Turkey.   Finally, both sides agreed to
enforce freedom of navigation in the Canal as specified by
the 1888 Constantinople treaty.[44]   The Anglo-Egyptian pact
was not accomplished without the assistance of the United
States.   Colonel Gamal Abdel Nasser, who had succeeded
General Naguib in September 1953, acknowledged the aid of
the United States as did Foreign Secretary Eden.[45]

The conclusion of this accord in the summer of 1954
encouraged Dulles to move ahead with the establishment of a
regional collective security system for the Middle East. As
he explained in his 1 June 1953 speech to the American people: "No such system can be imposed from without.   It
should be designed and grow from within out of a sense of
common destiny and common danger."[46]   The initial step in
this direction came in April 1954 when Turkey and Pakistan
signed a treaty of friendship and cooperation for the purpose
of mutual security.   This was not a military alliance, but,
as intended by American diplomacy, it was to serve as an
initial step toward regional security.[47]   The pact was in accord with Article 51 of the United Nations Charter, which
provided for regional collective security arrangements.   It
resulted from United States promises of aid to both Turkey
and Pakistan.[48]

The reaction in the Arab world to the American-Turk-
ish-Pakistani arrangement was instantaneous.   Iran, Jordan,
and Syria initially approved, as did Saudi Arabia.   But the
pact aroused fears in Egypt, where accords with Western
Powers recalled the years of British occupation.   Egypt was
concerned lest Iraq join and break up Arab solidarity.[49]
Egyptian fears were not idle, for the United States and Iraq
exchanged notes on 21 April 1954 whereby the U.S. promised military assistance to Iraq.   This move was followed by

the arrival of an American military mission to Iraq to survey
that country's military needs. The 9 June election endorsed
the pro-Western stance taken by Prime Minister Nuri al-
Said.[50] Not unexpectedly, Iraq signed the Baghdad Pact with
Turkey on 24 February 1955. This instrument pledged the
two nations to cooperate fully for mutual security.[51] The
creation of the Baghdad Pact, based on the "northern tier"
concept, was different than the Suez-centered strategy because
it isolated Egypt from Britain and other Arab states.[52] It
represented a revolution in U.S. Middle Eastern policy. Instead of a defense organization based on the Suez Canal Zone,
Dulles had effected an indigenous defense arrangement based
on the needs of the northern tier states.

    Reaction to the announcement of the Baghdad Pact
came almost immediately. Nasser opposed it as a breach of
Arab solidarity, and Cairo Radio filled the air waves with
abusive criticism.[53] Saudi Arabia, with its traditional hatred
of the Hashemite dynasty in Iraq, turned toward Egypt in opposition to the pact, while Lebanon greeted it with only half-
hearted acclaim. Syria followed Egypt. By and large, the
pact stirred up suspicions among the Arabs as a whole, for
they viewed it as a means of Western domination.[54] Most of
the Arab states tended to follow Nasser, who had been con-
tending with Nuri of Iraq for leadership in the Arab world.
The Arab states might not have reacted as negatively as they
did had the United States joined the Baghdad Pact.

    John Foster Dulles refused to adhere to the instrument
that was his brainchild. Historians have debated the Secretary's decision. John C. Campbell seems to sum up best the
reasons for it: he suggested that Dulles wished neither to
close out U.S. options with Egypt and Saudi Arabia nor to
provoke recriminations on the part of Russia. Further, he
did not want to antagonize Israel, and, finally, adherence to
the pact would require Senate approval, and he did not look
forward to a debate that might disrupt his Middle Eastern
handiwork. Domestic politics would surely have entered the
picture, for the Zionist lobby opposed the pact.[55] While the
U.S. did not join, Britain did so on 4 April 1955. At the
same time the Foreign Office signed with Nuri of Iraq a bilateral treaty that provided for Iraq's assumption of control
over the two bases at Habbaniya and Shu'aiba. The British
promised to assist with the maintenance of the bases and with
the training of the Iraqi air force.[56] But the British attempt
to associate Jordan with the Baghdad Pact became a cause
célèbre and had enormous repercussions in the Middle East.

Britain offered to revise her 1946 bilateral treaty with Jordan as an inducement to join, and she sent Sir Gerald Templer, chief of the Imperial General Staff, to Jordan to persuade the Jordanian King to join the alignment. The reaction of the Jordanian masses was instantaneous and violent. Agitated by Radio Cairo and stimulated by Saudi Arabian funds, nationalists loudly proclaimed opposition to Jordan's adhering to the Baghdad Pact. A few weeks later the Jordanian King dismissed General John Bagot Glubb, British commander of Jordan's famed Arab Legion, and this event brought about a marked change in British foreign policy,[57] for Sir Anthony Eden, now British Prime Minister, believed that Hussein's action stemmed from Nasser's influence. Eden now hoped to isolate Nasser.

Pakistan adhered to the Baghdad Pact in September 1955 and Iran joined in October. While Pakistan's accession to the pact was not unexpected, that of Iran was somewhat of a surprise, given the strength of post-war nationalism and the anti-British sentiment that had prevailed in that country during the oil crisis several years earlier. The signatories of the Pact met at Baghdad in November 1955 in order to establish a formal organization, which included a Council of Ministers, military planning committees, and special sections on economic cooperation, communications, and countersubversion. The members set up headquarters in Baghdad, elected a Secretary General, and appointed an advisory staff. The United States was represented by a special observer who gave the proceedings his official sanction.[58]

Dulles had created a collective security organization consisting of five nations, including some of the strongest states in the Middle East. It filled the geographical gap between NATO in Europe and the Southeast Asia Treaty Organization in the Far East. It represented a new defense concept, for it was not based on a NATO-type structure dominated by the Western Powers, but was an indigenous organization, the U.S. and Britain excepted, and was founded on the strength of the northern tier states and not the British base complex at Suez. It was not effective as a defense organization, because aside from Britain and Turkey the other members were relatively weak. This creation of John Foster Dulles was not wholly well received in the Arab world, where the emergence of post-war nationalism led to a distrust of pacts with Western Powers. Doubts were left in the minds of many Arab leaders about U.S. motives, with a resulting decline in the American reputation in the Middle East.

*   *   *   *   *

Between 1949 and 1955 the United States assumed a
larger role in the Middle East.   With the decline of British
power in that region, Washington felt it incumbent upon itself
to take the initiative for the defense of the Middle East.
While it hoped to use technical assistance and later military
and economic aid as the means for deterring the expansion
of Communism into the region, it later felt compelled to rely
on the creation of a defense organization to prevent Soviet incursion into the area.   At first American policy-makers tried
to form a Middle East Defense Command.   This effort proved
fruitless.   With the advent of the Eisenhower administration,
Secretary Dulles, realizing that a Western-organized defense
structure would not work in the Middle East, set out to create a collective security system for that region based on the
needs of regional states.   The Baghdad Pact was the result.
The signing of this Pact was dysfunctional.   It caused a historical chain reaction that resulted in Russian entry into the
Middle East, the rapid demise of British and French power
in the region, the exacerbation of Arab-Israeli hostility, the
1956 Suez crisis, and, with all of that, the emergence of the
U. S. as the sole defender of Western interests in the Middle
East.

Chapter 14

THE "HONEST BROKER" IN THE SUEZ CRISIS, 1956

The Baghdad Pact was an important factor leading to the Suez crisis of 1956, but there were others and they must be considered in order to understand the unfolding of the sequence of events. Israel reacted immediately, fearing that Egypt would adhere to the Pact and thus orient it in an anti-Israeli direction. The Israelis launched a raid into the Gaza Strip on 28 February, hoping to blunt any hostile notions Nasser might have. Finding none in the West, he turned to Moscow and received assurances of a bountiful supply. Russia acquired entry into the Middle East via the arms deal.

By the spring of 1956 all of the important events leading to the Suez imbroglio had taken place. Jordan's dismissal of General Glubb determined Eden of Britain to bring about the downfall of Nasser, whom he regarded as responsible for the ouster. John Foster Dulles could not tolerate Nasser's recognition of China and he decided to withdraw aid for the Aswan High Dam project. Dulles' reneging on the Aswan Dam offer on 19 July 1956 led to Nasser's seizure of the Suez Canal and to the ultimate conflict in which British and French forces, operating in collusion with the Israelis, sought to reverse the trend of events. The crisis led to the rapid demise of British and French power in the Middle East and to a corresponding rise in American prestige for having used its efforts to bring about a ceasefire. Following Suez the United States became the sole defender of Western interests in the Middle East.

*   *   *   *   *

It is indeed ironic that John Foster Dulles took such pains to create a collective security organization in the Middle East, because it ultimately resulted in Russian incursion

into the region, an event the Baghdad Pact was designed to
prevent. But Dulles was human and could not determine the
course of events. Israeli leaders announced on 26 February
that the pact was hostile to Israel's interests. David Ben-
Gurion had returned to Israel's Defense Ministry with plans
to deter any aggressive tendencies that Nasser might harbor
toward Israel.[1] On 28 February, just four days after the
signing of the pact, Israel mounted a heavy military raid in
the Gaza Strip. One writer has characterized it as "one of
the most fateful dates in Middle East history."[2] If Israel
hoped to deter Nasser she was wrong, for the Egyptian now
turned his attention to the enemy across the Sinai.

Nasser was opposed to the Baghdad Pact, which broke
up Arab solidarity, and he regarded pacts with Western Powers as anathema.[3] Iraq's accession to the pact challenged
Nasser's leadership in the Arab world, and this was intolerable to the man who hoped to unite the Arabs. Stung by the
Gaza Raid, Nasser launched fedayeen raids across the border against the Israelis, and he began a search for arms to
bolster the Egyptian military. Nasser feared Israel might
launch a full-scale war, a reality all the more plausible
since the return of Ben-Gurion. On 10 March Nasser called
on U.S. Ambassador Henry A. Byroade to request $27 mil-
lion worth of weapons that would enable him to withstand an
Israeli onslaught. But the U.S. willingness to grant arms to
Nasser had strings attached, for Washington demanded cash,
the right to supervise weapons usage, and Egyptian association with the Western collective security effort.[4] Nasser
found it impossible to meet these conditions. His effort to
secure arms in Britain was also unfruitful. But Nasser's
attendance at the Bandung Conference of neutral states in
April 1955 converted him to neutralism,[5] which offered him
a vista to the East. In June Nasser made an initial approach to the Russian ambassador for arms, and the Soviets
directed him to send a delegation to Prague to deal with the
Czechs. Although Nasser announced on 27 September that he
had made an agreement with Czechoslovakia for a supply of
arms in exchange for cotton and rice, it was well-known
that Russia was a party to the deal. The Egyptian procurement of arms from the Soviet bloc was an epochal incident
that won for Nasser the acclaim of the Arab world.[6] The
arms pact with Russia outraged Dulles and he sent George
V. Allen, the assistant secretary of state for Middle Eastern
affairs, to Cairo to dissuade Nasser from completing the
deal. Allen's talks with Nasser were futile. Both Dulles
and President Eisenhower warned the Russians that the arms

pact was likely to heat up the Middle East and bring about a
renewal of hostilities. 7   The Secretary also sent messages
to American ambassadors in the Middle East, instructing
them to meet with Arab officials to warn that the Soviets were
using the arms agreement with Egypt as a means of entering
the Middle East, an event that could have untoward consequences for them. 8

      With Russian entry into the Middle East via the arms
agreement a reality, the United States hoped to woo Nasser
away from the Soviet bloc using a proposed high dam at Aswan as bait.   It was announced on 17 December 1955 that the
U.S. and Britain would supplement a $200 million loan from
the World Bank with a $70 million grant ($56 million from
the United States and $14 million from Britain).   The Egyp-
tians were assured of support for the latter phases of the
construction project. 9   Completion of the Aswan Dam was a
popular project because it promised flood control, hydroelec-
tricpower, and more acres under cultivation in Egypt.   Since
Britain and the United States continued to adhere to the 1950
Tripartite Declaration that placed an embargo on arms shipments to the Middle East, Washington and London hoped that
the promise of aid for the Aswan Dam would be more than
adequate to undermine the growth of Soviet influence and to
dampen the animosity between Egypt and Israel. 10   Negotiations between the U.S. and Egypt continued into 1956 to iron
out details on financing the dam.   But shortly after the first
of the year events took a turn for the worse.   President
Eisenhower and Secretary Dulles hoped that an Egyptian-Israeli treaty would be forthcoming, and they dispatched Robert
B. Anderson, a Texas oil man, to the Middle East to negotiate.   Anderson contacted Ben-Gurion and Nasser, but his
mission failed because the Israelis had determined to launch
a preventive war against Egypt. 11   Eugene Black, president
of the World Bank, went to Cairo in January to negotiate with
Nasser the details for financing the dam, but American enthusiasm for the project had waned.   In early February Britain Prime Minister Sir Anthony Eden and Foreign Secretary
Selwyn Lloyd came to Washington for talks with Eisenhower
and Dulles.   While the American and British leaders were
not in complete accord on Middle Eastern affairs, they did
agree that support for the Aswan Dam was not a good proposition.   Nasser had mortgaged Egypt's cotton crop to Czechoslovakia for the arms, and the Egyptian economy did not offer high hopes for financing the Egyptian end of the dam
scheme.   By February Western leaders had begun to lose
their enthusiasm for the Aswan project. 12   Events in Jordan

also had a bearing on the unfolding crisis.   Hoping to bring
Jordan into the Baghdad alignment, the British sent General
Sir Gerald Templer, chief of the Imperial General Staff, to
Jordan to talk to King Hussein.   The Templer mission was
doomed.   Cairo Radio castigated it, saying that it was a plot
to bring Jordan into the Western pact.   Riots broke out in
Jordanian towns in opposition to Hussein's adherence to the
Baghdad Pact.   A number of people were killed and injured
and two cabinets fell.   The King continued to favor joining the
Pact, but Cairo propaganda and Saudi money built up a storm
of protest the King could not overlook.   Finally, on 1 March
King Hussein dismissed General John Bagot Glubb.   The dismissal of Glubb, a man of great stature in the Middle East,
had a bad effect on Anthony Eden.   Faced with a domestic
political rebellion within his party's ranks and suffering from
bad health, Eden took the dismissal of Glubb personally.   In
his mind that move was Nasser's doing, and he now pursued
a policy to bring about Nasser's downfall.[13]   Some historians
agree that Glubb's dismissal affected Eden emotionally, and
Anthony Nutting, then serving as Minister of State for Foreign
Affairs, claims that Eden lost his balance, was driven by
pride and emotion, and struck out wildly at his Egyptian adversary in a parliamentary address.[14]

If the dismissal of General Glubb was an important
factor in Eden's decision to oust Nasser, it was the Egyptian's
16 May 1956 decision to recognize Red China that caused Secretary Dulles to cool toward Egypt.   Nasser's recognition of
China was the other side of the coin of his reception of arms
from the Soviet bloc.   It was consistent with his newly adopted
policy of neutralism, but to Dulles it made him appear as a
compliant tool in the hands of international Communism.[15]
By the spring of 1956 Britain and the U.S. were not the only
nations turning away from Nasser, for by this time French
officials had concluded that the Egyptian leader could not be
trusted to cease arms shipments to the Algerian rebels
against whom the French then waged a colonial war.   To Guy
Mollet, French Prime Minister, and Christian Pineau, French
Foreign Secretary, Nasser must go.[16]

The American, French, and British leaders' hatred of
Nasser was matched by that of David Ben-Gurion, who became
Israeli Minister of Defense on 16 June.   The fiery Israeli was
determined to carry out a preventive war, for he could not
tolerate Egypt's acceptance of arms from the Soviet bloc.   A
re-armed Egypt constituted a menace to Israeli security.   As
early as the summer of 1955 the Israelis had begun to acquire

arms from France to balance the Egyptians. By the spring
of 1956 the Israelis and the French were planning a joint
war against the Egyptians. [17]

By the summer of 1956 the outlook for President Nasser was not good, but even though the Russians were willing
to finance the Aswan Dam, Nasser preferred to receive economic assistance for this project from the West. To receive
arms and assistance for the dam from the Russians would
place him in the Eastern bloc, and he deemed this position
to be at odds with the doctrine of neutralism. Nasser advised Dulles that Egypt preferred to deal with the West. [18]
But Dulles had become disenchanted, and on 15 July 1956,
just four days before Dulles announced his intention to withdraw American aid for the Aswan Dam, the State Department
announced the transfer from Cairo of the pro-Nasser American ambassador, Henry Byroade. On 19 July 1956 Egyptian
Ambassador Ahmed Hussein called on Secretary Dulles and
learned of the American's intention to withdraw American aid
from the Aswan scheme. While the Secretary's attitude toward the ambassador was kindly, the withdrawal was abrupt,
and Hussein left the Secretary's office deeply humiliated. [19]

Historians have debated the motives behind Dulles' action. An explanation frequently offered is that Nasser's recognition of Red China in May 1956 so affronted Dulles that he
determined as early as the spring to withhold American aid
from the Aswan Dam. [20] Another view is that Dulles was
convinced that the Egyptian President was negotiating with the
Russians, hoping thereby to obtain a better offer from the
United States. In Dulles' opinion the United States would not
submit to this form of international "blackmail," and he chose
to withhold American support. [21] A number of historians
claim that Dulles was motivated by the imperatives of domestic politics, claiming that the Senate Appropriations Committee had already placed restrictions on the use of funds for the
dam. Further, they point out that a number of senators from
the cotton-producing states were opposed to aiding a project
that would enable Egypt to compete with American cotton on
the world market at a time when there was already a surplus
of that commodity. [22] Still another interpretation is that
Dulles did not really believe that Russia would make good on
her offer to support Nasser's dam, and he wanted to call the
Soviet "bluff" by withdrawing U.S. support for Aswan. [23] However, several commentators on the Suez crisis have recorded
the view that Dulles withheld support because he did not feel
that the Egyptian economy was sufficiently healthy to sustain

the financial burden. Nasser had mortgaged Egypt's cotton
crop for Soviet bloc arms and it was poor business to make
a transaction with a partner who did not have the requisite
financial backing.[24] One writer had speculated that Dulles
might have been going along with Eden and the French, hoping that Nasser "could be toppled from power, or driven into some rash act of adventure before his army was ready for
combat."[25] Deputy Under Secretary of State Robert Murphy
has suggested that the Egyptian ambassador presented Dulles
with an "ultimatum" for money to build the dam, a project
unpopular with Congress. He says Dulles did not consult
with his advisers in the Department.[26] Dulles did offer an
explanation for his actions. In a letter to President Eisenhower, dated 15 September 1956, he said that there was little support for American financial aid to Egypt in the Senate
where a resolution had been passed "directing that there
should be no support for the Aswan Dam without approval of
the [Senate Appropriations] Committee." Further, Dulles
observed that the Egyptians had carried on "flirtations with
the Soviet Union ... and they had tried to bluff us by pretend-
ing to [accept] Soviet 'offers'."[27] Historians have also criticized Dulles for so abruptly withdrawing American aid, an
action that humiliated President Nasser and led to his nationalization of the Suez Canal on 26 July 1956 in response.[28]
Although Dulles has been chastised for reneging on the dam
offer, some writers believe that Nasser had determined to
seize the Suez Canal long before Dulles' precipitate action in
July.[29] This is an interesting speculation, but the general
consensus among historians is that Dulles' action led directly
to Nasser's reaction--i.e., the seizure of Suez.[30]

     Anthony Eden reports that the British government dis-
cussed Nasser's nationalization of the Suez Canal on the
morning of 27 July. He relates that the government could
not tolerate this action and "determined that our essential interests in this area must be safeguarded, if necessary by
military action, and that the needful preparations must be
made."[31] Although polls showed that less than 50 per cent
of the British public favored the use of force, an articulate
element in the Conservative Party supported Eden's decision
to use military means. The Labor Party opposed the use of
force, but it seems that the British public, press, and political structure divided on the question of force along partisan
lines.[32]

     What can be said of the American reaction to the
British decision to settle the Suez question by military means?

Did the United States clearly define its position on this question? There is considerable disagreement on this point. President Eisenhower recorded in his memoirs that "In my telephonic and other communications with Prime Minister Eden I frequently expressed the opinion that the case as it stood did not warrant resort to military force."[33] Numerous historians agree that Eisenhower and Dulles made it clear that the U.S. opposed a military solution. They believe that Eden had determined to use force and blame him for not having Parliamentary support to do so.[34] There is also Eden's point of view. He relates that Dulles and Robert Murphy engaged in talks with him on 1 August and he found it "encouraging that the United States government should be thinking in the context of military action...." Eden said that Dulles brought a letter from Eisenhower which "did not rule out the use of force." He reported that Dulles told him that the seizure of Suez was "intolerable" and that Nasser must be compelled to "disgorge."[35] A number of writers have concluded that Eden construed Dulles' words to mean that the U.S. would countenance the use of force to compel Nasser to give up the Suez Canal. This argument rests on what has been characterized as Dulles' imprecision in expressing his views to Eden. Last of all, critics of Dulles hold that he misled the British into thinking the U.S. would not oppose the use of force.[36] Supporters of this thesis frequently argue that the psychological barrier between the two men made it practically impossible for Dulles to communicate clearly and concisely with Eden.[37]

It appears that while Secretary Dulles and Eisenhower might not have clearly defined their position in opposition to the employment of force at the outset of the crisis, over the months between Dulles' withdrawal of the assurance of American aid for the Aswan Dam and the Israeli-Anglo-French attack on Egypt they did make the United States position indisputably clear. It also seems that Eden, Mollet, and Ben-Gurion decided amongst themselves in a manner befitting the secret cabinet diplomacy of the European states of the nineteenth century to carry out a military operation that would compel Nasser to give up the Suez.

Following Nasser's seizure of Suez and Eden's discussions in the House of Commons concerning the use of military force, Eisenhower acted quickly. Realizing that Nasser's actions could lead to war, the President called a high-level White House meeting. Dulles was absent, but Eisenhower told Deputy Under Secretary of State Robert Murphy, and

Under Secretary of State Herbert Hoover, Jr., that the Suez issue was not cause for military action or some other precipitate move. With Dulles out of the country, Eisenhower instructed Robert Murphy to go to London to relate his views to Anthony Eden. Eisenhower records that he was instructed "to discourage impulsive armed action."[38]

Murphy arrived in London and engaged in conversations with Anthony Eden and with Christian Pineau, the French Foreign Secretary. Murphy claims he had no "formal instructions," but that he did not encourage the British and French to feel that the United States had a "common identity of interest" on the Suez question.[39] Eden apparently suffered from the misapprehension that the United States shared the British concern about Suez.[40] Of the three men, Pineau was apparently the most aggressive and the most intent on action. The French leader was critical of Eisenhower for sending Murphy and claimed that the Russians were definitely behind Nasser's action to seize Suez.[41]

Dulles arrived in London on 1 August and consulted with Eden and Pineau. During the conference he made it clear that the United States was against intervention. While he did not rule out the use of force, he made it absolutely clear that the United States would not participate in any military ventures. He also established the position that the United States would not consent to the use of force.[42] But he did tell Eden that Nasser's actions were intolerable and that the Egyptian must be made to "disgorge." Eden relates in his memoirs that these words made an indelible impression on him. "They rang in my ears for months," he records.[43] The Secretary of State proposed to Eden and Pineau a meeting of maritime powers, including Egypt and the Soviet Union, in London on 16 August.[44] However, Dulles clearly stated that the United States opposed carrying the Suez question to the United Nations, because it would be too slow to act on the matter. Dulles apparently did not relish the idea of the United Nations' establishing a precedent that would later permit it to interfere in the U.S. control of the Panama Canal.[45]

Two weeks later the delegations from twenty-two countries met in London between 16 and 23 August. Egypt and Greece refused to send delegations. The conference decided by a vote of 18 to 4 to adopt a scheme for the organization of an international management body that would be authorized to exercise control over the Canal. According to the plan drawn up by Dulles, this international body would seek to maintain continued transit through the canal, unhindered by politics of any one nation, but offering an equitable return to Egypt for the continued use of the Canal.[46]

Two days after the conference was over, Robert Menzies, the Prime Minister of Australia, heading a body of delegates from five nations, went to Cairo to convey the findings of the London conference to President Nasser of Egypt. Menzies negotiated with Nasser during the week of 3-10 September. But while their talks were proceeding the press declared that President Eisenhower had advised Anthony Eden that the United States favored the peaceful settlement of the dispute and was unalterably opposed to the use of force. A second letter to Eden on 6 September repeated Eisenhower's initial warning that the U.S. public opposed the use of military force.[47]

A number of critics of the Esienhower administration have concluded that Eisenhower's untimely comments to Eden ruined the chances of the success of the Menzies mission. They generally agree that Eisenhower's statements gave Nasser a clear view of the United States' intentions. Without U.S. support for a final resort to force, the Egyptian could reject the five points set forth in the London declaration.[48] One writer even criticized Dulles, claiming that the Secretary gave a press conference following his return from London and that his statement that the Suez Canal was not of vital concern to the United States was also damaging to the Menzies mission.[49] However, on the other side of the coin are those who believe that Nasser had already made up his mind to reject the plan of the London conferees and the Menzies mission was foredoomed to failure. Nasser could not accept the five-point plan because it amounted to a form of "collective colonialism."[50] Although Menzies later told Eisenhower that he had "pulled the rug clean out from under his feet," the Australian Prime Minister also wrote Eden that Nasser bluntly rejected the London proposals because they smacked of "collective colonialism," a slogan that would lead one to conclude that Nasser could not accept the proposals of the London powers and be true to the demands of Egyptian nationalism.[51]

Following Menzies' outright failure, Eden and Selwyn Lloyd determined to take the Suez question to the United Nations. It seems that the British and French had arranged for all of the pilots of the Suez Canal Company to walk off their jobs. Dulles was adamantly opposed to Britain's taking the

matter to the U.N., because with the pilots not working, the
British and French would have a pretext to make use of force
to keep the Canal open. [52]

With the Menzies mission a failure and the British
about to go to the U.N., Dulles worked up a new alternative
to the use of force. In a meeting with Eisenhower at the
White House on 8 September, the Secretary proffered another
plan: the Suez Canal Users Association (SUCA). [53] The
Users Association would consist of the eighteen nations that
had agreed at the London conference for international control
of the Canal. The User plan suggested by Dulles provided
that when the Suez Canal pilots went on strike, the Users
Association could then step in to help operate the Canal and
negotiate with Nasser for some new approach to the problem.
It could employ its own pilots, coordinate the traffic, collect
tolls, and work to achieve cooperation with the Egyptians. [54]

Delegates from fifteen of the eighteen powers assembled for the second London conference on 19 September.
Dulles was the dominant figure at the conference and he outlined the six main ideas for the establishment of SCUA. The
final details for the establishment of SCUA were worked out
by the ambassadors of the fifteen nations on 2 October. [55]

Dulles has been criticized for giving two press conferences on the intent and purpose of SCUA, because, his critics
claim, his statements actually weakened the effectiveness of
the proposed Users Association. On 13 September Dulles
said: "We do not intend to shoot our way through; we might
have the right to do it but the U.S. does not intend to do it.
If we are met by force, we do not intend to get into a shooting war." At a second press conference on 2 October, the
Secretary said: "There is talk about teeth being pulled out of
the plan, but I know of no teeth; there were no teeth in it,
so far as I am aware." [56] Dulles' critics claim that his
statements emasculated the proposed Users Association. [57]
But the Secretary's supporters claim that he never intended
that SCUA would utilize force; therefore, it cannot be said
that he deceived Anthony Eden, as the British Prime Minister
claimed. Too, it has been pointed out that when the Suez
Canal pilots walked off their jobs on 15 September the Egyptians kept the Canal traffic flowing and thus undermined the
real reason for the creation of the Users Association. [58]

With the Users Association a dead letter, the British
and French now decided to continue their fight against Nasser

in the United Nations. On 5 October there began three days
of public debate on the Suez question. Then on 9 October
Lloyd and Pineau met with Egyptian Mahmoud Fawzi, Egyptian Foreign Minister, and Dag Hammarskjold, U.N. Secretary General. They agreed to the "Six Principles" of the
Suez settlement:

> (1) There should be free and open transit through the
>   Canal without discrimination, overt or covert.
>
> (2) Egypt's sovereignty should be respected.
>
> (3) The operation of the Canal should be insulated from
>   the politics of any one country.
>
> (4) The manner of fixing tolls and charges should be
>   signed by agreement between Egypt and the users.
>
> (5) A fair proportion of the dues should be allotted to
>   development.
>
> (6) In case of dispute, the matter should be settled by
>   arbitration. [59]

Egyptian Foreign Minister Fawzi received these proposals in
a positive manner. The Security Council accepted them on
13 October, and historians are generally agreed that Nasser
would have accepted the "Six Principles" as a formula for the
settlement of the Suez issue.[60] If Nasser was willing to ne-
negotiate on the basis of the "Six Principles," what went
wrong?

     By mid-October British, French, and Israeli leaders
had decided that negotiation with Nasser was no longer desirable, because they intended to obtain their objectives by military means. On 14 October General Maurice Challe, chief
of the French Air Staff, and Albert Gazier, a junior French
minister, crossed the Channel to meet with Eden. Challe had
already worked out a plan for cooperation between Israel and
the two Western Allies. On 10 October French and Israeli
leaders had designed an offensive in which Israel's invasion
of Egypt would be coordinated with the Anglo-French operation "Musketeer." Ben-Gurion would give the pretext for the
Anglo-French seizure of the Canal by attacking Egypt across
the Sinai Peninsula. The Israelis had been reinforced by
French planes, tanks, guns, and munitions. Following the
Israeli attack from the East, Anglo-French forces would in-

tervene to maintain continued transit through the Canal by
separating the Israeli and Egyptian forces. The two French-
men met with Eden and Anthony Nutting at Chequers, the official country estate of the Prime Minister, and they had
come to gain Eden's endorsement of the plan. Eden replied
that he would give his answer within two days.[61]

Not only was the majority of the British public opposed to military action, but Eden had neither the full support of his cabinet nor the endorsement by Parliament. Eden
was also out of contact with the United States and kept Washington in the dark about preparations for the forthcoming military operation in the Suez.[62] Nevertheless, Eden gave the
French his approval.

Final plans for the use of military force were made
on 24 October when representatives of the British, French,
and Israelis met at Sèvres, just outside Paris, to sign the
accord that would lead to the invasion at the end of the
month. The Sèvres accord was signed on 24 October by David Ben-Gurion, Christian Pineau, and Patrick Dean, the chairman of the Joint Intelligence Committee of the Foreign Office. The tripartite accord called for Israel to attack on 29
October. The British and French would then intervene to
preserve the security of the Canal in accordance with the prearranged operation "Musketeer"--this on 31 October.[63]

Historians have discussed the 1956 Suez crisis in
terms of collusion between the British, French, and Israelis.
There seems to be a general consensus that the French
hatched the scheme whereby an Israeli attack would serve as
a pretext for Anglo-French intervention. France acted as the
intermediary between Britain and Israel. France also supplied Israel with arms, while the United States and Britain
adhered to the 1950 Tripartite Declaration that placed an embargo on the introduction of offensive weapons into the Middle
East.[64] But other historians question the assertion that there
was a concrete plan whereby the Anglo-French operation
would take place as a reaction to the initial Israeli attack.[65]

The final step on the road to the 1956 Suez crisis came
on 24 October when King Hussein of Jordan, battered by count-
less Israeli border raids, joined the Egyptian-Syrian defense
alliance. By creating what Ben-Gurion called the "ring of
steel," Israel now had good reason to launch a preventive war
to escape the tight encirclement forged by the hostile Arab
states.[66]

On the evening of 29 October Israeli forces attacked Egypt across the Sinai Peninsula, moving swiftly toward the Suez Canal. On the following day the British and French issued their ultimatum to both Israel and Egypt, urging both sides to halt their military actions and to withdraw their forces for a distance of ten miles from the Suez Canal. Nasser rejected the ultimatum, and the British and French launched air raids against Egyptian air fields, preparatory to the joint Anglo-French airborne assaults that would follow on the 5th of November.

The United States reacted quickly. On 30 October Eisenhower cabled Eden, urging that no action be taken and repeating the U.S. support of a peaceful settlement.[67] On that same day Secretary of State Dulles instructed Cabot Lodge, the American representative to the United Nations, to advise the U.N. to order a ceasefire and the withdrawal of all Israeli forces. The British and French vetoed this resolution when it was introduced in the Security Council.[68]

On the following day the pace increased as the British and French stepped up their bombing attacks. By that day the fast-moving Israelis had fought their way to the Egyptian positions west of the main stronghold that lay across the roads to al-Arish and Ismailiya. At the United Nations, Yugoslavia moved in the Security Council on 30 October 1956 that the General Assembly be called into session to invoke a "Uniting for Peace" resolution, a measure resorted to when the Security Council was unable to act due to lack of unanimity among its members. This stratagem had not been used since 1950 at the time of the Korean conflict. Since it was a procedural matter it was not subject to veto, and the United States cast the seventh affirmative vote, thus siding with Russia, Nationalist China, Cuba, Iran, Yugoslavia, and Peru. Britain and France abstained.[69]

When the United Nations General Assembly convened on 1 November to consider the Suez question, Dulles made a strong speech to the body. He condemned the use of force by the British, French, and Israelis. He urged the assembled body to act quickly to "deal with this situation."[70] On 31 October President Eisenhower made a nationally televised address. He said that the United States had from the outset opposed the use of force. He observed that the United States had not been consulted by the three aggressor states. He cautioned that the United States would not become involved in the conflict, but that it would use its good offices to end the matter by peaceful means.[71]

The 2nd of November was an eventful day, for as Israel mopped up the Sinai and Gaza Strip, the Egyptian forces withdrew.   Syria blew up the pipelines from Iraq to the Mediterranean and by now the Suez Canal had been closed as the Egyptians sank some thirty-two vessels in the Canal freeway. That afternoon the General Assembly adopted the U. S. draft resolution, calling for an immediate ceasefire, the prompt withdrawal of all military forces, and recommended that member states refrain from sending military supplies into the combat zone.[72]   In response to this action, neither the British nor the French complied, but Israel, having achieved her military goals, agreed to the ceasefire within twenty-four hours.

But on the 3rd of November Israel reneged on her agreement to carry out the ceasefire and continued her operations in compliance with Anglo-French wishes.   The British and French continued to plan their offensive operations in the Suez.

On 4 November the General Assembly adopted a Canadian resolution, establishing a United Nations Emergency Force to take over the Canal Zone.   On that same day the Security Council was the scene of a Russian veto that condemned a U. S. resolution calling on the Russian Government to remove its forces from Hungary where Soviet forces were in the process of quelling a revolt.[73]

On 5 November Israeli forces completed their operations as they gained complete control of Aqaba Straits.   It was ironic that the British and French finally launched their attack at this time, with Anglo-French forces converging on the Canal from Port Said.   Within a short time the Soviet Union reacted, with Nicholai Bulganin announcing in messages to Eden, Mollet, and Ben-Gurion that the Russians would use force to crush the aggression in the Suez and to restore peace.   At the same time he wrote Eisenhower, urging that the United States and Russia join forces to put an end to the fighting.[74]

The 6th was an equally momentous day, for Eisenhower won re-election, Anglo-French forces agreed to a ceasefire after advancing into the Canal Zone, and President Eisenhower began to apply pressure to the British and French to abide by the ceasefire agreement on midnight of the 6th.   Dulles was ill, having been stricken with cancer, a tragedy that required hospitalization and operation.   Eisenhower took the lead to

end hostilities.   He applied U.S. fiscal pressure in the form
of an American withdrawal of a vast sum of dollars from the
International Monetary Fund in order to buy up British pounds.
This move shook the British.   Secretary of the Treasury
George Humphrey then promised the British adequate finan-
cial help provided they abided by the ceasefire resolution.[75]
Britain adhered to her promise.

While the United States might have informed the British and French and Israelis during the month of October what
it would do in the event they resorted to military force, the
United States nevertheless played the leading role in bringing
about the ceasefire.   There is general agreement among historians that Eisenhower's role in the crisis was chiefly responsible for compelling the British and French to lay down
their arms.[76]   However, it has been suggested that the Russian warning was more than just so much bombastic rhetoric
and that it was Bulganin's "missile rattling" messages that
brought an end to the conflict.[77]   Another writer suggests
that it was neither American nor Russian pressure that
caused Eden to pull back, but rather domestic economic and
political pressures and his failing health.[78]

*   *   *   *   *

The results of the Suez crisis were far reaching.   The
American stand behind Egypt and against the Anglo-French-
Israeli aggressors gained for the United States a new measure of respect among the Arab states.   British and French
influence in the Middle East dropped to an all-time low ebb.
The British and French began to withdraw their forces--com-
plete withdrawal was effected by Christmas--and the United
Nations Emergency Force went into Egypt to supervise the
withdrawals.   It was a sad day for Britain, a nation that had
dominated the Middle East for so long, and in the following
January Prime Minister Eden resigned from office, an event
reminiscent of David Lloyd George's resignation earlier in
the century over the abortive Greco-Turk war.   Nasser
emerged from the struggle stronger than before, in spite of
the poor showing of Egyptian armed forces.   Israel of course
emerged a victor, having obtained all of her predetermined
goals.   While Israel began her pullback in the Sinai in December, she was reluctant to return all of the Sinai, the
Gaza Strip, and control of the Gulf of Aqaba to Egypt.   Israel needed the right of passage through the Gulf.   When the
United Nations threatened to apply sanctions to Israel, Secre-

tary Dulles stepped in.   He made an agreement with the Israelis whereby they would remove all forces from Sharm-el-
Sheikh and the Gaza Strip in return for a guarantee of the
right of freedom of passage through the Straits of Tiran.[79]

The United States won a temporary measure of respect from the Arab states in bringing about the peace and
ensuring the withdrawal of the Anglo-French and Israeli
forces.   It might have capitalized on that fortunate turn of
events by supporting Egypt and using Arab nationalism as a
bar to further Soviet encroachment in the Middle East.   The
United States seems to have been unable to fathom Nasser's
neutralism and unable to understand the growth of Arab nationalism.   Instead of relying on Arab nationalism as a check
on a further Soviet incursion, Eisenhower opted to take another tack.   With Anglo-French influence and power on the
decline and Soviet power on the rise, Eisenhower chose to
go the route that Truman had followed in the previous decade.
He elected to issue the Eisenhower Doctrine, an American
policy statement that would guarantee the political sovereignty
and territorial integrity of all states in the Middle East.

Chapter 15

CONTAINMENT III:
THE EISENHOWER DOCTRINE, 1957-1959

The United States became the chief guardian of Western interests in the Middle East with the decline of British and French power after the Suez crisis. American strategists viewed a Russian threat as probable, either through military force or political subversion. This necessitated the continuation of the policy of defending the Middle East. While the Eisenhower administration refused to join the Baghdad Pact, it agreed to pursue another alternative to satisfy the needs of the northern tier states. In an address to Congress, the President requested authority to give economic and military aid to any state requesting it and to use military forces in the event of aggression or subversion. The Senate and House approved what came to be known as the Eisenhower Doctrine. Intended to complement the Truman Doctrine, Eisenhower's strategy was designed more specifically to defend the Arab states in the core of the Middle East. Unlike the Truman Doctrine, the Eisenhower measure was not well received. It was put to the test in Jordan, Syria, Iraq, and Lebanon, but it proved dysfunctional. The United States in 1959 reevaluated its policy for the Middle East and discarded the policy of defense for a new approach that set the standard for the decade of the 1960s.

*   *   *   *   *

The theme of anti-Communism dominated the thinking of the Eisenhower administration in the aftermath of the Suez crisis. That the U.S. would continue to defend the Middle East was forecast by Eisenhower's 8 November 1956 memorandum. He asserted that the nation must be "ready to take any kind of action ... that will exclude from the area Soviet influence." Further, he suggested that the U.S. provide eco-

204

nomic and military assistance to the states of the Middle
East. As the President recorded in his memoirs, these recommendations "pointed toward a Mid-East doctrine" that the
United States would implement in early 1957.[1] This memorandum was useful to administration policy planners, but Turkey, Iraq, Iran, and Pakistan--signatories of the Baghdad
Pact--were apprehensive lest the Soviets attempt a further
incursion into the region, and they requested Washington to
make a firm commitment to the northern tier states. On 29
November 1956 the State Department publicly declared the
American intention to guarantee the territorial integrity of the
Baghdad Pact members and to regard any threat to them
"with utmost gravity."[2] Other problems faced the administration.

The United States pressured the British and French to
continue their withdrawal from Suez. When the Arab states
cut off the flow of oil to Britain and France, the United
States declared that it would make oil available only when the
British and French complied with United Nations directives
ordering their withdrawal.[3] With compliance assured, the
United States acted quickly to overcome the oil shortage in
Europe. Tankers from the American "mothball" fleet were
pressed into service, and by early December the United
States had delivered some 16.2 million barrels of oil to western Europe.[4] But the administration neglected to heed Egyptian requests for emergency supplies of food, clothing, fuel,
and drugs. The Russians shipped the needed supplies, and
the United States lost a golden opportunity to the Soviets, who
made gains in the Middle East in the aftermath of the Suez
crisis.[5] The President later said of the Soviets: "The leaders of the Soviet Union, like the Czars before them, had
their eyes on the Middle East.... The Soviet objective was,
in plain fact, power politics: to seize the oil, to cut the Canal and pipelines of the Middle East, and thus seriously to
weaken Western civilization."[6] The Red menace caused Eisenhower to act.

The President and Dulles met a group of leaders from
both parties in Congress on 1 January 1957 to draft a new
statement on the U.S. position in the Middle East. Eisenhower
advised that a declaration of American policy was necessary
following the Suez debacle. He declared that he would ask
Congress to authorize the expenditure of funds for economic
and military aid to Middle Eastern countries. Since U.S. intelligence deemed a Soviet attack in the Middle East possible,
the President said it would be expedient to use American

military force to contain the Soviets.[7] On 5 January the
President addressed a special message to Congress. He requested authority to use military force to secure the integrity
of states in the Middle East and to extend military aid and
economic assistance to those countries requesting help.[8]
Later that day the Administration's bill, House Joint Resolution 117, was introduced into Congress, but its reception was
not without criticism. Dulles testified before the Senate Foreign Relations Committee that unless Congress acted swiftly
that the Middle East might be lost to the West. Senator J.
W. Fulbright, the Arkansas Democrat, demanded a full ac-
counting of U.S. Middle Eastern policy since the refusal of
funds for Aswan. Other senators claimed that the United
States was attempting to by-pass the United Nations. Some
maintained that the administration was acting too swiftly.[9]
After twelve weeks of hearings and debate, the House passed
the resolution 355 to 61 on 30 January. A Senate debate
dragged on and it was 5 March before it passed the resolution by a vote of 75 to 19. The President signed it into law
on 9 March.[10]

It was apparent that the United States intended to follow the path chosen by Harry Truman a decade earlier, and
that U.S. force would be applied to the Middle East to maintain stability and fill the vacuum created by the decline of
British and French power after the Suez crisis. While the
British and French gave the Eisenhower Doctrine a good reception in the Arab world the reaction was mixed. In order
to ensure that the United States was sincerely committed to
maintenance of regional stability and guaranteeing the Doctrine's credibility among Arab nations, it was necessary for
the Eisenhower administration to use its power to enforce Israeli compliance with the United Nations resolutions requiring
Israel to withdraw her forces to the pre-Suez lines.

American pressure on Israel to observe the wishes of
the United Nations was relentless, because without American
pressure and Israeli compliance the Arab world would regard
the United States as pro-Zionist and the Eisenhower Doctrine
as worthless paper. Secretary Dulles instructed Henry Cabot
Lodge, U.S. ambassador to the U.N., to support two United
Nations resolutions, calling on Israel to withdraw her forces
from Gaza and urging Egypt and Israel to observe the armistice. Lodge complied on 2 February.[11] Dulles then advised
President Eisenhower to put pressure on David Ben-Gurion,
and on 3 February the President urged the Israeli leader to
comply with the resolutions, adding that the United States

would support further measures in the United Nations to effect withdrawal.[12] The President's message implied the use of sanctions, and on 5 February Dulles addressed himself to this topic in a press conference. He said that sanctions would not be applied unilaterally but that if the United Nations called for their application the United States would have to "give them very serious consideration...."[13] Eventually, on the 11th of February Dulles sent an aide mémoire to Israel. The Secretary went to the point, leaving little doubt about his intentions. This document agreed that if Israel would withdraw her forces from Gaza the United States would seek to have the United Nations Emergency Force placed in the Gaza Strip to prevent further Egyptian fedayeen attacks and would also work to effect the right of free passage through the waters of Aqaba.[14]

American public opinion favored Israeli withdrawal, King Saud demanded it, and failure to effect it would, as President Eisenhower said, "spell the failure of the Eisenhower Doctrine even before it got under way."[15] Anxious to achieve Israeli compliance, the President called a White House conference on 20 February. Partisan politics entered the discussions, with several pro-Israeli senators urging caution.[16] A worried President then decided to take his case to the country. In a nationally televised appearance, he said that he would dislike having to support measures in the U.N. that would adversely effect American relations with Israel. He concluded with the words: "The United Nations must not fail."[17] The message was clear. The U.S. would support sanctions if they were introduced in the U.N.

On 22 February a resolution was introduced in the General Assembly by Charles Malik, Foreign Minister of Lebanon, sponsored by Afghanistan, Indonesia, Iraq, Lebanon, Pakistan, and Sudan, calling for the imposition of economic sanctions on Israel. Assured that the United States would support this measure, the Israelis gave in, and on 1 March Golda Meir the Israeli Foreign Minister, addressed the General Assembly, and announced Israel's plans for "full and complete withdrawal" of all military forces.[18]

The issue was resolved, and at a press conference on 7 March the President made an important statement to the effect that the United States would ensure free passage through the waters of the Gulf of Aqaba. The United States, he said, was determined to uphold the international "character of the Gulf." These words constituted commitment that would cause the United States to become involved in the 1967 Arab-Israeli war.

With Israeli withdrawal from Gaza and the passage of the Eisenhower Doctrine, the President sent James P. Richards, a South Carolina Democrat who had been chairman of the House Committee on Foreign Affairs, on a special mission to the Middle East. He instructed Richards to work out ways and means of making agreements for assistance to countries requesting it. Richards was instructed to find out which countries desired aid. He departed the United States with a small staff in March and visited fifteen countries of the Middle East.[19] Reaction was mixed.

While it is true that twelve of the countries visited by Richards gave the Eisenhower Doctrine a favorable reception, there was hostile reaction in some others. Nasser of Egypt regarded the American policy as a piece of imperialism.[20] Syria was openly hostile. The Iraqi leadership was not enthusiastic, but Richards found that Prime Minister Nuri gave the doctrine his warm approval. As a result Iraq received aid, both economic and military.[21] In Lebanon, President Camille Chamoun also gave Richards a warm reception and a hearty endorsement of the Eisenhower Doctrine. Like Nuri of Iraq, Chamoun was pro-western in his outlook, and in spite of Nasser's blunt denunciation of the Doctrine, he approved it.[22] The Eisenhower Doctrine was also given a good reception in Libya, Turkey, Iran, Pakistan, Afghanistan and Saudi Arabia. Of course, the northern tier states of the Baghdad Pact were enthusiastic.[23] King Saud visited the United States in early 1957, and on receiving the promise of American economic and military aid, he agreed to explain the meaning of the doctrine to his fellow Arab rulers.[24]

It was in Jordan, one of the least stable states of the Middle East, that the Eisenhower Doctrine was first applied. Jordan's instability stemmed from the fact that King Hussein, pressured by Nasser of Egypt and his own Arab nationalists, severed ties with Britain in March 1957, an action that resulted in the cessation of British subsidies to Jordan and the removal of British forces. Jordan was moving closer to the Syrian-Egyptian camp, and Egypt, Syria, and Saudi Arabia had promised to provide funds to replace the British subsidy. Unfortunately for King Hussein, Saudi Arabia was the only state to live up to its obligations. Facing financial difficulties, and aware of a definite pro-Nasser trend in Jordan--one that might result in Jordan's absorption by Egypt and/or

Syria--and faced with a prime minister who announced his intention to establish relations with the Soviet Union, the King decided to move. A test of strength took place between King Hussein and Prime Minister Suleiman Nabulsi in April. On the 13th Hussein, assured of the army's support, forced Nabulsi and several of his military supporters to flee to Syria, where they vowed to bring about Hussein's downfall.

While historians have debated the applicability of the Eisenhower Doctrine to the Jordanian crisis, [25] it does appear that the integrity of that small Arab state was at stake. Whether it was an international test between East and West, or an inter-Arab struggle, President Eisenhower and Dulles issued the announcement that they regarded the "independence and integrity of Jordan as vital" to American security. [26] The United States conveyed to Hussein a willingness to give support. Asked by President Chamoun of Lebanon on 24 April to take swift action to save Jordan, Eisenhower advised that he had acted. On the 25th he ordered the Sixth Fleet to the Eastern Mediterranean and Secretary Dulles advised that action was being instituted in behalf of Jordan due to the threat of international communism. [27] While the King had not requested the assistance, the sending of the Sixth Fleet to the Eastern Mediterranean was designed to bolster the regime of King Hussein who was beset by Syria and Egypt, both of whom were receiving shipments of Soviet aid. [28] With Hussein's victory, the United States made available a grant of $10 million.

While some historians have criticized the Eisenhower administration for intervening in what might be termed an Arab affair, it nevertheless remains true that the Jordanian episode proved that the Eisenhower Doctrine was no mere paper pronunciamento. The United States was willing to use its military force and economic assistance to maintain stability in a region fraught with internecine strife and disturbed by the influx of Soviet weapons and influence. The Jordanian story is another milepost in the decline of British power in the Middle East and the assumption by the United States of the role of chief peacekeeper.

Although the Jordanian incident resulted in what might be considered a victory for the Eisenhower Doctrine, the same conclusion cannot be drawn when the United States applied the doctrine to a situation that developed in Syria in August 1957. In the summer of 1957 there occurred in Syria a complex series of events that led officials in Washington to conclude that a "takeover by the Communists would soon be completed." This could result in the establishment of a "strong Soviet outpost" in the Middle East.[29] The Syrian Ministry of Defense arranged for closer relations with the Soviet Union, which led to increased trade and entitled Syria to some $500 million of economic and military aid. The Syrian government then announced a conspiracy in the American Embassy against the regime of President Shukri el-Kuwatly and it promptly called for the expulsion of three American officials who were supposedly involved. General Afif Bizri, a pro-Soviet, anti-western officer took over as chief of staff of the Army.[30]

That the Communists were effecting an assumption of power in Syria was an inference drawn not only in Washington, but also in Turkey, Lebanon, Iraq, Israel, Jordan, and Saudi Arabia.[31] From the confusing course of events in the Middle East, officials in Washington came to the conclusion that Syria's neighbors feared the emergence of a Soviet satellite in their midst and wanted the pro-Russian Syrian regime removed.[32] The White House then began to view developments in Syria as a cause to implement the Eisenhower Doctrine, and a number of preliminary steps were taken to meet a possible subversive action on the part of the Russians. First, the United States assured Turkish Premier Adnan Menderes that if Turkey found it necessary to meet aggressive acts stemming from Soviet infiltration of Syria it could depend on arms shipments from the United States. Similar assurances were given to King Hussein of Jordan and King Faisal of Iraq. The United States urged Israel to refrain from capitalizing on developments in Syria by seizing territory in the Golan Heights region. U.S. air forces were sent from Europe to the large American base at Adana in Turkey, and the Strategic Air Command was placed on alert. Finally, the Sixth Fleet was instructed to proceed to Eastern Mediterranean waters.[33]

With these actions taken, the President dispatched Ambassador Loy W. Henderson, Deputy Under Secretary of State, to Ankara to confer with Prime Minister Adnan Menderes, King Hussein, and King Faisal. Henderson reported on 4 September that all of Syria's neighbors feared that the Russians might bring down the regime of each of the countries after exploiting the Syrian crisis. The Turks, reported Henderson, were determined to take action against Syria. In fact, Turkish forces were massing on the Syrian border.[34]

By late summer 1957 the situation in the Middle East
was ripe for a conflict, for the forces of Iraq, Turkey, Jordan, and Lebanon were massed on the borders of Syria.
Eisenhower claims that the United States "had done everything we felt it possible to do."[35] But historians have
raised questions about these American actions. Did the
United States assemble the forces of states adjacent to Syria
for the purpose of overthrowing a supposedly pro-Soviet regime that might soon become a Russian satellite? A number
of historians answer this question in the affirmative, claiming that this was indeed the case, and British Prime Minister Harold Macmillan claimed that he had to urge restraint
on Washington, "which was interpreting the new 'Eisenhower
Doctrine' with all the enthusiasm of recent converts."[36]
However, another group of historians claim that the United
States had no intention to bring down the Syrian regime, but
that it was merely standing by in the event of a Soviet takeover of that country.[37] This group would agree with Eisenhower that "All we could do now was to watch the situation
closely for the next sign of a move--either a major aggression on the part of the Syrians or some evidence that the
situation was relaxing."[38] In other words, it would appear
that Washington's policy was not aggressive but merely re-
sponsive to the developments in the Middle East.

But no untoward event happened and by mid-September
1957 all of the Arab governments with the exception of Lebanon had abandoned ideas of collective action against Syria.
Iraq, the country most logically suited to attack Syria, would
not do so for fear that the Syrians would destroy the valuable
oil pipeline running from the Kirkuk oil fields to the Mediterranean. Jordan and Lebanon, chastised by Cairo Radio,
announced their support of Arab solidarity, even though they
had received hurried shipments of American arms. King
Hussein took off on a vacation trip to Italy, while the King
of Iraq visited Damascus and announced that no difficulty existed between Syria and Iraq, and King Saud warned
Washington that it was creating an unnecessary crisis situation in the Middle East.[39]

Having aroused Arab nationalism by actions that can
be construed as counter productive the United States decided
to back down quickly, but it still had Turkey to deal with.
The Turks were reluctant to demobilize their forces and had
in fact massed some 50,000 troops on the Syrian border.[40]
Nikita Khrushchev gave a press interview to James Reston
and claimed that the United States was trying to stir up a

war situation over Syria. He claimed that having failed to
get the Arabs to attack Syria the U.S. was now pushing the
Turks to launch an attack. [41]   The United States urged restraint on the Turks but at the same time gave them assurances of U.S. support. [42]

The President claimed that steps were taken to refute
the Soviet leader's accusations, but Khrushchev was assured
that the United States would stand by Turkey as a co-ally of
NATO. [43] Gradually, the situation simmered down after Henry Cabot Lodge presented, on 22 and 25 October 1957, the
American side of the situation in the United Nations, a presentation that received a favorable reception. [44] By late October developments in the Syrian crisis indicated that the
United States might have over-reacted. The American effort
to build up an Arab coalition to counter what appeared to be
a Communist takeover in Syria resulted in an adverse reaction of Arab nationalism and neutralism. Instead of creating
a friendly group of Arab states, Washington seems to have
stimulated Arab solidarity, a phenomenon that resulted in the
formation by Syria and Egypt of the United Arab Republic in
February 1958. Russia, too, tended to over-react, by posing as a champion of the Arab state of Syria. The Soviets
gained prestige in the Arab world while Washington lost the
goodwill it had gained as a result of Eisenhower's role in the
Suez crisis the previous year. [45]

The quickening of Arab nationalism following the American application of the Eisenhower Doctrine to Syria was repeated in July 1958 when the United States used the doctrine
to justify the sending of American military forces to Lebanon.
The pro-western regime of President Camille Chamoun was
anathema in the eyes of Nasser and pro-Nasser elements in
Lebanon. For example, in 1956 Chamoun had incurred Arab
wrath when he refused to break off relations with Britain and
France during the Suez crisis. In 1957 Chamoun's acceptance of the Eisenhower Doctrine caused an adverse reaction
in Egypt and Syria. With the creation of the UAR in February there was an increase in anti-Chamoun sentiment in Lebanon. The political cleavage in Lebanon seems to have been
along religious lines, with the country's Christian element
generally in favor of the President, and the Muslims opposed.
But the conflict did not run solely on religious lines, for
some of the foremost leaders of the Christian community
were against Chamoun. This group included the Maronite
Patriarch.

In April the anti-government forces solidified their opposition to Chamoun when he inadvisedly announced his wish
to amend the Lebanese constitution with a view to succeeding
himself in office.   In May this opposition took the form of a
full-scale civil war.   Muslims, incited by Nasser's propaganda, not only opposed Chamoun's desire to remain in office,
but also believed that he wished to strengthen his ties with the
West. [46]   Thus domestic and foreign policies of an unpopular
nature stirred up the forces of rebellion.

The American reaction was that the force underlying
the political rebellion was Communist.   On 13 May Eisenhower and Dulles conferred to discuss a cable from Chamoun,
inquiring what assistance the United States would render if it
were requested.   The reply was that the sending of U.S.
troops to Lebanon would be based on the need to protect
American life and property.   But the President also took preliminary steps in moving elements of the Sixth Fleet to the
Mediterranean, alerting American airborne elements in Europe
and taking other steps precursory to meeting an international
emergency.   The President and his Secretary of State thus
construed developments in Lebanon as of such a nature as to
bring the Eisenhower Doctrine into play. [47]

The crisis seemed to have been settling down, but then
on 21 May President Chamoun filed a complaint with the Arab
League Council, claiming that he had "innumerable proofs,
formal and irrefutable" that the United Arab Republic was interfering in the affairs of Lebanon.   He claimed that the rebellion was being supported by men, weapons, and supplies
coming in from Syria. [48]   On 6 June Dr. Charles Malik, the
Lebanese Foreign Minister, leveled formal charges in the Security Council at the UAR, alleging that it was guilty of
"massive, illegal and unprovoked intervention."[49]   The United
States, Iraq, and Britain supported the Lebanese charges.
With the conclusion of a Security Council debate, it was decided to dispatch an observation team to Lebanon.   The Observation Group reported to the Secretary General in a number of reports between 1 July and 25 September that there
was no massive intervention by the UAR in Lebanese affairs. [50]

While the Observation Group was doing its work in
Lebanon, the Lebanese crisis seems to have been subsiding.
Then on 14 July a revolution led by General Abdel Karim
Kassim overthrew the Iraqi government, and murdered the
king, the crown prince, and the prime minister.   This inci-

dent galvanized the Eisenhower administration. The President called a conference at the White House, where he learned from Allen Dulles of the Central Intelligence Agency that President Chamoun had requested through Robert M. McClintock, U.S. ambassador in Lebanon, that the United States and Britain intervene within forty-eight hours. Dulles advised that Chamoun was bitter because the United States had not yet taken steps to stabilize the situation.[51] Eisenhower and Dulles agreed that the situation had gotten out of hand in Iraq, but that there was still time to take remedial steps in Lebanon. The President announced to Dulles: "Foster, I've already made up my mind. We're going in."[52] The President based his actions on the United Nations Charter and also on the Eisenhower Doctrine, which provided for intervention so requested by a regional state.[53]

That afternoon the President, with Dulles at his side, conferred with leaders of both houses of Congress. Informed of the President's decision to intervene in Lebanon, the congressional delegation gave him a mixed reaction. On the one hand Senator J. W. Fulbright doubted that the Eisenhower Doctrine was applicable because he did not feel that there was a Communist conspiracy. Speaker Sam Rayburn said it looked like a civil war to him and that the U.S. should avoid intervention. There was little outspoken support for the decision, although Congressman Carl Vinson, the Georgia Democrat who chaired the powerful House Armed Services Committee, said in endorsement of the President's decision that we must "go the distance."[54]

The President also conferred with Prime Minister Harold Macmillan, who announced that Britain would dispatch troops to Jordan to support the unsteady regime of King Hussein. Having touched base with Britain, the President on the following day advised Congress, the American public, and the United Nations of the steps he had taken. On the morning of the 15th he announced to the press that American troops, conveyed by elements of the Sixth Fleet, had landed in Beirut, Lebanon, to "protect American lives" and "to encourage the Lebanese government in defense of Lebanese sovereignty and integrity."[55] In a radio-television address to the American people, the President announced that he had no intention of bypassing the United Nations. He hoped that his action would "preserve Lebanon's independence" and allow the early withdrawal of American forces.

In addition to alerting the Strategic Air Command and

army battle elements in Europe for air lifting to the Middle
East, the President also took steps on the diplomatic front.
He sent Robert Murphy, Deputy Under Secretary of State,
on a mission to Lebanon to work with President Chamoun's
government and the U.S. military forces. Dulles instructed
him to work closely with all American elements involved,
and the President urged him "to promote the best interests
of the United States incident to the arrival of our forces in
Lebanon."[56] Murphy reached Beirut on 19 July and began to
work toward a compromise solution in Lebanon. He also
visited President Kassim in Baghdad and President Nasser in
Egypt. Ultimately, Murphy played a large role in bringing
an end to the Lebanese crisis.

The United States representative in the Security Council requested on 16 July the dispatch of a United Nations military force to replace the U.S. expedition, but it met a Soviet veto.[57] Khrushchev countered with a proposal that a summit meeting should be called to settle the matter. This did
not meet with the approval of Eisenhower, who believed that
the United Nations was the arena to be used for a settlement.
Ultimately, a special session of the United Nations General
Assembly was called at the request of Khrushchev after his
suggested summit meeting was cast aside.

The British introduced troops into Jordan on 17 July,
the Russians announced military maneuvers on the Turkish
and Iranian borders, and Dulles assured the Baghdad Pact
powers on 28 July of American support. The situation in the
Middle East began to ease, because Robert Murphy in Lebanon was bringing about a compromise solution on the domestic front and the United Nations had agreed to meet on 12
August to settle the international implications of the crisis.

Murphy worked with both sides to the political dispute
in Lebanon, shuttling back and forth between Chamoun and
the rebels. Murphy determined that the conflict was related
to domestic politics and that Communism "was playing no direct or substantial part in the insurrection...." He urged
Chamoun that arrangements should be made for a special
election of a new President in accordance with the present
constitution of Lebanon.[58] But the American diplomat realized the necessity of meeting with the rebels to convey his solution. Colonel William A. Eddy, then a consultant with
Arabian-American Oil, arranged for a secret meeting outside
Beirut with associates of Saeb Salaam, a former Premier who
directed the anti-government forces. Murphy learned that the

Lebanese were not receiving aid from Syria. Murphy's talks
were successful, for the shooting soon subsided in Beirut.
He also met with other leaders and advised them that the
United States was not just a mere prop for Chamoun's regime. Ultimately, the skillful efforts of the American diplomat produced a settlement on 31 July, when both parties
agreed to hold a special election that would ensure the victory of General Fuad Chehab, a candidate acceptable to both
sides. On the 31st Chehab was elected President by the Lebanese Parliament by a vote of 48 to 0.[59] After bringing
about a solution in Lebanon, Murphy embarked on a tour of
the Middle East to explain the U.S. position.

He visited Jordan, Israel, Iraq, and Egypt. In Iraq
Murphy learned from Kassim that the Iraqi revolution was
domestic in nature and not dominated by Nasser. Kassim
said that he feared that the Americans intended to invade
Iraq. Murphy assured Kassim that this was not the case,
whereupon the Iraqi leader expressed the wish that the two
countries could enjoy better relations. He also asserted the
wish to ship more Iraqi oil to the West.[60] Murphy also met
with Nasser who informed him that the United States had
"played fast and loose with Egypt" on the Aswan Dam project. The Russians, on the other hand, were more understanding.[61]

On the basis of Murphy's reports the United States extended diplomatic recognition to Kassim's regime on 2 August,
and as a result of Murphy's mission the groundwork was laid
for a solution to the Lebanese crisis in the United Nations.
The United Nations convened on 12 August by which time a
number of American troops had already departed Lebanese
shores. On the 13th Eisenhower addressed the General Assembly, presenting a six-point peace plan that Dulles had
drawn up. It called for the dispatch of a U.N. peacekeeping
force to replace American and British forces, which would be
withdrawn. It suggested that new measures be taken to control the influx of arms into the region, and it urged that
propaganda broadcasts should be curtailed.[62] During the following week an all-Arab resolution was introduced in the General Assembly, calling on the Secretary General to bring
about the early withdrawal of American and British forces
and pledging the Arab states to respect each other's integrity.
Both the United States and the Soviet Union supported this
measure, which brought the Lebanese crisis to an end.

Although President Chamoun retained his office until

23 September and the American and British troops remained
in Lebanon and Jordan until October, the crisis had come to
a resolution with Murphy's mediation efforts and the General
Assembly resolution of 21 August. However, the repercussions of the crisis were more lasting for the United States.

An assessment of the American action during the Lebanese crisis indicates a lack of wisdom in dispatching American forces to a country that was fraught with political problems and not faced with Communist subversion.[63] Coming as
it did just a few short years following the Anglo-French landing at Suez, intervention could only redound to the discredit
of the United States. Arab nationalism would not tolerate
what has been termed "gunboat diplomacy." Reaction in the
Arab world was highly unfavorable. However, the dispatch
of American forces to Lebanon did give credibility to the
Eisenhower Doctrine, and the early recognition of Kassim's
government did assuage Arab hard feelings against the United
States.

Although the Eisenhower Doctrine was pressed into use
during the Lebanese crisis, the President and his advisers
were reluctant to do so in the case of the Iraqi revolution,
even though the official Washington reaction was that this incident was brought on by pro-Nasser, Communist forces. It
seems that on 14 February, shortly after the establishment
of the UAR, King Faisal of Iraq and King Hussein of Jordan,
members of the Hashemite dynasty, formed a counterfedera-
tion known as the Arab Union. This action considerably annoyed Nasser who regarded himself as the leader of the Pan-
Arab movement, and it also set in motion a long period of
fraternal strife in the Middle East as Egypt and Iraq contested
for the leadership of the Arab world.

The downfall of Faisal's regime in Iraq and the death
of Premier Nuri al-Said, a veteran politician with a pro-
Western orientation, came as a shock to the Eisenhower administration, which regarded Iraq "as a bulwark of stability
and progress in the region."[64] The President called a high-
level meeting in his office on the morning of the 14th. On
the surface it appeared to be a Nasser-inspired, pro-Communist conspiracy, one that could result in the loss of the Iraqi
oil fields to the West in addition to the loss of a valuable
link in the Baghdad Pact. Allen Dulles, director of the Central Intelligence Agency, reported that the coup was the work
of pro-Nasser elements. He reported that King Saud
wanted the Baghdad Pact powers to intervene in Iraq. But

John Foster Dulles warned that the Russians would probably demonstrate on the Turkish and Iranian borders. He said he had no evidence that pro-Nasser elements were involved. [65]

Ultimately, the United States took action in Lebanon, but decided to accept General Kassim's coup as an accomplished fact. Following his work in Lebanon, Robert Murphy visited Kassim in Baghdad and on the basis of Murphy's report the United States extended recognition to the Kassim regime on 2 August and included an expression of best wishes. [66]

The Iraqi regime had American recognition, but its presence in Baghdad was a blow to Washington. In March 1959 Kassim withdrew officially from the Baghdad Pact and in that same month signed an agreement with the Soviet Union that provided for a twelve-year Soviet credit of $137.5 million. At the same time Kassim ended his military and economic assistance agreements with the United States. [67] Although he had received shipments of military supplies from the Soviets and had now accepted economic assistance, he had no intention of becoming a Soviet satellite. Nor was he a dupe of President Nasser of Egypt, with whom he broke in October. By that time an Arab "cold war" was under way, with Nasser accusing Kassim of following the Soviet Union, a non-Arab power, and Kassim charging Nasser with intervention in Iraq's internal affairs. The Soviets had a dilemma, for they wanted Iraq as a satellite state and also wanted to work closely with the UAR--as evidenced by the Soviet's 1958 agreement to build the Aswan High Dam for Egypt. [68]

To counter the spread of Soviet influence the United States made a new commitment to the Baghdad Pact powers. Having already in March 1957 agreed to participate on the military committees of the Pact, the United States in March 1959 signed a series of separate bilateral pacts with Turkey, Pakistan, and Iran. At the meeting of the Pact Council in London, Secretary of State Dulles pledged to cooperate with the members "for their security and defense. "[69]

By the end of 1958 the American Middle Eastern policy based on the Eisenhower Doctrine was in shambles. Egypt, Syria, and Iraq were openly hostile to the United States, while Lebanon was cool. Only Jordan and Saudi Arabia retained cordial relations with the U.S. The doctrine had proven counter productive, for it was designed to keep the Soviets out of the Middle East, and yet 1958-1959 found Russia the

dominant power in the region.   The doctrine was a unilateral
policy that has been characterized as not being in conformity
with the United Nations definition of collective security.
American policy-makers had simply overestimated Soviet aggression and underestimated Arab nationalism, which regarded Israel as a more formidable threat than Russia.   Coalition diplomacy to bar the entry of the Soviet Union into the
Middle East had failed.[70]   Thus in the latter years of the
Eisenhower administration a new approach was sought to deal
with Middle Eastern problems.

*   *   *   *   *

         By not long after the death of John Foster Dulles in
1959, it was apparent that the defense of the Middle East had
failed.   The United States needed a new approach to Middle
Eastern affairs.   Historians disagree as to whether the new
approach was initiated by the Eisenhower administration or
by the Kennedy administration.   What seems clear is that
President Eisenhower's speech to the United Nations on 13
August 1958 presented a different American view of the Middle East, one that has been characterized as containing the
"outlines of a longer-term approach" to Middle Eastern problems.   The President took cognizance of the surge of Arab
nationalism and of the right of the Arabs to determine their
own future.   He pledged the United States to support the
Arab's right of development and progress.[71]

         The new approach to the Middle East accounted for
rapprochement between the United States and Egypt that saw
the U.S. ship vast quantitites of wheat to feed Nasser's people.   It implied an "even-handed" treatment of Arabs and Israelis.   It envisioned that the United States would stand aloof
from intra-regional quarrels.   It meant that the U.S. would
extend aid to Arab peoples with no strings attached and no
attempt to bind Arab regimes to adhere to an American line.
It involved the discarding of coalition diplomacy, an approach
that had included the establishment of a pro-American group
of states on the periphery of the Soviet Union for the purpose
of containing the Russian thrust toward the Middle East.   It
recognized the practice of "positive neutralism."[72]   However,
a smaller group of historians claim that the change in American foreign policy came with John F. Kennedy's entry into
the White House.   As a sign of this change they point to the
appointment of John Badeau as American ambassador to
Egypt.[73]

At all events, the decade of the 1950s ended the period during which the United States saw the Middle East mainly in terms of the need to defend that region from Soviet incursion.   It also rang down the curtain on the period when American policy-makers equated Arab nationalism and/or neutralism as evidence of a Pro-Russian stance.   The decade of the 1960s would present new challenges.

Chapter 16

THE 1960s: NEW APPROACHES
AND OLD MISCONCEPTIONS

Although the period following the Iraqi coup gave rise
to the need to review American-Middle Eastern policy--a review that resulted in the discard of coalition diplomacy and
the acceptance of Arab nationalism as a bar to the incursion
of the Soviets--nevertheless, the United States leadership continued to view the Middle East through a myopic vision. Although U.S. policy-makers adopted an enlightened view of the
force of Arab nationalism, they continued to perceive the
Arab-Israeli crisis only by the dim light reflected from the
Star of David. Pro-Zionist activities in the United States
continued to raise questions in the minds of Arab leaders as
to the credibility of a new American approach to the Middle
East.

But what is important is that policy-makers in Washington did recognize the validity of Arab nationalism in the
latter days of the Eisenhower years.[1] Some Arab nationalists looked forward, expecting to achieve many of the accomplishments of the West, while others looked backward,
hoping to preserve much that was good in Islam. At all
events, this force made for instability, because new leaders
were arriving on the scene to bring about modernization and
progress to the Arab world.[2] Since Arab nationalism had
been spawned on Western ideas, Western leaders must meet
the Arab nationalist on a basis of equality, since he has used
Western ideas to throw off reactionary regimes and old traditions that stand in the way to modernity.[3] With the emergence of the "new men"--those whose aim it was to erase the
poverty, backwardness, and unsanitary conditions of the region to bring on progress and modernization--a new social
and political and economic element was introduced into the
Middle Eastern picture. The "new men" have many similar
traits and characteristics. Western-educated, reared by the

middle class, schooled in the military, this "new man" is
pragmatic, hoping to achieve progress and modernization.
He is motivated by a sense of mission. The Western concept of private enterprise does not seem to serve his ends.
Arab Socialism is more functional and more beneficial to the
greatest number of people. While he acknowledges the superiority of the West, he also recognizes that there is a
clash between East and West. He readily looks to the Russians for aid, because the Soviet Union is not associated
with Western imperialism as the United States is, with its
long pro-British tradition. Revulsion for the past history
of domination by the West unites many in the Arab world,
and there has developed a fierce resentment of pro-Western
pacts and politically-oriented aid programs.[4]

American diplomacy with the Middle East during the
early 1960s can be described by the terms continuity, impartiality, and the "even hand." The U.S. continued to perceive
the need to defend the Middle East, a perception indicated
by the formation of the Central Treaty Organization (CENTO)
to replace the moribund Baghdad Pact. But U.S. policy-
makers were aware that continuity of the policy of defense
could also be achieved by new tactics based on the premise
that the force of Arab nationalism was a good deterrent to
Soviet expansion. It realized that the "new men" were as
unlikely to bend to the wishes of Washington as to those of
Moscow. In support of this emerging nationalism, the United
States agreed to assist the Arab leaders with economic aid,
hoping to promote progress and orderly change. The U.S.
continued to regard a steady flow of oil to the West as important in the early part of the decade but did not require
large imports of Middle Eastern oil for domestic needs.

American strategists also realized that the new approach to the Arab world must be based on impartiality.
The Cold War between the United States and Russia in the
Middle East was being replaced by what has been called the
"Arab Cold War," a phenomenon of intra-regional strife
among the Arab states after 1958. In the early years of this
episode the United States took an impartial approach to the
Arab nations engaged in the conflict, showing impartiality to
the radical Arab states, such as Egypt, Syria, and Iraq, and
the conservatives, such as Saudi Arabia, Jordan, and Kuwait,
and the neutrals, such as Lebanon and Tunisia.

But toward the middle of the 1960s there occurred a
marked change in U.S.-Middle Eastern policy. CENTO be-

came weaker as Turkey and Iran established closer relations
with Russia, and as Pakistan sought rapprochement with
China in her struggle with India. Toward the end of the decade it became increasingly apparent to American oil experts
that Middle Eastern oil would be required in greater quantities in the future to meet domestic industrial needs. Reli-
ance on the principle of impartiality also dwindled, because
the United States found it more difficult to work with the radical Arab states, notably Egypt, and found it advantageous to
cultivate stronger ties with the more conservative nations
such as Saudi Arabia. [5]

    Inasmuch as the United States' concern with the states
of the Middle East was initially with those of the northern
tier, it seems fitting to discuss first the American response
to nationalism in Turkey, Iran, and Iraq. Then a discussion
of the American reaction to the nationalism of the states of
the Arab core will follow.

                *   *   *   *   *

    American relations with Turkey in the post-war period
have been good, although during the 1960s Turkish nationalism has cooled her ardor toward the United States. In the
years after World War II Turkish nationalism was sufficiently
advanced and the Soviet threat sufficiently real to compel Turkey to request American assistance to cope with the complexi-
ties of the post-war world. A number of factors accounted
for the good reception given the Americans in Turkey. During the interwar era Americans maintained many social, cultural, economic, and technical contacts with Turkey. [6] A
sound diplomatic basis existed between the U.S. and Turkey in
the aftermath of World War II when the Soviets exhibited aggressive tendencies that caused the Turks to want American
aid. Turkey was the recipient of Truman Doctrine assistance,
Marshall Plan aid, Point Four funds, and Mutual Assistance
money, giving her a total of $5 billion in American aid from
1947 to 1971. In addition Turkey cooperated with the United
States in Korea, joined NATO in 1952, signed the Baghdad
Pact in 1955, and received a number of American military
missions. These missions updated the Turkish Army, inaugurated educational programs to erase illiteracy, trained officers, trained Turkish soldiers in weapons usage and military
organization, and also built a system of roads and increased
the capacity of Turkish ports. The U.S. relationship with
Turkey in the years 1947-1959 was sound, because the Turks

realized that U. S. aid and assistance was not only necessary
to Turkish defense but also to her domestic development.[7]
Furthermore, the Turks accepted the Eisenhower Doctrine
and called for U. S. assistance under this doctrine during the
Syrian crisis. Turkish leaders also supported the U. S. landing in Lebanon in 1958.[8] The signing of a Turco-American
treaty of mutual defense paved the way for the introduction
of American intermediate range ballistic missiles into Turkey. To cap it off, the U. S. granted Turkey a loan of
$359 million, with the U. S. donating $234 million, the Organization of European Economic Cooperation $100 million,
and the International Monetary Fund $25 million. These
funds were earmarked for projects to strengthen the Turkish
economy.[9] But times changed.

The government of Adnan Menderes encountered domestic opposition for supporting the Lebanese landing and for
signing the mutual assistance pact with the United States.[10]
Application of the Status of Forces Agreement to U. S. military personnel stationed in Turkey, the uncovering in 1959
of an American black-market ring, and resentment of the af-
fluence of American military and civilian personnel also
made for bad feeling.[11] Another factor causing discontent
was the financial crisis that emerged in 1958. The Turkish
economy experienced a trade deficit of some $200 million.
The Turks had experienced difficulties before, and the U. S.
had encouraged retrenchment and reform. While the U. S.
approved the $359 million loan in 1959, the ouster of the
Menderes regime in the following year left a legacy to the
Turkish people that associated the U. S. government with the
bankrupt condition of the Turkish economy under the Menderes regime.[12] It was not unexpected that a finely-honed
Turkish nationalism took a definite anti-American orientation
during the 1960s. While a number of incidents are involved
in this feeling, the new trend is best seen in the American
involvement in the Cyprus issue.[13]

The Cyprus question did the most damage to Turkish-
American rapport in the 1960s. A British crown colony
since 1878, Cyprus had a large Greek majority, with the
Turks constituting about 20 per cent of the population. A
Greek political movement, nationalistic and chauvinistic in nature, emerged in the 1950s as Cypriots sought to achieve independence from Great Britain and Union (enosis) with Greece.
In 1959 Britain, Greece, and Turkey worked out a compromise whereby Cyprus would become independent on 19 February 1960. The government would be shared proportionate-

ly by Greeks and Turks.   Britain would retain a naval base
on the island, and contingents of Turkish and Greek forces
would also be stationed there.   The Turkish minority would
enjoy special privileges. [14]

The United States inevitably became involved in the
thorny Cyprus question, because Archbishop Makarios, president of the island republic, proposed in 1963 repudiation of
the special privileges for the Turkish residents.   The rise
of hostility between the Greek and Turkish communities
caused the United States to suggest the introduction of NATO
forces into Cyprus to keep peace and to maintain law and order.   Washington was reluctant to intervene directly, as it
did not wish to complicate relations with its NATO partners
Greece and Turkey. [15]   The American caution with respect to
Cyprus was well advised, because one facet of Turkish nationalism in the decade of the 1960s was the desire to annex
Cyprus to Turkey.   After all, Cyprus had been an integral
part of the Ottoman Empire prior to 1878.   As late as December 1963 the United States remained neutral, but shortly
thereafter President Lyndon B. Johnson sent a number of
high-level advisers, including Ambassador Raymond Hare,
Senator J. W. Fulbright, the Arkansas Democrat who chaired
the Senate Foreign Relations Committee, and Under Secretary
of State George Ball to urge upon Ankara and Athens a peaceful settlement acceptable to all parties to the dispute.   But
reaction was immediate and strong.   The Turks construed the
American effort as anti-Turkish, complaining that the Americans were preventing Turkish military intervention while allowing a military build-up among Greek Cypriots who were
equipped with arms and could easily massacre the Turkish
community. [16]   But matters grew worse, and the Turkish ire
rose to fever pitch when on 5 June 1964 President Johnson
wrote to Prime Minister Ismet Inönü, advising that the United
States could not "agree to the use of any United States supplied military equipment for a Turkish intervention in Cyprus
under present circumstances."   Inasmuch as the President also raised doubts that Turkey's NATO allies would intervene
on her behalf in the event that the Soviet Union entered the
dispute, the Turks began to raise questions about the value of
the alliance with the United States.   President Johnson's letter
caused bitter feelings among Turkish officials and led to a
widespread, intense resentment toward the people of the United
States among the Turkish citizenry. [17]   The Turkish government was gravely concerned over the turn of events, and
Turkish Prime Minister Ismet Inönü came to Washington for
conversations in June 1964 to attempt to find some way out of

the impasse.[18]   These talks resulted in President Johnson's
appointment of Dean Acheson to mediate the dispute.

Acheson went to Cyprus in July.   Following a lengthy
fact-finding mission, the former Secretary of State proffered
a rather complex plan to solve the Cypriot problem, which
was fraught with much emotion.   He recommended a union between Cyprus and Greece, a Turkish military installation on
the island, and adequate compensation for all Turks migrating to Turkey.   Acheson's plan proved unacceptable to both
Turks and Greeks, and the mission was a failure.[19]

The Cypriot question continued to plague U. S. - Turkish
relations, for American inability to solve the problem resulted in greater Turkish antipathy toward the United States,
and many Turks began to reassess the value of continuing the
special relationship with the U. S.   Ultimately, President
Johnson sent Cyrus Vance as a personal emissary, to mediate.   He arrived to settle an issue that had caused heated,
anti-American demonstrations and signaled discontent with the
American alliance.   But Vance persevered and was able to
work out an interim agreement.   Greek and Turkish troops
were pulled back and the opposing ethnic vigilante forces
cooled off.[20]

The Cyprus issue was not settled in 1967, and the decade of the 1960s had witnessed the rise of a Turkish nationalism that increasingly challenged the American-Turkish alliance.   Other issues were involved.   The Cuban missile
crisis in 1962 deepened the growing cleavage between the
United States and Turkey, in spite of the fact that President
John F. Kennedy's charismatic qualities made for good feelings otherwise.   During the diplomatic bargaining related to
the crisis, President Kennedy agreed to withdraw American
missiles in Turkey in return for which the Russians would
remove their rockets from Cuba.   The American willingness
to barter defense commitments in Turkey for advantages in
the Western Hemisphere caused many in Turkey to doubt the
quality of the American commitment to Turkey.[21]   Another
factor in the growing gap between the U. S. and Turkey was
the call for greater independence by the radical left in the
universities.   On the extreme left appeared slogans urging
Turkish withdrawal from NATO and an end to the special relationship with the United States.[22]   As the gap between the
U. S. and Turkey grew in response to the sharpening of Turkish nationalism, Ankara agreed to bargain with the Russians.
The understanding with the Soviet Union led to Soviet economic
assistance.

While Ankara's willingness to look to Moscow was a result of the cooling of American-Turkish relations, there were other factors involved in the weakening of these ties. Many Turks took a dim view of the American intervention in the Dominican Republic and in Vietnam. There was also a growing suspicion that the Central Intelligence Agency was actively pursuing American policy objectives in Turkey. As the tide of anti-American sentiment grew, there developed an antipathy toward the American Peace Corps, and the extreme leftist elements saw this group of young Americans as an adjunct to the CIA whose real motives were suspect. So intense was the opposition, that Ankara announced the termination of the work of the Peace Corps in 1966.[23]

The role of the American military was also a cause for dissatisfaction in Ankara. The Turks did not too readily accept American suggestions for the future development of the Turkish military arm during the missile age. Authorities in Ankara also expressed a desire to exercise a greater measure of control over the bilateral relationship between the two countries. For example, the Turks expected to assert the right to abrogate the bilateral pacts upon giving adequate notice. The continued visits of ships of the Sixth Fleet to Turkish ports also proved a strain on relations between Washington and Ankara. Radical students demonstrated against visits of the fleet to Istanbul and Izmir, and eventually American visits were limited to single ships visiting small ports. The American determination to exercise freedom of the seas by regularly sending Sixth Fleet warships through the Turkish Straits also proved to be a bone of contention. In imposing the provisions of the Montreux Convention, the Turks claimed that American vessels carrying anti-aircraft missiles did not fall within the restrictions of the Convention. After 1966 the United States ceased requesting permission for ships armed with missiles to pass through the Straits.[24]

By the mid-1960s another problem had arisen to disturb American-Turkish relations. American officials began trying to deal with the rising drug abuse at home by urging the Turkish government to restrict and then ban the production of opium. At first Ankara was not enthusiastic, but eventually it agreed to reduce the number of provinces where the poppy could be legally cultivated. In 1968 the United States made a $3 million loan to the Turkish government to support research for crops to take the place of the poppy. But by the turn of the decade the opium issue was becoming an acute problem between Washington and Ankara, because

the United States was trying to pressure the Turks into closing down all of the poppy fields. The issue caused a broader cleavage in the summer of 1970 when Congressman Charles
V. Mitchell suggested that the United States impose economic
sanctions on the Turks in order to emphasize its wishes with
respect to the opium problem. Other members of Congress
took up the crusade, arguing that Turkey had received $5
billion in aid from the United States and should therefore
willingly comply with American wishes to curtail poppy culture. Finally, on 18 August 1971, the Turkish Parliament
passed a bill that enforced strict licensing procedures for
poppy cultivation. Eventually, Turkish Prime Minister Nihat
Erim agreed to prohibit the planting of poppies in Turkey after the harvesting of the 1972 crop. The United States, for
its part, agreed to provide $35 million over a three-year
period to compensate the farmers affected by the prohibition
and for the purpose of turning the farmers to the cultivation
of diversified crops. [25]

And so it has been that the United States had had to
adjust its relations with the Turks in the last decade in order
once again to accommodate to a Turkish nationalism that had
adopted an anti-American orientation. This was due in part
to the declining American image, but was also due to the
growing discontent among students and radicals that Turkey
was but a colony of the imperialistic United States. That the
U.S. had bestowed billions in aid on Turkey in the post-war
era was immaterial. But given the growth of nationalism in
the Middle East in the 1960s, perhaps it was only natural
that American-Turkish relations would feel additional strains.

Just as the 1960s witnessed Turkey's turning toward
the Soviet Union as relations with the United States cooled,
so it was that Iran tended to follow a similar pattern. Even
so Iran still retains her age-old apprehension of Soviet intentions, in spite of the Soviet-Iranian rapprochement during the
last decade. But since World War II Iran has looked to the
United States for support against the overweening aspirations
of the British and Russians. Iranian nationalism cultivated
better relations with the United States. But Iran's inability
to obtain the $250 million loan from the U.S. to implement
the Seven-Year Plan in the 1940s was due to Iran's unwillingness to carry out internal political reforms desired by Washington. Eventually, U.S. pressure did bring about reform in
Iran, [26] but in the summer of 1950 an American refusal to
grant financial aid to Iran led to a hardening of relations.
Anti-American sentiment developed and the growth of this

feeling was accompanied by the Shah's signing a trade agreement with the Soviets, an act indicative of a growing rapprochement with Moscow.   But in 1953 the U.S. assumed an
important role in retaining the Shah on his throne, settling
the oil dispute, and extending large-scale economic assistance to Iran.   Since 1954, Iranian-American relations have
enjoyed a greater degree of mutual agreement.[27]   One factor
in the development of better relations is the realization that
Washington has provided $1.1 billion foreign aid between 1945
and 1961, the bulk of which has been for economic assistance.[28] American Point Four aid, grants to cover periodic
balance of payments deficits, and extension of funds to the
Iranian army have also favorably colored Iran's feeling toward the U.S.   The Shah's attitude toward the U.S. has also
been positive because of the participation of the American oil
companies in the Western consortium.[29]

     But at the same time Iran has seen fit to improve re-
lations with Russia, a move that resulted in a 1954 commercial agreement.   During the 1960s Soviet-Iranian relations improved with the signing of a non-aggression pact in return for
Soviet aid for the development of oil, natural gas, industry,
and mining.   At the same time that the U.S. was curtailing
aid programs to Iran, the Shah's government fulfilled some of
its military needs in Moscow.[30]   In a new departure that the
Shah has described as his policy of "positive nationalism,"
the Iranian leader seems to have been motivated by a desire
to obtain Soviet assurance that Russia would surrender the
right of intervention in Iran in exchange for Iranian promises
not to threaten Russian security through her ties with the
United States.   Too, the Shah obviously hoped to play the
game of "neutralism" whereby he could play Russia off against
the United States, thereby maximizing the advantages that
would accrue to Iran.[31]   At all events, the Shah's flirtation
with Russia so alarmed Washington that American policy-
makers agreed to make a bilateral pact committing the United
States to assist Iran in the event of Soviet aggression.[32]   A
free Iran was vital to the economic health of the West.

     As the decade of the 1960s progressed, the Persian
Gulf became a world economic focal point with nations in Eu-
rope and Asia growing increasingly dependent on the oil that
flowed through the Strait of Hormuz.   The United States and
Britain depended upon Iran to preserve stability in the Persian
Gulf.   The Nixon Administration increased arms shipments to
Iran to maintain an equilibrium in and establish an American
sphere in the Gulf, to promote internal political order, and

to reduce the possible growth of Soviet and Chinese influence. [33]

While the United States continued to enjoy good relations with Turkey and Iran, the same cannot be said of the relationship with Iraq, the other northern tier state. Iraq had been a consistently strong supporter of the United States during the period when Nuri al-Said dominated Iraqi politics, but the pro-Western leaning did not continue in the era following the 1958 coup. [34] The rise of nationalism in Iraq during the 1950s found the Iraqi masses restive with Nuri's pro-Western orientation. General Kassim's coup on 14 July 1958 clearly had the support of the Iraqi populace. Kassim proclaimed that the revolution would deliver the country from imperialism. The United States promptly recognized the Kassim regime, but Kassim was his own man. He tried his hand at positive neutralism and obtained a pledge from the Soviet Union for support of a plan of economic development that included aid for dams, railroads, mining operations, and agricultural and industrial projects. [35] He promptly withdrew from the Baghdad Pact and terminated U.S. aid programs. Kassim was neither a pro-Nasser follower nor completely sold on solidarity with Russia. He maintained a constant political battle with pro-Nasser politicians and kept an eye on the strongly pro-Communist element that was growing in Baghdad. Kassim's regime seems to have been the genuine expression of Iraqi nationalism, a force that disliked the West, obtained aid from the Russians, acknowledged the role of Nasser as an Egyptian leader, but would tie her cock boat to no single man-of-war. [36] Kassim took measures to eliminate Communist influence in various trade unions and professional associations. [37] Following the ouster and death of Kassim, the Baathists came to power and carried out a systematic elimination of Communists. Colonel Abdul Salam Aref assumed the presidency, and Iraq turned more pro-Nasser, and Iraqis considered union with Egypt. Arab socialism was much in evidence in the post-Kassim era, for Colonel Aref nationalized many industrial and commercial enterprises, banks, and insurance companies. The public sector took charge of over one-half of the commercial transactions with foreign firms and assumed control of three-fourths of the country's manufacturing. The Soviets continued to provide aid and the United States accepted the new trend in Iraq by supplying loans for economic development. [38]

Iraq's post-1958 era was marked by non-alignment, neutralism, anti-Western sentiment, and a desire to achieve

progress and modernization. Iraq broke old ties with the
U.S. and Britain and sought aid from the Soviets, an act that
expressed the new-found positive neutralism that had come to
the Middle East via Nasser of Egypt.

Indicative of the new U.S. approach to Egypt and to
the new American approach to Arab nationalism in 1959 was
the negotiation of an American-Egyptian agreement for the
sale of $58 million in surplus wheat to Egypt. Highlighting
the growing rapprochement with the West was the World Bank
loan to Nasser in December 1959 to aid in clearing the Suez
Canal. Thus the United States began to clear the air between Cairo and Washington by large-scale agricultural and
economic assistance that tended to counter the growth of
Soviet influence and to make amends for the Eisenhower Doctrine, which had sorely tried American-Egyptian relations.[39]

While Nasser continued to practice his "positive neutralism," which the Eisenhower Administration had come to
accept, he could also count on American assistance to facilitate his success with Arab socialism. American support for
Arab nationalism and socialism amounted to an effort to neutralize the continued increase of Soviet influence in Egypt.
But the rapprochement between Washington and Cairo began
to cool off after 1964.

A number of factors accounted for the growing distance between the U.S. and Egypt. Just as the United States
had opposed Kassim's efforts to annex Kuwait, so it also opposed Nasser's involvement in the Yemen civil war. Civil
war broke out in September 1962 between republican and royalist forces, following a coup by Brigadier Abdulla al Sallal,
commander of the army and a republican leader. Egypt entered the conflict and sent forces to aid the republican cause.
Jordan and Saudi Arabia joined the fray by giving assistance
to the royalist forces. The two monarchical states resented
the rise of Nasser's influence, despite Syria's breaking away
from the UAR in 1961, and felt compelled to support the royalist form of government.

The United States soon became involved in the conflict,
because the Egyptian-Saudi Arabian confrontation might have
resulted in the growth of instability in Saudi Arabia where the
U.S. had large oil interests that could be threatened should
the throne of King Saud be toppled by republican forces.[40]
Jordanian entry into the war might also have resulted in an
unstable situation that might threaten or bring down the pro-

Western government of King Hussein, an eventuality that
would be contrary to American interests. [41] It was in America's interests to curtail the conflict and to restore stability
to the region.   In this, the first Middle Eastern crisis for
the Kennedy administration, the United States extended recognition to the republican government on 19 December and then
set about the task of effecting a disengagement. [42] The Kennedy administration suggested that the U.N. intervene.   Secretary General U Thant sent in Ralph Bunche as a special
mediator, and the U.S. dispatched Ellsworth Bunker to facilitate negotiations.   A withdrawal agreement was signed in
April 1963, but the protagonists continued the conflict.   Withdrawal of UAR forces and cessation of Saudi aid was not completed until late 1967.   The point is that the American inability to bring about an early disengagement soured American-
Egyptian relations. [43]

The end of good feelings between the U.S. and Egypt
was brought on by the Egyptian role in the Yemeni conflict,
the pro-Israeli stance of the administration of President Lyndon B. Johnson, who quite willingly sent substantial amounts
of weapons to Israel to balance the arrival of Soviet arms in
Egypt, and by the growing congressional opposition to continued food shipments to Egypt where Nasser openly denounced
American Middle Eastern policy.   The ending of American aid
to Egypt in 1965 brought to an end the rapprochement begun
by Eisenhower and nurtured by Kennedy. [44]

While the United States incurred criticism from Saudi
Arabia for failing to put pressure on Nasser to withdraw
from Yemen, American relations with Saudi Arabia have generally been good in the post-war era.   President Roosevelt
laid the groundwork for a solid relationship between the
United States and Saudi Arabia by the wartime extension of
Lend-Lease aid to King Ibn Saud.   Cordial relations between
the King and ARAMCO officials reinforced this relationship.

Following the war this relationship matured and Saudi
Arabia fast became the United States' trustworthy ally in the
region.   In 1946 the Saudi government received a $10 million
loan from the Export-Import Bank.   In the following year
Crown Prince Emir Saud visited Washington and received from
President Truman a decoration for meritorious service to the
Allied cause during the war.   In 1949 Washington raised the
American legation in Jidda to the status of an embassy.   In
1951 Point Four technical aid was extended to the Saudi gov-
ernment, and in that same year the two nations moved closer

together by signing a defense agreement that gave the U.S.
an extended lease on the air base at Dhahran in exchange for
the sending of American military aid to Saudi Arabia and
supplying the King's army with a military mission. Saudi
Arabia also qualified for aid under the Mutual Assistance Act
of 1951.[45] During the decade of the 1950s the United States
shipped military equipment to Saudi Arabia, including mech-
anized weapons and jet air planes. In 1957 Washington obtained a renewal of the lease to the Dhahran base, in exchange for a promise to train a Saudi navy. Oddly enough,
King Saud advised Washington in 1961, the year before Saudi
Arabia faced a confrontation with Egypt in Yemen, that the
base lease would not be renewed. This reluctance stemmed
from the growth of Nasser's influence.[46] During the Yemen
conflict the United States extended additional aid to Saudi
Arabia in the form of jet fighter air craft, and an American
military mission trained Saudi paratroopers. Although Washington remained neutral in the conflict, nevertheless good relations continued. During the decade of the 1960s the Saudis
continued to receive large arms shipments from the United
States.[47]

     Other factors entered the good relationship between the
United States and Saudi Arabia. In 1952 an American Point
Four program provided for the reorganization of the Saudi
currency and for the creation of more efficient fiscal procedures in the government. For example, provision was made
for the establishment of an annual budget.[48] The United
States Government had also participated in the negotiations
between ARAMCO and the Saudi Government that led to the
granting of a new concession in 1950 which provided for much
higher revenues for the Saudi government. This appreciable
increase in revenue and ARAMCO's participation in numerous
public works projects increased the harmonious relationship
between the two governments. The Buraimi oasis dispute, involving Saudi Arabia and Great Britain in 1953, did not result
in damage to the good relations between the United States and
Saudi Arabia, even though ARAMCO was a party to the dispute. The U.S. government urged arbitration, but largely remained aloof from the dispute.

     But in the mid-1950s there developed some strain on
American-Saudi relations. When the Eisenhower administration effected the Baghdad Pact in 1955, Saudi Arabia joined
with Egypt and announced her opposition to the pact. Saudi
Arabia promptly associated with Syria and Egypt in the formation of the Damascus Pact. In 1956 the Saudi government

signed with Yemen and Egypt the Jidda Pact.   In 1957 she
made with Egypt, Jordan, and Syria an Arab agreement of
solidarity.   In 1956 Saudi Arabia favored Nasser's nationalization of the Suez Canal.   But after 1956 Saudi Arabia
moved away from rapprochement with Nasser of Egypt, for
the latter's continued vaunting of Arab nationalism and his
willingness to accept a cooperative attitude with the Soviets
was too much for the Saudi government. [49]

In 1957 King Saud made a determined effort to reori-
ent Saudi foreign policy, and, following the enunciation of
the Eisenhower Doctrine, he visited Washington.   The President explained to him the fundamental premises of the doctrine and an agreement was made that extended American aid
to Saudi Arabia, renewed the Dhahran air base lease, and
promised American aid in developing the port of Dammam.
The King returned promptly to the Middle East and there negotiated an informal agreement with Iraq and Jordan.   Saudi
relations with Egypt continued to cool until the break in 1962
over the Yemeni civil war. [50]

During the 1960s the United States continued to show
interest in aiding the Saudis to achieve reform and progress.
With oil royalties growing annually, the Kennedy administration held talks with Prince Faisal in 1962 with a view to encouraging and implementing a program of reform in Saudi
Arabia.   Spurred on by American support, Prince Faisal issued on 6 November a ten-point program, pledging the Saudi
government to carry out political, social, and educational reforms.   Faisal proceeded to bring about a number of reforms within the government.   Fiscal reform, public works
projects, welfare and educational programs were soon forthcoming.   Finally in November 1964 he assumed the throne
and continued the program of reform. [51]

The United States also kept a good relationship with
the other conservative Arab states of Lebanon and Jordan.
Prior to the mid-1950s Jordan had been a British client, receiving subsidies and military aid on a regular basis according to the bilateral pact governing the relations between the
two states.   But all that changed when Britain tried to induce
Jordan to join the Baghdad Pact.   Sir Gerald Templer's mission to Jordan to achieve this goal touched off major riots in
Amman and in other towns.   The capital teemed with an Arab
nationalism that expressed defiance of the Western imperialists, an expression that had definite anti-American overtones.
Britain's overtures to King Hussein were to no avail, for the

King refused to adhere to the pact. In March 1956 the King promptly dismissed General John Bagot Glubb, senior British military adviser. While Jordan did not immediately terminate her alliance with Britain, a definite reorientation of Jordanian foreign policy was not long in the making. The October 1956 elections resulted in a pro-Egyptian victory, and the new leader of the Jordanian government, Suleiman Nabulsi, brought about a new Pan-Arab policy in Jordan. In company with Colonel Ali Abu Nuwar, a pro-Nasser officer, Nabulsi determined to abrogate the alliance with Britain, recognize the Soviet Union and the People's Republic of China, and seek closer identity with Egypt and Syria.[52]

The new departure in Jordanian foreign policy was marked on 19 January 1957 by Jordan's signing the Arab Solidarity agreement with Syria, Egypt, and Saudi Arabia, whereby these three states agreed to pay funds to Jordan to replace the loss of the British subsidy that would soon follow. On 13 February 1957 Britain and Jordan terminated the treaty, which resulted in the immediate departure of British troops and an end to British financial support.[53]

The departure of the British resulted in an increase in Communist political activity, which caused the King to warn Nabulsi about the rapid rate at which Communists were assuming positions in government. This led to a confrontation between the King and the pro-Egyptians who were determined to remove Hussein from his throne. In April the anti-Hussein faction attempted the Zerqa plot to oust Hussein, but the King rallied loyal troops to his cause, dismissed Premier Nabulsi, and soon restored order.[54] Having assured the safety of his regime on 13 April, Hussein dismissed other pro-Communist and pro-Nasser elements in the government and the army. On the 24th of April he appointed a new government. On that day President Eisenhower and Secretary Dulles announced that the integrity of Jordan was vital to American security and dispatched the Sixth Fleet to the Eastern Mediterranean. With the restoration of stability in Jordan, the United States extended $10 million in military aid to the King.[55]

Jordan now pursued a definite pro-Western policy, and American subsidies to Jordan increased, reaching the level of $50 million by 1960. The United States thus assumed the burden of supporting Hussein's pro-Western government, a regime that depended upon the army for support.

But having weathered the April 1957 coup, the King
had to face a similar crisis in 1958 during the Lebanese civil war. That the King now depended totally on the West is
evidenced by the British military occupation during the summer of 1958, an occupation that provided the buttress necessary to bolster a none too stable regime. While the British
troops remained in Jordan for several months following the
July crisis, it was American funds that provided the wherewithal to support the Jordanian Army and maintain order and
stability in the country. One of the benefits of this large outlay of funds was that the United States was able to exert a
restraining influence on the Jordanians who were careful not
to become too involved in the Pan-Arab, anti-Israeli movement.[56]

While the government of King Hussein was almost entirely dependent on the United States for financial assistance,
the government of Lebanon was far more financially stable,
but equally pro-Western. With the important Christian, mer-
cantile element in Lebanese society, there has always been
a pro-Western orientation. However, there is a large Muslim population with a Pan-Arab, pro-Nasser outlook. Thus
Lebanon had a pro-Western leadership but a large and vocal
Pan-Arab following among the populace.

Even after Camille Chamoun assumed the presidency
in 1952 with a platform based on radical reform, Lebanon remained essentially pro-Western in her outlook. Her economic and cultural ties with the West were strong and she received technical assistance from the United States. She received revenues from the TAPLINE, which had its Mediterranean terminus in the Lebanese port of Sidon. She also obtained revenue from the Iraq Petroleum Company, which had
its pipeline outlet on the Mediterranean at Tripoli in northern
Lebanon.

Relations with the United States had long been cordial,
and the American University of Beirut with its history of
service to the country was a large factor in this harmonious
relationship. Not only did Americans live and work in Lebanon, but many Lebanese had migrated to the United States.

In the year when the Baghdad Pact took shape, the
pro-Western government of President Chamoun would like to
have joined in order to obtain much needed military assistance. But pro-Nasser sentiment was strong, and the forces
of Pan-Arabism that infected the Lebanese populace was an

effective barrier to Lebanese adherence to the Pact.

However, in 1957 Lebanon was the only Arab state to accept the Eisenhower Doctrine, and on 16 March 1957 President Chamoun's government signed an agreement with the United States.[57] It was this acceptance of a Western alignment that caused the Pan-Arab elements in Lebanon to begin to take a harder look at Chamoun.   When he announced his intention to amend the constitution to seek re-election, a National Union Front coalesced around Saeb Salam, a former prime minister.   Claiming that his opposition was importing arms and men from Syria to overthrow his regime, Chamoun requested U.S. aid under the Eisenhower Doctrine.   A civil war broke out, and following the Iraqi coup, American military elements landed in Lebanon in July 1958.   Robert Murphy arrived in Beirut and worked out a solution that resulted in the election of President Fuad Chehab, an official acceptable to all parties.

After the creation of the UAR the so-called Arab Cold War erupted in which pro-Nasser forces contended with the followers of General Kassim of Iraq.   Lebanon's government chose to steer a path between the two conflicting groups.   It also followed a policy of non-alignment, and while pro-Western politicians with a bias for the United States could not expect to hold office long, Lebanon still maintained a Western orientation even though there was a growing trade with the Soviet bloc.[58]

If Lebanon was the Arab country that consistently maintained a friendly attitude toward the West, Syria was the nation that had sustained the most xenophobic feeling toward the West during the post-war era.   While directing her antipathy toward the French for the most part, Syrians have also adopted a strong anti-American bias.   Immediately after the conclusion of World War II, the United States embarked on a pro-Zionist policy that greatly antagonized Syria, a country where Arab nationalism was a potent force.   American support for Israel caused Syria to call a halt to the construction of TAPLINE.[59]   Because King Ibn Saud opposed the Greater Syria movement, popular in Syria following the war, and envisioning the union of Lebanon, Syria, Transjordan, Palestine, and Iraq, the United States also opposed this scheme.   This attitude earned the United States ill will in some circles in Syria, but the regime of Colonel Husni Zaim tended to be pro-American, since he, too, opposed the Greater Syria plan.[60]

But in 1949 the Zaim regime was ousted and Syria
turned away from the West, criticizing Washington and re-
nouncing American economic aid and technical assistance.
Thus by the early years of the 1950s Syria's anti-American
slant was most pronounced, and the government of Adid
Shishakli was bitter in its denunciation of the United States.

Syria reviled the Baghdad Pact, and the Eisenhower
Doctrine only exacerbated the anti-American feeling in Syria.
While Egypt enjoyed rapprochement with the United States in
the period after 1959, the same cannot be said of American-
Syrian relations. Syria looked to the Soviets for economic
and military assistance and at the outbreak of the 1967 Arab-
Israeli War, Syria maintained an anti-American posture and
her pro-Soviet stance made her a virtual Russian satellite in
the Middle East.

Perhaps one of the strongest expressions of Arab nationalism in the post-war era has been the Arab League.
Organized in 1945 at Cairo, the Arab League Pact has served
not so much as to create a focal point for Arab political
unity as to create a common bond and common attitude on
political, social, and economic questions. International relations has also interested the Arab League. Its opposition
to the creation of Israel, its strong anti-imperial stance, and
its denunciation of the Baghdad Pact and the Eisenhower Doctrine has tended to flavor the anti-Western posture of the
Arab states with a xenophobic attitude toward the United
States. 61

But if the Arab League has acted to channel Arab
antipathy toward the United States during the post-war era
when Arab nationalism and Pan-Arabism sharpened, the Organization of Petroleum Exporting Countries (OPEC) must also be viewed as a manifestation of Arab nationalism that has
had a profound effect on the United States and on the American oil companies that have concessions in the Middle East.
Organized at Baghdad in September 1960, OPEC, the brainchild of Sheik Abdullah Tariki, the Saudi Arabian Minister of
Petroleum, has caused American oil companies operating in
the Middle East to reconsider their relationship with the host
countries. The original membership of this organization consisted of Iraq, Iran, Kuwait, Saudi Arabia, and Venezuela,
and its members have pledged solidarity to demand stable
prices from the oil companies. This united approach to the
oil question and the revenues derived therefrom, was caused
when Standard Oil of New Jersey made a unilateral cut in

the posted price of oil in 1960, a cut that resulted in a dras-
tic decline in revenues for Saudi Arabia.   The host countries
needed a stable posted price in order to operate fiscally responsible governments, which depend to a large extent on oil
revenues to meet their obligations.   OPEC became a reality
with which the oil companies had to contend.   It voted itself
a budget of £150,000 and established its base of operations
and secretariat in Geneva, Switzerland. [62]

Although the Arab states had organized the Arab
League and OPEC, they remained unable to form a larger
unity and the years just prior to the 1967 Arab-Israeli war
attest to continued intra-regional strife.   But if the Arab nations were not agreed about political unity, they were agreed
about one thing: they all bore antipathy toward Israel.

In the years following the 1956 Arab-Israeli conflict
there was relative peace.   But beginning in early 1965 until
the outbreak of war in June 1967, border activity increased
as Arabs and Israelis launched a series of retaliatory raids.
Arab commando fedayeen had organized themselves into a political group called al-Fatah, which was composed primarily
of Palestinians who hoped to keep alive the Palestinian awareness of the Israelis who had taken their land.   Supported by
Syria, al-Fatah generally operated out of bases in Jordan and
at times from Lebanon.   During 1965 and 1966 Israel
launched raids against Jordan, Lebanon, and Syria to halt the
raids.   The intensity of these conflicts increased, and on 14
July 1966 Syrian and Israeli planes engaged in serial combat.
On 15 August both countries engaged in the Lake Tiberias
skirmish, which saw planes, tanks, artillery, and patrol
boats involved.   In the autumn of 1966 the Israeli-Syrian conflict subsided as both Russia and Egypt restrained the Syrian
government.   But on 13 November Israel launched the largest
reprisal since the 1956 war when Israeli forces attacked the
Jordanian towns of as-Samu, Jimba, and Khirbet Karkay.
This raid intensified Arab hatred, and Jordan took the matter
to the United Nations where Israel was censured.   The United
States voted to censure Israel and sent military aid to bolster
the forces of King Hussein's army.   But Israel disregarded
U.N. advice to exercise restraint.

As 1967 dawned neither the U.N. nor the major powers
seem to have been able to dampen the growing Arab-Israeli
antagonism.   By the spring of that year Arabs and Israelis
were once again drifting toward a war that could involve the
superpowers.   On 7 April took place one of the most serious

border skirmishes to date. This clash involved Israelis and Syrians and saw tanks, artillery, and air planes involved. [63] This action had important consequences, for Arab solidarity increased and there was an outgrowth of pressure on Nasser to stand by Syria with whom he had made an alliance in 1966. [64] The Egyptian leader was in a dilemma, because he had been trying to restrain his Syrian ally, and yet Arabs were urging him to make some concrete move that would indicate solidarity and decisiveness.

Nasser's freedom of action was soon to be restricted, for on 13 May he began to receive reports from diplomatic and intelligence sources that Israel was massing forces on the Syrian border for a strike at the Syrian capital of Damascus to unseat the government. He also learned that the Soviets would support the Syrians. [65] While some historians doubt that there was an actual Israeli build-up sufficiently strong to warrant a Middle Eastern crisis, [66] Nasser was convinced that these reports were true and he acted promptly. With many of his forces tied down in the Yemen conflict, Nasser had to move fast, and he placed his army on full alert on 15 May and on the following day he began to move large numbers of troops to the Sinai region. On the 16th he urged that the United Nations Emergency Forces leave their positions along the demarcation lines in order that Egyptian forces might take over their positions. Ultimately U.N. Secretary General U Thant withdrew all UNEF forces, and Israeli and Egyptian forces were on the brink of war. [67]

Nasser's mobilization did not necessarily mean that he intended to launch a preventive war against Israel. It seems that the Egyptian leader hoped to deter a possible Israeli attack on his Syrian ally to the north. But with UNEF forces withdrawn from Sharm el-Sheikh which overlooks the mouth of the Gulf of Aqaba, Nasser was subjected to additional pressures to prohibit Israeli ships from passing through the Strait of Tiran. On 22 May Nasser complied, and announced that Israeli ships could not pass the Strait of Tiran and that freedom of passage through the Gulf of Aqaba to the Israeli port of Elat was henceforth denied. [68] The Israeli reaction was prompt, and the government which had long regarded closure of the Strait of Tiran as a cassus belli, was subjected to pressure from powerful leaders like Moshe Dayan to take immediate military action to reopen the straits and end the blockade.

The Arabs strongly supported the actions of Nasser,

and in the United Nations Arab delegates accused Israel of
massing troops on the Syrian border.   Israel denied this ac-
cusation.   Soviet bloc delegates declared support for the
Arabs.   Although Russia was loud in her condemnation of Israel in the U. N. , Soviet diplomats privately urged restraint
on both sides. [69]

In the meantime Washington had not been idle.   Following the withdrawal of the UNEF and the movement of
Egyptian forces to the Sinai region, President Lyndon B.
Johnson cabled Prime Minister Levi Eshkol, urging restraint.
While Johnson hoped to use the U. N. to maintain peace, he
nevertheless took steps to restrain Israelis and Egyptians
alike, and on 22 May he cautioned President Nasser to avoid
war. [70]

Following Nasser's 22 May closure of the Straits of
Tiran, the decision-making process moved from the State Department to the White House, and on the 23rd President Johnson made a major policy statement.   Having conferred with
President Eisenhower who advised that his administration had
made a definite commitment to Israel to maintain freedom of
passage through the Gulf of Aqaba, Johnson flatly charged
that Nasser's blockade was a violation of international law.
He said that the United States was "firmly committed to the
support of the political independence" of all nations in the
Middle East and would oppose aggression in the region by any
state. [71]

On the 26th Johnson assured Israeli Foreign Minister
Abba Eban that the United States would stand by its commitment to keep the Strait of Tiran open.   He concluded, saying,
"You can assure the Israeli Cabinet we will pursue vigorously
any and all possible measures to keep the Strait open. "   But
he said that the United States expected to work through the
United Nations to seek out a solution to the problem.   He advised Eban that the United States had conferred with the British and they were considering the possibility of assembling an
international naval force to pass through the Strait.   But he
advised that Congress would have to approve such an action.
Johnson closed with the feeling that Israel would permit the
United States to assume the initiative to find a peaceful solution. [72]

On 31 May the United States introduced in the Security
Council a resolution urging all parties to the dispute to comply with U Thant's appeal to exercise restraint, to abstain

from belligerent actions, and to pursue peace by diplomatic
means. The Arabs opposed this measure and the Soviets rejected it.[73]

   Having failed to achieve success in the U.N., the
United States turned to traditional diplomatic means to accomplish policy objectives. By this time the U.S. had little
credibility with the Arab states who viewed Washington as
pro-Israeli.[74]   But the U.S. policy-makers at the White
House hoped to exercise some measure of restraint on Israel. Israel was cautioned not to attempt to force the blockade, and Washington believed that it had enough time to work
out a solution that would head off the possibility of war.[75]

   In late May the United States, persuaded that there
was some merit to the British suggestion that a multilateral
naval force be assembled to pass through the Strait of Tiran,
worked to assemble such a naval force. Unfortunately, the
European nations did not greet this suggestion with enthusiasm. Congress proved skeptical, and the British proved reluctant.[76] Even though the United States and Britain tried
to work out a compromise solution that would permit neutral
craft to pass through the Gulf carrying goods to Israel, Israel refused to accept this measure. Israelis wanted free passage and no compromise was acceptable.[77]

   By late May the Israelis were skeptical about U.S.
support. They viewed American actions as weak. They felt
isolated from the West. Jordan signed a treaty with Egypt
and Syria on 30 May. Lack of decisive U.S. action and the
feeling of diplomatic isolation determined the Israelis to fight
a preventive war. The re-organized Israeli cabinet voted for
war on 3 June and set the date for the 5th.[78]

   Historians have raised the questions: Why was it not
possible for the United States, Russia, and the United Nations
to maintain peace in June 1967? Did the United States exercise restraint on Israel or did a lack of restraint give Israel
the green light to launch a preventive war? What was Russia's responsibility?

   Historian Fred J. Khouri has suggested that none of
the responsible leaders wanted war, but once the unwanted
cycle or chain of events took place, "Grave miscalculations
... were made by all the principal parties directly and indi-
rectly concerned."[79] This estimate seems to coincide with
that of Nadav Safran who asserted that "a whole series of

miscalculations and misjudgments on the part of all interested
parties" brought on hostilities. [80] Those historians would both
agree that Washington miscalculated Israel's position vis-à-vis
Egypt, Syria, and Jordan. However, there is a consensus
among historians that the United States did attempt to restrain
both Israel and Egypt from using force to settle the issue at
hand. [81] This interpretation would agree with President Johnson's statement that "We threw the full weight of U.S. diplomacy into an effort to forestall war." [82] However, two historians claim American public opinion was so strongly pro-
Israel that the Israelis refused to make concessions. [83]
Looking at the issue from the Arab perspective, one Arab
historian claims that the American press was not only reluctant to criticize Israel, but that a well organized press campaign in the United States gave Israeli leaders freedom of
action. [84] With respect to American public opinion, another
historian viewing the issue from the Arab point of view claims
that only the American radical left seems to have evinced a
pro-Arab stance. This element of American society saw Israel as the aggressor in the Middle East just as it viewed the
United States in a similar role in Southeast Asia. [85]

If President Johnson did try to restrain the parties to
the dispute, one must also raise the question: Did he act de-
cisively to organize a multilateral force as a means of ensuring transit through the Strait of Tiran? Historians seem
to agree that the President was restricted by a Congress
that wanted no involvement in the Middle East that might
equal the American commitment in Vietnam. There seems to
be the feeling that he used the multilateral force approach to
buy time in hopes of working out a solution through traditional diplomatic avenues. [86]

But what can be said of the Russian role in the crisis?
The Soviet Union, more than any other power, had much to
gain by a renewal of the Arab-Israeli war. There is the
view that Russia tried to manufacture a situation that she
could control, one that would enable her to save the tottering
Syrian regime, pose as the champion of the Arabs, and eliminate Western influence in the Middle East. Russia was not
guilty of a conspiracy or plot to start a war, but setting in
motion a chain of events stemming from the report of an Israeli massing on the Syrian border, she miscalculated and
set in motion a diabolic cycle that led to war. [87] It has been
suggested, however, that Israel manufactured a crisis that
maneuvered Nasser into a position that enabled Israel to
launch a preventive war. [88] It has also been argued that

Syria was responsible for provoking an Israeli action, one
that would make an all-out war inevitable and result in an
Arab victory over Israel. [89]

At all events, war came on 5 June 1967 as Israel
launched early morning surprise air attacks on Egyptian airfields and later on those in Iraq, Syria, and Jordan. Israeli
strategy was based on the premise that destruction of Arab
air power would give Israeli ground forces freedom to ma-
neuver. With Arab air power neutralized, Israeli forces
overran in the short space of three days the Gaza Strip,
Sharm el-Sheik, and most of the Sinai Peninsula. The City
of Jerusalem fell as did the West Bank of the Jordan River.
An offensive against Syria gave Israel the strategic Golan
Heights. The Israeli victory was due to the element of surprise, superior military intelligence, control of the air, and
a well-conceived battle plan that completely overwhelmed the
inadequately trained Arabs. [90]

At approximately 8 a. m. on 5 June 1967, Secretary of
Defense Robert McNamara called the President to advise that
the "hot line" between Washington and Moscow had been acti-
vated to handle the Arab-Israeli crisis. [91] McNamara's words
carried an ominous note, because both the United States and
the Soviet Union feared a confrontation in the Middle East
that might result in a nuclear holocaust.

But events moved swiftly as the Israelis accompanied
their blitzkrieg offensive with a propaganda campaign designed
to win American support for their cause. Israel also carried
the issue to the United Nations where at the Security Council
all members seemed to have concurred that a ceasefire resolution would be desirable. But there was a difference of
opinion on the nature of the ceasefire. Russia, supported by
the Arabs, demanded an unconditional ceasefire and withdrawal of Israeli forces to the 5 June lines. The United States
took the Israeli view and demanded that any ceasefire resolution be unconditional. But on 6 June the Russians, only too
aware that the battle was going against the Arabs, decided to
accept a simple ceasefire resolution as an initial step toward
peace. This measure was unanimously approved by the Security Council on the 6th. [92]

The Arab states refused to accept this resolution, for
they wanted sanctions applied against the Israelis for launch-
ing a surprise attack, and they also accused the United States
of supplying Israel with intelligence information. Further,

the Arabs claimed that American carrier-based air craft had
assisted with air strikes. These latter charges were des-
perate measures, designed to bring the Russians in to the
conflict to neutralize the American Sixth Fleet. The charges
were without foundation, and for this reason the Russians did
not act. They did not act because Soviet ships maintained
a constant surveillance on the American naval force and knew
that air strikes were not being launched. [93] But even so, the
charges carried weight, for a number of Arab states broke
diplomatic relations with the United States and they also shut
down oil deliveries to the United States and Britain. Ultimately, they were the losers as revenue dropped and the
United States channeled sources of oil to Europe to make up
the shortfall. But oil was not an effective diplomatic weapon in the 1967 war. [94]

With the passage of Security Council Resolution 234,
demanding ceasefire at 10 p. m. Greenwich Time on 7 June,
first Jordan and then Egypt agreed to a ceasefire. But the
Jordanians and Egyptians claimed that the Israelis were continuing their operations. While Syria had agreed to the
ceasefire on 9 June, fighting continued on the Syrian front
until the 11th.

The Russians reacted sharply. Pressured by the
Arabs who felt left in the lurch by them, the U. S. S. R. broke
relations with Israel and then introduced a resolution in the
Security Council condemning Israel as an aggressor state.
The United States had little alternative but to press Israel
to adhere to the U. N. ceasefire resolution, which she did on
11 June. [95]

In the Security Council there began an effort to effect
a withdrawal. The Soviet Union on 14 June experienced a
setback as the Council voted down a Russian resolution condemning Israel and demanding her withdrawal to the 5 June
lines. The United States opposed this measure, but favored
a withdrawal based on conditions that would establish a viable peace. [96]

In the meantime the Arabs were castigating the United
States for having stalled the realization of a ceasefire in or-
der that Israel might achieve her military objectives. [97]
However, the State Department maintained that the United
States would observe neutrality, but the pro-Israel sentiment
in the United States did give the Israelis encouragement.
But as for the U. S. utilizing delaying tactics in the United

Nations, Arthur Lall claims that there is no truth in this
charge. He does criticize the United States for not calling
on Israel to withdraw beyond the armistice lines. He concluded that the United States demanded more of the losers
than of the winners.[98]

But even so, the high tide of pro-Israeli sentiment
in the United States, the double standard employed by the
American press in reporting the war in such a manner as
to cast a favorable light on the Israelis, and rumors that the
U.S. had aided the Israelis, caused the Arabs to turn to the
Russians, who were clearly the winners in the conflict.
Russia not only flew in and shipped in large quantities of
weapons to replace those lost by the Arabs during the Six
Day War, but she also undertook measures in the United Na-
tions to secure an Israeli withdrawal.[99]

On 19 June Aleksei N. Kosygin, chairman of the Soviet Council of Ministers addressed the General Assembly.
He submitted a resolution that condemned Israel's actions,
urged an immediate Israeli withdrawal to the armistice lines,
and appealed to the U.N. to take measures to put an end to
aggression. Kosygin's speech was lengthy, his resolution
had little chance of passage, and so the Russians then threw
their support behind a Yugoslav resolution that called on the
Israelis to withdraw to the positions they held prior to 5
June.[100] The Yugoslav resolution was unconditional and Israel opposed it as did the United States.

The United States elected to counter the Yugoslav
measure by encouraging several Latin American delegations
to present a resolution calling for withdrawal, but couched
in terms that called for parties to the dispute to end the
state of belligerency, guarantee freedom of transit in international waters, secure a solution to the refugee problem,
and establish demilitarized zones.[101] Since the Arabs
viewed the Yugoslav measure to be in their interests, and
the Israelis approved the Latin American resolution, there
was an impasse in the United Nations. Both were voted upon and defeated.[102]

While the United Nations was in deadlock and offering
little hope for a solution to the problem, President Johnson
continued to work for peace. On 19 June he made his nationally televised Five Great Principles speech. Johnson
urged first, the recognition of the right to national life;
second, justice for the refugees; third, innocent maritime

passage; fourth, limits on the arms race; and fifth, recognition of the political independence and territorial integrity for all nations.[103]

The President could support the Israeli position based on a conditional withdrawal, because the American people overwhelmingly supported Israel in spite of the heavy American investment in Middle Eastern oil. The effort of the Arab states to use oil as a diplomatic tool during the 1967 conflict failed to influence the attitude of the American public toward the Israelis.

Efforts to reach a solution in the United Nations failed and border clashes between Egyptian and Israeli continued on in to 1968, with disastrous results for the Egyptians. Nasser kept the Suez Canal closed, hoping thereby to force the Western countries to compel Israel to accept a peace that was satisfactory to the Arabs. Not only was Egypt a heavy loser in the conflict, but Jordan also sustained losses. Deprived of the fertile lands on the West bank area of the Jordan, and loss of the Old City of Jerusalem, which had provided Jordan with revenue from tourists, King Hussein's government was hard put to meet its obligations.

Although Abdul Nasser's forces were defeated in battle, nevertheless, Arab peoples rallied to his side. The wealthy Arab states with high revenues from oil were quite willing to award grants to Nasser to replace the loss of canal tolls. Kuwait, Saudi Arabia, and Libya provided Nasser with $75 million immediately after the war. Russia supplied badly needed economic and military aid.

While Israel was the victor, the war proved costly. Israel suffered in excess of 3000 casualties. By seizing some additional lands the Israeli government became responsible for caring for some 540,000 Palestinian Arabs, and about 500,000 Jordanians, Egyptians, and Syrians.

Although Israel made considerable gains, her victory did not settle the dispute, but only exacerbated old wounds, hardened Arab antagonisms, and made the task of the United States to find a peaceful solution all the more difficult. The United States in the Arab mind was clearly on the side of Israel. The U.N. Security Council resolution #242 of November 1967, containing in essence the points in President Johnson's 19 June speech, contained items for a peace favor-

able to all parties. The measure provided for free navigation in international waterways, justice for the refugees,
recognition of the sovereignty of all states within secure
borders, and the withdrawal of Israeli forces from all occupied territories. [104]

Not only did United States support the kind of peace
that was acceptable to Israel, but it also adopted a new policy
with respect to arms shipments to Israel. Given the enormous quantity of arms shipped to the Arabs by Russia, the
Johnson administration agreed on 27 December 1968 to ship
50 Phantom F4 jet aircraft to Israel. [105]

Although the United States supported U.N. Resolution
#242 and the efforts of U.N. mediator Gunnar Jarring to
achieve peace in the Middle East, the United States became
increasingly identified with Israel during the period following
the 1967 Arab-Israeli war. Israel came to count on a "special relationship" with the United States. The close identification with Israel was costly to the United States. The U.S.
lost diplomatic influence in the Arab world, which looked
more and more to the Soviet Union. American aid programs
came to a halt. The Arabs looked upon Israel as the pecul-
iar protégé of Washington. Many American private organizations in Arab lands, such as schools and universities, were
compelled to suspend their operations. Oil shipments were
temporarily halted. [106]

The growing American identification with Israel can be
readily understood in terms of widespread public support for
the Israelis. In a democratic polity the formulation of foreign policy must take into consideration the force of public
opinion. The American public's identification with Israel is
based on certain perceptions that have been formed over a
long period of time. These perceptions of Israel have been
shaped by the Zionist apparatus in the United States. [107] The
Zionist apparatus consists of the World Zionist Organization,
which is directed by the Joint Board of Development and Coordination. This board in turn determines the policy of the
Jewish Agency. In 1963 the Senate Foreign Relations Committee investigated the Zionist apparatus and determined that
it was an extension of the Israeli government and designed to
advance Israeli interests among those Jews living in various
nations. [108] Further, that its most important activity was
to create an identity of interests between the United States
and Israel. [109] The committee learned that the United Jewish
Appeal is an integral part of this apparatus and that it col-

lects money in the form of tax-exempt contributions to Israel. The Jewish Agency then funnels part of that money back
into the United States through the American Zionist Council
to avoid registration under the Foreign Agents Registration
Act. In so doing, the Jewish Agency violates the 1951
Treaty of Amity and Commerce between the United States
and Israel. [110] In addition to the aforementioned political
and fund-raising objectives, the apparatus utilizes the media
to condition the American people to accept the propriety of
Israel's internal and external goals and to feel that any criticism of Israel is morally wrong. [111] The apparatus also
employs the media to create a wide tide of sympathy for Israel in order to engineer the public consent to American
support for a policy vis-à-vis Israel harmonious with Israel
goals. By publications, radio, public rallies, meetings,
newspaper advertisements, letter-writing campaigns, the motion picture industry, and television, American Zionist
groups have gained the support of the American Jewish community and contrived a climate of public opinion conducive to
the achievement of Zionist ends. [112]

     This public support is based on a set of perceptions
that view the Israelis as a democratic people who would enjoy the fruits of peace if only the Arabs would leave them
alone to live in the land of Palestine that is rightfully theirs
by virtue of historical tradition.

     These perceptions require close examination. Al-
though American Jews enjoy a secular, non-racial, pluralis-
tic society which guarantees fundamental rights under the
U.S. Constitution, this climate of equality under the law does
not fully obtain in Israel. The Zionist character of Israel
makes for an exclusive state--one in which Jews enjoy many
privileges with respect to land-ownership, housing, education, and jobs. Furthermore, the non-Jewish inhabitants of
Israel suffer discriminatory practices that some observers
have characterized as similar to the South African system of
apartheid. [113] For example, Palestinian Arabs who live in
Israel are subject to residence restrictions and travel and
curfew regulations. They are not allowed to purchase land
held by the Jewish National Fund. They suffer disadvantages
in the acquisition of education, housing, and jobs. The Zionist nature of Israel is based on the Status Law and the
Law of Return which stipulates that Jewish people in the dia-
spora may return to Israel. But these laws exclude the Palestinian Arabs who formerly resided in Palestine and in so
doing they stand in contrast to the American principle of the

separation of church and state, and are wholly unlike the
First Amendment freedoms guaranteed American Jews under
the U.S. Constitution. [114]

The American public is also convinced that the Israelis are entitled to the land of Palestine, failing to realize
that the Palestinian Arabs had inhabited that land for thirteen centuries prior to their dispossession at the time of the
creation of Israel. Furthermore, the American people have
obviously overlooked the fact that the Israelis have violated
the Balfour Declaration and the 1947 U.N. resolution that
partitioned Palestine by denying the Palestinian Arabs the
right of self-determination. The Balfour Declaration ex-
pressly says that the Jewish people will clearly understand
that "nothing shall be done which may prejudice the civil and
religious rights of existing non-Jewish communities in Palestine...."[115] In addition the American populace has forgotten
that the U.N. partition resolution awarded the Jews, with
one-third of the population of Palestine, 56 per cent of the
land. In the hostilities that followed, the Israelis annexed
an additional 28 per cent of the land. There is no Palestinian state as provided by the Balfour Declaration and the
U.N. resolution, and today the Israelis refuse to recognize
the Palestinians as a people entitled to a national existence,
rationalizing this refusal on the grounds that the Palestinians
are little more than a group of terrorists bent on the destruction of Israel.

But this refusal to recognize the Palestinians is inconsistent with Israeli history, because after the 1948 partition
of Palestine went into effect, the Israelis declared their
statehood and used terror to forcibly expel some 750,000
Palestinians from their homes in order to ensure the exclu-
sively Zionist character of Israel. Haganah, the Israeli
army, supported by Jewish terror groups--Irgun and the
Stern Gang--forced the Arabs to flee Haifa, Jaffa, Lydda,
Ramle, Beersheba and Besan. On 11 July 1948 the much-
vaunted Moshe Dayan drove his motorized column into Lydda
shooting up the town and compelling 30,000 Arabs to flee in
terror.[116] But the height of Israeli use of terror came at
the little town of Deir Yassin, where in April 1948 the Stern
Gang deliberately butchered 250 Arab old men, women, and
children and threw their bodies into a well.[117]

To cover the expulsion of the Palestinians, Israeli
leaders concocted the myth that the Palestinians voluntarily
exiled themselves to take up homes in surrounding Arab

states.   But the Israeli government has never once cited a
single bit of direct probative evidence supporting its claim.[118]

The Israeli government has perpetrated a second myth
to cover the sad plight of the Palestinian refugees, arguing
that the governments of the surrounding Arab states have
forced the refugees to remain unsettled, untrained, and un-
employed largely because their governments wanted to hold
the refugees as hostages for political purposes.   This myth
is punctured by Dr. John W. Davis, the commissioner-gener-
al of the United Nations Relief and Works Agency, which su-
pervised the care of the Palestinian refugees in the Arab
countries.   Davis claims the Arab states were largely agrar-
ian, and they simply could not integrate into their already
strained economies the vast influx of refugees.[119]   As there
were in 1970 the large number of some two million Palestinian Arabs--400,000 in the Gaza Strip, 300,000 in Israel, 1.3
million in Jordan, and 150,000 in Lebanon and Syria[120]--it
can be readily understood that the refugee problem is of considerable complexity of shear numbers alone.

While the American public has the view that the Israelis are a peaceloving people who want only to realize their
own destiny but have to remain on the defensive against a hostile Arab world that seeks to destroy Israel, the Arabs perceive Israel as a creature of Western imperialism that aims
to aggrandize itself at the expense of Arab lands.   They view
Zionism as a brand of nineteenth-century nationalism that con-
doned colonialism, and they see the Palestinian Arabs as a
colonial people, deprived of their rightful home and the subjects of Israeli masters.   This perception is held by many
peoples of the Afro-Asian Third World who equate Israel with
South Africa.   The new left also adheres to this view.   Today
Arabs construe Israel as bent upon the creation of a Greater
Israel, stretching from the Sinai to the Euphrates and rationalizing its expansion on the need to accommodate an ever increasing number of immigrants coming in from the Soviet Union.[121]

*   *   *   *   *

Although the United States began the decade of the
1960s with a new approach to the Arab world, one that offered
high hopes of a more meaningful relationship with Arab nations,
the decade closed on a dismal note.   While Washington had
been willing to accommodate to the thrust of Arab nationalism

in the years of the Kennedy administration, Johnson's pro-
Israeli stance antagonized the Arabs and served as a prod to
Arab antagonism toward the U.S.   Clearly the outcome of the
1967 Arab-Israeli conflict was costly to the United States.
Although Arab efforts to effect an oil embargo in 1967 had
few adverse consequences for the United States, with the passage of time and the growing dependence on Middle Eastern
oil a future embargo might have disastrous results for the
American economy.

his successor Richard M. Nixon continued to seek a resolution of the Arab-Israeli dispute. Nixon gave high priority to finding a Middle Eastern settlement, for in his initial press conference on 27 January 1969, he announced: "I believe we need new initiatives and new leadership on the part of the United States in order to cool off the situation in the Mideast. I consider it a powder keg, very explosive. It needs to be defused." Nixon defined his "new initiatives" to mean that the United States would continue to support the Jarring mission, to carry on bilateral and four-power talks in the United Nations, to maintain discussions with Israel and the Arab states, and to offer regional economic assistance.[1] Nixon was as good as his word, and he made a concerted effort early in his first year in office to find a peaceful solution to the Arab-Israeli impasse. In April American and Soviet diplomatic representatives began a series of bilateral talks, with the Russians calling for unconditional Israeli withdrawal from occupied territory, and the United States agreeing to withdrawal only under certain conditions that would ensure Israeli security. These talks were non-productive.[2] On 3 April the U.N. representatives of the United States, Britain, France, and Russia began a series of four-power talks in a search for peace. These conversations endorsed the 22 November Security Council resolution and reaffirmed support for the Jarring mission. Although these exchanges continued through the autumn of 1969, nothing of consequence was achieved.[3] At length Secretary of State William Rogers set forth a series of proposals on 9 December 1969 that became the basis for United States policy toward the Arab-Israeli controversy for the next two years. Rogers asserted that the United States supported the 22 November Security Council resolution and endorsed the efforts of the Jarring peace mission.[4] Four-power and bilateral talks proved unfruitful, and during 1970 conditions along the Suez Canal deteriorated. Incidents of Egyptian-Israeli artillery duels, increased shipments of Soviet military supplies to Egypt, reports of Soviet pilots flying fighter aircraft from Egyptian bases, the placing of Russian anti-aircraft missiles along the western bank of the Suez Canal, and a devastating Israeli raid against Palestinian guerrillas in Lebanon caused the United States great concern.[5]

To prevent the Middle East from erupting into another full-scale war, the United States undertook bilateral talks with President Gamal Abdel Nasser of Egypt in the late spring of 1970. On 25 June Secretary of State Rogers announced that the United States had initiated a new diplomatic

effort to bring about a halt to the "shooting" and a beginning
of talks with Ambassador Jarring along the lines of the 22
November U.N. Resolution. The Secretary suggested that
Israel, Egypt, and Jordan observe a ninety-day ceasefire in
order to conduct the talks. This new peace initiative was
productive.[6] President Nasser announced Egypt's acceptance
of the U.S. proposal on 23 July and Jordan followed suit on
26 July. Israel's affirmative response came on 4 August. A
formal ceasefire went into effect on 7 August,[7] and on 25
August Ambassador Jarring commenced a series of exchanges
between diplomatic agents of Israel, Egypt, and Jordan. But
after the conversations got under way, Israel recalled her
U.N. ambassador, claiming the Egyptians and Russians were
using the ceasefire to build up Egyptian forces along the Suez
Canal. The United States investigated and found that Israel
had also been guilty of a violation. But peace talks were
broken off with the outbreak of civil war in Jordan. The war
was concluded on 27 September and on the 28th President
Nasser died of a heart attack.[8]

After President Anwar Sadat had settled in office and
receovered from the death of his predecessor, the United
States initiated a new diplomatic offensive designed to recom-
mence peace talks. On 28 December 1970, the Israeli government announced its willingness to resume negotiations with
Egypt and Jordan under the direction of Ambassador Jarring.
President Sadat proved agreeable and peace talks were reopened on 5 January 1971.[9] Jarring obtained from Egypt,
Jordan, and Israel agreements to extend the ceasefire. On
8 February Ambassador Jarring delivered aide mémoires to
Egypt and Israel, requiring them to meet certain precondi-
tions leading to a peaceful settlement. Israel was to agree
to withdraw from Egyptian territory, and Egypt was to affirm
that she would make a peace treaty with Israel that would
guarantee her territorial integrity and political sovereignty.[10]
Although Sadat regarded Israel as an imperialist state, intent
on expanding her territorial boundaries and colonizing the newly acquired territory to make it a permanent part of Israel,[11]
he nevertheless proved willing to meet the pre-conditions set
forth by Ambassador Jarring. On 15 February he stated
categorically that Egypt would make peace with Israel, provided Israel withdrew from the occupied territory and agreed
to find a solution to the refugee problem. The Egyptian leader declared that he hoped that the settlement would lead to
the opening of the Suez Canal.[12] Israel replied on 26 February that she would enter negotiations leading to a settlement.
On the matter of withdrawal, Israel asserted that she would

meet this obligation by the evacuation of "Israeli armed
forces from the Israel-U.A.R. ceasefire line to the secure,
recognized and agreed boundaries to be established in the
peace agreement. Israel will not withdraw to the pre-June
5, 1967 lines."[13] To facilitate this new peace initiative, the
United States urged Israel to assume a more flexible posture.
Israel accepted the 22 November United Nations resolution as
a basis for peace and she also agreed to negotiate with Egypt
through Jarring. The United States had every reason to believe during the summer of 1971 to expect a forthcoming
peace settlement.[14] Unfortunately, the new peace initiative
was not fruitful, for, when Joseph Sisco, Assistant Secretary
of State for Middle Eastern Affairs, visited Israel in July,
he learned that Israel would not comply with the terms of the
agreement. Inasmuch as 1972 was an election year, the
United States proved unwilling to continue to apply pressure
to Israel to go ahead with the negotiations. The Nixon administration wanted peace but it also wanted the Jewish vote.
It seems that domestic politics played no small role in producing an impasse on the diplomatic scene.[15]

But Secretary Rogers continued to work for a settlement, and in a speech to the United Nations General Assembly on 4 October 1971, he outlined a six-point plan to effect
an interim agreement on the Suez Canal. First, the Canal
agreement would be the initial step to implement Resolution
242. Second, it was hoped the ceasefire would help "to find
common understanding between the parties on this issue."
Third, that "the most significant aspect of an interim agreement might prove to be that it established the principle of
withdrawal looking to an overall settlement as a fact rather
than as a theory." Fourth, ways must "be found for altering
and strengthening the supervisory mechanisms which have existed in the area for the past two decades." Fifth, arrangements must be made to permit the stationing of Egyptian
forces on the east bank of the Canal. Sixth, the Canal must
be "open to passage for all nations without discrimination."[16]
The 1971 American peace initiative failed to achieve concrete
results. Prime Minister Golda Meir asserted that Rogers'
plan for an interim agreement was merely a reprise of his
1969 scheme, and it "most regrettably, failed to contribute
to the advancement of the special arrangement for the opening of the Suez Canal."[17] With 1972 being an election year,
the Nixon administration could ill-afford to pressure Israel
to accept the Rogers' plan. Ultimately, President Nixon did
receive what amounted to an endorsement by the Israeli ambassador to the United States.[18]

The American effort to bring about peace based on
U. N. Resolution 242 proved futile, but inasmuch as the
United States and the Soviet Union regarded the Middle East
impasse as one that might result in a nuclear Armageddon
between the superpowers, diplomatic agents of the two nations made a new approach. In May 1972 Russia and the
United States arranged a détente. Henry Kissinger, President Nixon's adviser on foreign affairs, and one of the architects of the compacts leading to détente, drafted an agreement
whereby the two powers agreed on 29 May to avoid military
confrontation that would lead to war. On 22 June representatives of the two nations affirmed their willingness to enter
consultation in the event that a situation might arise that
could result in war. In the Middle East the U. S. and the
Soviet Union had cautioned Arabs and Israelis alike to avoid
taking rash actions that might lead to a renewal of hostilities.[19] For her part, the Soviet Union refused to reequip
Egypt with offensive weapons that would enable her to make
a successful crossing of the Suez Canal to carry the war to
Israeli soil. The Russo-American pact to limit the introduction of offensive weapons in the Middle East came at a time
when radicals in the Arab world were calling for Sadat to
end the "no war, no peace" condition. Russia would not accommodate Sadat, because she did not wish to antagonize the
United States and run the risk of rupturing the détente.[20]

Failing to obtain offensive weapons from his Russian
mentor and benefactor, President Sadat ejected his Soviet
military advisers in July 1972, an act that was clearly based
on his disappointment at Russian failure to deliver the requisite arms.[21] Unfortunately, the United States was unable
to capitalize on this turn of events, for the nation was then
involved in a Presidential election. The Nixon administration was reluctant to make a move toward Egypt because of
"constraints of domestic politics." Republicans had high hopes
of winning 40 per cent of the Jewish vote.[22]

Following the election of 1972, President Nixon was
once again in a position to pursue a peace initiative in the
Middle East. In a television interview in November Secretary of State Rogers said, "We are going to do what we can
diplomatically to see if we can get negotiations started between Egypt and Israel...." He reaffirmed American adherence to U. N. Security Council Resolution 242.[23] But prospects for peace in 1973 were unpromising, for Israel was
unwilling to release her grip on the Golan Heights, the Old
City of Jerusalem, the Gaza Strip, the West Bank of the

Jordan, and the Sinai Peninsula. Not only would she not
surrender these parcels of territory, but she took steps to
tighten her grip on them. She colonized and fortified the
Golan Heights, settled the Sinai with Israeli citizens, brought
the agriculture of the West Bank into the Israeli economy,
and erected high-rise buildings in Old Jerusalem.[24] But in
spite of Israeli reluctance to come to terms on the basis of
Resolution 242, the Arabs looked to the United States in 1973,
with Nixon safely assured of another four years in the White
House, to put pressure on Israel to agree to peace. They
had good cause to be optimistic, because by 1973 the energy
crisis was a reality in the United States and the Arabs hoped
that the growing American need for Middle Eastern oil would
result in increased U.S. pressure on Israel.[25] But unfortunately the past record of U.S. identification with Israel was
too strong. American arms shipments to Israel to maintain
the so-called arms balance in the Middle East insulted the
intelligence of Arab radicals. The Arab left raised the question: Who benefitted from this balance? Clearly Israel benefitted, for the continued existence of Israel depended on her
military superiority, a condition that could be maintained only with U.S. support. The continued American identification
with Israel tended to push Arab radicals closer to the Russians and Chinese, a development that could have serious
consequences for the U.S. position in the region of the Persian Gulf.[26]

Stability in the Persian Gulf remains most necessary
to the United States, because 60 per cent of the oil bound for
Western industrial nations passes through the Strait of Hormuz. But with the British withdrawal from the region in
1972, there was a growing restiveness in the Gulf. Iraq opposed Iran's claim to the islands of Abu Musa, Greater
Thumb, and Lesser Thumb, three islands that guarded the
passage through the Strait. Iraq also continued to maintain
her claim to Kuwait, and disputed Iran's claim to the province of Khuzistan. Iran and Saudi Arabia disagreed about oil
exploration rights in the Gulf. Saudi Arabia continued to assert her right to the Buraimi Oasis. And to complicate matters further, the Russians and Chinese entered the picture,
hoping to capitalize on a complex situation to the detriment of
the Western nations.[27] Although Iran had sought closer ties
with Russia in the 1960s and received some $840 million in
economic assistance from the Soviet bloc,[28] she nevertheless
remained apprehensive about the Russians and continued to
look to the U.S. for support. Believing it unwise to attempt
to impose peace on the Gulf states by the resurrection of the

Eisenhower Doctrine, Washington had grown to depend on
Iran to maintain stability in the Persian Gulf. [29] In June
1973 Secretary Rogers announced that shipments of American
arms to Iran "would be a stabilizing influence for peace in
this rich oil-producing area." The United States worked
through CENTO to effect this Persian Gulf policy, and some
$2 billion in sales of Phantom jet air craft, missile systems,
ships, and helicopters was made to implement this policy. [30]
The American utilization of CENTO to accomplish diplomatic
aims in the Gulf demonstrates that the policy of containment,
based on the northern tier concept, was not wholly defunct
in the 1970s. But what is clear is that Iran, while willing
to soften her relationships with the Soviet Union, continues
to look to the United States for economic assistance and security. [31] But Iraq, another northern tier country, is clearly leaning toward the Soviet bloc. In April 1971 she made a
deal with the Soviets whereby Russia would supply $210 mil-
lion to help construct oil facilities, erect hydro-electric stations, and build fertilizer plants. In April 1972 Iraq and
Russia signed a pact of friendship whereby Russia agreed to
market the oil of the IPC, which Iraq nationalized in the summer of 1972. [32] Although Turkey, the third northern tier
state, also had better relations with the Russians in the
1960s during the time that Turco-American relations experienced some difficulty, she nevertheless continues her membership in NATO and adheres to "the primacy of the American connection within that grand alliance." The recipient of
over $5 billion in economic and military assistance from the
U.S. between 1946 and 1971, Turkey seeks to improve her
relations with the Soviet Union and yet maintained her alliance with the West. [33]

    Just as American economic assistance has been neces-
sary to maintain Turkish stability in the 1960s, so it has also been needed to sustain Jordan. Since the 1967 conflict,
the Jordanian economy has been in dire straits. Loss of the
Old City of Jerusalem with its tourist revenue and the West
Bank of the Jordan River, which produced about 40 per cent
of her GNP, has strained King Hussein's financial structure.
Too, his government must now care for an additional 245,000
new Palestinian refugees. [34] The states of Kuwait, Saudi
Arabia, and Libya have provided grants to sustain the Jordanian economy, but Hussein has continually looked to the United
States. Since 1957 when Britain terminated her treaty with
Jordan and ended economic subsidies, the United States has
assumed the burden of maintaining stability in Jordan by economic, military, and diplomatic support. Between 1952 and

1970, the U.S. extended in excess of $500 million in econ-
omic aid and about $200 million in military assistance.[35]
Jordan will continue in all probability to look to the United
States for economic and military aid until she can recover
the Old City of Jerusalem and the West Bank. Further evidence of the American commitment to maintain stability in
Jordan came in September 1970 during the conflict between
Hussein's army and the forces of the Palestinian Liberation
Organization. In what has been characterized as a civil war,
Syria threatened to intervene in behalf of the PLO. Washington reacted quickly, moving elements of the Atlantic Fleet
and the Sixth Fleet to the Eastern Mediterranean. Military
units in the United States and Europe were alerted. Because
the U.S. considered the situation as a threat to Jordanian
political sovereignty, policy-makers in Washington took a
firm stand against Syria's threat to intervene. In a strongly
worded communiqué to the Soviet Union, the U.S. warned
"of the serious consequences which could arise if Syria did
not withdraw." In addition President Nixon extended $10
million in emergency aid to Jordan.[36] On 18 November 1970
he requested Congress to authorize $30 million to nourish
the Jordanian economy, saying that "a stable and viable Jordan is essential if that nation is to make a positive contribution toward working out an enduring peace settlement which
would serve the interests of all nations in the Middle
East."[37]

The American reaction to the Jordanian crisis of 1970
was symptomatic of the growing American concern for a
stable Middle East, because in the period following the 1967
conflict it was becoming more evident that the United States
would require greater amounts of Arab oil to meet domestic
needs. As early as 1968 George Lenczowski warned that
"it would appear that Middle Eastern petroleum could become
a factor of considerably more importance to the United States
in the years ahead...."[38] This prediction was verified in
the summer of 1971 by petroleum expert Walter J. Levy,
who declared that by 1980 the United States would require 21
million barrels of oil per day. Since U.S. production could
not possibly meet the anticipated demand, Levy suggested the
U.S. would need to look to the Middle East to meet its growing demand for oil.[39] But in the spring of 1973 James E.
Akins, a State Department petroleum specialist, sounded an
even more ominous note, warning that by 1980 the United
States would consume some 24 million barrels of oil per day.
Of that amount only one-half would come from domestic
sources, while approximately 35 per cent would come from

the Middle East. [40]   With 300 of 500 billion barrels of proven reserves of oil located in the Middle East, it becomes apparent that the U.S. must reconsider its special relationship with Israel.   King Faisal of Saudi Arabia, a long-time friend of the United States during his life-time, "repeatedly" warned that the pro-Israeli stance taken by the United States will "ultimately drive all Arabs into the Communist camp. . . . "[41] During the year 1972 Arab oil and political officials made numerous threats to use oil to coerce foreign policy of countries in the West, and frequently they mentioned the United States as a prime target. [42]   Not only have the Arab states threatened to use oil as a diplomatic tool, but they now have the power and the organization to make good that threat.   The Organization of Petroleum Exporting Countries has exhibited the ability in the period following the 1967 conflict to use its power. [43]   At the Teheran Conference in February 1971 OPEC members obtained huge increases in revenues from the oil companies. [44]   OPEC officials have raised the question of participation, a method of operation in lieu of nationalization whereby host countries would take part in the management of the oil companies and obtain a percentage of their stock.   In effect, that was an alternative that would tie the interests of the producing countries to those of the oil concerns. [45]   Sheikh Ahmed Zaki Yamani, the Saudi Arabian Minister for Petroleum and a leading light in OPEC, is the strongest advocate of participation as an alternative to nationalization.

   But unfortunately for the oil companies, militant Arabs, led by Sheikh Abdullah Tariki, the founder of OPEC, favor total nationalization.   Tariki's persuasive arguments in favor of nationalization proved fruitful in Algeria, Iraq, and Libya.   Following President Houaria Boumedienne's nationalization of European oil holdings in Algeria, Ahmed Hassan Bakr, President of Iraq, nationalized the Iraq Petroleum Corporation on 1 June 1972.   Shortly thereafter Syria seized IPC's pipeline and terminal. [46]   Bakr's action was followed on 11 June 1973 by Libyan leader Colonel Muammar el-Qaddafi's announcement that Libya was taking over the Bunker Hunt Oil Company of Dallas, Texas, an action that Qaddafi characterized as a "slap in the face" for the pro-Israeli United States. [47]   Some petroleum experts in the West have suggested that the oil-consuming countries unite to present a solid front to OPEC.   But others have discouraged this move, suggesting that such a scheme would be counter productive and lead only to a confrontation that would have disastrous results. [48]   By the summer of 1973 American

Middle Eastern oil companies faced an increasingly militant Arab world. Rising oil prices, participation, and the ever-present threat of nationalization was a constant reality. Some sources predicted that the United States would ultimately have to choose between continued support of Israel or face the possibility of a loss of oil assets in the Arab world.[49] With the threat of an effective embargo added to the above possibilities, oil companies faced the loss of concessionary and accessionary rights. To make matters worse, the summer of 1973 found Arab-Israeli tensions mounting.

On 13 September Israeli sources claimed the destruction of thirteen Syrian air craft in action over Latakiya, while Syrian spokesmen declared that Syrian pilots shot down five Israeli planes. On 18 September Syrian troops had moved up to the ceasefire line in the Golan Heights. During the week prior to the outbreak of hostilities on 6 October, Israeli Premier Golda Meir conversed with Austrian Chancellor Bruno Kreisky in Vienna about Austria's closing Schonau Castle as a transit facility for Jews migrating from Russia to Israel. Simultaneously with these talks, Syrian and Egyptian troops were building up on the ceasefire lines. Just a few days before the resumption of the Arab-Israeli conflict, Russia withdrew some 3000 Soviet military advisers from Syria. Moscow issued no public statement, but the Soviets, possibly aware of the renewal of hostilities, chose to leave the country rather than be associated with Syrian military ventures. Although American and Israeli intelligence units were aware of the Syrian and Egyptian troops concentrations, they were not concerned, for the movements were regarded as routine in nature.[50] But these were not routine troop movements, for on 6 October at 1:50 p.m. Egyptian tanks and infantry forces crossed the Suez Canal at five points and they were accompanied by a Syrian attack in the Golan Heights. The Arab attack did not include air strikes aimed at knocking out Israeli air forces on the ground. Syria committed six divisions of about 100,000 men and approximately 1000 tanks to the battle, while in the south, the Egyptians sent 120,000 men into battle along with approximately 1900 tanks.[51]

The onset of war in the Middle East presented Secretary of State Henry Kissinger with his first major crisis. Caught unawares by the conflict, Kissinger commenced a diplomatic effort to bring about a halt to the conflict and to prevent it from spreading to other sectors of the Middle East. Acting on orders from President Nixon, the Secretary con-

tacted Israeli Foreign Minister Abba Eban and Egyptian Foreign Minister Muhammad al-Zayyat, both of whom were in
New York attending a U.N. General Assembly meeting. After trying in vain to obtain a cessation of the fighting, Kissinger flew to Washington, there to meet with a Special Action Group, a team of advisers consisting of representatives
from the Departments of State and Defense, the Central Intelligence Agency, and the National Security Council.[52] But
the Secretary also made a determined effort to preserve détente with the Soviet Union, and his diplomatic offensive included talks with Anatoliy F. Dobrynin, the Soviet Ambassador. Kissinger's goal was to maintain contact pursuant to
the May 1972 agreement whereby U.S. and Soviet diplomats
agreed to consult in the event that a crisis arose that might
result in confrontation.

In spite of efforts to restrain the combatants, a full-
scale war continued to rage in the Sinai Desert and on the
Golan Heights on Sunday, 7 October. On the Suez front, the
Israelis claimed the destruction of at least nine of the eleven
bridges over which Egyptian forces had crossed the Canal.
But even so, Egyptian sources claimed that 400 tanks had
crossed the Canal to the east bank. On the Golan front Syrian tanks and infantry attacked Israeli forces along the entire
line. Syria had committed about 1000 tanks to the battle.[53]
Unfortunately for the Arab forces seeking to liberate former
Egyptian and Syrian territory, the Israelis enjoyed air superiority on both fronts. Although reliable sources show
that Egypt and Syria had a total of some 946 air craft to 488
for Israel, the Israelis continued to make most effective use
of their air arm to blunt the combined Egyptian-Syrian offensive.[54] While war continued in the Middle East, the
United States continued to seek a peaceful solution, and Robert J. McCloskey, State Department spokesman, reported
that the U.S. had called for a meeting of the U.N. Security
Council. However, he advised that no draft resolution had
been drawn up and it was not the immediate intent of the
U.S. to move for a ceasefire. McCloskey's remarks can be
interpreted to mean that Washington supported a return to the
1967 ceasefire lines.[55] Commenting on U.S. Middle Eastern
policy, Senator J. W. Fulbright, the Arkansas Democrat who
chaired the Senate Foreign Relations Committee, said that
the U.S. should compel Israel to abide by a settlement in
accordance with U.N. Resolution 242. But he said this was
not possible, because Israeli "influence is dominant" in the
Congress.[56] Although continuing to work through the U.N.,
American policy-makers alerted the Sixth Fleet which had

moved to Eastern Mediterranean waters. The President's
Special Action Group continued to meet under the chairman-
ship of Henry Kissinger. The Committee was worried about
the effects of the war on American oil interests in the Middle
East. It had good cause for concern. The Bechtel Corporation, an American construction firm, had only recently signed
$345 million agreement with Egypt to build an oil pipeline
from the Suez to the Mediterranean. On the day that Bechtel signed with Egypt, Radio Baghdad announced that the
Iraqi government had decided to nationalize the interests of
Mobil and Exxon Oil Companies because "aggression in the
Arab world necessitates directing a blow at American interests in the Arab nation."[57] The tenuous position of American oil concerns in the Middle East caused action in another
quarter. A Senate-House conference committee announced
that it was ready to report out a bill that would make possible the beginning of construction on the 800-mile Alaskan
pipeline from Prudhoe Bay to the port of Valdez.

The 8th of October found the war escalating in the
Middle East, but Lieutenant General David Elazar, the Israeli
Chief of Staff, declared that Israel had mobilized her armored
reserves, that the initiative was now in Israeli hands, and
that "we shall break and destroy completely all of the attacking forces."[58] Elazar asserted that Israel would not respect
the ceasefire lines in its pursuit of enemy forces. On the
Suez front the Egyptians had established three bridgeheads,
one near Kantara, a second in the proximity of Ismailia, and
a third near the town of Suez in the south. The Egyptians
had placed 400 tanks across the Canal but were giving them
little air cover. In the Golan Heights sector the Syrians had
moved up about 1,000 tanks and had penetrated the heavily
fortified Israeli line in three places. But as on the Suez
front, the Israelis commanded the air space, but this advantage was not without loss. Reports from the battle front advised that 40 to 50 Israeli jets had been shot down by missiles launched from the ground.[59] In the meantime, the
United States called for a ceasefire, urging Security Council
members to support this measure that would require a return
to the lines that were in effect before the outbreak of hostilities. U.S. Ambassador John A. Scali set forth three principles upon which to work out a settlement. First, there was
to be a halt to all military operations. Second, parties to
the conflict should resolve their differences at the peace table.
Third, U.N. Resolution 242 should be used as a basis for establishing a peaceful settlement.[60] The State Department declared that the United States was in agreement with China and

the Soviet Union that the conflict should not spread beyond
the region.   Department spokesman Robert McCloskey asserted that the United States was in contact with the Soviet
Union and the two nations agreed that all precautions should
be taken to avoid military confrontation in accordance with
the principles set down in the 29 May 1972 agreement. [61]
While the U.S. and Russia were in accord, there were additional indications that the conflict would adversely affect the
Western industrial powers.   Representatives of the Persian
Gulf oil exporting countries met in Vienna, and Abderrahman
Khene, the secretary general of the Organization of Petroleum Exporting Countries, announced that members were in
agreement that the Gulf nations should ask for a rise in the
price of crude oil. [62]

        The war continued unabated on 9 October as Egyptian
forces compelled the Israelis to abandon the Bar-Lev defense
line on the east bank of the Suez Canal.   Although the Israelis claimed to have destroyed a large number of Egyptian
tanks that had crossed the Canal, Egypt continued to send
men and supplies across the waterway.   U.S. observers estimated that Egypt had about 50,000 men and 500 tanks on the
east bank of the Canal.   Egyptian sources claimed that the
Israeli counterattack in the Sinai had been effectively repelled. [63]   But on the Syrian front Israeli fighter bombers
struck at Damascus and at other targets deep inside Syria.
Israeli planes bombed the Soviet cultural center in the Syrian
capital, although Israelis advised that it was their intention
to hit the Syrian Defense Ministry.   Israel also claimed that
the Syrian attack had been broken in the Golan. [64]   While
the war took its bloody course, diplomats were no closer to
a solution, for the U.N. Security Council was the scene of
bitter exchanges between Egyptian, Syrian, and Israeli representatives.   Syria and Egypt denounced the Israeli air raids
that had killed many civilians, and Soviet Ambassador Jacob
Malik accused the Israelis of committing "a barbaric gangster
act."   Nixon administration sources announced that the United
States was unable to arrange a ceasefire at the U.N. and that
such an event would probably have to await a decisive turn
of events on the battlefield.   It was apparent that neither side
was willing to accept a ceasefire.   Meanwhile, Arab solidarity was fast becoming a reality as Kuwait called for an immediate meeting of Arab oil ministers to discuss the possibility of using oil as a diplomatic weapon.   It was an ominous
note, for the United States was becoming more dependent on
Arab oil to meet its burgeoning domestic needs--a reality
that was brought home by John A. Love, director of the

White House Energy Policy Office. Love advised members
of the House of Representatives that the United States faced
the possibility of fuel rationing for a period of five years. [65]

     The fifth day of the war, 10 October, found Egyptian
troops, tanks, and armored vehicles continuing to cross the
Canal without a challenge from the Israelis. Egyptian
sources asserted that tank battles were taking place nine to
ten miles from the Canal on the east bank. But on the
Golan front the Syrian advance had not only been halted, but
Israelis recaptured the Golan and drove their Syrian adver-
saries beyond the ceasefire line. But to sustain their Syrian
neighbors, Iraq declared that it was committing its air force
to the war and was sending 16,000 Iraqi troops and 100 tanks
to the Golan front. [66] The war threatened to escalate further,
for King Hussein of Jordan declared that he was calling up
Jordan's reserves and mobilizing the country's resources for
a war effort. Jordan's 70,000-man army is reputedly the
best trained of the Arab forces. Another gloomy note was
sounded when Washington officials announced that the Russians were air-lifting supplies to both Syria and Egypt. To
further complicate the situation, Soviet and American naval
movements were reported in the Mediterranean. A Russian
cruiser and two guided missile destroyers passed through the
Dardanelles, and major elements of the U.S. Sixth Fleet
steamed into the Eastern Mediterranean. But in spite of
these naval movements, the Soviet-American détente continued in force, even though the Russians supported Syria and
Egypt with military supplies and despite the fact that they
probably knew of the impending attack when they withdrew
their military personnel from Syria just prior to the attack
and failed to advise the U.S. Russian support of the Arabs
and reluctance to advise the U.S. of the probable outbreak
of war constituted violations of the 1972 agreements signed
at Moscow by American and Soviet diplomatic agents. To
meet the Russian arms replenishment, Senator Henry Jackson, the pro-Israeli Democratic senator from Washington,
had already urged that the U.S. supply arms to Israel. But
even then the United States was giving consideration to re-
supplying the Israeli air force which had suffered high losses
to Egyptian missiles. [67] Meanwhile on another quarter of the
home front, officials in Washington were growing concerned
about the effects of the war on the American energy situation. Egypt urged King Faisal of Saudi Arabia to halt oil
production at American wells if the United States agreed to
replace Israeli losses. Faisal agreed and sent a warning to
Washington, asserting that Saudi Arabi would embargo oil

shipments to the United States if American supplies were
sent to Israel. Secretary of Transportation Claude S. Brin-
egar advised that "even if a few tanker loads of fuel get
held up," the U.S. might "have to go to a rationing program."[68]

The 11th of October was uneventful on the battlefront.
Israeli and Egyptian jets engaged in dog fights over the Suez
Canal near Kantara. But the war on the ground was like a
"Sitzkrieg." In the Golan Heights Israeli forces penetrated
approximately six miles beyond the 1967 ceasefire line into
Syrian territory. Israeli planes bombed and strafed eight
Syrian airfields. Syrian and Israeli air craft engaged in
aerial combat over the Golan, and naval elements of the two
combatants fought along the Mediterranean coastline. In
Washington Secretary Kissinger contacted Soviet Ambassador
Anatoliy F. Dobrynin, urging Moscow to restrain her arms
build-up in the Middle East. While urging caution upon the
Russians, the U.S. was considering arms support to Israel
to cover plane and tank losses.[69]

The fourth Middle Eastern conflict continued apace on
12 October. On the Suez front Egyptians maintained a steady
build-up of forces on the east bank of the Canal, preparatory
for the anticipated Israeli counterthrust. Egyptian ground
forces continued to use surface-to-air missiles with great effect, and Cairo claimed the downing of 15 Israeli planes.
Heavy fighting continued on the Syrian front, where Israelis
continued to penetrate in an effort to place Damascus under
artillery fire. On the diplomatic front little of note was accomplished. Although the Security Council had met four
times in the first week of the 1973 conflict little of consequence was forthcoming. The main cause for the U.N.'s inability to end the war seems to be that neither side favored
a cessation of hostilities until a decisive victory had been
achieved on the field of battle. The U.N. had been the scene
of heated debate, and on the 10th the nonaligned states, unable to introduce a ceasefire resolution, expressed their collective support for Egypt and Syria and demanded an immediate Israeli troop withdrawal from the occupied territories,
precursory to seeking a peace settlement in the Middle
East.[70] On that morning Henry Kissinger declared at his
initial news conference as Secretary of State that it was the
intention of the United States to end hostilities and preserve
peace. He noted that the Soviet arms build-up had been
"fairly substantial" but yet "moderate" and said that Russian
behavior in the present conflict was much less provocative

than in the 1967 crisis. He affirmed that "the United States
has a traditional friendship with Israel" and that it would
maintain that condition in the present crisis. He observed
that the U.S. has "an ongoing military relationship with Israel" and that American military planners were engaged in
discussions with Israeli leaders. He said that the U.S. was
perfectly aware of Arab views on the conflict.[71] Kissinger
was saying that the United States was giving consideration
to the dispatch of U.S. logistical support to Israel even
though Arab leaders called for an oil embargo in the event
that this support was forthcoming. Given the growing Ameri-
ican energy crisis and the burgeoning American need for
Arab oil, these were brave words indeed. It should be clear
that U.S. aid for Israel was based on factors other than considerations of the national interest. American economic
prosperity required imports of Arab oil to meet the needs of
the American populace and industry. To render support to
Israel and court the disastrous consequences of an Arab oil
embargo begs the question: Did the Nixon administration
view the Middle Eastern crisis in terms of domestic politics
or in terms of the American interest? Coincidentally, Saudi
Arabia's King Faisal conferred with Egyptian President Sadat,
and sent an urgent warning to the United States to the effect
that American aid for Israel would bring about an Arab oil
cutoff.[72] This communiqué was but a harbinger of things to
come in a conflict that continued to rage in the Middle East.

    Heavy tank battles marred the sands of the Sinai Des-
ert on 13 October as Egyptian forces tried to break through
the Israeli line. The day was also punctuated with heavy
artillery duels. Egyptian units had driven the last Israeli
stronghold from the east bank of the Canal. Cairo disclosed
that Egyptian troops did not seek territorial gains, but had
set for themselves the goal the infliction of losses on the Israelis and the creation of a situation from which to begin new
negotiations toward a settlement. On the Golan front Israel
claimed the destruction of an Iraqi division along with approximately 80 tanks and other armored vehicles. Jordan
backed its Arab allies by a mobilization on the 13th. King
Hussein's 70,000 soldiers posed a distinct threat at the belly
of Israel. Jordan became the second pro-Western Arab state
to enter the picture, for earlier Saudi Arabian contingents
had joined the fray in Syria. But even with the assistance of
Iraqi and Saudi units and the promises of help from Jordan,
Israeli military elements pushed ever closer to Damascus.
Israeli artillery shells fell on the outskirts of the Syrian capital. While the battles continued, State Department person-

nel feared the war could destroy the détente with the Soviet
Union. Secretary Kissinger announced at his press conference on the 12th that a continuation of the conflict could possibly involve the two superpowers. For the reason Kissinger
had been in close touch with Soviet Ambassador Dobrynin
since the outbreak of hostilities. [73] He also met with Israeli
Foreign Minister Abba Eban and advised that the U. S. , along
with Russia, would now work for a ceasefire in place on both
the Suez and Golan fronts. He said the U. S. would honor
its military logistical relationship with Israel, but he warned
that the conflict should not be allowed to go on. [74] At a
press briefing, State Department spokesman Robert McCloskey denied as "false ... mischievous and groundless reports"
that the United States was involved militarily in the war.
"There is no truth whatsoever" to these rumors, McCloskey
declared. [75] The rumors of American participation had emanated from Cairo, where on the 13th Egyptian President Sadat urged King Faisal to use his "oil weapon" against the
United States. The King complied and sent his foreign minister Omar Al-Saqqaf to Washington with a warning that continued
American aid to Israel could result in an embargo on Arab
oil to the United States. At the same time President Sadat
sent a representative to visit the oil-producing countries of
Kuwait, Bahrain, Qatar, and Abu Dhabi, urging that the
Arabs employ oil as a diplomatic foil. Sadat also sent messages to Arab leaders in Libya, Tunisia, Algeria, and Morocco. The rising Arab pressure on King Faisal placed the
Saudi monarch in a dilemma. He had long been a loyal
friend of the United States. He had repeatedly warned that
the American pro-Israeli policy would drive the Arab world
into the Soviet camp. He disliked placing an embargo on
oil to the United States. Yet he had to satisfy the Arabs who
viewed oil as a legitimate means of accomplishing diplomatic
goals. That oil was an efficient diplomatic arms is evidenced by the oil squeeze placed on Europe by the shutdown
of the IPC oil terminal at Banias, Syria, and with a reduction in the flow of TAPLINE's flow from Saudi Arabia to the
Lebanese port of Sidon. [76]

On 14 October the focus of the Middle Eastern conflict
shifted from Syria to the Sinai Desert where the Egyptians
launched a large-scale armored offensive all along the hun-
dred-mile front east of the Suez. The Israelis repelled this
all-out attack, and many officials in Washington regarded this
battle as being decisive. Its outcome would result in an
early ceasefire. But just as the Israelis had blunted the
Egyptian offensive in the Sinai, so the Syrians slowed down

the Israeli advance on the Syrian front. The Syrian retreat
was not pell-mell, and its orderly retirement forced the Israelis to fight for every inch of ground taken. But even so,
the Israelis could now claim to hold a salient beyond the
1967 ceasefire line that was at least 15 miles wide and 20
miles deep. But to beef up the Syrian forces, Iraq's President Ahmed Hassan Bakr disclosed that Iraqi forces would
continue to support the Syrians. Western military observers
estimated that Iraq had dispatched some 12,000 troops, 200
tanks, and two squadrons of MIG-21 jet fighters to Syria.[77]
This announcement caused Senator Henry M. Jackson to criticize Secretary Kissinger for "withholding from Israel the
arms she needs to defend herself," while the Soviets continue
to nourish the Egyptian and Syrian forces with weapons.
Jackson seems to have overlooked the fact that the U.S. had
been shipping bombs, missiles, artillery shells, and other
equipment via Israeli commercial airliners and chartered
American planes. Talks of arms replenishment caused Kuwait to call for a meeting of the Organization of Arab Petroleum Exporting Countries for 16 October to discuss the use of
oil to coerce the United States.[78]

By 15 October military activity on the Sinai front had
subsided considerably as the Egyptian attack was halted by
Israeli air, armored, and infantry forces. The Egyptians
had aimed their offensive at the strategic Gidi and Mitla
passes, hoping to achieve a breakout into the Sinai Desert,
which is ideal terrain for the deployment of tanks and other
armored vehicles. Israeli defensive forces had knocked out
some 116 of 200 Egyptian tanks. Meanwhile, on the Syrian
front, Israel maintained a slow advance, compelling the Iraqi
to retreat. But heavy fighting continued around the Syrian
town of Sasa, which overlooks the road to Damascus. Official Washington disclosed on the 15th that the U.S. was sending approximately 150 M-60 tanks and 16 Phantom jets to Israel. The tanks would help replace Israeli tank losses which
were estimated at between 550 and 650. The planes would
aid the Israeli air force which had suffered the destruction
of about 100 planes. Speaking for the State Department, Robert J. McCloskey declared that the United States' resupply
of Israel aimed to restore the arms balance to the Middle
East.[79]

Inasmuch as the Arab states were meeting on the 17th
to discuss the imposition of an oil embargo on the United
States, it would seem that the American extension of military
aid to Israel was badly timed. Given the increasing Ameri-

can dependence on Arab oil, military assistance could hardly
be described as fulfilling national interests. Using the need
to sustain an "arms balance" as a rationale for the dispatch
of aid to Israel has been interpreted as a euphemism for
maintaining Israeli military superiority. While the United
States continued an arms airlift to Israel, the Nixon administration urged the Russians to use restraint in sending military equipment to the Syrians and Egyptians. At the same
time Washington protested the Yugoslavian government's decision to permit Soviet airplanes carrying equipment to Syria
and Egypt the right of passage through Yugoslav air
space. [80]

On 16 October Israeli Prime Minister Golda Meir
stated that Israeli armored forces were operating on the west
bank of the Suez. The Israeli task force struck at Egyptian
missile and artillery batteries. The task force was operating in the central sector near Ismailia. The SA-6 surface-
to-air missiles that the Egyptians had used so effectively
against the Israelis were deployed north and south of Ismailia.
These missiles had enabled the Egyptians to neutralize Israeli jets that might otherwise have interfered with the movement of Egyptian forces across the Canal. Israeli jets also
bombed targets in the Nile Delta, some 100 miles north of
Cairo, while at the same time heavy tank battles raged in
the Sinai. [81] While the Israelis were carrying the war to
Egyptian soil in the south, Israeli units repelled three Syrian
and Iraqi counterattacks in the northern sector. Israeli Defense Minister Moshe Dayan announced that Israel had
achieved two of its three objectives on the Syrian front. First,
Israeli forces had pushed the Syrians off of the Golan Heights.
Second, they had compelled them to retreat well within Syrian territory. He said the third objective was to fight a war
of attrition and destroy large segments of the Syrian army.
Surprisingly enough, while Israeli units on the Syrian front
had encountered Iraqi forces, they had not yet been opposed
by Jordanian troops. Most of the heavy fighting on the Syrian front was taking place near the strategic town of Sasa.

That the war was entering the stage when political
leaders were willing to discuss ceasefire was indicated by
President Sadat's announcement that Egypt was ready to seek
a lasting peace based on Israeli withdrawal from all territories occupied in the 1967 war. His declaration came in an
open letter to President Nixon given in an address to the
Egyptian Parliament. At the same time he asserted that
Egypt possessed missiles capable of striking at the very heart

of Israel. While Sadat was voicing his views in Cairo, President Nixon met with foreign ministers of Saudi Arabia, Kuwait, Algeria, and Morocco to hear Arab protests of U.S. arms shipments to Israel. Doubtless, the ministers carried a threat to embargo oil shipments to the United States should arms assistance to Israel continue. However, State Department official Robert J. McCloskey announced that the United States would continue to meet Israel's military needs regardless of the consequences. [82]   At the same time, President Nixon's White House adviser Melvin R. Laird declared that the continued Soviet arms replenishment in the Middle East jeopardized the détente. But officials at the State Department viewed the build-up as moderate and refused to take a hard line that would jeopardize diplomatic relations with the Soviet Union. McCloskey said that the United States was in constand touch with Russia. [83]   Although maintaining close contact with officials in the Kremlin, the State Department announced that the American resupply of Israel was going ahead. Replenishment of the Israeli army had been delayed by repeated warnings by American oil company officials, who said that the Arabs would embargo oil shipments to the United States. Israeli Ambassador Simca Dinitz delivered a message in Washington from Prime Minister Golda Meir, declaring that Israel could lose the war unless the United States undertook immediate steps to send arms to Israel. Although American C-140 and C-5A transport planes were denied landing rights in Britain and Spain, the large aircraft were lifting ammunition and tanks to replace Israeli losses, estimated at more than one-third of an inventory of 1800 tanks. Phantom fighters were being flown direct to Israel to replace about one-third of Israel's 488 military air craft which had been shot down by missiles. [84]   The decision to resupply Israel had the support of the U.S. Senate, but senators warned against the dispatch of American military units to the war zone. Senate Majority Leader Mike Mansfield, the Montana Democrat, declared that he would agree to the U.S. maintaining an arms balance in the Middle East, but said, "I do not believe that we should become involved with American forces anywhere except as our national interests and security are at stake. One Vietnam is one Vietnam too many." [85] American support of Israel was accompanied by the sending of additional U.S. warships to the Eastern Mediterranean. The build-up of the Sixth Fleet was an effort to match the Soviet task force in the Mediterranean, which numbered approximately 70 vessels. But American backing for Israel was not without adverse results, for the representatives of the Arab nations met in Kuwait to discuss an embargo on oil to

the U.S. to modify American support of Israel. Algerian
Oil Minister Belaid Abdelsalam issued a statement, saying
that the Western nations must be made to recognize the
"weight of the Arab world."[86]

As the Arab oil ministers met in Kuwait on 17 October, one of the largest tank battles of the war was being
fought on the east bank of the Suez opposite the city of Ismailia. Israeli forces reduced the Egyptian bridgehead,
which had been five miles deep, but Egypt continued to maintain some 1000 tanks on the east bank, chiefly around Kantara in the north and near the town of Suez in the south.
In spite of heavy losses the Egyptian army units fought with a
fervor and an expertise not usually associated with the Egyptian military arm. In addition to the heavy tank warfare
raging on the north-south axis of the east-bank--a tank battle
compared to that of El Alamein in World War II--the Israelis continued to move forward their task force on the west
bank of the Canal. But on the Syrian front intense artillery
fire from Syrian batteries drove Israeli forces back from the
fortified positions around Sasa. The intensity of the war in
this area seems to have subsided somewhat as the Israelis
concentrated their major efforts on the Suez front. Syrian
troops held a second line of defense, centered on the town of
Sasa, 23 miles from Damascus. On the diplomatic scene,
Israeli Foreign Minister Abba Eban rejected Egyptian President Sadat's formula for a ceasefire. Eban said the ceasefire negotiations must be separated from the final peace settlement. The United States and Russia increased efforts to
obtain a standstill ceasefire that would be linked to a final
settlement. Secretary Kissinger remained in touch with Soviet Ambassador Dobrynin. Although there was no solution
that had found perfect agreement with both the Americans and
the Soviets, Robert J. McCloskey said the possibility of a
settlement was at hand.[87] There was also an indication that
relations between the United States and the Arab nations were
improving, for both President Nixon and Secretary Kissinger
talked with the foreign ministers of Algeria, Morocco, Kuwait, and Saudi Arabia. Speaking for the visiting dignitaries,
Saudi Foreign Minister Omar al Saqqaf said: "We ... have
been received well and we had a very good exchange of views
and discussions with His Excellency, Mr. Nixon." He said
that the conversations were "fruitful" and that he reposed
faith in the Americans to bring about a peace.[88] Simultaneous with the U.S.-Arab talks in Washington was the announcement of the Arab oil ministers to cut back oil shipments to
U.S. companies at the rate of 5 per cent a month until the

Israelis withdrew from the Arab lands they had occupied in
the 1967 war.   They also agreed to a 17 per cent increase
in the posted price of oil, from about $3 per barrel to
$3.65.   Although Treasury Department officials said the Mid-
dle East oil producers did not have the power to hurt the
American economy severely, the U.S. imported 1.5 to 2
million barrels of Middle Eastern oil per day.   While the
curtailment of oil would not damage the American economy
severely, it would have an adverse effect on Europe and Japan.   But as events were to show, the Arab embargo did
have a deleterious effect on the American economy. [89]   Aware
that the Arab cutback could have serious consequences for
the American people, a House-Senate conference committee
agreed on a bill to pave the way for American oil firms to
commence work on the Alaska oil pipeline.

Activity on the Syrian front remained static on 18 October, but the war took a dramatic turn on the Suez front as
Israeli tanks crossed the Canal in force.   The Israelis
pierced the Egyptian lines on the east bank of the Canal between Ismailia and the Bitter Lakes.   They had thrown a
pontoon bridge across the Canal, and more than 40 tanks
crossed quickly to the west bank.   Not only had all of the
Egyptian bridges in the center of the Suez sector been put
out of action, but Israeli Defense Minister Dayan asserted
that the Israelis had seized the initiative in the Suez region.
He said that Israel was confident of victory against the Egyptians.   As the war escalated, Secretary Kissinger announced
to the cabinet that the United States and Russia were seeking
a formula for a ceasefire linked to a final settlement.   He
noted: "We are engaged in very serious, very open-minded
consultations with many countries....   We believe that there
exists an opportunity for a decent and just settlement fair to
all parties, which must be reached first by bringing about an
end to all hostilities...."[90]   Meanwhile, on Capitol Hill in
excess of two-thirds of the Senate and more than half of the
House membership introduced resolutions supporting the
American resupply of Israel.   In the Senate a bipartisan
group of 67 members introduced a resolution endorsing the
dispatch of aid to Israel, and in the House 220 members
joined Thomas P. O'Neill, the Massachusetts Democrat, in
sponsoring a resolution supportive of aid to Israel. [91]   In response to the congressional support of arms assistance to
Israel, Saudi Arabia announced it would reduce by 10 per
cent its oil production to pressure the U.S. to reconsider its
backing for Israel.   Further, the Saudis warned that the
flow of oil from Saudi Arabian oil fields would be completely

shut down if the U.S. continued to send arms to Israel. But
the small Persian Gulf sheikhdom of Abu Dhabi went one
step further. It declared an embargo of its oil exports to
the United States. In Tripoli, the Libyan news agency called
for all Arab countries to levy an embargo on the flow of oil
to the United States. Sensing the threat of a total Arab oil
embargo, a House-Senate conference committee gave final
approval to a bill that would result in the building of the
Alaskan pipeline. The bill forbade further lawsuits against
the pipeline construction because of environmental considerations. [92] Another sign of the times was the statement by
United Air Lines, Trans-World Airlines, and American Airlines of the elimination of 44 flights in order to conserve jet
fuel. A spokesman for the three companies said this would
conserve 6.6 million gallons of jet fuel per month. [93]

Action on the Suez front took a decisive turn on the
19th when the Israelis moved 13,000 troops and about 300
tanks and armored vehicles across the Suez Canal. The purpose of this operation was to destroy Egyptian missile sites
on the west bank in order to create a missile-free corridor
that would permit Israeli armored forces to attack those of
Egypt under an umbrella of Israeli planes that would not have
to face the devastating Egyptian missiles. The vanguard of
the Israeli task force succeeded in advancing up to 15 miles
on the west bank and destroyed 10 missile batteries. The
Israelis confronted the Egyptians with the possibility that their
forces on the east bank would be cut off from their bases of
supply. To relieve the hard-pressed Egyptians the Syrian
and Iraqi forces launched a spirited counterattack against Israeli position along the Golan Heights, but an offensive aimed
at reducing the Israeli salient around Sasa was not effective.
On the diplomatic front the American and Russian arms build-
up posed a definite threat to détente. Soviet Premier Alexei
N. Kosygin held three days of private conversations with
President Sadat, and Nixon administration sources credited
the Soviet official with urging upon Sadat acceptance of a
ceasefire in place. This goal was acceptable to both the
U.S. and the U.S.S.R. But Hassanein Heikal, editor of the
influential Egyptian daily newspaper Al Ahram, said that a
ceasefire in place was wholly unacceptable to Egypt. [94]

In response to repeated Israeli requests for arms support, President Nixon asked Congress to appropriate $2.2
billion to prevent a military imbalance in the area that would
result in the defeat of Israel. In his special message to
Congress, the President advised that he was working through

diplomatic channels to achieve a ceasefire and a peaceful settlement to the long-standing Arab-Israeli dispute. [95] But an ominous note was sounded in the Arab world when Libya declared that it was curtailing the flow of oil to the United States and doubling the price of its crude oil to $8.95 per barrel. This carried a threat to the American east coast where 200,000 barrels of high-grade Libyan petroleum arrived per day. This oil is low in sulphur content and does not add to the pollution problem that obtains in the American eastern megalopolis. The Libyan announcement, following so closely on Saudi Arabia's cutback of 10 per cent and Abu Dhabi's embargo on oil to America, posed a definite threat to the American economy which was already feeling the effects of the energy crisis. [96]

On 20 October Israeli military units broadened their breakthrough into Egypt and had moved approximately 18 miles beyond the Suez Canal. Israeli Minister of Defense Dayan said that the Israeli war effort was going well on both fronts and Israel was little disposed to a ceasefire. In spite of the setbacks on the two fronts, there was a new sense of pride in the armies of Egypt and Syria, for in none of the previous Arab-Israeli conflicts had the Arabs demonstrated the ability to fight so well as they had in the current war. While neither Arabs nor Israelis were inclined toward ceasefire talks, Secretary Kissinger arrived in Moscow on the 20th for direct consultations with high Soviet officials with a view to bringing about an end of the war. His arrival in the Soviet capital was pursuant to an invitation extended by Communist Party chief Leonid I. Brezhnev to President Nixon after the former's Cairo talks with President Sadat. Both the Soviets and Americans were disposed toward arriving at a ceasefire linked to a final settlement. That the U.S. hoped to achieve positive results from the meeting was indicated by the large entourage of State Department officials accompanying the Secretary. [97] But news from the Persian Gulf was not good, for Saudi Arabia, America's closest ally in the Arab world, declared that it had placed an embargo on all oil deliveries to the U.S. because of American military support of Israel. At the same time, the tiny Persian Gulf sheikhdom of Bahrain announced its termination of an agreement with the United States granting the U.S. Navy homeport facilities. More bad news came from the other end of the Arab world as Algeria declared its intention to reduce oil production by 10 per cent. [98] In response, President Nixon declared that the United States did not intend to modify its policy toward Israel. But Saudi officials declared that

the U. S. had failed to perceive the intensity of Arab opposition to American arms deliveries to Israel. [99]

By 21 October Israeli forces controlled approximately
24 miles of the west bank of the Suez. They had thrown
three bridges across the Canal and were operating from two
well-developed bridgeheads. But on the northern front the
Syrian forces had stopped the Israeli offensive and driven Israeli units back three to four miles toward the Golan Heights.
Nothing of consequence occurred on the diplomatic scene on
the 21st, but that date was a black letter day for American
officials charged with solving the energy problem. Kuwait,
Qatar, Bahrain, and Dubai announced a total embargo of oil
to the United States. [100] The U. S. was now cut off from
Middle Eastern sources of petroleum, an event that would
plague the American people for some months to come, giving
the lie to those idle claims that the United States did not require Middle Eastern oil.

Although the 21st proved dismal, the 22nd saw the
U. N. Security Council pass a joint U. S. -Soviet sponsored
resolution #338, calling for a ceasefire in place. The resolution was to take effect no later than twelve hours after the
adoption of the resolution. The vote was 14 to 0 with China
abstaining. Israel and Egypt accepted the measure, but the
Syrians did not. Iraq rejected it, but Jordan accepted. [101]
Actually neither side observed the ceasefire and fighting continued, but a résumé of the conflict discloses some interesting facts and raises several engrossing questions. Clearly,
Israel had the military advantage, having placed some 500
tanks and 15,000 men on the west bank of the Suez. The
cream of the Egyptian army, 80,000 to 100,000 troops, was
trapped on the east bank. On the Syrian front, Israeli
forces had driven the Syrians back to within 30 miles of Damascus. To achieve the victory on both fronts, the Israelis
chose to take the initiative on the Syrian front at the outset.
A Syrian breakthrough on the Golan Heights would have
placed major Israeli targets in jeopardy. During the first
week of the conflict, the Israelis placed the majority of their
air and armored forces on the Syrian front. The Israeli
strategy worked, for the Syrian advance was turned back, and
during that time the Egyptians did not exploit their initial advantage on the east bank of the Canal. The Egyptians apparently did not have well-defined objectives and they failed
to move ahead vigorously in the Sinai. Having halted the
Syrian offensive, the Israelis were then able to contain the
Egyptian advance in the Sinai, and then cross the Canal in

force to destroy Egyptian missile sights and cut off the Egyptian Third Army on the east bank.[102]

Casualties on both sides were heavy. Combined Arab forces suffered some 15,000 to 16,000 killed and wounded, while Israel lost around 3500 to 4000 in killed and wounded. Material losses on both sides were enormous. The combined Arab losses are estimated to have been 450 planes and approximately 2000 tanks. The Israelis lost about 125 planes and between 800 and 900 tanks in the 17-day conflict.[103] From the heavy losses, we can deduce that the Arab forces put up a stiff fight. Never before in the twenty-five years of Arab Israeli warfare had the Arabs shown such a marked ability to engage in full-scale war with the Israelis. They inflicted such heavy losses on their adversary that American resupply of planes, tanks, weapons, and munitions became necessary to prevent an Israeli collapse. With congressional approval, the President felt free to offer extensive aid to Israel.[104] But it should be noted that America's European allies opposed the shipment of material from their harbors and airports.[105]

It is interesting to speculate on several questions. Why did the Soviets, who were perhaps aware of the impending attack, not give advance notice to the United States in accordance with the provisions of détente? Why was American intelligence caught unaware by the onset of hostilities? Further, why did the Arabs not commit their air force to the battle early in the game to knock out Israeli air forces which had so clearly dominated past wars? Doubtless, these questions and others will cause observers of the Middle Eastern scene to engage in considerable debate.

*   *   *   *   *

The inability of the United States to arrange a settlement to the Arab-Israel conflict and maintain stability in the Middle East resulted in the resumption of hostilities in 1973, with dire consequences for the American people. U.S. support for Israel courted the displeasure of the Arabs who embargoed the flow of oil to the United States and its European allies. Not only did the embargo prove costly to the American economy and result in a recession, but it also strained diplomatic relations with America's NATO allies.

Following the ceasefire American policy-makers were

compelled to reassess American Middle Eastern policy. It
was imperative that relations with the Arab world be repaired in order that the embargo would be lifted and that the
ceasefire be enforced and a disengagement be obtained. But
policy-makers in Washington faced a dilemma. How could
the United States arrange for a peace settlement that would
preserve the territorial integrity of Israel and yet satisfy the
Arab states? The task that faced the State Department
seemed momentous indeed.

Chapter 18

THE AMERICAN SEARCH FOR STABILITY
AND A NEW IDENTITY IN THE MIDDLE EAST

In the months following the 1973 Arab-Israeli war, United States foreign policy-makers attempted to obtain an acceptance of the ceasefire and an ultimate disengagement of forces on the Suez and Golan fronts, a lifting of the Arab oil embargo, a strengthening of the ties with European allies, a new identity with the Arab states, and the initiation of steps toward a peace settlement. Secretary of State Henry Kissinger shuttled back and forth between the Syrian, Egyp-. tian, and Israel capitals in pursuit of peace and disengagement that the Arabs would renew the flow of oil so vital to the American economy. He also sought to achieve a more even-handed posture in the Middle East, one that recognizes an identification of interests with the Arab oil-producing states. In so doing, the Secretary accomplished what had been characterized as a "diplomatic revolution." At length, he initiated a step-by-step settlement of the Arab-Israeli dispute, one that involved Israeli withdrawal from territories occupied in the 1967 conflict. The accomplishment of these goals led to a reassessment of the American special relationship with Israel and resulted in a debate both in government and at the grass-roots level.

*   *   *   *   *

Secretary of State Kissinger's immediate task was to obtain observation of the ceasefire by the various parties to the dispute and a disengagement of both fronts. In spite of the heavy losses suffered by both sides during the 17-day conflict, and regardless of the ceasefire, fighting continued beyond the deadline established by the U.N. ceasefire resolution. Israeli forces on the west bank of the Suez turned south, surrounded the city of Suez, and completely isolated

the Egyptian Third Army on the east bank of the Canal.
While the Egyptian forces in the south were cut off from
their sources of supply, Egyptian military elements in the
northern sector retained their logistical support and continued to wage war. However, the Israelis sustained a drive
to broaden their salient on the west bank from about 500
to 700 square miles.

On the diplomatic scene the Egyptians requested the
U.S. and the Soviet Union to implement the ceasefire, thereby hoping to relieve the isolated Third Army and redeem the
honor of the Egyptian military arm. Secretary of State Kissinger returned to Washington and initiated an intensive effort to achieve observance of the ceasefire. State Department official McCloskey said that the U.S. was seeking every
avenue possible to bring about a ceasefire in terms of the
Security Council resolution that was adopted on the 22nd.
Meanwhile, at the United Nations, the Security Council
passed resolution #339, confirming its call for a ceasefire
and urging the disposition of U.N. observers to supervise
the ceasefire demarkation line. To brighten the situation
at the U.N., Syria announced its intention to accept the
ceasefire, provided Israel withdrew from territory occupied
during the 1967 war. [1]

On 24 October the war was winding down on both the
Suez and Syrian fronts as the ceasefire began to take hold.
But with Egypt's Third Army cut off from its supply base
and its plight worsening by the hour, Egyptian President Anwar Sadat renewed his request via the Security Council for
the U.S. and Russia to dispatch forces to supervise the
ceasefire. At the White House, Deputy Press Secretary Gerald Warren said the United States had "no intention" of dispatching troops to the Middle East. Clearly, the U.S. did
not want the introduction of Soviet forces into the troubled
region. Although the United States opposed the sending of
American and Russian forces to the area, Secretary Kissinger advised that peace talks would be conducted under "Soviet and American auspices." Obviously, Kissinger was making it clear that the U.S. and the Russians had made an
agreement at Moscow to carry out the ceasefire and that negotiations would be conducted in the presence of American
and Soviet diplomats. [2]

But despite the move toward negotiations, on 25 October the 1973-Middle East crisis took a foreboding turn as
President Nixon placed all American military forces on alert

at 3:00 a.m. in response to the Soviet Union's announced intention to take unilateral action and send Russian troops to
the Middle East.   The alert of U.S. forces was "precaution-
ary" and did not put the nation on a war footing.   In essence,
it meant that leaves were canceled for military personnel,
men were ordered to return to their units, and preparations
were made to move forces to the Middle East.   By mid-af-
ternoon the cause for alarm subsided. [3]

Secretary of State Kissinger at a 12:00 noon press
conference said that the United States would push for a settlement to the crisis.   He said that the U.S. was opposed
to the "unilateral introduction by any great power ... of
forces into the Middle East, in whatever guise."   But he
made it clear that the United States would work with the Soviet Union to restore the peace. [4]   The necessity for unilateral big power action was soon negated.   At the United Nations,
the Security Council passed Resolution 340 to dispatch a
multi-national security force to the Middle East.   American
and Soviet troops would not be included in this force.   This
move headed off the necessity of American leaders assuming
the responsibility for denying Russian forces entry into the
Middle East.

Although the alert ended without further incident,
there was one bad consequence.   America's European allies
depended on Middle Eastern oil.   The Arab oil embargo had
harmed Europe's economic health by severely cutting back
production.   The White House announcement of the alert was
not accompanied by an advisory communiqué to America's
NATO allies.   The alert coming shortly behind the oil embargo had placed the severest strain on American-European
relations.   West European officials were outraged that the
State Department did not consult with them during the Soviet-
American confrontation. [5]

Thus the Arab-Israeli conflict had not only produced
a hard feeling for the United States in the Arab world that
resulted in the oil embargo, but it also resulted in a pronounced strain on American-European relations.   These adverse consequences, added to the confrontation with the Soviet Union and the eventual slowdown in the American economy, caused many Americans to question the wisdom of continuing the "special relationship" with Israel.

Although Secretary Kissinger had declared that the
"special relationship" between the U.S. and Israel would

continue, he set about restoring peace to the troubled Middle
East and at the same time repairing the rift between the U.S.
and the Arab states. In the closing days of October and the
early days of November it became apparent that the United
States was undertaking a serious effort to broaden its ties
with the Arabs. During that time American diplomatic pressure resulted in Israel's agreement to allow the resupply of
the trapped Egyptian Third Army. Under the auspices of the
United Nations, trucks carrying food and water were permitted to replenish the Egyptians on the east bank. Israeli Defense Minister Moshe Dayan announced that this agreement
resulted from American pressure. Simultaneously with the
resupply, Egyptian Foreign Minister Ismail Fahmi left Egypt
on 28 October for talks with President Nixon and Secretary
Kissinger in Washington. In prolonged conversations with
these American officials, Fahmi enlarged upon the need to establish a permanent corridor to the beleaguered Egyptian
troops. Fahmi's visit, said one State Department spokesman,
heralded the beginning of a new era in American-Egyptian relations. That the United States was assuming a more even-
handed treatment of Arabs and Israelis was soon apparent by
the announcement of Secretary Kissinger's forthcoming visit
to five Arab states. President Sadat of Egypt reacted en-
thusiastically, saying it appeared to him that a new departure
was in the making.[6]

Although President Nixon reassured Israeli Prime Minister Golda Meir, who made a fleeting trip to Washington, of
continued U.S. support, Kissinger's meeting with Fahmi and
with Syrian Deputy Foreign Minister Muhim Ismail indicated
that an American rapprochement with the Arab states was
forthcoming. As Kissinger was making preparation for his
tour of Middle Eastern states, the U.N. peacekeeping force
had taken up positions on the Suez front where tensions had
eased considerably. Just prior to the Secretary's departure,
word leaked to the press that American-Israeli relations had
dimmed. In essence, Secretary Kissinger strongly urged
Prime Minister Meir that as a preliminary concession she
should permit the establishment of a resupply corridor from
Egypt to the trapped Egyptian army which Israeli forces had
cut off after the ceasefire.[7]

Kissinger's initial trip to the Middle East as Secretary
of State came on a somber note, for by early November it
was becoming increasingly evident that the United States suffered from the recent Arab-Israeli conflict. On the one hand,
relations between the U.S. and her European allies were

strained. Europeans had opposed the American resupply of
Israel and many European officials denied the Americans access to ports and airfields to implement the resupply. Too,
this American aid had resulted in the Arab oil embargo,
which had a disastrous result on the European economy which
depended for at least 60 per cent of its petroleum imports
from the Middle East. On the other hand, the U.S. was
faced with dire consequences, for the Arab oil embargo
cost the American economy some three million barrels of oil
per day. Many observers reported that by the year's end
the effects of this shortfall would be felt in many areas of
the country. Too, the price of oil was rising at a rapid rate.

And so Kissinger arrived in the Middle East determined to effect a lifting of the embargo. Following a one-
day stopover in Morocco for talks with King Hassan, the Secretary arrived in Cairo on 6 November, a date that also saw
Israel agree to permit additional truckloads of supplies to go
through to the Egyptian Third Army. On 7 November Kissinger met with President Sadat for three hours. At the conference it was agreed that the U.S. and Egypt would resume
diplomatic relations, broken since the 1967 war, and that
Egypt would make some major concessions to meet Israeli
demands. First, Egypt would return Israeli prisoners of war
and agree to initiate direct peace talks. In return for this,
Sadat could expect from Israel a promise to open a permanent access corridor to the Third Army and a promise from
Kissinger that he would personally obtain an eventual Israeli
withdrawal from much of the Sinai. The urgency of Kissinger's mission is perhaps best revealed by Assistant Secretary of State Joseph Sisco. Queried by a high Egyptian official whether the U.S. could be trusted, Sisco replied: "Oil
and our strategic interests. I am convinced that Congress,
despite the Israeli lobby, is now beginning to see the situation much more clearly. The mood is changing in the U.S.
in favor of the Arabs."[8]

Following the Cairo conference Sisco flew to Tel Aviv,
there to present the peace plan worked out by Kissinger and
Sadat. Under considerable pressure from Sisco and U.S. Ambassador Kenneth Keating, Israel agreed to the terms of the
plan.[9]

On the 9th of November the U.S. turned over to U.N.
Secretary General Kurt Waldheim the six-point agreement
drawn up by Kissinger and Sadat, as accepted by Israel.
This plan called for, first, observance of the ceasefire by

both sides; second, both sides would agree to a disagreement
of forces under the auspices of the U.N.; third, Suez would
receive adequate supplies of water, food, and medicine;
fourth, there would be a permanent corridor to permit food
and water to proceed through Israeli lines to the Egyptian
Third Army; fifth, the U.N. would assume control of all
checkpoints on the Cairo-Suez road; and, sixth, all prisoners
of war would be exchanged. [10]

Although the terms of the agreement were acceptable
to both sides, Secretary Kissinger learned from King Faisal
on the 9th that Saudi oil production limits would not be lifted
until such time as Israel withdrew from territory occupied
during the 1967 war.   This meant that the oil embargo, with
its adverse consequences for the U.S. economy, would continue. [11]   All was not lost, however.

A major step toward peace on the Suez front came on
11 November.   In no man's land on the Cairo-Suez road Israeli Major General Aharon Yariv and Egyptian General Muhammad Abd al-Gani el Gamasy signed the ceasefire accord.
Simultaneously with the signing, the United States urged the
convening of an Arab-Israeli peace conference at Geneva in
December.   Unfortunately, the Egyptians and Israelis could
not come to a meeting of the minds on the implementation
of the ceasefire accord.   Although they did agree to an exchange of prisoners of war on the 14th, there was no agreement on the details of the disengagement.   By the 22nd the
POW exchange had been completed, but Egyptian and Israeli
generals meeting at Kilometer 101 on the Suez-Cairo road
reached no accord on the anticipated troop withdrawal. [12]

While military leaders could reach no formula on the
military withdrawal in the Sinai, Secretary Henry Kissinger
exuded confidence in Washington.   Kissinger fully expected
to convene a peace conference at Geneva by mid-December.
He announced that "Sufficient progress has been made on the
ceasefire negotiations so that we can look forward with some
confidence to the beginning of negotiations. "[13]   Kissinger appears to have had control over the progress of the talks.
The Egyptians wanted the Israelis to withdraw to the lines
held on 22 October, but they refused to do so.   Oddly enough,
Kissinger was responsible for the Israelis' refusal.   He
wanted them to agree to a withdrawal at the Geneva peace
talks in order to open the conference on a positive note.   Although sporadic fighting accompanied the diplomatic impasse
on the Suez front, there was one positive development during
early December. [14]

Representatives of fifteen Arab states met at Algiers
for a summit conference in the opening days of December.
This conference spelled a new spirit of Arab unity. But
what is more important, the representatives agreed for the
first time to recognize the right of Israel to exist as a sovereign state. Although the Arabs called for the Israeli withdrawal from occupied territory and for a solution to the Palestinian refugee problem, their willingness to discuss terms
of a peace settlement with Israel was remarkable. [15]

However, the road to the Geneva meeting was marred
by continued fighting on both the Suez and Syrian fronts and
by reluctance on the part of Israel, Syria and Jordan to attend the conference. Although Israel had agreed to send a
delegate, the Israelis were opposed to the return of any part
of Jerusalem to Arab control and to the surrounding of the
West Bank of the Jordan River to the Palestinian Liberation
Organization. Syria announced that it would not officially attend the conference. Jordan wanted no dealings with the Palestinians. To make matters worse for the U.S., Sheik Ahmed Yamani, the Saudi oil minister, declared that the opening of the peace convention at Geneva would not of itself
guarantee the lifting of the oil embargo. [16]

Undeterred by the obstacles to a peace settlement,
Secretary of State Kissinger set off on a tour of the Middle
East to visit Algiers, Saudi Arabia, Egypt, Syria, Jordan,
Lebanon, and Israel in an effort to talk up the forthcoming
Geneva meeting. Clearly, the Secretary hoped to achieve a
withdrawal of Israeli forces in the Sinai, thinking that this
might lead to at least a partial end of the Arab oil embargo.
The Secretary's tour had a salutary affect on the Middle
Eastern diplomatic atmosphere. [17]

As the Secretary anticipated, the Geneva conference
opened on 21 December. Although Secretary General Kurt
Waldheim chaired the sessions, the United States and the
Soviet Union set the tone and shape of the conference. However, it opened on a bad note, for the Egyptians and Jordanians claimed there could be no settlement unless Israel withdrew to its pre-1967 borders. Egyptian Foreign Minister
Ismail Fahmi joined Jordanian Ambassador Abedel Mioneim
el Rifai in stating the Arab case. But Israeli Foreign Minister Abba Eban declared that Israel's need for secure boundaries precluded her compliance with these Arab demands.
He said that Israel was willing to give up some but not all
of the Arab territory. [18]

Behind the scenes Secretary of State Henry Kissinger held private talks with Soviet Foreign Minister Andrei Gromyko and Egyptian Foreign Minister Fahmi, with a view to obtaining a disengagement of forces on the Suez front. Kissinger hoped that Israel would agree to pull back to the mountain passes in the Sinai and permit control of the Canal to pass back into the hands of the Egyptians. But the Secretary was disappointed. Israeli Prime Minister Golda Meir simply refused to offer concessions on a withdrawal until after the Israeli national elections.[19]

On the 22nd the initial round of talks at Geneva ended with agreement to move the negotiations on troop disengagement from Kilometer 101 to Geneva and to establish several ad hoc committees to deal with the details of the disengagement. It was agreed that these committees would continue to function until the conference was reconvened in mid-January. The Geneva conference had made little headway toward implementing a settlement, because it was agreed that further negotiations would have to await the outcome of the Israeli elections. However, military talks continued at Geneva, and during the first week of January a spokesman for the conference announced that the parties to the dispute had agreed on the "principles" that would dictate the separation of the armed forces. But he claimed that disengagement would have to await the course of the elections.[20]

While the military conversations continued at Geneva, sporadic exchanges of gunfire occurred on both the Suez and Syrian fronts. On 25 December the U.N. peacekeeping force reported 44 shooting incidents on the Suez front alone. U.N. observers reported a lengthy small-arms battle on the 29th between Egyptians and Israelis. On 2 January there was intermittent skirmishing on the Syrian front as well as exchanges of fire on the Suez front.

To make matters worse for the United States, the Arab oil ministers meeting at Kuwait on 25 December decided to increase by 10 per cent the flow of oil to Japan and Europe. Nothing was said of lifting the embargo on the flow of Middle Eastern oil to the U.S.[21] In Washington Secretary of Defense Schlesinger announced on 7 January that there was the possibility that the embargo might cause the U.S. to use "force." This announcement caused a quick reaction in the Middle East as Kuwait's Foreign Minister Sheikh Sabah al-Ahmad al-Sabah said that Kuwait would sabotage its installations should any foreign power utilize force to obtain oil.[22]

During the second week in January expectations for a disengagement rose, for the Israelis went to the polls, gave Golda Meir's party a plurality with 40 per cent of the vote. This vote was expected to affect the peace talks, for observers anticipated that Israel would now willingly make concessions leading to a disengagement. In fact, Israel's Defense Minister Moshe Dayan held talks with Kissinger during the week and was reported ready to pull back Israeli forces in the Sinai to the Mitla and Gidi passes. Officials in Washington now hoped for a disengagement in the near future.[23]

It was at this juncture that Secretary of State Kissinger decided to make a third trip to the Middle East to hasten the process leading to disengagement. But prior to his departure, he announced his intention of calling a meeting of oil producing nations in Europe and North America as well as Japan for the express purpose of working out a solution to the problem caused by the oil embargo and the rapid rise in oil prices. Kissinger warned that the rise in oil prices faced the industrial nations with economic hardship. Oil consultant Walter Levy declared that energy costs would rise from $4.5 billion to more than $20 billion for the U.S. in 1973. But many experts said that a consumers' league would not be effective, since nations affected by the oil crisis were likely to make private arrangements to ensure a steady flow of petroleum. Sheikh Ahmed Zaki Yamani, the Saudi oil minister, warned that the formation of a consumers' consortium would likely lead to a confrontation with the oil producing nations that could have disastrous consequences.[24]

Although the Geneva talks had reached an impasse and the oil picture looked grim for the United States, Kissinger's "shuttle diplomacy" in the Middle East was productive. He met with Sadat on the morning of 12 January and then flew to Israel to confer with Golda Meir. Israeli leaders approved a plan for the disengagement of forces and Kissinger returned to Cairo to present it to Sadat. Israel was prepared to withdraw to the Mitla and Gidi Passes in the Sinai Desert and wanted Egypt to reduce its forces on the east bank of the Suez, reopen the Canal, rebuilt and repopulate the cities of Suez, Ismailia and Port Said. Further, Israel desired that Egypt make a declaration of non-belligerency. In return, Egypt demanded that Israel make a unilateral withdrawal to the passes and assert that this withdrawal was precursory to an eventual Israeli evacuation of all Egyptian territory.[25]

While the two sides were not yet in agreement on a

disengagement formula, Kissinger announced on 14 January
that there "was very good progress in his talks in Egypt"
and he shuttled back to Israel to convey the Egyptian response to the proposed agreement.[26] Following further talks
with the Israelis and a return trip to confer with Sadat, an
accord was reached. On 17 January it was announced in
Egypt, Israel, and the United States that the Egyptians and
Israelis had arrived at mutually acceptable terms on a disengagement formula. A triumph for Kissinger, the disengagement blueprint called for Israel to withdraw into the Sinai, leaving small skeleton forces at the Giddi and Mitla
Passes. Egypt would maintain a small force of 7000 troops
on the east bank of the Canal. There would be arms restrictions on Egyptian and Israeli forces along the U.N. buffer
zone. On 18 January the chiefs of staff of Egypt and Israel
Muhammad al-Gamasi and David Elazar, met at Kilometer
101 and signed the disengagement agreement.[27]

The disengagement was epochal. It marked the first
time in a generation that Arabs and Israelis had been able
to reach a meeting of the minds. Sadat was clearly the win-
ner. Israel withdrew her 25,000-man force from the west
bank of the Canal, and now Sadat, bent on a program of economic development for Egypt, would be able to reopen the
Canal, which would supply his economy with badly needed
revenues. Too, his trapped, ill-supplied Third Army could
return from the east bank without further complications.[28]

While in the Middle East, Kissinger met with Jordan's
King Hussein and discussed the possibility of talks between
Jordan and Israel, and also conversed at some length with
President Hafez Assad of Syria. He departed for Washington
where there was speculation that the disengagement might
lead to an end of the oil embargo.

By late January the United States economy was feeling
the pinch that resulted from the approximate three million
barrel per day shortfall of Arab oil. Automobile sales
dropped and thousands of auto workers were laid off. Many
airlines were compelled to reduce their schedules due to the
dearth of jet fuel. This reduction was accompanied by a
lay-off of many airline employees. Restaurants and motels
in winter resort areas were in a fit of economic doldrums.
Fuel shortages pushed the American economy to the verge of
a recession.[29]

On 22 January Kissinger announced in Washington that

he hoped the disengagement would result in the termination
of the Arab oil embargo.   But the word from Kuwait was that
talk of an end to the embargo was premature and that it was
still tied to the promise of an Israeli withdrawal from the occupied territories and the restoration of the sovereign rights
of the Palestinian Arabs.   But even so, Kissinger said on the
31st that several Arab leaders would work for the lifting of
the embargo when the Arab oil ministers convened in Libya
in mid-February. [30]

That the Secretary of State was growing more concerned about the deleterious effects of the oil embargo on the
American economy is made clear by his increased diplomatic
activity aimed at lifting the cutoff.   Although the Israelis had
begun their three-stage withdrawal from the west bank, there
was little hope for a disengagement on the Syrian front where
Syrians and Israelis continued their long-range artillery duels.
Kissinger hoped that the disengagement on the Suez front
would lead to a resumption of the oil flow, but he was disappointed to learn that Saudi and Kuwaiti officials pledged to
President Assad of Syria that the oil embargo would continue
until a disengagement could be worked out between Syria and
Israel. [31]   On 6 February Kissinger announced that the American effort to restore peace to the Middle East was producing
desired results and that the continued oil embargo would constitute a "form of blackmail" which would have a bad effect
on the American attitude toward the Middle East. [32]

Although frustrated by the continued embargo, Kissinger could view with encouragement the disengagement on the
Suez front.   By the terms of the agreement, the Israelis
were withdrawing their troops.   During the initial phase, they
were to evacuate the 25,000 troops and 300 tanks on the west
bank of the Canal.   During the second phase (due to be completed by 5 March), Israel agreed to pull back to a new ceasefire line some thirteen miles east of the Canal.   By that time
the Egyptians would have placed a force of 7000 men and
some 30 tanks on a five-mile strip of land along the east
bank, with the United Nations Emergency Force occupying the
buffer zone in between. [33]

While the disengagement on the Suez front was proceeding smoothly, there was little cause for enthusiasm on
the Syrian front, for Syrian President Assad made it clear
that he would not be pressured by Henry Kissinger, the Russians, or President Sadat into making an early settlement
with the Israelis.   Assad was being subjected to domestic

political pressures that precluded his treating with the hated
Israelis. Syrian Foreign Minister Abdel Halik Khaddam, one
of those opposed to unconditional negotiations with Israel, announced that Syria would accept disengagement only if Israel
would agree to a total withdrawal from Syrian territory.
There was little hope that a disengagement on the Syrian
front would be soon forthcoming and the artillery duels continued intermittently. [34]

As Syria exhibited a reluctance to come to the conference table, pessimism was growing in Washington where it
was becoming more apparent that an economic recession was
being hastened by the continued oil embargo. The President's
economic advisers presented a dismal forecast for the American economy during 1974. With talk of recession on every
hand, growing lines of automobiles at gasoline stations, industrial cutbacks in production, and little likelihood that Syria
would come to terms with Israel, Secretary Kissinger approached the oil embargo on a new tack. Having tried unsuccessfully for four months to bring about a resumption of oil
shipments from the Middle East, the Secretary called for a
meeting in Washington of the major oil-consuming nations,
including the nine members of the Common Market, plus Nor-
way, Japan, and Canada. On 11 February Kissinger addressed the conference, saying the continued energy crisis
could produce economic anarchy on the world scene. The
Secretary presented a seven-point program that included, first,
conservation of energy sources; second, a search for alternative energy sources; third, extended research and development; fourth, emergency sharing of available energy sources;
fifth, international financial cooperation; sixth, aid to the less
developed countries which require massive oil imports; and
seventh, the creation of a cooperative environment between
consumer and producer nations. [35]

The majority of the delegates gave Kissinger's plan a
favorable reception, but French Foreign Minister Michel Jobert reacted negatively, saying France would make her own
oil arrangements in the future. Jobert's effort to undermine
the effectiveness of the conference was headed off by President Nixon's suggestion that the United States might cut back
its military establishment in Europe should the European
states prove uncooperative during the energy crisis. Nixon's
threat carried the day, and the conference agreed to implement Kissinger's proposals, in spite of French objections. [36]

But while the oil consumers were meeting in Washington, the Arab oil-producing countries were preparing to meet in Algiers. News from the Algiers conference was not encouraging for an energy-short United States. Syrian President Assad persuaded the assembled delegates to continue the oil embargo until such time as Israel pulled back her forces on the Golan Heights. However, the conference did end on one bright note. Although the oil boycott continued, nevertheless at the conclusion of the meeting, the Egyptian and Saudi Arabian foreign ministers hastened to Washington for conversations with Secretary Kissinger. The two envoys brought with them a plan which provided that if Kissinger could bring about a disengagement on the Syrian front, the Arab states would end the embargo. [37]

Following talks with the Arab emissaries, Kissinger prepared for a fourth trip to the Middle East. During the first week in March the Secretary achieved almost immediate success. In exchanges with President Hafez Assad of Syria, he obtained a list of Israeli prisoners of war held by the Syrians, and he was authorized by Assad to deliver this list to Jerusalem. This marked a major concession on the part of Assad, and it paved the way for further negotiations, for the Israelis had refused to discuss disengagement with the Syrians until the list of POWs was handed over. Furthermore, Assad assured the Secretary that he was quite willing to meet the second Israeli demand by permitting the International Red Cross to send observers to visit the prisoners to determine if they had been ill treated by the Syrians. At the conclusion of Kissinger's mission, a U.S. official announced that Syria and Israel had agreed to dispatch envoys to Washington within the near future to discuss terms of disengagement on the Golan Heights. Perhaps the major key to the breakthrough was President Assad's political acumen in overcoming domestic opposition to negotiation with the Israelis. Kissinger had learned from the Syrian leader that negotiations could go forward, provided the Syrian government could return the 170,000 refugees who fled the occupied areas during the recent conflict. Too, Assad wanted Israel to return the city of Quneitra, the principal city of the Golan region, to Syria. Assad also agreed to the placement of a United Nations force in a buffer zone along the line of disengagement. Although the government of Golda Meir was not yet ready to make major concessions due to the political configuration in Israeli, Kissinger could view his recent mission with some degree of enthusiasm. [38]

Kissinger could also congratulate himself on the on-

going disengagement on the Suez front and the announcement
of the resumption of diplomatic relations between the United
States and Egypt on 28 February. [39] This exchange of diplomatic officials was indicative of a new status between the two
countries. President Sadat, who frequently referred to Kissinger as "my friend Henry," had achieved a heightened status in Egypt. Sadat was now bent on economic development
in Egypt, and the hotels in Cairo were full of Western entrepreneurs seeking new opportunities for expansion and investment. Reports from Cairo indicate that Sadat envisaged rebuilding the cities along the Suez Canal, deepening the Canal
to permit passage of the larger oil tankers, and encouraging
the industrial development of the Land of the Nile. Middle
Eastern sources claim that the rebuilding of the Suez Canal
Zone would greatly dampen the Arab-Israeli strife and add to
the security of Israel. Egypt could hardly afford to become
engaged in another conflict with Israel, for a highly-devel-
oped Canal Zone would come under heavy Israeli fire and face
destruction. [40]

During the second week in March William Simon,
White House energy expert, announced that the energy shortage had reached crisis proportions. This announcement came
as little comfort to the 250,000 American workers who had
been laid off during the time of the oil embargo. Simon declared that the 15 per cent gasoline shortfall might reach as
high as 20 per cent if the embargo is not lifted. The auto
industry had laid off some 80,000 workers, while the airlines
had separated over 15,000 employees. Hotels, motels, and
restaurants had fired thousands of workers. [41] The outlook
for the American economy was grim, indeed.

But news from the Middle East was looking up, for
Egyptian and Saudi Arabian officials had been arguing for
some time that the United States should be rewarded for its
diplomatic efforts by a lifting of the oil embargo. Meeting
at Tripoli, the capital of Libya, Arab officials finally agreed
on 18 March to lift the oil embargo and resume oil shipments
to the United States. But the Arab leaders attached a pro-
viso to their decision, adding that the embargo could be rein-
stated if further progress toward a disengagement in the Golan Heights were not forthcoming. [42] While the news was
greeted with enthusiasm, it would be some six weeks before
tankers could reach U.S. ports from the Persian Gulf.

The Arab effort to utilize oil as a tool of diplomacy
had been successful, for the United States had exerted strong

diplomatic pressure on Israel to bring about a ceasefire and disengagement on the Suez front. But given the Arab oil ministers' promise to review their decision to lift the embargo in two months, and in light of the continued artillery duels that had been raging in the Golan Heights since mid-March, Kissinger had his task cut out for him. However, by late March he was confident that he would be able to effect a disengagement in the Golan Heights.

But March gave way to April, and the 5th of the new month marked the twenty-fifth day of fighting between Syria and Israel in the Golan Heights. Mount Hermon was the scene of much of the fighting, for Israel wanted this strategic geographic eminence from which to obtain a commanding view of military movements in Syria. Fighting continued through the month of April, but by the last week of the month, reports emanated from Syria to the effect that President Assad was ready to negotiate with Israel under the auspices of Secretary of State Kissinger. To heighten prospects for peace, Yitzhak Rabin, the new Israeli Prime Minister, began to form a new government in the closing days of April --one that would enable him to arrive at terms satisfactory to Syria. Rabin exhibited a more flexible attitude than his predecessor, and, although he would under no circumstances surrender the entire Golan Heights region to Syria, he indicated a greater willingness to negotiate a settlement acceptable to the Syrians. To give impetus to the movement toward peace, a joint United States-Russian statement issued on the 29th declared that the two nations would coordinate efforts to obtain a settlement to the outstanding Israeli-Syrian dispute. In this regard, Kissinger received an able assist from Soviet Foreign Minister Andrei A. Gromyko. So bright did the chances for peace appear in late April, that President Anwar Sadat announced that Kissinger, whom he termed "a man of miracles," would succeed in obtaining a disengagement between the two belligerents in the Golan region. Heralding the new relationship between the United States and Egypt and indicating a new departure in Soviet-Egyptian relations, Sadat attacked the Soviet Union and declared that Egypt was turning to new sources for arms and assistance.[43]

To implement the Egyptian turn away from the Soviets toward the West, the Nixon administration planned to ask Congress for a $250 million appropriation for economic assistance and a second grant of some $15 million to clear the Suez Canal. A State Department official announced that this readiness to aid Egypt was due to the improved diplomatic

relations with that country that had come about in the past
six months.   Moreover, the United States would assist in
the clearing of the Canal by supplying technical assistance to
implement the work and to train Egyptian personnel to complete the reopening of the waterway.   Aid to Egypt is a cor-
nerstone of the Kissinger peace plan.   Although the State Department expected opposition from Jewish elements and conservatives in Congress, the reopening of the Suez Canal
would greatly benefit the United States.   Since the U.S. had
no superports to accommodate the great supertankers being
used to transport oil from the Persian Gulf to the West,
American imports of Arab oil would need to come via the
smaller tankers which could pass through the Canal on the
way to American eastcoast ports.   Although no American official had been present to witness the opening of the Suez
Canal in 1869--so minor did the U.S. government regard the
incident--a century later found the U.S. willing, ready, and
able to cooperate with Britons and Egyptians to reopen the
101-mile Canal that had been blocked since the 1967 Arab-
Israeli war.   So vital to American national interests is the
clearing of the waterway that by late April there were already
some 300 U.S. Air Force, Army, and Navy personnel assisting Egyptians with the engineering feat.   In addition to the
technical assistance rendered to Egypt, U.S. Ambassador
Herman F. Eilts presented his credentials in Cairo on 20
April, the day after Ashraf Ghorbal, the new Egyptian ambassador, was received at the White House. [44]

While American promises of assistance to Egypt indicated a brighter future in American-Egyptian relations and an
up-turn in the Egyptian economy, the picture of the American
domestic economy looked very dismal indeed.   The oil embargo that resulted from American aid to Israel during the
late war brought about a decline in the American gross national product of some 6.3 per cent during the first quarter
of 1974.   Such a marked downturn caused officials in Washington to wonder if this did not mark the beginning of a recession.   High prices for imported oil resulted in a $171.3
million deficit trade balance during the month of April--the
first such deficit in nine months.   The embargo cost the
American auto industry dearly.   General Motors Corporation
reported that earning for the first three months of 1974
dropped by 85 per cent.   G.M. officials declared that this
was the worst slump since 1948.   To make matters worse,
the auto industry laid off some 92,000 workers.   The net result of the embargo continues to be felt by American consumers in the form of higher utility rates.   The increased

rise in oil prices has led to higher costs in the production
of goods in the petro-chemical industry as well.[45]

That the United States is now partially dependent on
Arab oil is a new fact of life. The United States currently
consumes about 20 million barrels of oil per day. Domestic
supplies can meet about two-thirds of this demand. The remaining 6.7 million barrels must be imported. Of that
amount about three million barrels per day come from the
Middle East.[46] The shortfall resulting from the Arab oil
embargo had so adversely affected the American economy
that by May Secretary Kissinger stepped up his efforts to obtain a disengagement between Syria and Israel to ensure that
the Arab states would not renew the oil embargo at some
future date.

The month of May saw Kissinger shuttling back and
forth between the Egyptian, Syrian, and Israeli capitals in
an effort to procure a desired settlement that would restore
stability to the Middle East. May opened with the Israelis
and Syrians carrying on their struggle for control of the strategic Mount Hermon, marking the fifty-first day of the battle
that had raged since mid-March. On the diplomatic front
Secretary Kissinger continued his talks in Alexandria with
President Sadat in an attempt to enlist his support for the
separation of Israeli and Syrian forces. Following conversations with Sadat, the Secretary returned to Israel on Saturday,
4 May. He spent ten hours with high Israeli officials working out a disengagement plan. It called for an Israeli withdrawal from Syrian territory occupied in the 1973 war; a
partial pullback from territory seized during the 1967 conflict; the establishment of a buffer zone to be occupied by
U.N. troops; release of Israeli prisoners and the return of
Syrian refugees to the Golan Heights. But an unidentified
U.S. official said that the disengagement was complicated by
the fact that Israel had established seventeen settlements in
the Golan area.[47]

In spite of the difficulties, U.S. officials reported
that Kissinger was "very confident" of completing a settlement within the month. Not only had he met with Soviet
Foreign Minister Gromyko on the island of Cyprus to solicit
his support in pressuring Assad of Syria to listen to reasonable terms, but the Secretary was also willing to use economic power to facilitate the settlement. Economic power
was part of the Kissinger peace plan for the Middle East.
He anticipated a congressional appropriation of $250 million

for Egyptian economic development and he expected an additional appropriation of $100 million for use in Syria. Just as Kissinger hoped that economic development in Egypt would prove a stabilizing influence in Egyptian-Israeli relations, so he also hoped that American aid to Syria would achieve a similar end in Syrian-Israeli relations.[48] In spite of his use of economic incentives as a means of restoring peace, and despite his shuttling from Damascus to Jerusalem and thence to Cairo, the chances of a peace settlement by 10 May seemed remote indeed. The roadblock to success was the protest of Israeli settlers in the Golan Heights who were reluctant to give up their property rights.

But by 20 May State Department officials announced that there now seemed a ray of hope that Kissinger would achieve reconciliation before departing the Middle East. Israeli sources declared that the Kissinger compromise formula called for Israel to restore to Syria the 300-square-mile salient captured during the recent war and a partial withdrawal from land taken in the 1967 conflict. It also envisaged U.N. control of strategic Mount Hermon. The gap between Syrian and Israeli demands hinged over the placement of the line of demarcation. Kissinger closed the gap following a conference with the Israeli cabinet.[49]

But by 24 May the impetus toward peace had slowed, and there was some doubt that Kissinger would achieve the desired disengagement. It seems that Syria and Israel disagreed about troop and arms limitations and the size of the U.N. peacekeeping force. However, during the final week in May, the shuttling Secretary of State moved rapidly toward a settlement. He obtained an agreement on the drawing of the demarcation line and Syrian acceptance of Israeli retention of the settlements in the Golan Heights and the crests of certain strategic hills; in exchange he secured Israeli acquiescence to the return of Queneitra to Syria and permission for Syrian troops to take up positions in the vicinity of that city; U.N. troops would fill the buffer zone between the opposing sides.[50] Finally, success came as Israeli and Syrian officials signed an agreement at Geneva on 31 May that provided for a cessation of hostilities and a disengagement. The reconciliation was made in the council chamber of the Palace of Nations, the same chamber in which Egyptians and Israelis agreed to their January disengagement.[51]

The signing of the accord marked an end to Kissinger's extended 33-day trip to the Middle East, a trip that involved

some 24,230 miles of travel. His achievement was remarkable. In bringing about a disengagement, Kissinger had
utilized the assistance of Soviet Foreign Minister Gromyko
and President Sadat of Egypt. Gromyko's assistance was
proof that the Soviet-American détente remained in force.
Kissinger said, "Relations between the United States and
Egypt have improved and will continue to improve." The
United States had achieved a new identity in the Middle East,
proof of which came with Sadat's laudatory remarks about
Kissinger and President Nixon.

Additional indication of the new American identity in
the Middle East came with the announcement that President
Nixon would visit Egypt, Saudi Arabia, Jordan, Syria, and
Israel during the month of June. The White House announced
that the trip was Nixon's bid to strengthen American ties with
the Middle East and to promote peace in the region. Although Secretary Kissinger announced that the United States
has no intention of expelling Soviet influence in the Middle
East, an Egyptian newspaper declared that the U.S. had replaced the Soviet Union as "The Arabs' sweetheart No. 1"[52]
--a remarkable observation given the spirit of discord which
has so frequently plagued American relations with the Arab
world during the past twenty years.

Kissinger continued his efforts to formulate a permanent settlement. In August 1974 President Nixon resigned
over the Watergate disclosures and his place was taken by
Gerald Ford who depended on Kissinger's advice and expertise
in the realm of foreign affairs. The Secretary came close
to achieving a second-stage agreement between Egypt and Israel in March 1975, only to see his efforts go to waste.
But in the early summer he began to put together a basic
plan that held out hope for acceptance by the Israelis and
Egyptians. It called for an Israeli withdrawal in the Sinai
to a position extending roughly from Al Arish to Sharm el
Sheikh. This would return the Abu Rudeis oil fields, the
strategic Mitla and Gidi passes, and sufficient east bank territory to Egypt to permit the reopening of the Suez Canal.
A demilitarized zone between Israeli and Egyptian forces
would be established, with a U.N. Emergency Force serving
in the buffer zone. The road to a second-stage disengagement was a rocky one, strewn with objections based on tech-
nicalities and points of agreement. After months of negotiation, with false hopes and real frustration, prospects for
peace seemed bright by mid-August. Ultimately, Kissinger
was successful, for the accord was initialed on 1 September

at Jerusalem by representatives of Israel and at Alexandria
by representatives of Egypt and signed at Geneva on 4 September.   The Sinai accord, as it came to be known, provided that the Egyptians and Israelis agreed to observe the
ceasefire and not to use force or military blockade against
the other party; that Israeli forces will be withdrawn from
some 2000 square miles of Egyptian territory in the Sinai
including the oil fields and the passes; that Egyptian forces
will be deployed west of an agreed upon demarcation line;
that a United Nations Emergency Force would serve in the
buffer zone; that 200 American technicians would maintain an
early-warning and surveillance network between the two parties; that non-military cargoes have the right of transit
through the Suez Canal, both to and from Israel; and that the
agreement "is a significant step toward a just and lasting
peace.   It is not a final peace agreement."[53]   The signing
of the accord was accompanied by the negotiation of a Memorandum of Agreement between Israel and the United States,
pledging the U.S. to supply Israel with military equipment
and oil supplies to make up for sources of oil lost by surrendering of the Abu Rudeis oil field in the Sinai.   The U.S.
also agreed to extend aid to Egypt.   The signing of the Sinai
accord was followed by brief House and Senate hearings on
that portion of the accord pertaining to the use of American
forces to operate the early-warning network.[54]   The House
approved the joint resolution permitting the use of Americans
in the early-warning network by a vote of 341 to 69, while
the Senate approved by a vote of 70 to 18.   The President
signed it on 13 October.

*   *   *   *   *

Although the Sinai accord marked a milestone on the
road to a Middle Eastern settlement, it left many questions
unanswered.   First, there was the question of the Ford administration's obtaining congressional approval of a $2.4
billion agreement with Israel, and a $650 million aid pact
with Egypt.   Although the administration gained early congressional approval of the early-warning agreement, there
was every indication that it would meet opposition in obtaining approval for aid to Israel and to Egypt.   Second, while
Egyptians had reason to be satisfied with the accord, there
was dissent in the Middle East, where Syrians, Jordanians,
and Palestinians registered vocal disapproval.   This negative
attitude stemmed from the belief that Israel would view the
agreement as final and not just as a stepping stone to further

concessions that would bring about an ultimate settlement
agreeable to all parties to the Arab-Israeli conflict.   The
burden was clearly on the United States to ascertain that the
Sinai accord was indeed merely one stage on the road to a
final settlement.

torian must pose the question: Will American foreign policy-
makers view the Middle East, and particularly the Arab-Israeli dispute, in terms of the national interest or will they
continue to regard this problem in terms of domestic political considerations. It would be hoped that the five-month
Arab oil embargo, with its deleterious effects on the American economy, and the confrontation with the Soviet Union on
25 October, would provide adequate food for thought on this
question. Moreover, it seems fitting to ask if the time is
not now ripe for the United States to recognize the Palestine
Liberation Organization as the official representative of the
Palestinian Arabs? In view of the resounding endorsement
that the Arab states gave to the PLO at the Rabat conference
in October 1974, the United Nations' invitation to PLO leader
Yasir Arafat to address the U.N. General Assembly, recognition by India, Indonesia, and several other nations, and the
diplomatic courtship by France and Italy, this might not be
an unwise course. The Palestinian tragedy is at the core of
Arab nationalism. The Arab states are finally committed to
the establishment of a Palestinian entity, because the emergence of Palestinian nationalism since the 1967 conflict has
become too strong a force in Middle Eastern politics to be
ignored. [4] To ensure its new role in the Arab world in the
period following the 1973 war, the United States must establish some sort of working relationship with the PLO, work
to influence that organization to accept the existence of Israel
as a fait accompli and to be content with the establishment
of a Palestinian state in the Gaza Strip and the West Bank of
the Jordan River. [5] One good reason for recognition is that
justice demands it. Another is that the Palestinian question
is so inextricably bound up in the complicated oil question,
which brings us to the high price of oil charged by the Arab
oil-producing countries. This raises a final question: Will
the formulation of an equitable settlement to the Arab-Israeli
dispute bring about a reduction in oil prices. It is now well
established in public statements given by the late King Faisal
and Sheikh Ahmed Zaki Yamani of Saudi Arabia, by Senator
J. W. Fulbright in a speech at Fulton, Missouri, and by oil
expert Marcos Y. Namj that a Middle Eastern settlement
based on U.N. resolution 242, calling for Israel to evacuate
all territory seized in the 1967 war, would in all probability
lead to a reduction in Arab oil prices. [6] Although in the
period following the 1967 war many have agreed that the United
States has been content to permit Israel to retain the territory acquired in the 1967 conflict, there is every indication
that the Middle Eastern situation is now ripe for Washington
to impose acceptance of Resolution 242 and a solution to the

Palestinian Arab problem on Israel. There is adequate
precedent for U.S. pressure on Israel. In 1953 Secretary of
State John Foster Dulles ended economic aid to Israel to
compel that state to end its efforts to unilaterally divert the
Jordan River. In 1956 President Eisenhower forced the Israelis to withdraw from the Sinai following the Israeli-French
-British aggression against Egypt.

As the United States achieves its bicentennial year of
1976 it is also nearing the year 1984, a year that will mark
two hundred years of American diplomatic relations with the
Middle East. During this period American intercourse with
the Middle East has evolved from the casual contacts of merchants, missionaries, archaeologists, technicians, mariners,
archaeologists, military advisers, and philanthropists to the
real and vital relationship based on the growing American
need for Arab oil which is necessary, at least for the foreseeable future, to sustain the high rate of productivity of the
American economy. During all but the past generation,
American diplomacy with the Middle East was based upon
certain basic guiding principles and upon the concept of the
national interest. But in the post-World War II period the
United States has deviated from these principles and this concept and has formed a special relationship with one state, to
the detriment of its overall Middle Eastern policy. In closely associating with Israel, the U.S. has placed in jeopardy
the traditional, good working relationships with the Arab
states. It is now necessary that the United States normalize
its relationship with Israel, and, as a rationale for this process, one need only recall George Washington's admonition in
his noted Farewell Address:

> So, likewise, a passionate attachment of one nation
> for another produces a variety of evils. Sympathy
> for the favorite nation, facilitating the illusion of
> an imaginary common interest in cases where no
> real common interest exists, and infusing into one
> the enmities of the other, betrays the former into
> a participation in the quarrels and wars of the latter
> without adequate inducement or justification. It
> leads also to concessions to the favorite nation of
> privileges denied to others, which is apt doubly to
> injure the nation making the concessions by unneces-
> sarily parting with what ought to have been retained,
> and by exciting jealousy, ill will, and a disposition
> to retaliate in the parties from whom equal privi-
> leges are withheld.... [7]

By normalizing its relations with Israel and strengthening its ties with the Middle Eastern oil-producing countries, the United States will in effect be turning away from
the "special relationship" with Israel, which is based on no
real identity of interests, and basing its policy on interests
that are real. The United States has numerous interests
that coalesce with those of the Arab oil-producing states.
Not only does the United States have increasing need for imports of oil and liquid natural gas from Arab lands, but it
requires that this oil be shipped, for the foreseeable future
at least, through the Suez Canal. The Very Large Crude
Carriers which now move oil from the Persian Gulf via the
Cape of Good Hope cannot find adequate deep water port facilities in the United States which must still depend on the
smaller tankers that can use the Canal. Prior to the 1967
closure of the Canal, the United States was the fourth largest
volume user of that waterway. With the Canal reopened, the
United States will probably become the number one user, because the smaller tankers up to 70,000 dead weight tons
which the Canal can accommodate will be plying to and fro
from the Gulf to the U.S. east coast ports carrying the crude
oil and liquid natural gas that American consumers so vitally
need. [8] The reopened Canal will also save American transit
costs, for the closure of the Canal in 1967 cost the United
States around $3 billion in added transportation charges. [9]
Another area in which the U.S. has mutual interests with the
Arab states is in the field of technology. The Arab nations
have developing economies and an abundance of capital to invest. With the growth of stability in the Middle East and the
restoration of normal conditions, the U.S. can expect to sell
its goods and services to the Arab states, thus reducing its
balance of payments deficit which has risen along with the
rising price of oil. Middle East markets constitute a real
goal for the American entrepreneur. [10] In addition to new
markets, there is the distinct prospect for American investment capital to find lucrative projects in the Middle East.
For example, President Sadat of Egypt has been courting
American business men for some time, seeking the funds necessary to develop the Canal Zone. [11] The Saudis are amen-
able to joint economic ventures in which American business
men match Saudi capital with American capital and technology.
Finally, in the period following the October War, the U.S.
has reoriented its Middle Eastern policy in a manner that has
resulted in renewed diplomatic ties with Egypt, and sustained
close relations with Saudi Arabia and Iran, three of the most
important nations in the region. [12] In the case of Iran and
Saudi Arabia, the United States has made numerous arms

sales with a view to establishing stability in the region of the
Persian Gulf.[13]   In the case of Egypt, the U.S. has rendered
substantial assistance to reopen the Suez Canal.   But the State
Department has also negotiated with all three countries agreements providing for Joint Commissions on economic cooperation.   These commissions are vitally important to these developing countries.[14]   It would appear that the continuation of
sound relations with Egypt, Saudi Arabia, and Iran would be
valuable to the United States in assuring accessionary rights
to Middle Eastern oil and equal opportunity in the markets
that are becoming increasingly enriched by oil revenues.[15]

Thus it is conceivable that as the United States re-
assesses its policy toward Israel and continues to have sound
relations with Egypt, Saudi Arabia, and Iran, that the nation's policy-makers will effect a policy based on real and
vital interests associated with oil, trade, the Suez Canal link,
transportation and communication routes, and stability.   In
so doing it will establish a policy based on a true community
of interests that are concrete and not permit the apparent interests between the United States and Israel to obstruct the
achievement of those goals lying within the scope of the American national interest.

CHAPTER NOTES

PREFACE

1. Charles A. Beard, The Idea of National Interest: An Analytical Study in American Foreign Policy (New York, 1934), p. 134.

2. This suggestion is contained in John A. DeNovo, "Researching American Relations with the Middle East: The State of the Art, 1970," in Milton O. Gustafson, ed., The National Archives and Foreign Relations Research (Athens, O., 1974), p. 246. I read Professor DeNovo's essay in typescript in 1969 and began at that time to do the research upon which this book is based.

CHAPTER 1

1. Robert A. Rutland, et al., eds., The Papers of James Madison (Chicago, 1973), VIII, 315.

2. James A. Field, Jr., America and the Mediterranean World, 1776-1882 (Princeton, N.J., 1969), p. 19.

3. On the importance of trade in the Confederation era, see Chapter 9 of Merrill Jensen, A History of the United States during the Confederation, 1781-1789 (New York, 1958).

4. H. G. Barnby, The Prisoners of Algiers (New York, 1966), p. 83.

5. Charles Oscar Paullin, Diplomatic Negotiations of American Naval Officers, 1778-1883 (Baltimore, 1912), pp. 47-48, and Ray W. Irwin, The Diplomatic Relations of the United States with the Barbary Powers, 1776-1816 (Chapel Hill, N.C., 1931), pp. 8, 18.

6. Field, Mediterranean World, p. 32; Gardner W. Allen, Our Navy and the Barbary Corsairs (Cambridge, Mass., 1905), pp. 26-29; Irwin, Diplomatic Relations, p. 27; Paullin, Diplomatic Negotiations, pp. 49-52; The Diplomatic Correspondence of the United States, September 10, 1783-March 4, 1789, I, 501-502, 628, 652-53, and 656-674.

7. Luella J. Hall, The United States and Morocco, 1776-

1956 (Metuchen, N.J., 1971), pp. 67-70; Allen, Our Navy, pp. 28-29; Field, Mediterranean World, pp. 32-33; Irwin, Diplomatic Relations, p. 33; Hunter Miller, ed., Treaties and Other International Acts of the United States of America (Washington, 1931-1948), II, 212-219.

8.   Allen, Our Navy, pp. 35-41; Field, Mediterranean World, pp. 34-35; Irwin, Diplomatic Relations, pp. 46-52.

9.   Field, Mediterranean World, p. 36; Allen, Our Navy, pp. 43-44; Irwin, Diplomatic Relations, pp. 64, 66-68.

10.   Field, Mediterranean World, p. 36; Paullin, Diplomatic Negotiations, p. 53; and American State Papers: Foreign Relations, I, 100-105.

11.   Paullin, Diplomatic Negotiations, pp. 53-54; Allen, Our Navy, pp. 46-48; and American State Papers: Foreign Relations, I, 292-294.

12.   Barnby, Prisoners of Algiers, pp. 110, 113-115, and 303; Wayne S. Cole, An Interpretative History of American Foreign Relations (Homewood, Ill., 1968), p. 27.

13.   Field, Mediterranean World, p. 37; Paullin, Diplomatic Negotiations, p. 55; and Miller, Treaties, II, 229-304.

14.   Louis B. Wright and Julia H. MacLeod, The First Americans in North Africa (New York, 1945), p. 20.

15.   Milton Cantor, "Joel Barlow's Mission to Algiers," Historian, XXV (1963), 172-194; Irwin, Diplomatic Relations, Chapter 5.

16.   Paullin, Diplomatic Negotiations p. 56; Miller, Treaties, II, 364-368.

17.   Paullin, Diplomatic Negotiations, pp. 56-57; Allen, Our Navy, pp. 59-64; and Miller, Treaties, II, 402-414.

18.   Wright and MacLeod, First Americans, pp. 20-21.

19.   Allen, Our Navy, pp. 90-91.

20.   Field, Mediterranean World, pp. 49-50; Paullin, Diplomatic Negotiations, pp. 62-68; and Allen, Our Navy, pp. 97-102.

21.   Paullin, Diplomatic Negotiations, pp. 62-68; Irwin, Diplomatic Relations, pp. 112-123.

22.   Paullin, Diplomatic Negotiations, pp. 68-82; Allen, Our Navy, pp. 188-197.

23.   Wright and MacLeod, First Americans, Chapter 7.

24. Allen, Our Navy, pp. 198-214, 222-265; Paullin, Diplomatic Negotiations, pp. 82-88.

25. Allen, Our Navy, pp. 267-270; Paullin, Diplomatic Negotiations, pp. 90-121.

26. Field, Mediterranean World, p. 57.

27. Miller, Treaties, II, 637-640.

28. Allen, Our Navy, pp. 281-287; Paullin, Diplomatic Negotiations, pp. 110-115.

CHAPTER 2

1. Edward Mead Earle, "Early American Policy Concerning Ottoman Minorities," Political Science Quarterly, XLII (Sept. 1927), 340.

2. Myrtle A. Cline, American Attitude Toward the Greek War of Independence, 1821-1828 (Atlanta, 1930), pp. 83, 163, 178.

3. Carl Seaburg and Stanley Paterson, Merchant Prince of Boston: Colonel T. H. Perkins, 1764-1854 (Cambridge, Mass., 1971), pp. 313-14, and Merle Curti, American Philanthropy Abroad: A History (New Brunswick, N.J., 1963), p. 27.

4. Field, Mediterranean World, p. 132, and Earle, "Ottoman Minorities," 343.

5. Harris John Booras, Hellenic Independence and America's Contribution to the Cause (Rutland, Vt., 1934), pp. 159-61; Edward Mead Earle, "American Interest in the Greek Cause, 1821-1827," American Historical Review, XXXIII (Oct. 1927), 45, and Field, Mediterranean World, p. 122.

6. Earle, "Ottoman Minorities," 345.

7. Curti, American Philanthropy, pp. 22-25; Cline, American Attitude, pp. 21-31, 89-111; Stephen A. Larrabee, Hellas Observed: The American Experience of Greece, 1775-1865 (New York, 1957), pp. 67-70; and Earle, "Greek Cause," 49-54.

8. Earle, "Ottoman Minorities," 345-46; Annals of Congress, 17 Cong, 2 Sess, pp. 457 et seq.

9. Earle, "Ottoman Minorities," 346.

10. James D. Richardson, ed., A Compilation of the Messages and Papers of the Presidents (Washington, 1896), II, 193.

11. Booras, Hellenic Independence, p. 163, and American

State Papers: Foreign Relations, V, 255-256.

12.   Earle, "Ottoman Minorities," 348-49.

13.   Booras, Hellenic Independence, pp. 164-65; Earle, "Ottoman Minorities," 348-49; Cline, American Attitude, p. 159; and American State Papers: Foreign Relations, V, 257.

14.   Cline, American Attitude, pp. 150-51; Earle, "Ottoman Minorities," 350.

15.   Cline, American Attitude, p. 151.

16.   Ibid., p. 151; Dexter Perkins, A History of the Monroe Doctrine (Boston, 1941), pp. 43-44; Charles Francis Adams, ed., Memoirs of John Quincy Adams, Comprising Portions of His Diary from 1795 to 1848 (reprinted ed., Freeport, N.Y., 1969), VI, 197.

17.   Richardson, ed., Messages and Papers, II, 218-19.

18.   Earle, "Ottoman Minorities," 351-353.

19.   Cline, American Attitude, p. 162; Larrabee, Hellas Observed, p. 70.

20.   Annals of Congress, 18 Cong, 1 Sess, p. 806.

21.   Ibid., pp. 1084-1099.

22.   Earle, "Ottoman Minorities," 355.

23.   Annals of Congress, 18 Cong, 1 Sess, pp. 1181-1191; 1127-1132; 1132-1139; 1150-1155; 1165-1170; 1158-1160, and 1197-1200.

24.   Earle, "Ottoman Minorities," 357.

25.   Annals of Congress, 18 Cong, 1 Sess, pp. 1136-1139.

26.   Earle, "Ottoman Minorities," 358.

27.   Annals of Congress, 18 Cong, 1 Sess, pp. 849, 870-872, 917.

28.   S. E. Morison, "Forcing the Dardanelles in 1810: With Some Account of the Early Levant Trade of Massachusetts," New England Quarterly, I (1928), 224.   Perkins and Co. dominated the opium trade at this time.   See Jacques M. Downs, "American Merchants and the China Opium Trade," Business History Review, 42 (winter, 1968), 432.

29.   Earle, "Ottoman Minorities," 361; Larrabee, Hellas Observed, p. 71; and Cline, American Attitude, p. 198.

30. Robert L. Daniel, American Philanthropy in the Near East, 1820-1960 (Athens, O., 1970), p. 11.

31. Cline, American Attitude, pp. 138-140; Daniel, American Philanthropy, pp. 5-6.

32. Daniel, American Philanthropy, p. 1-8; Cline, American Attitude, pp. 140, 217; and Field, Mediterranean World, p. 132.

33. Earle, "Ottoman Minorities," 366-67.

34. The U.S. negotiated a treaty of commerce and navigation with Greece in 1837. Miller, Treaties, IV, 107-121.

CHAPTER 3

1. David H. Finnie, Pioneers East: The Early American Experience in the Middle East (Cambridge, Mass., 1967), p. 33.

2. Paullin, Diplomatic Negotiations, pp. 123-24.

3. Leland James Gordon, American Relations with Turkey, 1830-1930: An Economic Interpretation (Philadelphia, 1932), pp. 41-42.

4. Ibid., p. 8.

5. Paullin, Diplomatic Negotiations, p. 130. A good account of Bainbridge's cruise is in Allen, Our Navy, pp. 75-86.

6. Finnie, Pioneers East, pp. 25-26; L. C. Wright, United States Policy Toward Egypt, 1830-1914 (New York, 1969), pp. 27-28; Gordon, American Relations with Turkey, pp. 8-9; Paullin, Diplomatic Negotiations, pp. 133, 135, 137.

7. Field, Mediterranean World, p. 138.

8. Paullin, Diplomatic Negotiations, pp. 144-50; Frank E. Hinckley, American Consular Jurisdiction in the Orient (Washington, 1906), pp. 22-23; Miller, Treaties, II, 617-623.

9. Finnie, Pioneers East, p. 64.

10. On the arrival of Commodore Porter and the exchange of ratifications see: James E. DeKay, Sketches of Turkey in 1831 and 1832, by an American (New York, 1833), pp. 289-90, 298; David Porter, Constantinople and Its Environs, by an American (New York, 1835), I, 43-45; David Dixon Porter, Memoirs of Commodore David Porter of the United States Navy (Albany, N.Y., 1875), pp. 400-402; and Archibald D. Turnbull, Commodore David Porter (New York, 1921).

11. See DeKay, Sketches, pp. 282-283, on the office of dragoman.

12. Finnie, Pioneers East, pp. 93-100.

13. Andor Klay, Daring Diplomacy: The Case of the First American Ultimatum (Minneapolis, 1957), p. 113.

14. Ibid., p. 132.

15. Finnie, Pioneers East, p. 68.

16. Ibid., p. 81, and Field, Mediterranean World, p. 170.

17. Gordon, American Relations with Turkey, p. 44.

18. Field, Mediterranean World, pp. 186-196.

19. Ibid., p. 189; Finnie, Pioneers East, pp. 133, 129; and Joseph L. Grabill, Protestant Diplomacy and the Near East: Missionary Influence on American Policy, 1810-1927 (Minneapolis, 1971), p. 40.

20. Grabill, Protestant Diplomacy, p. 293.

21. A number of studies related to missionaries and Middle Eastern diplomacy are: Edward Mead Earle, "American Missions in the Near East," Foreign Affairs, VII (April 1929), 398-417; Grabill, Protestant Diplomacy; Field, Mediterranean World; Finnie, Pioneers East; Stephen B. L. Penrose, That They May Have Life: The Story of the American University of Beirut, 1866-1941 (New York, 1941); and Clifton Jackson Phillips, Protestant America and the Pagan World: The First Half Century of the American Board of Commissioners for Foreign Missions, 1810-1860 (Cambridge, Mass., 1969).

22. A number of writers seem to feel that the missionaries were responsible for evoking cultural nationalism: Daniel, American Philanthropy, pp. 87, 111; Grabill, Protestant Diplomacy, pp. 46-51; George Sarton, The Incubation of Western Culture in the Middle East (Washington, 1951), p. 42; Lewis V. Thomas and Richard N. Frye, The United States and Turkey and Iran (Cambridge, Mass., 1951), p. 141; William Yale, The Near East: A Modern History (Ann Arbor, Mich., 1958), p. 195; and George Antonius, The Arab Awakening: The Story of the Arab National Movement (New York, 1946), pp. 13-27. But A. L. Tibawi, American Interests in Syria, 1800-1901: A Study of Educational, Literary and Religious Work (Oxford, 1966), p. 308, disputes this point, declaring that the Protestant press had no influence in reviving Arab cultural nationalism. But Field, Mediterranean World, p. 359, and N. Marbury Efimenco, "American Impact Upon Middle East Leadership," Political Science Quarterly, 69 (1954), 6-9, assert that the Americans had influence on the political leadership as well.

23. Tibawi, American Interests, p. 75.

24. Secretary of State to Porter, 2 Feb. 1842, Department of State Instructions, Turkey. Microfilm collection. National Archives.

25. Tibawi, American Interests, pp. 89, 128, and Field, Mediterranean World, p. 288.

26. Wright, United States Policy, pp. 34, 39, and Field, Mediterranean World, p. 192.

27. Patterson to Livingston, 19 June 1833, Department of State Despatches, Turkey.

28. Hodgson to McLane, 14 June 1834, Ibid.

29. Hodgson to McLane, 25 Aug. 1834, 28 Sept. 1834 and to Forsyth, 2 Mar. 1834, Ibid. Also see Thomas A. Bryson, "William Brown Hodgson's Mission to Egypt, 1834," West Georgia College Studies in the Social Sciences, XI (June 1972), 10-18. This author is currently preparing a diplomatic biography of Hodgson, giving emphasis to his role as a consular official in the Middle East.

30. Hodgson wrote numerous despatches on the diplomatic and consular practice of the Middle East. See ibid. He also wrote a Biographical Sketch of Mohammed Ali, Pacha of Egypt, Syria, and Arabia (Washington, 1837) and numerous scholarly essays on Oriental languages, of which he was a student.

31. Roy E. Nichols, "Diplomacy in Barbary," Pennsylvania Magazine of History and Biography, LXXIV (1950), 113-141.

32. Roy E. Nichols, Advance Agents of American Destiny (Philadelphia, 1956), p. 116.

33. Miller, Treaties, II, 617-623; Nichols, "Diplomacy in Barbary," 127; and Nichols, Advance Agents, p. 127.

34. Nichols, "Diplomacy in Barbary," 136-137.

35. Ibid.

36. Hall, United States and Morocco, pp. 90, 158-60, 176, and Charles F. Gallagher, United States and North Africa: Morocco, Algiers, and Tunisia (Cambridge, Mass., 1963), p. 235.

CHAPTER 4

1. Gordon, American Relations with Turkey, pp. 13-15.

2. Department of State, Papers Relating to the Foreign Re-

lations of the United States, 1866, II, 230-239. Hereafter cited as
FRUS.

3. Wright, United States Policy Toward Egypt, pp. 62-65.

4. FRUS, 1907, II, 1052-1053.

5. Gordon, American Relations with Turkey, pp. 44-48, and
Field, Mediterranean World, pp. 310-313.

6. Field, Mediterranean World, pp. 248-253.

7. Ibid., pp. 311-313.

8. Ibid., pp. 355-359; Penrose, That They May Have Life,
pp. 20-25; and Tibawi, American Interests in Syria, pp. 160-170.

9. Gordon, American Relations with Turkey, pp. 223-233.

10. Ibid., pp. 233-239; Hinckley, American Consular Jurisdiction, pp. 23-29; and Nasim Sousa, The Capitulatory Regime of
Turkey: Its History, Origins, and Nature (Baltimore, 1933), p. 130.

11. Sousa, Capitulatory Regime, p. 137.

12. Tibawi, American Interests in Syria, pp. 221, 262, 270,
272, 292, 298.

13. Ralph Elliott Cook, "The United States and the Armenian
Question, 1884-1924," unpublished Ph.D. dissertation, Fletcher School
of Law and Diplomacy, 1957, pp. 35, 84; Gordon, American Relations with Turkey, p. 233.

14. Field, Mediterranean World, p. 359.

15. Ibid., p. 317.

16. FRUS, 1866, II, 253-255.

17. Field, Mediterranean World, p. 321.

18. Ibid., pp. 359-362; Daniel, American Philanthropy, p.
124.

19. Daniel, American Philanthropy, p. 129.

20. Ibid., p. 129; Field, Mediterranean World, pp. 365-369.

21. Field, Mediterranean World, pp. 371-372.

22. Irving McKee, "Ben-Hur" Wallace: The Life of General
Lew Wallace (Berkeley, Calif., 1947), p. 201.

23.   Field claims that American missionaries in Constanti-
nople were responsible.   Field, Mediterranean World, p. 359.
Richard Hovannisian suggests that it was Russian influence that led
to this activity.   Richard G. Hovannisian, Armenia on the Road to
Independence, 1918 (Berkeley, Calif., 1969), pp. 15-17.   But Louise
Nalbandian asserts that it was French influence.   Louise Nalbandian,
The Armenian Revolutionary Movement: The Development of Armen-
ian Political Parties (Berkeley, Calif., 1967), pp. 37, 75-76, 96.

24.   Cook, "Armenian Question," p. 46.

25.   See Gordon, American Relations with Turkey, Ch.
XVIII, and Cook, "Armenian Question," pp. 11-26.

26.   FRUS, 1894, I, 719.

27.   Cook, "Armenian Question," pp. 47-48.

28.   FRUS, 1894, I, 719-720.

29.   Ibid., 721-722; Congressional Record, 54 Cong, 1 Sess,
p. 11.

30.   FRUS, 1895, II, 1340, 1344-1345.

31.   Congressional Record, 54 Cong, 1 Sess, p. 854.

32.   Cook, "Armenian Question," pp. 65-66.

33.   FRUS, 1895, II, 1238, 1243.

34.   Ibid., 1893, 712; 1894, I, 725-726; Cook, "Armenian
Question," pp. 81-85.

35.   Cook, "Armenian Question," p. 85.

36.   Grabill, Protestant Diplomacy, p. 46; Cook, "Armenian
Question," pp. 103, 105, 108, 110.

37.   Cook, "Armenian Question," pp. 89-91; Ernest R. May,
Imperial Democracy: The Emergence of America as a Great Power
(New York, 1961), pp. 29-30.

38.   May, Imperial Democracy, pp. 53-54; Alfred L. P. Dennis, Adventures in American Diplomacy, 1896-1906 (New York,
1928), pp. 450-451; FRUS, 1896, 848-938.

39.   Cook, "Armenian Question," p. 91.

40.   Congressional Record, 54 Cong, 2 Sess, pp. 2-3.

41.   FRUS, 1898, I, 1113; Oscar Straus, Under Four Administrations: From Cleveland to Taft (Boston, 1922), pp. 125, 141-142;

Lloyd Griscom, Diplomatically Speaking; Memoirs of Constantinople
and Persia (New York, 1940), pp. 156-174.

42. Dennis, Adventures, p. 446.

43. Ibid., p. 139, and David R. Serpell, "American Consular Activities in Egypt, 1849-63," Journal of Modern History, X (Sept. 1939), 341.

44. Wright, United States Policy, pp. 142, 197, 206, 209-212.

45. Ibid., p. 146.

46. Ibid., pp. 40-48.

47. Ibid., pp. 52-56.

48. Ibid., pp. 44-46; Field, Mediterranean World, p. 292; Edwin DeLeon, Thirty Years of My Life on Three Continents (London, 1890), I, Chapter 11.

49. Wright, United States Policy, pp. 151-154.

50. Ibid., pp. 65-71 and Edward Mead Earle, "Egyptian Cotton and the American Civil War," Political Science Quarterly, 41 (1926), 520-545.

51. Wright, United States Policy, pp. 68-70.

52. FRUS, 1862, I, 784, 853, 856.

53. Wright, United States Policy, Chapt. 5; Field, Mediterranean World, Chapt. 11; Frederick J. Cox, "American Naval Mission in Egypt," Journal of Modern History, XXVI (June 1954), 173-178; Pierre Crabitès, Americans in the Egyptian Army (London, 1938); and William Hesseltine and Hazel C. Wolf, The Blue and the Gray on the Nile (Chicago, 1969).

54. Crabitès, Egyptian Army, p. 52; Wright, United States Policy, p. 73.

55. Hesseltine and Wolf, Blue and the Gray, p. 22, and Wright, United States Policy, p. 75.

56. Ibid., pp. 75-76.

57. Ibid., p. 81.

58. Ibid., pp. 88-90.

59. Ibid., pp. 94-100; Hinckley, Consular Jurisdiction, pp. 153-55.

60. Wright, United States Policy, pp. 116-117.

61. Ibid., pp. 119-125; McKee, "Ben-Hur" Wallace, pp. 203-204; Field, Mediterranean World, p. 431.

62. Wright, United States Policy, pp. 125-131.

63. Abraham Yeselson, United States-Persian Diplomatic Relations, 1883-1921 (New Brunswick, N.J., 1950), p. 21.

64. Miller, Treaties, VII, 446-449.

65. Yeselson, Diplomatic Relations, p. 22; Richardson, Messages and Papers, V, 435.

66. Yeselson, Diplomatic Relations, pp. 25-28.

67. Richardson, Messages and Papers, VIII, 251.

68. Yeselson, Diplomatic Relations, p. 29.

69. Richardson, Messages and Papers, VIII, 301.

70. Yeselson, Diplomatic Relations, p. 32.

71. FRUS, 1887, 913, 916, 918; 1888, II, 1359.

72. Yeselson, Diplomatic Relations, pp. 42-51.

73. Ibid., pp. 53-61.

74. Ibid., p. 59.

75. Ibid., p. 60.

76. Field, Mediterranean World, pp. 339-343 and "A Scheme in Regard to Cyrenaica," Mississippi Valley Historical Review, 44 (June 1957), 445-468.

77. Field, Mediterranean World, pp. 381-383.

78. Hall, United States and Morocco, pp. 220-224.

CHAPTER 5

1. On the missionary role in the Middle East, see John A. DeNovo, American Interests and Policies in the Middle East, 1900-1939 (Minneapolis, 1963), pp. 8-16.

2. Gordon, American Relations with Turkey, pp. 233, 246, and DeNovo, American Interests, p. 8.

3. Gordon, American Relations with Turkey, pp. 58, 155-156, and DeNovo, American Interests, pp. 16, 24, 25, 38-41.

4. Gordon, American Relations with Turkey, p. 15; William C. Askew and J. Fred Rippy, "The United States and Europe's Strife, 1908-1913," Journal of Politics, 4 (1942), 73-74.

5. Askew and Rippy, "Europe's Strife," 75-79.

6. Cook, "Armenian Question," p. 106.

7. Ibid., p. 107.

8. For a lengthy discussion of this problem, see Gordon, American Relations with Turkey, Ch. XVIII.

9. Straus, Under Four Administrations, pp. 296-297.

10. Ibid., pp. 297-298.

11. Cook, "Armenian Question," pp. 106-107.

12. Ibid., pp. 111-112.

13. Straus, Under Four Administrations, p. 297.

14. John A. DeNovo, "A Railroad for Turkey: The Chester Project of 1908-1913," Business History Review, 33 (autumn, 1959), 322.

15. F. M. Huntington Wilson, Memoirs of an Ex-Diplomat (Boston, 1945), p. 223.

16. Gordon, American Relations with Turkey, pp. 14-15.

17. Askew and Rippy, "Europe's Strife," 73.

18. For background material on the Chester plan, I have depended heavily on Gordon, American Relations with Turkey, pp. 257-264; DeNovo, "A Railroad for Turkey," 300-329 and American Interests, Ch. 3.

19. FRUS, 1909, 595; DeNovo, American Interests, pp. 65-66.

20. DeNovo, American Interests, pp. 66-67.

21. Ibid., pp. 73-74.

22. Ibid., pp. 74-76, and Huntington Wilson, Memoirs, pp. 227-230.

23. See A. J. P. Taylor, The Struggle for Mastery in Europe,

1848-1918 (Oxford, 1954), pp. 427-428, for this interpretation.

24.   Luella Hall asserts that American-Moroccan trade was not a factor.   Hall, United States and Morocco, pp. 158-164.   A. L. Dennis discounted the American Treaty with Morocco and the American signing of the 1880 Madrid Convention as factors, and, like Joseph Bishop, suggests that American participation resulted from Roosevelt's fear that a war might ensue that would endanger American security, a conclusion also expressed by Raymond Esthus and Howard K. Beale.   Dennis, Advenures, pp. 485-493; Joseph Bucklin Bishop, Theodore Roosevelt and His Time (New York, 1920), I, 467; Raymond A. Esthus, Theodore Roosevelt and the International Rivalries (Waltham, 1970), pp. 108-109; and Howard K. Beale, Theodore Roosevelt and the Rise of America to World Power (Baltimore, 1956), pp. 333, 389.

25.   Harold E. Davis suggests that Roosevelt was prepared to support the French position at Algeciras, this by virtue of his treatment of the Perdicaris episode.   Harold E. Davis, "The Citizenship of John Perdicaris," Journal of Modern History, XIII (1941), 517-526.

26.   Yeselson, Diplomatic Relations, pp. 61-62; Griscom, Diplomatically Speaking, pp. 206-216.

27.   Yeselson, Diplomatic Relations, pp. 68-82.

28.   FRUS, 1904, 658-659.

29.   Yeselson, Diplomatic Relations, pp. 75-80.

30.   Ibid., p. 87.

31.   Ibid., p. 89.

32.   Ibid., p. 91.

33.   Ibid., p. 94.

34.   Ibid., p. 113, and William M. Shuster, The Strangling of Persia (New York, 1912), p. 3.

35.   Robert A. McDaniel, The Shuster Mission and the Persian Constitutional Revolution (Minneapolis, 1974), p. 197.

36.   Yeselson, Diplomatic Relations, pp. 114-115, 120-121; DeNovo, American Interests, p.55; McDaniel, Shuster Mission, p. 179.

37.   Wright, United States Policy Toward Egypt, Ch. 15, and John A. DeNovo, "Petroleum and the United States Navy before World War I," Mississippi Valley Historical Review, 41 (March 1955), 641-656.

CHAPTER 6

1. Laurence Evans, United States Policy and the Partition of Turkey, 1914-1924 (Baltimore, 1965), p. 27.

2. DeNovo, American Interests, pp. 91-93; FRUS, 1914, 1090-1094.

3. Evans, United States Policy, pp. 29-31.

4. DeNovo, American Interests, p. 93; FRUS, 1914, Supp., 771-772.

5. Henry Morgenthau, Ambassador Morgenthau's Story (Garden City, N. Y.: 1922), p. 118 and All in a Lifetime (Garden City, N. Y., 1922), p. 203.

6. Grabill, Protestant Diplomacy; Caleb Frank Gates, Not to Me Only (Princeton, N. J., 1940); Mary Mills Patrick, Under Five Sultans (New York, 1929).

7. DeNovo, American Interests, p. 97.

8. On the missionary influence on the Wilson Administration, see Joseph L. Grabill "Missionary Influence on American Relations with the Near East, 1914-1923," Muslim World, LVIII (April 1968), 141-54; Robert L. Daniel, "The Friendship of Woodrow Wilson and Cleveland Dodge," Mid-America, 43 (July 1961), 182-96.

9. Morgenthau, Morgenthau's Story, pp. 327-28; FRUS, 1915, Supp., 982-984.

10. Grabill, Protestant Diplomacy, pp. 69-70; FRUS, 1915, Supp., 983.

11. For a complete study of Near East Relief, see James L. Barton, Story of Near East Relief, 1915-1930: An Interpretation (New York, 1930).

12. DeNovo, American Interests, p. 103.

13. Grabill, Protestant Diplomacy, p. 78.

14. Ibid., pp. 74-75.

15. William Yale, The Near East: A Modern History (Ann Arbor, Mich., 1958), p. 265.

16. Selig Adler, "The Palestine Question in the Wilson Era," Journal of Jewish Social Studies, X (1948), 303; Frank E. Manuel, The Realities of American-Palestine Relations (Washington, D. C., 1949), p. 116.

17. Manuel, American-Palestine Relations, p. 120.

18. Ibid., p. 123.

19. Ibid., pp. 127-131.

20. Ibid., pp. 138-142.

21. Ibid., pp. 142-144.

22. Ibid., pp. 144-146.

23. Congressional Record, 65 Cong, 2 Sess, pp. 18-21.

24. Evans, United States Policy, p. 42.

25. Grabill, "Missionary Influence," 52; Penrose, That They May Have Life, p. 162; Paul C. Helmreich, From Paris to Sèvres: The Partition of the Ottoman Empire at the Peace Conference, 1919-20 (Columbus, Ohio, 1974), p. 20; Daniel, "Friendship of Woodrow Wilson," 43; Lewis Einstein, A Diplomat Looks Back (New Haven, Conn., 1968), p. 137. But Dr. Barton claims that the ACRNE was non-political and did not even discuss U.S. entry into the war. Barton, Near East Relief, p. 55.

26. Sousa, The Capitulatory Regime of Turkey, p. 256.

27. FRUS, Lansing Papers, II, 17-19.

28. William Yale, "Ambassador Henry Morgenthau's Special Mission of 1917," World Politics, I (1944), 308-20.

29. Selig Adler asserts that Colonel House and Secretary Lansing opposed Zionist aspirations and that Justice Brandeis swung Wilson over in favor of Zionist goals. Adler, "Palestine Question," 307 et seq. But Herbert Parzen says that House was responsible for influencing Wilson. Herbert Parzen, "Brandeis and the Balfour Declaration," Herzl Yearbook, V (1963), 309-50. Milton Plesur suggests that it was Brandeis, ably assisted by Rabbi Stephen Wise, who converted Wilson. Milton Plesur, "The Relations between the United States and Palestine," Judaism: A Quarterly Journal of Jewish Life, III (1954), 474. Leonard Stein asserts that Brandeis converted House and that the latter influenced Wilson. Leonard Stein, The Balfour Declaration (New York, 1961), pp. 196-197. But George Lenczowski claims that a number of "eminent men in American official circles" influenced Wilson. He suggests that William Jennings Bryan, Secretary Lansing, Newton Baker, Josephus Daniels, Colonel House, and Norman Hapgood were responsible. George Lenczowski, Middle East in World Affairs (Ithaca, 1956), pp. 79-80.

30. Richard Ned Lebow, "Woodrow Wilson and the Balfour Declaration," Journal of Modern History, 40 (Dec. 1968), 506-514, 522-523.

31. Lawrence Gelfand, The Inquiry: American Preparations for Peace (New Haven, Conn., 1963), pp. 248-49.

32. Congressional Record, 65 Cong, 2 Sess, pp. 680-681.

33. Seth P. Tillman, Anglo-American Relations at the Paris Peace Conference of 1919 (Princeton, N.J., 1961), p. 368; FRUS, 1919, Paris Peace Conference, III, 787-791, 795-796, and 807-808. Hereafter cited as PPC.

34. For British motives for offering the mandate to the U.S., see Thomas A. Bryson, "An American Mandate for Armenia: A Link in British Near Eastern Policy," Armenian Review, XXI (1968), 23-41; Helmreich, From Paris to Sèvres, pp. 12-14; E. L. Woodward and Rohan Butler, eds., Documents on British Foreign Policy, 1919-1939, (1st series), XII, 557, 563, 565, 577-580, and 560-591. Hereafter cited as British Documents.

35. FRUS, 1919, PPC, V, 482-583-585.

36. Harry N. Howard, The King-Crane Commission: An American Inquiry in the Middle East (Beirut, 1963), pp. 24-26.

37. See Harry N. Howard, "An American Experiment in Peacemaking: The King-Crane Commission," Muslim World, XXXII (1942), 122-146.

38. Helmreich, From Paris to Sèvres, pp. 90-93; DeNovo, American Interests, p. 117; Evans, United States Policy, pp. 172-173; Howard, King-Crane Commission, pp. 233-234; and FRUS, 1919, PPC, V, 106-108, 135-136, 149-150, 202-203, 222, 254, 412, 535-538, and 733-734.

39. Tillman, Anglo-American Relations, p. 368; David Lloyd George, Memoirs of the Peace Conference (2 vols. New Haven, Conn., 1939), II, 568; James B. Gidney, A Mandate for Armenia (Kent, Ohio, 1967), pp. 90-91; and FRUS, 1919, PPC, V, 622.

40. See Thomas A. Bryson, "Mark Lambert Bristol, U.S. Navy, Admiral-Diplomat: His Influence on the Armenian Mandate Question," Armenian Review, XXI (1968), 3-22.

41. Evans, United States Policy, p. 195; FRUS, 1919, PPC, VI, 729.

42. See Thomas A. Bryson, "Walter George Smith and the Armenian Question at the Paris Peace Conference, 1919," Records of the American Catholic Historical Society, XXXI (March 1970), 3-26 and Walter George Smith (Washington, D.C., 1976), Ch. 5.

43. Harold Nicolson, Curzon: The Last Phase, 1919-1925-- A Study in Post-war Diplomacy (New York, 1939), p. 67; Lloyd George, Memoirs, II, 817, 818, 820, and 878; and Helmreich,

From Paris to Sèvres, p. 125.

44. See Thomas A. Bryson, "Woodrow Wilson and the Armenian Mandate: A Reassessment," Armenian Review, XXI (1968), 18-22. Also see William Linn Westermann, "The Armenian Problem and the Disruption of Turkey," in Edward Mandell House and Charles Seymour, eds., What Really Happened at Paris: The Story of the Peace Conference, 1918-1919 (New York, 1921); and Helmreich, From Paris to Sèvres, p. 328, in which is refuted the view that Wilson delayed handling the Armenian question.

45. For the report of this commission, see Howard, King-Crane Commission, Ch. 7, and "Experiment in Peacemaking," 138-142; and FRUS, 1919, PPC, XII, 751-863.

46. For the work of this commission see Peter M. Buzanski, "The Interallied Investigation of the Greek Invasion of Smyrna, 1919," Historian, XXV (May 1963), 325-343 and "Admiral Mark L. Bristol and Turkish-American Relations, 1919-1922," unpublished Ph.D. dissertation, University of California, 1960, Ch. 4.

47. Bryson, "The Armenian Question," 6-9.

48. For the work of the Harbord Mission, see John Philip Richardson, "The American Military Mission to Armenia," master's thesis, George Washington University, 1964; and James H. Tashjian, "The American Military Mission to Armenia," Armenian Review, 1949-1952, Issues 5-17; and Gidney, A Mandate for Armenia, Ch. 8.

49. Thomas A. Bryson, "Woodrow Wilson, the Senate, Public Opinion and the Armenian Mandate Question, 1919-1920," unpublished Ph.D. dissertation, University of Georgia, 1965, p. 172; FRUS, 1919, II, 841-889.

50. Bryson, "Woodrow Wilson," 95-98. Speeches are in Senate Documents, 66 Cong, 1 Sess, Vol. 11.

51. Evans, United States Policy, pp. 232-233.

52. Robert L. Daniel, "The Armenian Question and American-Turkish Relations, 1914-1927," Mississippi Valley Historical Review, XLVI (Sept. 1959), 263-64. Also see Thomas A. Bryson, "John Sharp Williams: An Advocate for the Armenian Mandate, 1919-1920," Armenian Review, XXVI (1973), 23-42 for a brief resumé of the work of Senator Williams on this committee.

53. Grabill, Protestant Diplomacy, pp. 89-105.

54. Concerning this committee, see Thomas A. Bryson, "Armenia-America Society: A Factor in American-Turkish Relations, 1919-1924," Records of the American Catholic Historical Society, 82 (1971), 83-105 and "Walter George Smith and the International Philarmenian League: A Note on the Armenian Question before the

League of Nations, 1920," in Robert Thomson, ed., Recent Studies in Modern Armenian History (Boston, 1972), pp. 71-82.

55. Daniel, "The Armenian Question," 264.

56. DeNovo, American Interests, p. 125.

57. Lloyd George, Memoirs, II, 855-858.

58. FRUS, 1920, III, 748-750.

59. Bryson, "Woodrow Wilson and the Armenian Mandate Question," p. 121; FRUS, 1920, III, 750-753.

60. Bryson, "Woodrow Wilson and the Armenian Mandate Question," p. 122.

61. FRUS, 1920, III, 779-783.

62. Evans, United States Policy, pp. 283-85, 297; Woodward and Butler, British Documents (1st Series), IV, 501-503.

63. Gidney, A Mandate for Armenia, p. 221; FRUS, 1920, III, 783.

64. Gidney, A Mandate for Armenia, p. 226; Congressional Record, 66 Cong, 2 Sess, pp. 7533-7534.

65. For the Senate debate on the mandate question, see Bryson, "Woodrow Wilson and the Armenian Mandate Question," pp. 167-203; Congressional Record, 66 Cong, 2 Sess, pp. 7875-7890; 7960-62; 7964-71; 8051-73.

66. Kirk H. Porter and Donald B. Johnson, National Party Platforms, 1840-1956 (Urbana, Ill., 1956), p. 222.

67. Bryson, "International Philarmenian League," pp. 76-78.

CHAPTER 7

1. Daniel, "The Armenian Question and American-Turkish Relations," 264.

2. On the work of this society, see Bryson, "Armenia-America Society."

3. Gordon, American Relations with Turkey, pp. 33-34.

4. Ibid., pp. 33-34; Bryson, "Armenia-America Society," 101; and Richard Washburn Child, A Diplomat Looks at Europe (New York, 1925), p. 93.

5. On the growth of the "Terrible Turk" image, see Robert L. Daniel, "The United States and the Turkish Republic before World War II: The Cultural Dimension," Middle East Journal, 21 (1967), 52-63; Roger R. Trask, The United States Response to Turkish Nationalism and Reform, 1914-1939 (Minneapolis, 1971), pp. 12, 82-92, 243-244, and "The 'Terrible Turk' and Turkish-American Relations in the Interwar Period," Historian, XXXIII (Nov. 1970), 40-53.

6. Daniel, "The Armenian Question and American-Turkish Relations," 273.

7. FRUS, 1926, II, 993-1000; 1927, III, 794-798.

8. Gordon, American Relations with Turkey, p. 246.

9. Trask, United States Response, Ch. 7, and "Unnamed Christianity in Turkey during the Ataturk Era," Muslim World, 55 (1965), 66-76, 102-111.

10. Daniel, American Philanthropy, p. 279.

11. Grabill, Protestant Diplomacy, p. 260.

12. Joseph C. Grew, Turbulent Era: A Diplomatic Record of Forty Years (2 vols. London, 1953), II, Ch. XXVI.

13. George Horton, The Blight of Asia (New York, 1926), p. 236, and Edward Hale Bierstadt, The Great Betrayal (New York, 1924), p. 175, disagree, declaring that the U.S. bartered the rights of the Armenians for economic rights. However, Edward M. Earle, Nasim Sousa, and Harry Howard agree that the Turks granted the Chester Concession to gain American diplomatic support against the European Powers. Edward Mead Earle, Turkey, the Great Powers, and the Baghdad Railway: A Study in Imperialism (New York, 1923), pp. 334-44; Sousa, The Capitulatory Regime of Turkey, p. 256; and Howard, The King-Crane Commission, p. 307.

14. Child, A Diplomat, pp. 93, 117; Gordon, American Relations with Turkey, p. 280.

15. Trask, "The Terrible Turk," 40 and United States Response, p. 243.

16. Trask, "The Terrible Turk," 44-48.

17. Gordon, American Relations with Turkey, p. 61.

18. Thomas A. Bryson, "Admiral Mark L. Bristol, An Open Door Diplomat in Turkey," International Journal of Middle East Studies 5 (1974), 453.

19. DeNovo, American Interests, pp. 210-211.

20.   Ibid., pp. 211-216.

21.   Ibid., pp. 217-225; Evans, United States Policy, pp. 344-345; and FRUS, 1923, II, 1215-1240.

22.   DeNovo, American Interests, p. 227; FRUS, 1923, II, 1251-1252.

23.   See Buzanski, "Admiral Mark L. Bristol and Turkish-American Relations."

24.   Evans, United States Policy, pp. 270-277; FRUS, 1923, II, 884.

25.   Bryson, "Armenia-America Society," 98-100.

26.   Evans, United States Policy, p. 397.

27.   DeNovo, American Interests, pp. 138-140.

28.   Ibid., p. 143; Bryson, "Armenia-America Society," 100.

29.   Grew, Memoirs, II, 558-559, and DeNovo, American Interests, p. 148.

30.   Grew, Memoirs, II, 603-605; DeNovo, American Interests, p. 152; FRUS, 1923, II, 1153-1166.

31.   Trask, United States Response, pp. 39-44.

32.   DeNovo, American Interests, pp. 157-158.

33.   Daniel, "The Armenian Question and American-Turkish Relations," 273, and Congressional Record, 69 Cong, 2 Sess, p. 1468.

34.   Trask, United States Response, pp. 49-55.

35.   Grew, Memoirs, II, 807, 837; Trask, United States Response, pp. 109-114; FRUS, 1929, III, 823-825.

36.   Trask, United States Response, pp. 99-102.

37.   Ibid., pp. 108, 137-139; Trask, "United States and Turkish Nationalism: Investments and Technical Aid during the Ataturk Era," Business History Review, 38 (Spring, 1964), 68-70.

38.   Trask, United States Response, pp. 115-22.

39.   Ibid., pp. 139-145.

40.   Ibid., pp. 147-151, and "Unnamed Christianity," 66-71.

41. Grew, Memoirs, II, 758-789.

42. Ibid., pp. 852-858.

43. Trask, United States Response, pp. 245-247.

44. Ibid., pp. 194-200; FRUS, 1931, II, 1537-1544.

45. Trask, United States Response, pp. 200-211.

46. Ibid., pp. 175-177.

47. Ibid., p. 242.

48. FRUS, 1919, II, 700.

49. Yeselson, Diplomatic Relations, p. 167.

50. Ibid., pp. 169, 178.

51. Ibid., pp. 173-174.

52. Ibid., pp. 181-189.

53. DeNovo, American Interests, pp. 281-282; A. C. Mills-paugh, The American Task in Persia (New York, 1925), pp. 19-20; and FRUS, 1927, III, 527.

54. DeNovo, American Interests, pp. 282-283; Millspaugh, American Task in Persia, p. 310.

55. DeNovo, American Interests, p. 283; M. K. Sheehan, Iran: Impact of United States Interests and Policies, 1941-1954 (Brooklyn, N.Y., 1968), p. 4.

56. Sheehan, Iran, p. 4.

57. DeNovo, American Interests, pp. 297-302.

58. Ibid., pp. 288-297.

59. For an account of the German influence in Iran in this period, see George Lenczowski, Russia and the West in Iran, 1918-1948 (Ithaca, N.Y., 1949), pp. 158-162. For the breach in rela-tions, see DeNovo, American Interests, pp. 306-309.

60. Sheehan, Iran, p. 4.

61. DeNovo, American Interests, pp. 318-322.

62. Ibid., pp. 322-323; FRUS, 1924, I, 741-746.

63. DeNovo, American Interests, pp. 325-326.

64. Ibid., pp. 327-333.

65. Manuel, American-Palestine Relations, pp. 271-279.

66. Ibid., p. 271; DeNovo, American Interests, pp. 337-339; J. C. Hurewitz, Middle East Dilemmas: The Background of United States Policy (New York, 1953), p. 118; and FRUS, 1924, II, 203-222.

67. Manuel, American-Palestine Relations, pp. 300-304 and Samuel Halperin, The Political World of American Zionism (Detroit, 1961), pp. 12, 17.

68. Hurewitz, Middle East Dilemmas, p. 124; FRUS, 1929, III, 58.

69. Yale, The Near East, p. 395.

70. Ibid., pp. 395-396.

71. Cordell Hull, The Memoirs of Cordell Hull (2 vols., New York, 1948), II, 1529.

72. Ibid., p. 1529; Manuel, American-Palestine Relations, p. 307; DeNovo, American Interests, pp. 342-44.

73. DeNovo, American Interests, p. 346.

74. Ibid., p. 380.

75. FRUS, 1930, III, 302-305.

76. DeNovo, American Interests, pp. 355-357.

77. Karl S. Twitchell, Saudi Arabia: With an Account of the Development of Its Natural Resources (Princeton, N.J., 1953), pp. 211-216 and Joseph William Walt, "Saudi Arabia and the Americans, 1923-1951," unpublished Ph.D. dissertation, Northwestern University, 1960, pp. 84-86.

78. For the story of the establishment of U.S. diplomatic ties with Saudi Arabia, see Walt, "Saudi Arabia," pp. 184-205.

CHAPTER 8

1. Herbert Feis, Petroleum and American Foreign Policy (Stanford, Calif., 1944), p. 4; Benjamin Shwadran, The Middle East and the Great Powers (New York, 1955), pp. 205-206; Congressional Record, 66 Cong, 1 Sess, pp. 3304-3310.

2. John A. DeNovo, "The Movement for an Aggressive American Oil Policy, 1918-1920," American Historical Review, 66 (July 1956), 856.

3. Evans, United States Policy, pp. 295-296; FRUS, 1919, I, 250-252.

4. DeNovo, American Interests, p. 173; FRUS, 1919, II, 259.

5. Evans, United States Policy, p. 298. Text of the San Remo oil agreement is in FRUS, 1920, II, 655-58. For U.S. protest to Britain, see FRUS, 1920, II, 650-655.

6. Ibid., II, 658-659; Evans, United States Policy, p. 300.

7. Edward Mead Earle, "The Turkish Petroleum Company: A Study in Oleaginous Diplomacy," Political Science Quarterly, 39 (1924), 274.

8. DeNovo, American Interests, p. 181.

9. Gerald D. Nash, United States Oil Policy, 1890-1964 (Pittsburgh, Pa., 1968), p. 56.

10. DeNovo, American Interests, p. 185.

11. Ibid., p. 186.

12. Shwadran, The Middle East, pp. 209-210.

13. George Sweet Gibb and Evelyn H. Knowlton, The Resurgent Years, 1911-1927: History of Standard Oil Company (New York, 1956), p. 293.

14. DeNovo, American Interests, pp. 189-190; FRUS, 1922, II, 339-342.

15. DeNovo, American Interests, pp. 191-192; FRUS, 1922, II, 346-347.

16. Shwadran, The Middle East, p. 216; FRUS, 1922, II, 347-348.

17. DeNovo, American Interests, p. 193; FRUS, 1922, II, 348-49, 351-52.

18. DeNovo, American Interests, p. 197.

19. Ibid., p. 196.

20. Ibid., p. 198.

21. Shwadran, The Middle East, p. 237.

22. Ibid., pp. 244-247, and Halford L. Hoskins, The Middle East: Problem Area in World Politics (New York, 1957), pp. 201-203; Yale, The Near East, pp. 371-372.

23. DeNovo, "An Aggressive American Oil Policy," 875.

24. George W. Stocking, Middle East Oil: A Study in Political and Economic Controversy (Nashville, 1970), p. 56.

25. Gibb and Knowlton, The Resurgent Years, pp. 289-291. Leonard Mosley also credits Gulbenkian with using his influence at the Foreign Office to obtain U.S. membership. Leonard Mosley, Power Play: Oil in the Middle East (New York, 1973), p. 47.

26. DeNovo, American Interests, p. 200; Gibb and Knowlton, The Resurgent Years, p. 297; David H. Finnie, Desert Enterprise: The Middle East Oil Industry (Cambridge, Mass., 1958), p. 31; Stocking, Middle East Oil, p. 56. Benjamin Shwadran gives a different interpretation, saying the Open Door did provide an "ideal opening" but that the State Department agreed to the "practical solutions" needed to "overcome the abstract principles of the Open Door policy." Shwadran, The Middle East, p. 242. This explanation seems the most practical.

27. Yeselson, Diplomatic Relations, p. 201.

28. DeNovo, American Interests, p. 284.

29. Gibb and Knowlton, The Resurgent Years, p. 309; Yeselson, Diplomatic Relations, p. 213; and FRUS, 1921, II, 648-649.

30. Gibb and Knowlton, The Resurgent Years, pp. 310-311; Yeselson, Diplomatic Relations, p. 219; and FRUS, 1921, II, 653-654.

31. Gibb and Knowlton, The Resurgent Years, p. 311; FRUS, 1924, II, 541-545.

32. Gibb and Knowlton, The Resurgent Years, p. 312.

33. Ibid., pp. 312-313.

34. DeNovo, American Interests, pp. 285-286; FRUS, 1923, II, 713-714.

35. DeNovo, American Interests, p. 286.

36. Ibid., pp. 314-315.

37. FRUS, 1929, III, 80-82.

38. Shwadran, The Middle East, pp. 370-375; Stephen Hemsley Longrigg, Oil in the Middle East: Its Discovery and Development (New York, 1968), pp. 99-105.

39. FRUS, 1932, II, 1-29.

40. Shwadran, The Middle East, pp. 384-89; Longrigg, Oil in the Middle East, pp. 110-113.

41. Ibid., p. 107; Karl S. Twitchell, Saudi Arabia: With an Account of the Development of Its Natural Resources (Princeton, N.J., 1953), pp. 211-216; Joseph W. Walt, "Saudi Arabia and the Americans, 1928-1951," unpublished Ph.D. dissertation, Northwestern University, 1960, pp. 84-88.

42. Twitchell, Saudi Arabia, p. 219; Walt, "Saudi Arabia," pp. 90-96.

43. Walt, "Saudi Arabia," pp. 98-104.

44. Ibid., p. 127.

CHAPTER 9

1. For examples, see John C. Campbell, Defense of the Middle East: Problems of American Policy (New York, 1960), pp. 30-31; Ephraim Speiser, The United States and the Near East (Cambridge, Mass., 1952), pp. 242-247; Hurewitz, Middle East Dilemmas, pp. 1, 130; and R. H. Nolte, "The United States and the Middle East," in Georgianna S. Stevens, ed., The United States and the Middle East (Englewood Cliffs, N.J., 1964), p. 152.

2. Evidence of a U.S. policy independent of Britain is seen in Hull, Memoirs, II, pp. 1365, 1498-1541, and Gaddis Smith, American Diplomacy During the Second World War, 1941-1945 (New York, 1966), p. 99.

3. Historians claiming that the U.S. adhered to an aggressive policy include William Reitzel, The Mediterranean: Its Role in America's Foreign Policy (New York, 1948), pp. 14-22, 56; Joyce and Gabriel Kolko. The Limits of Power: The World and United States Foreign Policy, 1945-1954 (New York, 1972), pp. 235-36; George E. Kirk, The Middle East in the War (London, 1952), pp. 24-25; Lloyd C. Gardner, Economic Aspects of New Deal Diplomacy (Madison, Wis., 1964), pp. 220-230; Martin W. Wilmington, The Middle East Supply Centre (Albany, N.Y., 1971), pp. 164-65; and Mohammed Agwani, The United States and the Arab World, 1945-1952 (Aligarh, India, 1955), pp. 31, 44, and 47.

4. Herbert Feis, Churchill, Roosevelt, Stalin: The War They Waged and the Peace They Sought (Princeton, N.J., 1967), pp. 89-90.

5. T. H. Vail Motter, The Persian Corridor and Aid to Russia (Washington, D.C., 1952), p. 28.

6. For evidence of an aggressive, anti-British, American oil policy in wartime Saudi Arabia, see Howard M. Sachar, Europe

Leaves the Middle East, 1936-1954 (New York, 1972), pp. 391-394;
Shwadran, The Middle East, pp. 303-309; Smith, American Diplomacy,
pp. 108-09; Stocking, Middle East Oil, p. 97; Hull, Memoirs, II,
1514; Kirk, Middle East in the War, pp. 352-57, 367-69; Mosley,
Oil in the Middle East, pp. 146-55; Walt, "Saudi Arabia," Ch. VIII;
and R. F. Mikesell and Hollis B. Chenery, Arabian Oil: America's
Stake in the Middle East (Chapel Hill, N.C., 1949), Ch. VII.

7. Walt, "Saudi Arabia," p. 197.

8. Shwadran, The Middle East, pp. 301-303.

9. Walt, "Saudi Arabia," pp. 159-167; FRUS, 1941, III, 624-
627.

10. Walt, "Saudi Arabia," pp. 171-173; Mosley, Oil in the
Middle East, pp. 145-148; FRUS, 1941, III, 642-643.

11. Smith, American Diplomacy, p. 108, and Mosley, Oil
in the Middle East, pp. 149-150.

12. Shwadran, The Middle East, p. 308.

13. Ibid., p. 309.

14. Walt, "Saudi Arabia," pp. 218-219; FRUS, 1943, IV,
854-59. Saudi Arabia received a total of $33 million in Lend-Lease
funds.

15. Hull, Memoirs, II, 1512-1514; Walt, "Saudi Arabia," pp.
225, 280-293; and FRUS, 1943, IV, 830-854; 1941, III, 651-659; and
1942, 561-567.

16. Hull, Memoirs, II, 1514; FRUS, 1944, V, 676.

17. Feis, Petroleum and American Foreign Policy, p. 14.

18. Shwadran, The Middle East, pp. 310-314, and FRUS,
1943, IV, 925-30.

19. Shwadran, The Middle East, p. 314; Mikesell and Chenery, Arabian Oil, pp. 90-91.

20. Walt, "Saudi Arabia," pp. 240-246; Shwadran, The Middle East, pp. 314-317.

21. Shwadran, The Middle East, pp. 318-319; Walt, "Saudi
Arabia," pp. 251-252.

22. Walt, "Saudi Arabia," pp. 255-262; Shwadran, The Middle
East, pp. 319-322.

23. Walt, "Saudi Arabia," pp. 262-272.

24. Twitchell, Saudi Arabia, pp. 237-243.

25. Shwadran, The Middle East, p. 329.

26. Ibid., p. 331, and Walt, "Saudi Arabia," pp. 275-279.

27. William Hardy McNeill, America, Britain, and Russia: Their Cooperation and Conflict, 1941-1946 (reprint ed., New York, 1970), pp. 90-118.

28. Feis, Churchill, Roosevelt, Stalin, p. 48, and James MacGregor Burns, Roosevelt: The Soldier of Freedom, 1940-1945 (New York, 1970), p. 229.

29. Smith, American Diplomacy, pp. 25-26; Burns, Roosevelt, pp. 242-43.

30. Feis, Churchill, Roosevelt, Stalin, p. 54.

31. Ibid., pp. 89-90; McNeill, America, Britain and Russia, p. 196.

32. On the Anglo-Russian intervention in Iran, see Kirk, The Middle East in the War, pp. 129-141.

33. Hull, Memoirs, II, 1501-1502; FRUS, 1944, III, 419, 446-447, 406-07.

34. Kirk, The Middle East in the War, p. 139.

35. Ibid., pp. 139-140; Motter, The Persian Corridor, p. 11; and FRUS, 1944, III, 449-450.

36. Motter, The Persian Corridor, p. 6.

37. Ibid., p. 17.

38. Michael Kahl Sheehan, Iran: Impact of United States Interests and Policies, 1941-1954 (Brooklyn, N.Y., 1968), p. 19. FRUS, 1943, IV, 453-510; and R. K. Ramazani, Iran's Foreign Policy, 1941-1973 (Charlottesville, Va., 1975), p. 71.

39. Motter, The Persian Corridor, pp. 437-442.

40. Ibid., p. 28.

41. Ibid., pp. 91, 213, 241-242.

42. George Lenczowski, Russia and the West in Iran, 1918-1949 (Ithaca, N.Y., 1949), pp. 279, 383, and Ramazani, Iran's Foreign Relations, pp. 81.

43. Motter says the U.S. began to formulate policy about

January 1943. Motter, The Persian Corridor, pp. 443-446. This view is supported by Hurewitz, Middle East Dilemmas, pp. 22-23; Sheehan, Iran, p. 20; Hull, Memoirs, II, 1507; and FRUS, 1943, IV, 331-336, 343, 351-354, 377-78 and 400-405.

44. Arthur C. Millspaugh, Americans in Persia (Washington, 1946), pp. 8, 47, 208-209, 230-233; Halford L. Hoskins, The Middle East: Problem Area in World Politics (New York, 1957), p. 177; Motter, The Persian Corridor, pp. 4-5. The above writers suggest that the U.S. presence in Iran was designed mainly to win the war. But Kolko and Kirk argue the U.S. was interested primarily in obtaining new sources of oil. Kolko, Limits of Power, p. 236 and Kirk, The Middle East in the War, pp. 24, 367-369, 474.

45. Hull, Memoirs, II, 1504-1509; FRUS, 1943, IV, 625-629.

46. Millspaugh, Americans in Persia, pp. 47, 61; Motter, The Persian Corridor, pp. 163 et seq.; Lenczowski, Russia and the West, pp. 263-71; and FRUS, 1943, IV, 517-548.

47. Millspaugh, Americans in Persia, pp. 132-139; FRUS, 1943, IV, 517-543, and Ramazani, Iran's Foreign Relations, pp. 83-85.

48. Lenczowski, Russia and the West, p. 270, and FRUS, 1943, IV, 532-45.

49. Lenczowski, Russia and the West, p. 271, and Motter, The Persian Corridor, pp. 171-172.

50. Lenczowski, Russia and the West, p. 272; Motter, The Persian Corridor, p. 163 and Ramazani, Iran's Foreign Policy, pp. 73-76.

51. On the work of the PGSC, see Lenczowski, Russia and the West, pp. 273-76; Motter, The Persian Corridor, pp. 138, 139, 155, 251-52, 264, 282, 331-377, and 419.

52. Hull, Memoirs, II, 1506 and FRUS, 1943, IV, 400-405.

53. McNeill, America, Britain, and Russia, pp. 365-66, and FRUS, 1943, Conference at Cairo and Teheran, 646.

54. See Don Lohbeck, Patrick J. Hurley (Chicago, 1956), pp. 196-197; Motter, The Persian Corridor, pp. 442-445; and FRUS, 1944, V, 303-306.

55. Hull, Memoirs, II, 1506-07. Motter says that Hurley's influence was important in shaping Roosevelt's thinking on Iran. Motter, The Persian Corridor, pp. 442-43. But Russell Buhite discounts the influence of Hurley, saying that he was a mere gadfly with little influence of any kind on Roosevelt's thinking about the Middle

East. Russell Buhite, Patrick Hurley and American Foreign Policy (Ithaca, N.Y., 1973), pp. 314-315. See FRUS, 1943, IV, 420.

56. Hull, Memoirs, II, 1508, and FRUS, 1944, V, 343-345.

57. Millspaugh, Americans in Persia, p. 233.

58. Hull, Memoirs, II, 1508.

59. Ibid., 1508-1509; Shwadran, The Middle East pp. 64-65; and FRUS, 1943, IV, 625.

60. Shwadran, The Middle East, pp. 65-68; Kirk, The Middle East in the War, pp. 474-478; FRUS, 1944, V, 445-486; and Ramazani, Iran's Foreign Relations, p. 104.

61. Kirk, The Middle East in the War, p. 23.

62. Millspaugh, Americans in Persia, pp. 207-210.

63. Lenczowski, Russia and the West, pp. 279, 283.

64. Motter, The Persian Corridor, pp. 160, 443-446, and Sheehan, Iran, pp. 20-23.

65. Hull, Memoirs, II, 1528.

66. Richard Stevens, American Zionism and U.S. Foreign Policy (New York, 1962), pp. 62-64.

67. Ibid., p. 25.

68. Manuel, American-Palestine Relations, p. 310.

69. Stevens, American Zionism, pp. 6-12.

70. Ibid., pp. 13-24.

71. Ibid., pp. 30-33.

72. Hull, Memoirs, II, 1531-1532; Evan Wilson, "The Palestine Papers, 1943-1947," Journal of Palestine Studies, II (1973), 37; and FRUS, 1943, IV, 773-775, 781-785.

73. Wilson, "Palestine Papers," 38 and FRUS, 1943, IV, 786-787.

74. Hull, Memoirs, II, 1532-1533 and FRUS, 1943, IV, 795, 807-810.

75. Hull, Memoirs, II, 1533 and FRUS, 1943, IV, 802, 811.

76. Wilson, "Palestine Papers," 40 and FRUS, 1945, 692-709.

77. Manuel, American-Palestine Relations, p. 311.

78. Wilson, "Palestine Papers," 41; Hull, Memoirs, II, 1534-1536; and FRUS, 1944, V, 563-564.

79. Wilson, "Palestine Papers," 42, and Manuel, American-Palestine Relations, p. 312.

80. Hurewitz, Middle East Dilemmas, p. 130.

81. Stevens, American Zionism, pp. 81-85.

82. Ibid., p. 85.

83. Hull, Memoirs, II, 1536. In agreement with this interpretation are the following: Hurewitz, Middle East Dilemmas, p. 172; Stevens, American Zionism, p. 92; Manuel, American-Palestine Relations, p. 317; and Kirk, The Middle East in the War, p. 328.

84. Sumner Welles, Where Are We Heading? (New York, 1946), pp. 264-65; M. S. Agwani supports this conclusion. Agwani, The United States and the Arab World, pp. 61-62.

85. William A. Eddy, FDR Meets Ibn Saud (New York, 1954), pp. 34-35.

86. Sachar, Europe Leaves the Middle East, pp. 453-454. Russell Buhite claims that Hurley was responsible for Roosevelt's feelings on Zionism. Buhite, Hurley, p. 315.

87. Smith, American Diplomacy, pp. 113-114; Burns, Roosevelt, p. 397; and John C. Campbell, "American Efforts for Peace," in Malcolm H. Kerr, ed., The Elusive Peace in the Middle East (Albany, N.Y., 1975), p. 252.

88. Hurewitz, Middle East Dilemmas, p. 127.

89. Smith, American Diplomacy, p. 106; Hull, Memoirs, II, 1541; and FRUS, 1941, III, 795-797, 801-802, 807-808.

90. Smith, American Diplomacy, p. 107; Hull, Memoirs, II, 1545; Sydney Nettleton Fisher, The Middle East, (New York, 1969), p. 485; and FRUS, 1944, V, 774-782.

91. Kirk, The Middle East in the War, pp. 412, 433; Burns, Roosevelt, p. 322; and Hall, United States and Morocco, pp. 943, 1002. But Leon B. Blair's Western Window on the Arab World (Austin, Tex., 1970), pp. 96-97 and 301, questions the claim that Roosevelt encouraged the Moroccan leader to expect U.S. assistance in winning self-determination after the war.

92. Smith, American Diplomacy, p. 102; Fisher, The Middle East, p. 483; and FRUS, 1942, IV, 63-87.

93.   Fisher, The Middle East, pp. 486-487; Smith, American Diplomacy, p. 105; and FRUS, 1941, III, 492-514.

94.   Sachar, Europe Leaves the Middle East, pp. 398-406, and Hurewitz, Middle East Dilemmas, p. 79.

95.   Hull, Memoirs, II, 1547; FRUS, 1944, V, 660-66; and Department of State Bulletin, May 18, 1947, 96.

96.   Martin W. Wilmington, The Middle East Supply Centre (Albany, N.Y., 1971), p. 54, and "The Middle East Supply Centre," Middle East Journal, 6 (1954), 144-166.

97.   Wilmington, The Middle East Supply Centre, pp. 164-168; Kirk, The Middle East in the War, pp. 188-189; and FRUS, 1945, VIII, 85-87.

98.   McNeill, America, Britain, and Russia, p. 272; Winston S. Churchill, The Hinge of Fate (Boston, 1950), p. 699; and FRUS, Conferences at Washington, 1941-42 and Casablanca, 1943, 659-660.   Also see Harry N. Howard, Turkey, the Straits and U.S. Policy (Baltimore, 1974), p. 172.

99.   McNeill, America, Britain, and Russia, p. 272; Edward Weisband, Turkish Foreign Policy, 1943-1945: Small State Diplomacy and Great Power Politics (Princeton, N.J., 1973), pp. 133-138; and Howard, Turkey, p. 174.

100.   Hull, Memoirs, II, 1536, and FRUS, 1943, IV, 1060-1062.

101.   This point appears all the more plausible following a reading of Weisband, Turkish Foreign Policy, pp. 180-200.

102.   Hull, Memoirs, II, 1366-68, and FRUS, 1943, IV, 1064-1071.

103.   Weisband, Turkish Foreign Policy, p. 180.

104.   Ibid., p. 152, and FRUS, 1943, IV, 1057.

105.   Howard, Turkey, p. 177; Hull, Memoirs, II, 1368; and FRUS, Conferences at Washington and Quebec, 1943, 480.

106.   Howard, Turkey, pp. 182-188; Weisband, Turkish Foreign Policy, p. 108; and FRUS, Conferences at Cairo and Teheran, 1943, 123-125.

107.   McNeill, America, Britain and Russia, pp. 352-53; Feis, Churchill, Roosevelt, Stalin, pp. 265-266.   Harry Howard claims that Turkish entry into the war was an unpopular, unacceptable subject to the American Joint Chiefs of Staff, to the British Chiefs of Staff, and to the Soviet Government.   He notes, "Indeed,

with the possible exception of the period when Italy entered the war in June 1940 and the winter of 1943-44, despite Churchill's position, the evidence would seem to indicate that neither the United Kingdom nor the United States nor even the Soviet Union actually desired Turkey's entry into the 'shooting war'." Howard, Turkey, p. 208. Also see Harry N. Howard, "Historical Backgrounds," in Tareq Y. Ismael, ed., The Middle East and World Politics: A Study in Contemporary International Relations (Syracuse, N.Y., 1974), pp. 13-14, and "The United States," in ibid., pp. 119-120. See FRUS, 1943, I, 634-635, 644, and 655.

108.   Weisband, Turkish Foreign Policy, pp. 201-215.

109.   Howard, Turkey, p. 196; Weisband, Turkish Foreign Policy, pp. 220-230; Hull, Memoirs, II, 1371; and FRUS, 1944, V, 818.

110.   Weisband, Turkish Foreign Policy, p. 230.

111.   Ibid., pp. 256-269, and FRUS, 1944, V, 818-900.

112.   Weisband, Turkish Foreign Policy, pp. 302-315.

CHAPTER 10

1.   For a general discussion of the formulation of a post-war U.S. foreign policy for the Middle East, see Hurewitz, Middle East Dilemmas; Campbell, Defense of the Middle East; John S. Badeau, American Approach to the Arab World (New York, 1968); William R. Polk, The United States and the Arab World (Cambridge, Mass., 1965); William Reitzel, The Importance of the Mediterranean (Ithaca, N.Y., 1952); Speiser, The United States and the Near East; Ernest Jackh, "The Geostrategic Uniqueness of the Middle East," in Ernest Jackh, ed., Background of the Middle East (Ithaca, N.Y., 1952); and Dankwart A. Rustow, "Defense of the Near East," Foreign Affairs, XXXIV (Jan. 1965), 271-86. For an estimate of the aggressive Soviet aims in the post-war Middle East, see Adam B. Ulam, Expansion and Coexistence: The History of Soviet Foreign Policy, 1917-1967 (New York, 1968), pp. 389-390, 425-427.

2.   Sheehan, Iran, p. 29; Hurewitz, Middle East Dilemmas, p. 26; George Curry, James F. Byrnes (New York, 1965), p. 174; and FRUS, 1945, VIII, 448-450.

3.   George E. Kirk claims that Britain took the lead to contain the Soviets. George E. Kirk, The Middle East, 1945-1950 (London, 1954), p. 5.

4.   Hurewitz, Middle East Dilemmas, p. 27; Dean Acheson, Present at the Creation: My Years at the State Department (New York, 1969), p. 197; James F. Byrnes, Speaking Frankly (New York, 1947), pp. 118-120; FRUS, 1946, VII, 292-293, 306-308; and

Ramazani, Iran's Foreign Relations, pp. 125-128.

5. Sheehan, Iran, p. 31; Lenczowski, Russia and the West, p. 297; FRUS, 1946, VII, 340-342.

6. Harry S Truman, Years of Trial and Hope: Memoirs by Harry S Truman (2 vols. New York, 1956), II, 95. Truman claims that his "blunt message" to Stalin was responsible for the Soviet withdrawal.

7. John C. Campbell refutes the importance Truman has attached to his message, saying the evidence does not support his claim. Campbell, Defense of the Middle East, p. 33. Also see Ramazani, Iran's Foreign Relations, pp. 138-139.

8. John Lewis Gaddis, The United States and the Origins of the Cold War, 1941-1947 (New York, 1972), p. 312.

9. Hurewitz, Middle East Dilemmas, p. 29.

10. See Lenczowski, Russia and the West, pp. 307-311. This author claims that Ambassador Allen's remarks caused a turning point in Iranian-Russian relations. See FRUS, 1947, V, 951-952.

11. Truman, Memoirs, II, 93-96; Campbell, Defense of the Middle East, p. 34; and Lenczowski, Russia and the West, p. 314.

12. George Kirk claims Britain took the lead. Kirk, The Middle East, p. 5. But the following writers assert that the U.S. acted independently of Britain: Lenczowski, Russia and the West, pp. 306-311; Richard W. Cottam, Nationalism in Iran (Pittsburgh, 1964), p. 208; Hurewitz, Middle East Dilemmas, pp. 26-28; Halford L. Hoskins, The Middle East: Problem Area in World Politics (New York, 1957), p. 178; Sheehan, Iran, pp. 27-31; William B. Quandt, "United States Policy in the Middle East: Constraints and Choices," in Paul Y. Hammond and Sidney S. Alexander, eds., Political Dynamics in the Middle East (New York, 1972), pp. 489-525.

13. Concerning revisionist literature on Iran in the Cold War, see Richard W. Cottam, "The United States, Iran, and the Cold War," Iranian Studies, III (winter 1970), 2-22; Justus D. Doenecke, "Revisionists, Oil and Cold War Diplomacy," ibid. III (winter 1970), 23-33, and "Iran's Role in Cold War Revisionism," ibid., V (summer 1972), 96-111.

14. See Byrnes, Speaking Frankly, pp. 118-120, 304, about the U.S. role in supporting Iran's efforts to get this issue before the United Nations. Also see Curry, Byrnes, pp. 205-206.

15. This claim is made by Gabriel Kolko, The Politics of War: The World and United States Foreign Policy, 1943-1945 (New York, 1968), pp. 297, 313, 310, 495, 623 and Limits of Power, p. 236; Lloyd C. Gardner, Architects of Illusion: Men and Ideas in

American Foreign Policy, 1941-1949 (Chicago, 1970), pp. 210-215; Stephen E. Ambrose, Rise to Globalism: American Foreign Policy, 1938-1970 (Baltimore, 1971), p. 131; and Denna Frank Fleming, The Cold War and Its Origins, 1917-1950 (New York, 1961), I, 340.

16.   Mikesell and Chenery, Arabian Oil, p. 108.

17.   Sheehan, Iran, p. 37.

18.   Trask, United States Response, pp. 245-247; Howard, Turkey, p. 233.

19.   Harris, Troubled Alliance, pp. 15-19.

20.   Ibid., p. 15; FRUS, 1945, I, 1015-1017.

21.   Harris, Troubled Alliance, pp. 16-17; Howard, Turkey, p. 220; and FRUS, 1945, I, 1034.

22.   FRUS, 1945, I, 1034.

23.   FRUS, 1945, VIII, 1288.

24.   Truman, Memoirs, II, 97; Gaddis Smith, Dean Acheson (New York, 1972), pp. 33-34; Howard, Turkey, pp. 242-260; and FRUS, 1945, VIII, 1287-1289.

25.   Harris, Troubled Alliance, p. 19.

26.   Ibid., p. 20; Howard, Turkey, p. 244; and FRUS, 1946, VIII, 902-903.

27.   Truman, Memoirs, II, 97; Hurewitz, Middle East Dilemmas, p. 197; Acheson, Present at the Creation, p. 195; Walter Millis and E. S. Duffield, eds., The Forrestal Diaries (New York, 1951), pp. 192-193; and FRUS, 1946, VII, 847-848.

28.   Stephen Xydis, Greece and the Great Powers, 1944-1947: Prelude to the Truman Doctrine (Thessaloniki, Greece, 1963), p. 105, and FRUS, 1945, VII, 132-133.

29.   Xydis, Greece, p. 149; FRUS, 1945, VIII, 193-299.

30.   Xydis, Greece, p. 153; Byrnes, Speaking Frankly, p. 293; and Acheson, Present at the Creation, p. 217.

31.   Xydis, Greece, p. 156; Millis and Duffield, eds., The Forrestal Diaries, pp. 127, 158, 172.

32.   Xydis, Greece, p. 170.

33.   Acheson, Present at the Creation, p. 196; FRUS, 1946 VII, 847-48.

34. Xydis, Greece, p. 291.

35. Ibid., pp. 300-361; FRUS, 1946, VII, 208-209.

36. Xydis, Greece, pp. 346-425; FRUS, 1946, VII, 262-263.

37. Xydis, Greece, pp. 462, 470; Department of State Bulletin, 4 May 1947, Supplement, 898.

38. Acheson, Present at the Creation, p. 217.

39. Richard M. Freeland, The Truman Doctrine and the Origins of McCarthyism: Foreign Policy, Domestic Politics, and Internal Security, 1946-1948 (New York, 1972), p. 82; Acheson, Present at the Creation, p. 217; and FRUS, 1947, V, 43.

40. Joseph Marion Jones, The Fifteen Weeks (New York, 1955), pp. 132-138; Acheson, Present at the Creation, p. 218; Smith, Acheson, p. 45; and FRUS, 1947, V, 45-57.

41. Smith, Acheson, p. 46; Jones, Fifteen Weeks, pp. 138-143.

42. Jones, Fifteen Weeks, p. 164; FRUS, 1947, V, 71.

43. Truman, Memoirs, II, 105-106; Congressional Record, 80 Cong, 1 Sess, p. 1981; Public Papers of the Presidents of the United States: Harry S Truman, 1947, pp. 176-180. Hereafter cited as PPPUS:HST.

44. Jones, Fifteen Weeks, pp. 171-198.

45. Smith, Acheson, pp. 47-48.

46. Campbell, Defense of the Middle East, pp. 32-34; Halford L. Hoskins, "Some Aspects of the Security Problem in the Middle East," American Political Science Review, 47 (1953), 188-198; Mikesell and Chenery, Arabian Oil, pp. 107-108; Harry N. Howard, "The United States and the Soviet Union in the Middle East," in Ernest Jackh, Background in the Middle East (Ithaca, N.Y., 1952), pp. 178-187; Hurewitz, Middle East Dilemmas, pp. 198-200; and Harris, Troubled Alliance, pp. 15-30.

47. Campbell, Defense of the Middle East, pp. 32-34; Hoskins, The Middle East, p. 178; and Polk, United States and the Arab World, p. 263. For a different view, see Robert Strausz-Hupé, "United States in the Middle East," in Philip W. Thayer, ed., Tensions in the Middle East (Baltimore, 1958), p. 5.

48. Freeland, Truman Doctrine, pp. 5, 102, and Gaddis, Origins of the Cold War, p. 317.

49. George F. Kennan, Memoirs, 1925-1950 (2 vols. Bos-

ton, 1967), I, 314-24, 357-67.

50. Kolko, Limits of Power, pp. 339, 414, 426; Sidney Lens, The Forging of the American Empire (New York, 1971), pp. 341-54; Barton J. Bernstein, Politics and Policies of the Truman Administration (Chicago, 1970), p. 56; David Horowitz, The Free World Colossus: A Critique of American Foreign Policy in the Cold War (New York, 1956), pp. 52, 100; Lloyd C. Gardner, "From Liberation to Containment, 1945-1953," in William Appleman Williams, ed., From Colony to Empire: Essays in the History of American Foreign Relations (New York, 1972), p. 351.

CHAPTER 11

1. See Nash, United States Oil Policy, pp. 171-176; Feis, Petroleum and American Foreign Policy, p. 36; Shwadran, The Middle East, pp. 318-319; and Mikesell and Chenery, Arabian Oil, pp. 90-93.

2. Mikesell and Chenery, Arabian Oil, p. 90.

3. Finnie, Desert Enterprise, pp. 24-25, 43.

4. George Lenczowski, ed., United States Interests in the Middle East (Washington, D.C., 1968), pp. 39-40.

5. Finnie, Desert Enterprise, pp. 3-4.

6. James E. Akins, "The Oil Crisis: This Time the Wolf Is Here," Foreign Affairs, 51 (April 1973), 462-490.

7. Mosley, Oil in the Middle East, p. 158.

8. Ibid., pp. 163-175; Shwadran, The Middle East, pp. 331-338; Stephen Hemsley Longrigg, Oil in the Middle East: Its Discovery and Development (London, 1968), pp. 201-208; Stocking, Middle East Oil, pp. 105-107; and Walt, "Saudi Arabia," pp. 252-262.

9. See Finnie, Desert Enterprise, pp. 4-6; Fisher, The Middle East, pp. 557-558; Shwadran, The Middle East, pp. 344-364; and Walt, "Saudi Arabia," Ch. XIV.

10. Finnie, Desert Enterprise, pp. 3-4.

11. Mosley, Oil in the Middle East, pp. 192-196 and Ch. 17.

12. These figures are from Ibid., pp. 428, 430, 442, and Lenczowski, United States Interests, p. 68.

13. See Longrigg, Oil in the Middle East, pp. 214-216; Mosley, Oil in the Middle East, pp. 179-187; and Walt, "Saudi Arabia,"

pp. 391-394.

14.   Mosley, Oil in the Middle East, pp. 433-438.

15.   Sheehan, Iran, p. 42, and Council on Foreign Relations, Documents on American Foreign Relations, 1950, p. 664.

16.   Kolko, The Limits of Power, p. 417; Kirk, The Middle East, pp. 15-16; and Mosley, Oil in the Middle East, p. 201.

17.   Sheehan, Iran, p. 43.

18.   Longrigg, Oil in the Middle East, p. 166.

19.   Shwadran, The Middle East, p. 103, and Stocking, Middle East Oil.

20.   On U.S. mediation, see Council on Foreign Relations, Documents on American Foreign Relations, 1951, pp. 586-589.

21.   Dwight D. Eisenhower, Mandate for Change, 1953-1956: The White House Years (New York, 1963), pp. 160-161, and Ramazani, Iran's Foreign Relations, pp. 206-212.

22.   Eisenhower, Mandate for Change, p. 162, and Ramazani, Iran's Foreign Relations, pp. 247-248.

23.   Kolko, Limits of Power, p. 419, and Ramazani, Iran's Foreign Relations, pp. 248-250.

24.   Sheehan, Iran, pp. 61-65, and Mosley, Oil in the Middle East, pp. 212-229.

25.   Cottam, Nationalism in Iran, pp. 225-229.

26.   Works by Andrew Tully and by co-authors David Wise and Thomas B. Ross substantiate the active role played by the CIA in the Iranian coup.   See Andrew Tully, CIA, The Inside Story (New York, 1962), Ch. VII, and Wise and Ross, The Invisible Government (New York, 1964), pp. 110-134.   For Eisenhower's statement, see Eisenhower, Waging Peace, p. 164.

27.   Sheehan, Iran, p. 75.

28.   Ibid., p. 75, and Mosley, Oil in the Middle East, pp. 220-221.

29.   Sheehan, Iran, p. 72.   During the year 1965 the Justice Department required the five major oil companies to give 1 per cent each to a group of nine American independent companies to be called Iricon Agency, Ltd.   Mosley, Oil in the Middle East, p. 230.

CHAPTER 12

1.   Wilson, "The Palestine Papers," 44.

2.   See Stevens, American Zionism, p. 101; Samuel Halperin, The Political World of American Zionism (Detroit, 1961), p. 141,
and Ch. 10; Manuel, American-Palestine Relations, p. 318; Alfred
M. Lilienthal, The Other Side of the Coin: An American Perspective of the Arab-Israeli Conflict (New York, 1965), Ch. 5; Truman,
Memoirs, II, 132; and Margaret Arakie, The Broken Sword of Justice: America, Israel and the Palestine Tragedy (London, 1973),
pp. 32-34.

3.   Stevens, American Zionism, p. 125.

4.   FRUS, 1945, VIII, 704-705; Truman, Memoirs, II, 132-
135.

5.   Stevens, American Zionism, p. 130; Millis and Duffield,
eds., The Forrestal Diaries, pp. 188-189; and FRUS, 1945, VIII,
710-715.

6.   Truman, Memoirs, II, 134; Wilson, "Palestine Papers,"
710-715; and FRUS, 1945, VIII, 705-707, 709.

7.   See Ian J. Bickerton, "President Truman's Recognition of
Israel," American Jewish Historical Quarterly, 58 (1968), 187, wherein it is asserted that Truman did seek advice from close advisers.
But Dean Acheson says that Truman "was directing policy on Palestine" by himself.   Acheson, Present at the Creation, p. 167.

8.   Stevens, American Zionism, p. 131; FRUS, 1945, VIII,
716-717.

9.   Truman, Memoirs, II, 136.

10.   Ibid., pp. 137-138; Wilson, "Palestine Papers," 47.

11.   Quandt, "United States Policy in the Middle East," p.
497, and FRUS, 1945, VIII, 737-739.

12.   Kennan, Memoirs, I, 380; FRUS, 1945, VIII, 742.

13.   Millis and Duffield, eds., The Forrestal Diaries, p. 323.

14.   Stevens, American Zionism, p. 137.

15.   Herbert Feis, The Birth of Israel: The Tousled Diplomatic Bed (New York, 1969), pp. 23-24; FRUS, 1945, VIII, 775-776;
PPPUS: HST, 1945, pp. 467-69.

16.   For the work of this commission see Bartley C. Crum,
Behind the Silken Curtain (New York, 1947); James G. McDonald,

My Mission in Israel, 1948-1951 (New York, 1951); William Phillips, Ventures in Diplomacy (London, 1955); and Kirk, The Middle East, pp. 198-217.

17. Stevens, American Zionism, pp. 108-116.

18. See Halperin, Political World, pp. 253-280; Lilienthal, Other Side of the Coin, pp. 89-97; Stevens, American Zionism, p. 99; and W. F. Abboushi, The Angry Arabs (Philadelphia, 1974), pp. 232-240.

19. Crum, Silken Curtain, pp. 32-36; J. C. Hurewitz, The Struggle for Palestine (New York, 1968), p. 257; and McDonald, My Mission, pp. 19, 185.

20. FRUS, 1946, VII, 631-633.

21. Ibid., 588-589.

22. Stevens, American Zionism, p. 146.

23. FRUS, 1946, VII, 624-625; PPPUS: HST, 1946, p. 297.

24. Wilson, "Palestine Papers," 51. On the extent of Zionist terror in Palestine, see Kirk, Middle East, pp. 218-222.

25. FRUS, 1946, VII, 652-667.

26. Ibid., 682.

27. Wilson, "Palestine Papers," 51-52; Stevens, American Zionism, p. 155; and PPPUS: HST, 1946, pp. 442-444.

28. For this point of view, see James Batal, "Truman Chapters in the Middle East," Middle East Forum, XXXI (1956), 12; Stevens, American Zionism, p. 155; Hurewitz, Struggle for Palestine, p. 265; Welles, Where Are We Heading? p. 266; Agwani, The United States and the Arab World, p. 69; Manuel, American-Palestine Relations, p. 327; and John Snetsinger, Truman, the Jewish Vote, and the Creation of Israel (Stanford, Calif., 1974), pp. 31-34.

29. Wilson, "Palestine Papers," 45-46, 52. This view is shared by Frank Manuel, American-Palestine Relations, p. 328. On this point, Truman wrote in his memoirs, "The Balfour Declaration, promising the Jews the opportunity to re-establish a homeland in Palestine, had always seemed to me to go hand in hand with the noble policies of Woodrow Wilson, especially the principle of self-determination. When I was in the Senate, I had told colleagues, Senator Wagner of New York and Senator Taft of Ohio, that I would go along on a resolution putting the Senate on record in favor of the speedy achievement of the Jewish homeland." Truman, Memoirs, II, 134.

30. Bickerton, "Recognition of Israel," 173, 185.

31. Manuel, American-Palestine Relations, pp. 329-330.

32. United Nations, Official Records of the First Special
Session of the General Assembly: Plenary Meetings of the General
Assembly, 1947, I, 183.

33. Ibid., 17.

34. Stevens, American Zionism, pp. 161-165.

35. United Nations, Resolutions Adopted by the General Assembly During the First Session from 28 April to 15 May 1947, 6-7.

36. United Nations, Yearbook of the United Nations, (1947-
1948), Report of the United Nations Special Committee on Palestine,
pp. 227-31.

37. Ibid., p. 227.

38. Manuel, American-Palestine Relations, p. 332.

39. United Nations, Official Records of the Second Session of
the General Assembly: Plenary Meetings of the General Assembly,
II, 1947, 1424-1425.

40. Sumner Welles, We Need Not Fail (Boston, 1948), p. 63;
Stevens, American Zionism, pp. 183-185; Lilienthal, Other Side of
the Coin, p. 96; Batal, "Truman Chapters," 33-34; Polk, The United
States and the Arab World, p. 264; Campbell, Defense of the Middle
East, p. 36; Arakie, The Broken Sword, p. 64; Nadaf Safran, The
United States and Israel (Cambridge, Mass., 1963), p. 35; and
Snetsinger, Truman, the Jewish Vote, pp. 68-69.

41. Stevens, American Zionism, pp. 186-189.

42. Ibid., p. 197; Truman, Memoirs, II, 160.   Truman saw
Weizmann on 18 March to reassure him about continued support for
Zionist aims.

43. United Nations, Security Council Official Records, 1948,
p. 167.

44. Truman, Memoirs, II, 162.

45. Stevens, American Zionism, p. 202; PPPUS: HST, 1948,
pp. 190-91.

46. Ibid., p. 188.

47. Truman, Memoirs, II, 162.

48. Stevens, American Zionism, p. 188; Truman, Memoirs,
II, 161-163.

49. Stevens, American Zionism, pp. 198-202; Feis, Birth of Israel, pp. 53-62; J. C. Hurewitz, "The United Nations and Palestine," in Richard N. Frye, ed., The Near East and the Great Powers (Port Washington, N. Y., 1969), p. 94; Manuel, American-Palestine Relations, p. 345; and Milton Plesur, "The Relations Between the United States and Palestine," Judaism: A Quarterly Journal of Jewish Life and Thought, III (fall, 1954), 479.

50. Stevens, American Zionism, p. 203.

51. Ibid., p. 204.

52. Ibid., p. 204; Batal, "Truman Chapters," 12 et seq.

53. Stevens, American Zionism, p. 204; PPPUS: HST, 1948, p. 258.

54. Wilson, "Palestine Papers," 52; Welles, Where Are We Heading? p. 266; Phillips, Ventures in Diplomacy, p. 298; Stevens, American Zionism, p. 206; Agwani, United States and the Arab World, p. 77; Kirk, Middle East, pp. 267, 273; and Snetsinger, Truman, the Jewish Vote, pp. 34-35, 99, 106, 113, and 116.

55. Campbell, Defense of the Middle East, p. 37; Kermit Roosevelt, "The Partition of Palestine: A Lesson in Pressure Politics," Middle East Journal, II (1948), 2.

56. Bickerton, "Truman's Recognition of Israel," 173, 226-228.

57. Hurewitz, Middle East Dilemmas, p. 141.

58. Kirk, Middle East, pp. 294-301.

59. See Alan R. Taylor and Richard N. Tetlie, eds., Palestine: A Search for Truth: Approaches to the Arab-Israeli Conflict (Washington, 1970), pp. 91, 93, 183; John H. Davis, The Evasive Peace: A Study of the Zionist/Arab Problem (London, 1968), p. 41; and Christopher Sykes, Crossroads to Israel, 1917-1948 (Bloomington, Ind., 1973), p. 356.

60. Taylor and Tetlie, eds., Palestine, pp. 122, 161; Davis, Evasive Peace, pp. 56-62; Sykes, Crossroads, pp. 337-356; and Gary V. Smith, ed., Zionism: The Dream and the Reality (New York, 1974), p. 207.

61. FRUS, 1946, VII, 682; Truman, Memoirs, II, Ch. 10, 11, 12. George H. Gallup's polls of January 1948 and Oct. 1947 indicate that the American people strongly favored the partition of Palestine and the free migration of Jews to that land. George H. Gallup, The Gallup Poll: Public Opinion, 1935-1971 (New York, 1972), I, 554-666.

CHAPTER 13

1. Campbell, Defense of the Middle East, p. 200.

2. Ibid., p. 202; Polk, The United States and the Arab World, pp. 268-269; Hurewitz, Middle East Dilemmas, pp. 210, 227-228; Hoskins, The Middle East, p. 233; Sheehan, Iran, pp. 43-47; Badeau, American Approach to the Arab World, pp, 71, 86-88; and Truman, Memoirs, II, 232.

3. Kolko, The Limits of Power, pp. 240-241; Lens, The Forging of the American Empire, pp. 351-352; Howard Zinn, Post-war America, 1945-1971 (New York, 1973), p. 68; Lloyd C. Gardner, Architects of Illusion: Men and Ideas in American Foreign Policy, 1941-1949 (Chicago, 1970), pp. 206-227; Amaury de Riencourt, The American Empire (New York, 1968), pp. 96-98; John M. Swomley, Jr., American Empire: The Political Ethics of Twentieth-Century Conquest (New York, 1970), pp. 105-113; and Horowitz, A Critique of American Foreign Policy in the Cold War, p. 186.

4. William E. Warne, Mission for Peace: Point 4 in Iran (New York, 1956), p. 207.

5. Harris, Troubled Alliance, p. 178.

6. Agwani, The United States and the Arab World, pp. 101-102, and Polk, United States and the Arab World, pp. 335-336.

7. Truman, Memoirs, II, 233; George Hakim, "Point Four and the Middle East," Middle East Journal, 4 (1950), 190-91; and Arthur Z. Gardiner, "Point Four and the Arab World," Middle East Journal, 4 (1950), 302-03.

8. Hurewitz, Middle East Dilemmas, pp. 232-234; Polk, United States and the Arab World, pp. 267-268.

9. Robert L. Daniel maintains that Point Four was based on the work of the Near East Foundation. He claims that Point Four was anticipated by two decades by NEF which sponsored technical assistance programs during the interwar period. Daniel, American Philanthropy, p. 279.

10. Truman, Memoirs, II, 231-232, and Department of State Bulletin, XXIII, 93.

11. Truman, Memoirs, II, 232.

12. Daniel, American Philanthropy, p. 279.

13. PPPUS: HST, 1950, pp. 623-624.

14. Warne, Mission for Peace, pp. 312-313.

15. Hurewitz, Middle East Dilemmas, pp. 243-244.

16. Polk, United States and the Arab World, p. 269; Hurewitz, Middle East Dilemmas, pp. 236-244.

17. Ibid., p. 91.

18. With American oil production growing in Saudi Arabia, there was an increase in U.S. ships passing through the Suez Canal. In 1948 the Suez Canal Company named S. Pinkney Tuck, former American ambassador to Egypt, to its board of directors. Council on Foreign Relations, Documents on American Foreign Relations, 1945-1946, p. 671.

19. Acheson, Present at the Creation, pp. 562-563.

20. Ibid., p. 563; Hoskins, The Middle East, p. 73; Campbell, Defense of the Middle East, pp. 40-41; and Council on Foreign Relations, Documents on American Foreign Relations, 1951, pp. 589-590.

21. For the text of the proposal presented to Egypt, see ibid., 1951, pp. 269-276.

22. Campbell, Defense of the Middle East, p. 41.

23. Agwani, United States and the Arab World, p. 122.

24. Hoskins, The Middle East, p. 73.

25. Agwani, United States and the Arab World, pp. 122-123. For an excellent essay on the problem of Arab nationalism as a factor in western planning for regional defense in the Middle East, see Majid Khadduri, "The Problem of Regional Security in the Middle East: An Appraisal," Middle East Journal, 11 (1957), 12-22. For an enlightening study of Arab reaction to Western Civilization, see Bernard Lewis, The Middle East and the West (New York, 1964), pp. 134-135.

26. Agwani, United States and the Arab World, p. 123.

27. Hoskins, The Middle East, pp. 266-268.

28. Congressional Record, 82 Cong, 2 Sess, pp. 276-279.

29. Acheson, Present at the Creation, p. 566.

30. Ibid., p. 566.

31. Halford L. Hoskins, "Some Aspects of the Security Problem in the Middle East," American Political Science Review, 47 (1953), 195.

32.   Acheson, Present at the Creation, p. 567.

33.   Louis L. Gerson, John Foster Dulles (New York, 1967), p. 243.

34.   Dwight D. Eisenhower, Mandate for Change, 1953-1956: The White House Years (New York, 1963), p. 150.

35.   Gerson, Dulles, p. 244.

36.   Eisenhower, Mandate for Change, p. 152.

37.   Ibid., p. 152.

38.   Gerson, Dulles, p. 245.

39.   Eisenhower, Mandate for Change, p. 155.

40.   Gerson, Dulles, p. 245; Anthony Eden, Memoirs: Full Circle (London, 1960), pp. 28-281.

41.   Gerson, Dulles, p. 248; Eisenhower, Mandate for Change, p. 156; John Robinson Beal, John Foster Dulles, 1888-1959 (New York, 1956), p. 248.

42.   Gerson, Dulles, pp. 251-252.

43.   James W. Spain, "Middle East Defense: A New Approach," Middle East Journal, 8 (1954), 251-266; Polk, The United States and the Arab World, p. 271; Gerson, Dulles, pp. 252-255; Campbell, Defense of the Middle East, pp. 49-53.

44.   Gerson, Dulles, p. 256; Lewis Broad, Anthony Eden: Chronicle of a Career (New York, 1955), p. 241; Council on Foreign Relations, Documents on American Foreign Relations, 1954, pp. 388-390.

45.   Gerson, Dulles, p. 257 and Eden, Full Circle, p. 288.

46.   Gerson, Dulles, pp. 257-258.

47.   Campbell, Defense of the Middle East, p. 51; Council on Foreign Relations, Documents on American Foreign Relations, 1954, pp. 376-378.

48.   Spain, "Middle East Defense," 254.

49.   Ibid., 255-259.

50.   Ibid., 256.

51.   Campbell, Defense of the Middle East, p. 55; Council on Foreign Relations, Documents on American Foreign Relations,

1955, pp. 342-344.

52. Spain, "Middle East Defense," 260.

53. Jean Lacouture, Nasser: A Biography (New York, 1973), p. 154; Campbell, Defense of the Middle East, p. 55.

54. Leila M. T. Meo, Lebanon: Improbable Nation (Bloomington, Ind., 1965), p. 96; Campbell, Defense of the Middle East, p. 56; T. C. Bose, The Superpowers and the Middle East (New York, 1972), pp. 18-19.

55. Campbell, Defense of the Middle East, p. 60. For other interpretations, see Gerson, Dulles, p. 259; Lenczowski, The Middle East in World Affairs, pp. 293, 675; Kennett Love, Suez: The Twice-Fought War (New York, 1969), pp. 273-274; Waldemar J. Gallman, Iraq Under General Nuri: My Recollections of Nuri al-Said, 1954-1958 (Baltimore, 1964), p. 73; and Richard Goold-Adams, The Time of Power: Reappraisal of John Foster Dulles (London, 1962), pp. 201-202.

56. Campbell, Defense of the Middle East, p. 56.

57. Love, Suez, pp. 207-208.

58. Department of State Bulletin, 2 Jan. 1956, 16-18. For a good discussion of Iran's adherence to the pact, see Ramazani, Iran's Foreign Relations, pp. 274-278.

CHAPTER 14

1. Love, Suez, p. 200.

2. Guy Wint and Peter Calvocoressi, Middle East Crisis (Harmondsworth, England, 1969), p. 58.

3. Wilton Wynn, Nasser of Egypt: The Search for Dignity (Cambridge, Mass., 1959), pp. 52-53; Campbell, Defense of the Middle East, pp. 67-68; and Wint and Calvocoressi, Middle East Crisis, pp. 52-53.

4. Hugh Thomas, Suez, (New York, 1966), pp. 14-15; Goold-Adams, The Time of Power, p. 202; Wynn, Nasser, p. 117; Jean Lacouture, Nasser (New York, 1973), p. 160; Love, Suez, pp. 88-90. For the U.S. position on the sale of arms to Arab states, see Department of State Bulletin, 10 Oct. 1955, 560.

5. Georgianna G. Stevens, "Arab Neutralism and Bandung," Middle East Journal, 11 (1957), 139-152; Lacouture, Nasser, p. 157; and Love, Suez, p. 241.

6. Goold-Adams, Time of Power, p. 202; Dwight D. Eisen-

hower, Waging Peace, 1956-1961: The White House Years (New York, 1965), p. 25; and Love, Suez, p. 91.

7.   Eisenhower, Waging Peace, p. 25; Gerson, Dulles, p. 263.

8.   Gerson, Dulles, pp. 266-67.

9.   Michael A. Guhin, John Foster Dulles: A Statesman and His Times (New York, 1972), p. 267. For this announcement see Department of State Bulletin, 26 Dec. 1955, 1050-1051.

10.   Love, Suez, pp. 308-310; J. E. Dougherty, "The Aswan Decision in Perspective," Political Quarterly, LXXXIV (1959), 37. For the Tripartite Declaration, see Council on Foreign Relations, Documents on American Foreign Relations, 1950, pp. 658-659.

11.   Love, Suez, pp. 307-310.

12.   Goold-Adams, Time of Power, pp. 210-211.

13.   Terence Robertson, Crisis: The Inside Story of the Suez Conspiracy (New York, 1965), pp. 27-39; Love, Suez, pp. 203-207; and Anthony Nutting, No End of a Lesson: The Story of Suez (New York, 1967), pp. 27-35.

14.   Nutting, No End of a Lesson, p. 32.

15.   Of Dulles' biographers, Louis Gerson makes no mention of Nasser's actions on Dulles, while Michael Guhin dismisses it altogether. However John R. Beal says that Nasser's action did affect the Secretary, who viewed it as a "petulant" move. Kennett Love claims that Nasser's recognition of Red China was the most important factor that caused Dulles to withdraw aid for the Dam. Gerson, Dulles, pp. 272-77; Guhin, Dulles, p. 268; Beal, Dulles, p. 257; and Love, Suez, pp. 293-94. Eisenhower also took a dim view of Nasser's recognition of China. Eisenhower, Waging Peace, p. 31.

16.   Love, Suez, pp. 121-145 and Thomas, Suez, pp. 47-48.

17.   Gerson, Dulles, p. 277; Love, Suez, pp. 122-124, 143.

18.   Love, Suez, p. 302.

19.   Ibid., p. 315; Guhin, Dulles, p. 271.

20.   This explanation is supported by Love, Suez, p. 293; Herman Finer, Dulles over Suez: The Theory and Practice of His Diplomacy (Chicago, 1964), p. 51; Wint and Calvocoressi, Middle East Crisis, p. 67; Richard H. Nolte, "Year of Decision in the Middle East," Yale Review, XLVI (winter, 1957), 232; and Campbell, Defense of the Middle East, p. 73.

21.   The "blackmail" thesis is supported by Eisenhower, Waging Peace, p. 31; Carey B. Joynt, "John Foster Dulles and the Suez Crisis," in Gerald N. Grob, ed., Statesmen and Statecraft of the Modern West (Barre, Vt., 1967), pp. 209-210; Finer, Dulles over Suez, p. 51; M. A. Fitzsimons, "The Suez Crisis and the Containment Policy," Review of Politics, XIX (1957), 439; Gerson, Dulles, p. 281; Quandt, "United States Policy in the Middle East," p. 506; and Fisher, The Middle East, p. 710.

22.   See Harry B. Ellis, Challenge in the Middle East: Communist Influence and American Policy (New York, 1960), p. 47; Finer, Dulles over Suez, p. 51; Roscoe Drummond and Gaston Coblentz, Duel at the Brink: John Foster Dulles' Command of American Power (New York, 1960), p. 171; Guhin, Dulles, pp. 272-73; Robert Murphy, Diplomat Among Warriors (New York, 1964), p. 376; and Anthony Eden, The Suez Crisis, (Boston, 1960), p. 49.

23.   Beal, Dulles, pp. 258-60, and Robertson, Crisis, p. 62.

24.   Eisenhower, Waging Peace, p. 31; Wint and Calvocoressi, Middle East Crisis, p. 62; and Campbell, Defense of the Middle East, p. 73.

25.   Dougherty, "The Aswan Decision," 38.

26.   Murphy, Diplomat Among Warriors, p. 376.

27.   Eisenhower, Waging Peace, p. 33.

28.   Love, Suez, p. 315; Finer, Dulles over Suez, p. 54; and Michael Adams, Suez and After: Years of Crisis (Boston, 1958), p. 6.

29.   Lionel Gelber, America in Britain's Place: The Leadership of the West and Anglo-American Unity (New York, 1961), p. 232, and Dougherty, "The Aswan Decision," 42.

30.   Concerning the international legal aspects of Nasser's seizure of Suez, see A. L. Goodhart, "Some Legal Aspects of the Suez Situation," in Philip W. Thayer, ed., Tensions in the Middle East (Baltimore, 1958), p. 255, and Thomas T. F. Huang, "Some International and Legal Aspects of the Suez Canal Question," American Journal of International Law, LI (1957), 277-307. Goodhart claims that Nasser's action was legal, while Huang claims that it was a violation of international law.

31.   Eden, Suez, pp. 53-54.

32.   Leon D. Epstein, British Politics in the Suez Crisis (Urbana, Ill., 1963), pp. 41, 65-66, 141, and 173.

33.   Eisenhower, Waging Peace, p. 39.

34. Love, Suez, p. 368; Murphy, Diplomat Among Warriors, pp. 379-382; Merry and Serge Bromberger, Secrets of Suez (London, 1957), p. 18; Joynt, "The Suez Crisis," p. 216; Guhin, Dulles, p. 280.

35. Eden, Suez, pp. 63-66.

36. Goold-Adams, The Time of Power, pp. 218-222; Nutting, No End of a Lesson, p. 52; Robertson, Crisis, p. 93; Thomas, Suez, p. 55; Finer, Dulles over Suez, p. 92; and Wint and Calvocoressi, Middle East Crisis, p. 93.

37. Finer, Dulles over Suez, p. 87; Goold-Adams, Time of Power, pp. 216, 220; and Thomas, Suez, p. 54.

38. Eisenhower, Waging Peace, pp. 35-37; Gerson, Dulles, pp. 283-85.

39. Murphy, Diplomat Among Warriors, pp. 379-82.

40. Gerson, Dulles, p. 286.

41. Ibid., pp. 286-87.

42. Guhin, Dulles, pp. 279-280.

43. Eden, Suez, pp. 65-66.

44. Ibid., p. 67, and Council on Foreign Relations, Documents on American Foreign Relations, 1956, pp. 292-294.

45. Gerson, Dulles, p. 290.

46. Goold-Adams, The Time of Power, p. 227; Guhin, Dulles, p. 281; Eden, Suez, p. 93; Public Papers of the Presidents of the United States: Dwight D. Eisenhower, 1956, pp. 716-717. Hereafter cited as PPPUS: DDE.

47. Eisenhower, Waging Peace, p. 49; Thomas, Suez, p. 71.

48. For criticism of Eisenhower on this point, see Thomas, Suez, pp. 70-72; Finer, Dulles over Suez, p. 189; Gelber, America in Britain's Place, p. 236.

49. Goold-Adams, The Time of Power, p. 228.

50. Gerson, Dulles, p. 292; Wynn, Nasser, p. 174; Love, Suez, p. 416.

51. Thomas, Suez, p. 72 and Eden, Suez, p. 107.

52. Love, Suez, pp. 420-425; Thomas, Suez, p. 73. The U.S. held back support of a British draft resolution for the U.N. and without this support Britain would not go further. Guhin, Dulles, pp. 282-83.

53. Gerson, Dulles, p. 292.

54. Eisenhower, Waging Peace, pp. 50-51.

55. Eden, Suez, Chapter 5; Guhin, Dulles, pp. 283-84.

56. Quoted in Goold-Adams, The Time of Power, p. 232 and Guhin, Dulles, p. 284.

57. See Love, Suez, pp. 436-438; Thomas, Suez, p. 94; Goold-Adams, The Time of Power, p. 232; Finer, Dulles over Suez, p. 229; Robertson, Crisis, p. 119; Eden, Full Circle, p. 539; Adams, Suez and After, p. 53; and Nutting, No End of a Lesson, pp. 64-69.

58. Joynt, "John Foster Dulles," pp. 221-223; Gerson, Dulles, p. 292; and Guhin, Dulles, pp. 283-284.

59. Love, Suez, p. 445 and Goold-Adams, The Time of Power, p. 236.

60. Wynn, Nasser, p. 174; Love, Suez, p. 444; Nutting, No End of a Lesson, p. 75; and Finer, Dulles over Suez, pp. 308-310.

61. Love, Suez, p. 450; Thomas, Suez, p. 104; and Nutting, No End of a Lesson, pp. 80, 90-94.

62. Nutting, No End of a Lesson, p. 110; Love, Suez, p. 471; and Gerson, Suez, p. 294.

63. Love, Suez, pp. 461-66; Thomas, Suez, pp. 112-114.

64. Finer, Dulles over Suez, p. 348; Nutting, No End of a Lesson, pp. 80, 158; Wint & Calvocoressi, Middle East Crisis, p. 88; Love, Suez, pp. 450, 573; and Thomas, Suez, p. 134.

65. A. J. Barker, Suez: The Seven Day War (London: 1964), p. 39; Wynn, Nasser, p. 184; and Campbell, Defense of the Middle East, pp. 105-107.

66. Love, Suez, p. 467.

67. Eisenhower, Waging Peace, pp. 75-76.

68. Goold-Adams, The Time of Power, pp. 239-240.

69. United Nations, Security Council, Official Records, 1956, pp. 13-14.

70. Goold-Adams, The Time of Power, p. 241.

71. Eisenhower, Waging Peace, p. 83, and PPPUS: DDE, 1956, pp. 281-82.

72. General Assembly, First Emergency Special Session, 1-10 Nov. 1956, p. 2.

73. Goold-Adams, The Time of Power, p. 241; General Assembly, First Emergency Special Session, 1-10 November 1956, p. 2.

74. Eisenhower, Waging Peace, p. 89. Concerning the international legal aspects of the Israeli attack on Egypt and the Anglo-French intervention, see Quincy Wright, "Intervention, 1956," American Journal of International Law, LI (1957), 257-276.

75. Love, Suez, pp. 625-27.

76. Bromberger, Secrets of Suez, pp. 153-59; Love, Suez, p. 633; Eden, Full Circle, pp. 622-23; O. M. Smolansky, "Moscow and the Suez Crisis, 1956: A Reappraisal," Political Science Quarterly, 80 (1965), 592; Murphy, Diplomat Among Warriors, p. 390; and Nutting, No End of a Lesson, pp. 144-46.

77. Finer, Dulles over Suez, p. 411.

78. Thomas, Suez, pp. 145-47.

79. Campbell, Defense of the Middle East, pp. 117-119; Love, Suez, p. 666; and Eisenhower, Waging Peace, p. 184.

CHAPTER 15

1. Eisenhower, Waging Peace, pp. 96-97.

2. Harris, Troubled Alliance, p. 64; Department of State Bulletin, 10 Dec. 1956, 918.

3. Love, Suez, p. 651.

4. Ibid., p. 45; PPPUS: DDE, 1956, pp. 238-239; Beal, Dulles, pp. 290-291; and Mosley, Oil in the Middle East, pp. 260-266.

5. Love, Suez, p. 647; Meo, Lebanon, pp. 106-107.

6. Eisenhower, Waging Peace, pp. 177-178.

7. Ibid., p. 178.

8. Ibid., p. 180; Campbell, Defense of the Middle East, p. 122; and Congressional Record, 85 Cong, 1 Sess, pp. 224-227.

9. Townsend Hoopes, The Devil and John Foster Dulles (Boston, 1973), pp. 406-408; and Campbell, Defense of the Middle East, pp. 123-124.

10. Eisenhower, Waging Peace, p. 182, and Congressional Record, 85 Cong, 1 Sess, pp. 1323, 1329.

11. Eisenhower, Waging Peace, p. 184, and U.N. General Assembly, Official Records: Plenary Meetings, 11 Sess, pp. 1052-1053.

12. Eisenhower, Waging Peace, p. 184.

13. Finer, Dulles over Suez, p. 471.

14. PPPUS: DDE, 1957, p. 144; Eisenhower, Waging Peace, p. 184.

15. Eisenhower, Waging Peace, p. 185.

16. Ibid., p. 187.

17. Ibid., p. 188 and PPPUS: DDE, 1957, pp. 147-156.

18. Ibid., p. 189, and U.N. General Assembly, Official Records: Plenary Meetings, 11 Sess, p. 1193.

19. Eisenhower, Waging Peace, pp. 193-194; Campbell, Defense of the Middle East, p. 127; and Finer, Dulles over Suez, p. 500.

20. Campbell, Defense of the Middle East, p. 126.

21. Waldemar J. Gallman, Iraq Under General Nuri: My Recollections of Nuri al-Said, 1954-1958 (Baltimore, 1964), pp. 80-81.

22. Meo, Lebanon, p. 125.

23. Finer, Dulles over Suez, p. 500, and Bose, The Superpowers and the Middle East, p. 47.

24. PPPUS: DDE, 1957, pp. 138-140 and Department of State Bulletin, 25 Feb. 1957, 308-309.

25. Hoopes, Dulles, p. 411. He claims that the doctrine was not applicable. Bose, The Superpowers and the Middle East, p. 50, agrees, as does Finer, Dulles over Suez, p. 500. George Lenczowski says that the doctrine "was not tailored to fit the situation in the Arab world." Lenczowski, The Middle East in World Affairs, pp. 677-678. But the following writers find that the doctrine was applicable: Campbell, Defense of the Middle East, pp. 128-130 and Goold-Adams, The Time of Power, p. 254.

26. Eisenhower, Waging Peace, p. 195, and Department of State Bulletin, 13 May 1957, 767.

27. Campbell, Defense of the Middle East, p. 129.

28. Bose, The Superpowers and the Middle East, p. 50, and Department of State Bulletin, 22 July 1957, 146.

29. Eisenhower, Waging Peace, p. 197; PPPUS: DDE, 1957, pp. 556, 614.

30. Bose, The Superpowers and the Middle East, p. 51; Campbell, Defense of the Middle East, p. 131; Eisenhower, Waging Peace, p. 196; Hoopes, Dulles, p. 412; Gordon H. Torrey, Syrian Politics and the Military, 1945-1958 (Columbus, Ohio, 1964), p. 360.

31. Campbell, Defense of the Middle East, pp. 131-132; Eisenhower, Waging Peace, p. 197; and Hoopes, Dulles, p. 412.

32. Campbell, Defense of the Middle East, pp. 131-132; Eisenhower, Waging Peace, p. 197; Hoopes, Dulles, p. 412; and Department of State Bulletin, 23 Sept. 1957, 487.

33. Harris, Troubled Alliance, p. 64; Hoopes, Dulles, p. 412; and Eisenhower, Waging Peace, pp. 198-199.

34. Eisenhower, Waging Peace, pp. 201-203; Hoopes, Dulles, p. 413; Torrey, Syrian Politics, pp. 363-364.

35. Eisenhower, Waging Peace, p. 202.

36. Bose, The Superpowers and the Middle East, p. 51; Hoopes, Dulles, p. 477; Harold R. Macmillan, Riding the Storm, 1956-1959 (New York, 1971), p. 477; Goold-Adams, The Time of Power, p. 264. The latter said the Arabs viewed the doctrine as an imperialistic act.

37. Campbell, Defense of the Middle East, p. 132; Quandt, "United States Policy in the Middle East," p. 510; Lionel Gelber, America in Britain's Place: The Leadership of the West and Anglo-American Unity (New York, 1961), p. 279; and Torrey, Syrian Politics, pp. 362-363.

38. Eisenhower, Waging Peace, p. 202.

39. Ibid., pp. 202-203; Hoopes, Dulles, p. 413; and Campbell, Defense of the Middle East, p. 133.

40. Eisenhower, Waging Peace, p. 203.

41. Ibid., p. 203; Campbell, Defense of the Middle East, p. 133; and Torrey, Syrian Politics, pp. 365-366.

42. Harris, Troubled Alliance, p. 64; and Hoopes, Dulles, p. 413.

43. Eisenhower, Waging Peace, p. 203; and PPPUS: DDE, 1957, p. 226.

44. Eisenhower, Waging Peace, p. 204; and Hoopes, Dulles, p. 214.

45. For an assessment of this application of the doctrine in Syria, see Campbell, Defense of the Middle East, pp. 134-137; Finer, Dulles over Suez, p. 501; and Polk, The United States and the Arab World, p. 282. For Henry Cabot Lodge's presentation in the United Nations, see U.N. General Assembly, Official Records: Plenary Meetings, 12 Sess, pp. 357-358; 386-389.

46. Meo, Lebanon, pp. 120-176.

47. Eisenhower, Waging Peace, pp. 266-267; Hoopes, Dulles, p. 433.

48. Meo, Lebanon, pp. 177-178.

49. Hoopes, Dulles, p. 433; Campbell, Defense of the Middle East, p. 140; and U.N. Security Council, Official Records, 823rd Meeting, pp. 1-22.

50. This evaluation is supported by Campbell, Defense of the Middle East, p. 141; Hoopes, Dulles, p. 433; and Bose, The Superpowers and the Middle East, p. 42. But Leila Meo said that there was some Syrian infiltration but that it was not necessarily affiliated with the Syrian government. Meo, Lebanon, p. 180. Sharing the skepticism of Hoopes and Bose is C. W. Thayer, Diplomat (New York, 1959), p. 24.

51. Eisenhower, Waging Peace, pp. 269-270.

52. Hoopes, Dulles, p. 435.

53. Campbell, Defense of the Middle East, p. 142.

54. Eisenhower, Waging Peace, pp. 271-272; PPPUS: DDE, 1957, p. 550.

55. Eisenhower, Waging Peace, p. 274; Department of State Bulletin, 4 Aug. 1958, 181-182; and Congressional Record, 82 Cong, 2 Sess, House Doc. 422.

56. Murphy, Diplomat Among Warriors, p. 398.

57. U.N. Security Council, Official Records, 829th Meeting, pp. 1-4.

58. Murphy, Diplomat Among Warriors, p. 404.

59. Ibid., pp. 405-408.

60.   Ibid., pp. 412-414.

61.   Ibid., p. 414.

62.   Eisenhower, Waging Peace, p. 287, and U.N. General Assembly, Official Records: Plenary Meetings, Supplement 1, 1958, 3rd Emergency Special Session, pp. 7-10.

63.   Quincy Wright claims that the U.S. would have to prove that the conflict in Lebanon that caused President Chamoun to request intervention was due essentially to "subversive intervention" from external sources, a fact that Wright concludes would be "difficult to prove." Quincy Wright, "United States Intervention in the Lebanon," American Journal of International Law, LIII (1959), 112-125.

64.   Eisenhower, Waging Peace, p. 269.

65.   Ibid., pp. 270-271.

66.   Murphy, Diplomat Among Warriors, pp. 412-414, and Hoopes, Dulles, pp. 437-438.

67.   Majid Khadduri, Republican Iraq: A Study in Iraqi Politics Since the Revolution of 1958 (London, 1969), pp. 183, 157-158.

68.   Concerning the Arab Cold War, see Malcolm H. Kerr, The Arab Cold War: Gamal Abdal Nasir and His Rivals, 1958-1970 (London, 1971).

69.   Campbell, Defense of the Middle East, p. 147, and Bose, The Superpowers and the Middle East, p. 57.

70.   For this assessment, see Campbell, Defense of the Middle East, pp. 153-154; Richard H. Nolte, "United States Policy and the Middle East," in Georgianne Stevens, ed., The United States and the Middle East (Englewood Cliffs, N.J., 1964), pp. 170-77; Quandt, "United States Policy in the Middle East," p. 511; Lenczowski, The Middle East in World Affairs, p. 677; Polk, United States and the Arab World, p. 284; Nadav Safran, From War to War: The Arab-Israeli Confrontation, 1948-1967 (New York, 1969), p. 119; Clyde Eagleton, "The United Nations and the Suez Crisis," in Philip W. Thayer, ed., Tensions in the Middle East (Baltimore, 1958), p. 282; and Freda Utley, Will the Middle East Go West? (Chicago, 1957), pp. 133-134.

71.   PPPUS: DDE, 1958, pp. 606-616.

72.   The following agree that Eisenhower instituted the new departure: Harry B. Ellis, "The Arab-Israeli Conflict Today," in Stevens, ed., The United States and the Middle East, pp. 117-118; Nolte, "United States Policy and the Middle East," pp. 172-173; Lenczowski, United States Interests in the Middle East, pp. 22-23;

Safran, From War to War, p. 131; and Meo, Lebanon, p. 202.

73. Bose, The Superpowers and the Middle East, p. 67; Polk, United States and the Arab World, p. 285; and Badeau, The American Approach to the Arab World, p. 83. However, Harry N. Howard, "The United States," in Tareq Y. Ismael, ed., The Middle East in World Politics: A Study in Contemporary International Relations (Syracuse, N.Y., 1974), p. 127, says that there was no basic change in U.S. policy during this period.

CHAPTER 16

1. For a thumbnail sketch of Arab nationalism, see Halford L. Hoskins, The Middle East, pp. 148-152; Raphael Patai's The Arab Mind (New York, 1973), Ch. XVI, supplies a description of the Arab view of the West.

2. Campbell, Defense of the Middle East, pp. 16-19.

3. Albert Hourani, "The Decline of the West in the Middle East," International Affairs, XXIX (April 1953), II, 37-38.

4. Concerning the rise of the "new men" and the relationship of the Arab world to the West, see Bernard Lewis, The Middle East and the West (Bloomington, Ind., 1964), pp. 133-139; Badeau, American Approach to the Arab World, pp. 44 47; Polk, The United States and the Arab World, pp. 214-228 and "The Nature of Modernization: The Middle East and North Africa," Foreign Affairs, 44 (Oct. 1965), 100-110; and Patai, The Arab Mind, pp. 296-306.

5. Thomas A. Bryson, American Diplomacy in the Middle East (St. Charles, Missouri, 1975), p. 11.

6. Trask, United States Response, pp. 241-247.

7. See Hurewitz, Middle East Dilemmas, pp. 200-206; Harris, Troubled Alliance, pp. 27-53; Fisher, The Middle East, pp. 493-94; and Yale, The Near East, pp. 417-422.

8. Harris, Troubled Alliance, pp. 62-68.

9. Lenczowski, Middle East in World Affairs, p. 161; Department of State, United States Treaties and Other International Agreements, X, Pt. 1, 1959, 320-322.

10. Harris, Troubled Alliance, pp. 67, 70.

11. Ibid., pp. 54-61.

12. Ibid., pp. 72-85; Lenczowski, Middle East in World Affairs, pp. 162-165; and Fisher, The Middle East, pp. 501-503.

13. Harris, Troubled Alliance, p. 204. Also see Harry N. Howard, "Continuing Trouble in the Turkish Republic," Current History, 64 (Jan. 1973), 26-29.

14. Lenczowski, The Middle East in World Affairs, p. 162, and Fisher, The Middle East, p. 495.

15. Harris, Troubled Alliance, p. 109.

16. Ibid., pp. 110, 112.

17. Ibid., pp. 115-116.

18. Council on Foreign Relations, Documents on American Foreign Relations, 1964, p. 105.

19. Harris, Troubled Alliance, pp. 117-118.

20. Ibid., pp. 122-124.

21. Ibid., pp. 91-95.

22. Ibid., pp. 96, 128-129.

23. Ibid., pp. 132, 135-137, 188-189.

24. Ibid., pp. 154-157, 160-162, 163-168, 169-170, 171-172.

25. Ibid., pp. 191-197.

26. Sheehan, Iran, p. 56.

27. Ibid., p. 65.

28. Ibid., pp. 66-67, and Fisher, The Middle East, pp. 540-541.

29. Ibid., pp. 67-68.

30. Fisher, The Middle East, pp. 540-542. On Iran's new policy toward Russia, see Ramazani, Iran's Foreign Policy, Ch. XIII.

31. Lenczowski, The Middle East in World Affairs, p. 221.

32. Ibid., p. 22, and Department of State, United States Treaties and Other International Agreements, X, pt. 1, 1959, 314-316.

33. Ann T. Schulz, "A Leadership Role for Iran in the Persian Gulf," Current History (Jan. 1972), 25-30.

34. Gallman, Iraq Under General Nuri, Ch. X.

35. Majid Khadduri, Republican Iraq (London, 1969), pp. 157-158.

36. Lenczowski, The Middle East in World Affairs, p. 307, and "Iraq: Seven Years of Revolution," Current History, 48 (May 1965), 283-285.

37. Lenczowski, The Middle East in World Affairs, p. 306.

38. Fisher, The Middle East, p. 628.

39. Campbell, Defense of the Middle East, pp. 155-158, and Department of State, United States Treaties and Other International Agreements, X, 1959, 1386-1391.

40. Badeau, American Approach to the Arab World, p. 133.

41. Ibid., p. 134.

42. Department of State Bulletin, 21 Jan. 1963, 90-91.

43. Badeau, American Approach to the Arab World, pp. 144-147; Nadav Safran, From War to War: The Arab-Israeli Confrontation, 1948-1967 (New York, 1969), p. 133; United Nations Security Council, Official Record, 11 June 1963; and Council on Foreign Relations, Documents on American Foreign Relations, 1963, pp. 260-265.

44. Safran, From War to War, pp. 134-135. See John S. Badeau, "USA & UAR: Crisis in Confidence," Foreign Affairs, 43 (Jan. 1965), 281-296.

45. Lenczowski, The Middle East in World Affairs, pp. 554-555.

46. Fisher, The Middle East, p. 559.

47. Ibid., p. 560.

48. Ibid., p. 561, and Lenczowski, The Middle East in World Affairs, p. 558.

49. Lenczowski, The Middle East in World Affairs, pp. 565-566, and Fisher, The Middle East, p. 563.

50. Lenczowski, The Middle East in World Affairs, pp. 566-567; Department of State Bulletin, 25 Feb. 1957, 308-309; and PPPUS: DDE, 1957, pp. 138-140.

51. George Lenczowski, "Tradition and Reform in Saudi Arabia," Current History, 52 (Feb. 1967), 100-102.

52. Fisher, The Middle East, p. 677.

53. Lenczowski, The Middle East in World Affairs, p. 466.

54. Ibid., p. 468.

55. Ibid., p. 469; Council on Foreign Relations, Documents on American Foreign Relations, 1957, p. 231; and Department of State Bulletin, 22 July 1957, 146.

56. Fisher, The Middle East, p. 679, and Safran, From War to War, pp. 232-233.

57. Department of State, United States Treaties and Other Agreements, VIII, 1957, 943-945.

58. Fisher, The Middle East, pp. 597-601.

59. Walt, "Saudi Arabia," p. 354.

60. Lenczowski, The Middle East in World Affairs, p. 349.

61. Ibid., Ch. XVI, and Fisher, The Middle East, pp. 630-636.

62. Mosley, Oil in the Middle East, pp. 289-298.

63. Fred J. Khouri, The Arab-Israeli Dilemma (Syracuse, N.Y., 1968), pp. 229-243; Bose, The Superpowers and the Middle East, pp. 87-91; and Walter Laqueur, The Road to War: The Origin and Aftermath of the Arab-Israeli Conflict, 1967-1968 (Harmondsworth, England, 1968), pp. 68-108.

64. Theodore Draper, Israel and World Politics: Roots of the Third Arab-Israeli War (New York, 1967), pp. 45-48, and Khouri, Arab-Israeli Dilemma, p. 245.

65. Bose, The Superpowers and the Middle East, pp. 99-100; Khouri, The Arab-Israeli Dilemma, p. 245; Bernard Lewis, "The Arab-Israeli War: The Consequences of Defeat," Foreign Affairs, 46 (Jan. 1968), 323; Safran, From War to War, pp. 267-278; Charles W. Yost, "The Arab-Israeli War, 1967: How It Began," Foreign Affairs, 46 (Jan. 1968), pp. 305-308; Draper, Israel, p. 56; Laqueur, Road to War, p. 95; and Love, Suez, p. 68.

66. Safran, From War to War, p. 274; Bose, The Superpowers and the Middle East, p. 97; and Love, Suez, p. 683.

67. Khouri, Arab-Israeli Dilemma, pp. 245-246.

68. Ibid., p. 246.

69. Ibid., pp. 250-252.

70. Lyndon Baines Johnson, Vantage Point: Perspectives of

the Presidency, 1963-1969 (New York, 1971), pp. 290-291; PPPUS: LBJ, 1967, I, 561-562.

71. Quandt, "United States Policy in the Middle East," p. 519; Johnson, Vantage Point, p. 291; Khouri, Arab-Israeli Dilemma, p. 253; Bose, The Superpowers and the Middle East, p. 102; and PPPUS: LBJ, 1967, I, 561-563.

72. Johnson, Vantage Point, p. 293. Nadav Safran claims Congress caused Johnson to move from unilateral to collective action. William Quandt also notes that Congress clearly exerted considerable influence on the President. Safran, From War to War, pp. 296-297, and Quandt, "United States Policy in the Middle East," p. 521.

73. Khouri, Arab-Israeli Dilemma, p. 253; Bose, The Superpower in the Middle East, p. 104; United Nations Security Council, Official Records, 1967, 1345th Meeting, p. 4.

74. Khouri, Arab-Israeli Dilemma, p. 254; Bose, The Superpowers and the Middle East, p. 105; and Quandt, "United States Policy in the Middle East," p. 523.

75. Johnson, Vantage Point, p. 294, and Quandt, "United States Policy in the Middle East," p. 523.

76. Khouri, Arab-Israeli Dilemma, pp. 254-255, and Quandt, "United States Policy in the Middle East," pp. 522-523.

77. Khouri, Arab-Israeli Dilemma, p. 255.

78. Quandt, "United States Policy in the Middle East," p. 522, and Safran, From War to War, pp. 297-311.

79. Khouri, Arab-Israeli Dilemma, pp. 256-257.

80. Safran, From War to War, p. 267.

81. Draper, Israel, pp. 89, 93; Laqueur, Road to War, p. 197; and Bose, The Superpowers and the Middle East, pp. 103-104.

82. Johnson, Vantage Point, p. 290.

83. Bose, The Superpowers and the Middle East, p. 105; Khouri, Arab-Israeli Dilemma, p. 254.

84. Michael W. Suleiman, "American Mass Media and the June Conflict," in Ibrahim Abu-Lughod, The Arab-Israeli Confrontation of June 1967: An Arab Perspective (Evanston, Ill., 1970), pp. 139, 144, and 152.

85. Abdeen Jabara, "The American Left and the June Conflict," in ibid., p. 170.

86.   Laqueur, Road to War, p. 258; Quandt, "United States Policy in the Middle East," pp. 521-523; Bose, The Superpowers and the Middle East, pp. 106-107; Johnson, Vantage Point, pp. 292-293; and Safran, From War to War, pp. 296-297.

87.   Bose, The Superpowers and the Middle East, pp. 99-100; Lewis, "Arab-Israeli War," 323; Yost, "How It Began," 305-310; Draper, Israel, p. 130; and Safran, From War to War, p. 404.

88.   Love, Suez, p. 683.

89.   Laqueur, Road to War, p. 95.

90.   Khouri, Arab-Israeli Dilemma, pp. 259-261.

91.   Johnson, Vantage Point, p. 287.

92.   Khouri, Arab-Israeli Dilemma, pp. 262-264; Arthur Lall, The UN and the Middle East Crisis, 1967 (New York, 1967), p. 58; and U.N. Security Council, Official Records, 1347th Meeting and 1348th Meeting.

93.   Bose, The Superpowers and the Middle East, pp. 107-109 and Draper, Israel, p. 115.

94.   Mosley, Oil in the Middle East, pp. 343-346.

95.   Khouri, Arab-Israeli Dilemma, p. 265; Lall, Middle East Crisis, pp. 87-88; and U.N. Security Council, Official Records, 1351st Meeting.

96.   Khouri, Arab-Israeli Dilemma, pp. 265-266; Lall, Middle East Crisis, p. 102; U.N. Security Council, Official Records, 1060th Meeting.

97.   K. S. Abu-Jaber, "United States Policy toward the June Conflict," in Abu-Lughod, Arab-Israeli Confrontation, p. 157; Love, Suez, p.690; Khouri, Arab-Israeli Dilemma, p. 265.

98.   Johnson, Vantage Point, p. 299; Laqueur, Road to War, pp. 211-214; and Lall, Middle East Crisis, p. 63.

99.   Sueleiman, "American Mass Media," p. 152 in Abu-Lughod, Arab-Israeli Confrontation, p. 152; and Khouri, Arab-Israeli Dilemma, pp. 266-269.

100. Lall, Middle East Crisis, pp. 123-128, 160, and Khouri, Arab-Israeli Dilemma, p. 269.

101. Lall, Middle East Crisis, p. 270.

102. Khouri, Arab-Israeli Dilemma, p. 274.

103. Johnson, Vantage Point, p. 304, and PPPUS: LBJ, 1967, I, 632-33.

104. Lall, Middle East Crisis, p. 268, and U.N. Security Council, Official Records, 1382nd Meeting.

105. Bernard Reich, "United States Policy in the Middle East," Current History, 60 (Jan. 1971), 3.

106. Badeau, American Approach to the Arab World, pp. 163-164.

107. On the operation of the Zionist apparatus, see Alan R. Taylor and Richard N. Tetlie, eds., Palestine, A Search for Truth: Approaches to the Arab-Israeli Conflict (Washington, 1970), pp. 109, 217; W. T. Mallison, "The Legal Problems Concerning the Juridical Status and Political Activities of the Zionist Organization/Jewish Agency: A Study in International and United States Law," William and Mary Law Review, 9 (spring 1968), 556-629; John H. Davis, The Evasive Peace: A Study of the Zionist/Arab Problem (London, 1968), pp. 26-27; and Lilienthal, The Other Side of the Coin, pp. 79-80.

108. See U.S. Senate, Activities of Non-Diplomatic Representatives of Foreign Principals in the United States. Hearing before the Committee on Foreign Relations, U.S. Senate, 88 Cong, 1 Sess, Parts 9-12, May 23, 1963, Aug. 1, 1963, pp. 1211-1424, 1695-1782; and Mallison, "The Legal Problems Concerning the Juridical Status and Political Activities of the Zionist Organization," 583-584, 607.

109. Ibid., 564.

110. Ibid., 615-621.

111. Davis, The Evasive Peace, p. 106.

112. Halperin, The Political World of American Zionism, pp. 253-280; Lilienthal, The Other Side of the Coin, pp. 89-97; Abboushi, The Angry Arabs, pp. 232-240; Mallison, "The Legal Problems Concerning the Juridical Status and Political Activities of the Zionist Organization," 603; and Taylor and Tetlie, eds., Palestine, pp. 109-112.

113. Richard P. Stevens, "Smuts and Weizmann: A Study in South African-Zionist Cooperation," in Ibrahim Abu-Lughod and Baha Abu-Laban, eds., Settler Regimes in Africa and the Arab World: The Illusions of Endurance (Wilmette, Ill. 1974), p. 173.

114. W. T. Mallison, Jr., "The Zionist-Israel Juridical Claims to Constitute 'the Jewish People' National Entity and to Confer Membership in it: Appraisal in Public International Law," George Washington Law Review, 32 (June 1964), 983-1075; Lilienthal, The Other Side of the Coin, pp. 67, 212, 223; Taylor and Tetlie, eds., Palestine, pp. 160, 180, 181, 182, 212, and 240-245; Gary V.

Smith, ed., Zionism: The Dream and the Reality--A Jewish Critique (New York, 1974), pp. 210, 216, 227, 233, and 251, Neville Rubin, "The Impact of Zionism and Israel on the Political Orientation and Behavior of South African Jews," in Abu-Lughod and Abu-Laban, eds., Settler Regimes, pp. 171-172; and Israel Shahak, "What Are My Opinions?" Middle East International, (Jan. 1975).

115.   Mallison, "The Zionist-Israel Juridicial Claims," 1002, 1014, and 1029.

116.   Taylor and Tetlie, eds., Palestine, p. 93.

117.   Ibid., p. 91.

118.   Ibid., pp. 122, 161; Davis, The Evasive Peace, pp. 56-62; Christopher Sykes, Crossroads to Israel, 1917-1948 (Bloomington, Ind., 1973), pp. 337-356.

119.   Davis, The Evasive Peace, pp. 62-69.

120.   Taylor and Tetlie, eds., Palestine, p. 162.

121.   Ibid., pp. 9, 134, 139, 147, 281; Smith, ed., Zionism, pp. 186, 200, 253; Lilienthal, The Other Side of the Coin, pp. 48, 340; Abu-Lughod and Abu-Laban, eds., Settler Regimes, pp. 24-27, 197, 207.

CHAPTER 17

1.   Public Papers of the Presidents of the United States: Richard Nixon, 1969, p. 18.   Hereafter cited as PPPUS: RN.   See also Bernard Reich, "United States Policy in the Middle East," Current History, 60 (Jan. 1971), 3.   For a good summary of U.S.-Middle Eastern foreign policy from 1970 to 1973, see Barry Rubin, "U.S. Policy, January-October 1973," Journal of Palestine Studies, III (1974), 114-121.

2.   William B. Quandt, "Domestic Influences on United States Foreign Policy in the Middle East: The View from Washington," in Willard A. Beling, ed., The Middle East: Quest for an American Policy (Albany, N.Y., 1973), pp. 272-273; Department of State Bulletin, 21 April 1969, 337.

3.   Reich, "United States Policy," 4.

4.   Quandt, "Domestic Influences," p. 273.

5.   Department of State Bulletin, 1 June 1970, 675.

6.   Quandt, "Domestic Influences," p. 275; Reich, "United States Policy," 4; and Department of State Bulletin, 10 Aug. 1970, 178-179.

7. Reich, "United States Policy," 5; "Israel's Quest for Security," Current History, 62 (Jan. 1972), 3-4.

8. Quandt, "Domestic Influences," p. 275; Reich, "United States Policy," 5.

9. Reich, "Israel's Quest," 4.

10. Ibid., 4.

11. Anwar Sadat, "Where Egypt Stands," Foreign Affairs, 51 (Oct. 1972), 119, 121.

12. Quandt, "Domestic Influences," p. 276.

13. Reich, "Israel's Quest," 5.

14. Quandt, "Domestic Influences," p. 276.

15. Ibid., p. 276; Dwight J. Simpson, "Israel After Twenty-five Years," Current History, 64 (Jan. 1973), 3; and Tareq Y. Ismael, "Oil: The New Diplomacy," in Ismael, ed., The Middle East in World Politics, p. 235.

16. For Rogers' six-point plan, see Current History, 62 (Jan. 1972), 44, 47.

17. Reich, "Israel's Quest," 5.

18. Nixon gave Israel a firm commitment of U.S. support. See Lawrence L. Whetten, The Canal War: Four-Power Conflict in the Middle East (Cambridge, Mass., 1974), pp. 116-117; Quandt, "Domestic Influences," pp. 276-277; and Simpson, "Israel After Twenty-five Years," 3.

19. Roger E. Kanet, "Soviet-American Relations: A Year of Détente?" Current History, 63 (Oct. 1972), 159; PPPUS: RN, 1972, p. 633.

20. Alvin Z. Rubinstein, "The Soviet Union in the Middle East," Current History, 63 (Oct. 1972), 168; Oles M. Smolansky, "The Soviet Setback in the Middle East," Current History, 64 (Jan. 1973), 18; and George Lenczowski, "Egypt and the Soviet Exodus," Current History, 64 (Jan. 1973), 13-14.

21. Rubinstein, "Soviet Union," 168; Lenczowski, "Soviet Exodus," 14; and Smolansky, "Soviet Setback," 18.

22. Quandt, "Domestic Influences," p. 277.

23. Simpson, "Israel After Twenty-five Years," 4.

24. Ibid., 3.

25. Arnold Hottinger, "The Depth of Arab Radicalism,"
Foreign Affairs, 51 (Apr. 1973), 502-503.

26. George Lenczowski, "Arab Radicalism: Problems and
Prospects," Current History, 60 (Jan. 1971), 32-37, and Harry N.
Howard, "The United States," in Ismael, ed., The Middle East, pp.
128, 131, 135.

27. Ann T. Schulz, "A Leadership Role for Iran in the Persian Gulf," Current History, 64 (Jan. 1972), 25; David Holden, "The
Persian Gulf: After the British Raj," Foreign Affairs, 49 (Jul. 1971),
725 et seq; Roy E. Thoman, "Iraq and the Persian Gulf Region,"
Current Affairs, 64 (Jan. 1973), 23-25.

28. Philip M. Dadant, "American and Soviet Defense Systems in the Middle East," in Beling, ed., The Middle East, p. 191.

29. R. K. Ramazani, The Persian Gulf: Iran's Role (Charlottesville, Va., 1972), p. 107.

30. Schulz, "A Leadership Role for Iran," 28; New York
Times, 12 June 1973; and Ramazani, The Persian Gulf, pp. 106-107.

31. Ramazani, The Persian Gulf, p. 107.

32. Rubinstein, "The Soviet Union," 169.

33. Harry N. Howard, "Continuing Trouble in the Turkish
Republic," Current History, 64 (Jan. 1973), 29. The government of
Prime Minister Balent Ecevit has tried to ease Turkish resentment
of the opium pact by various means, and the arrangement with Turkey has now deteriorated. Atlanta Constitution, 26 May 1974.

34. Harry N. Howard, "Jordan in Turmoil," Current History, 63 (Jan. 1972), 15.

35. Ibid., 15.

36. Ibid., 18; Reich, "United States Policy," 5.

37. Ibid., 18; PPPUS: RN, 1970, p. 1076.

38. Lenczowski, United States Interests in the Middle East,
p. 40.

39. Walter J. Levy, "Oil Power," Foreign Affairs (July
1971), 652-53.

40. James E. Akins, "The Oil Crisis: This Time the Wolf
Is Here," Foreign Affairs, 51 (April 1973), 463; Ismael, "Oil: The
New Weapon," in Ismael, ed., The Middle East, p. 231.

41. Akins, "The Oil Crisis," 467.

42. Ibid., 467.

43. OPEC consists of Iran, Indonesia, Venezuela, Nigeria, Saudi Arabia, Iraq, Kuwait, Libya, Algeria, Abu Dhabi, and Qatar.

44. Levy, "Oil Power," 654; Akins, "The Oil Crisis," 473; and Mosley, Oil in the Middle East, p. 381.

45. Levy, "Oil Power," 657; Akins, "The Oil Crisis," 473; and Mosley, Oil in the Middle East, p. 395.

46. Newsweek, 12 June 1973.

47. New York Times, 12 June 1973.

48. Akins, "The Oil Crisis," 485; Janigir Amuzegar, "The Oil Story: Facts, Fiction, and Fair Play," Foreign Affairs, 51 (July 1973), 684.

49. National Observer, 16 June 1973.

50. Department of State Bulletin, 29 Oct. 1973, 534. Walter Laqueur, Confrontation: The Middle East and World Politics (New York, 1974), pp. 83-85 suggests that Russia knew the full details of the attack. Ron Hall et al., Insight on the Middle East War (London 1974), pp. 48-50, 53, contends that U.S. and Israeli intelligence were caught off-guard.

51. The best treatment of the October War to date is Hall, Insight on the Middle East War; Laqueur's Confrontation; and Whetten's The Canal War.

52. Time, 15 Oct. 1973; Newsweek, 15 Oct. 1973; Washington Post, 7 Oct. 1973.

53. Hall, Insight, pp. 63-73, and Whetten, The Canal War, p. 245.

54. New York Times, 8 Oct. 1973, and Washington Post, 8 Oct. 1973.

55. Washington Post, 8 Oct. 1973.

56. Ibid., 8 Oct. 1973.

57. Ibid., 8 Oct. 1973.

58. Ibid., 9 Oct. 1973.

59. Hall, Insight, pp. 85-86, 89-93, 93-95, and Washington Post, 9 Oct. 1973.

60. New York Times, 9 Oct. 1973.

61. Washington Post, 9 Oct. 1973.

62. New York Times, 9 Oct. 1973. On the use of oil as a tool of diplomacy, see Fuad Itayim, "Arab Oil--The Political Dimension," in Journal of Palestine Studies, III (1974), 84-97.

63. Hall, Insight, pp. 93-100; Whetten, The Canal War, pp. 261-65.

64. Hall, Insight, pp. 101-105.

65. New York Times, 10 Oct. 1973.

66. Hall, Insight, pp. 118-119, 120-124.

67. Washington Post, 10 Oct. 1973.

68. Ibid., 11 Oct. 1973.

69. Ibid., 12 Oct. 1973.

70. Ibid., 13 Oct. 1973.

71. Department of State Bulletin, 29 Oct. 1973, 534-541.

72. Washington Post, 13 Oct. 1973, and New York Times, 13 Oct. 1973.

73. Washington Post, 13 Oct. 1973.

74. Ibid., 14 Oct. 1973.

75. Ibid., 14 Oct. 1973.

76. New York Times, 14 Oct. 1973.

77. Hall, Insight, pp. 140-149; Whetten, The Canal War, pp. 269-272.

78. New York Times, 15 Oct. 1973; Itayim, "Arab Oil," 90; Hall, Insight, pp. 177-183. Walter Laqueur rejects the thesis that U.S. was responsible for the oil embargo. Laqueur, Confrontation, pp. 246-47.

79. Hall, Insight, pp. 134-136, and Rubin, "U.S. Policy," 109.

80. New York Times, 16 Oct. 1973.

81. Hall, Insight, pp. 159-176.

82. Washington Post, 17 Oct. 1973.

83. Ibid., 17 Oct. 1973.

84. Edmund Ghareeb, "The U.S. Arms Supply to Israel during the October War," Journal of Palestine Studies, III (1974), 114-121, and Whetten, The Canal War, p. 289.

85. Washington Post, 17 Oct. 1973.

86. Ibid., 17 Oct. 1973.

87. Ibid., 17 Oct. 1973.

88. New York Times, 18 Oct. 1973.

89. On the effects of the oil embargo, see U.S. House of Representatives, The Impact of the October Middle East War. Hearings before the Subcommittee on the Near East and South East Asia of the Committee on Foreign Affairs, 93 Cong, 1 Sess, pp. 83, 140, and U.S. House of Representatives, The United States Oil Shortage and the Arab-Israeli Conflict. Report of a Study Mission to the Middle East from October 22 to November 3, 1973 pursuant to H. Res. 267, 93 Cong, 1 Sess, pp. 9, 18, 22-23.

90. Washington Post, 19 Oct. 1973.

91. New York Times, 19 Oct. 1973.

92. Ibid., 19 Oct. 1973.

93. Washington Post, 19 Oct. 1973.

94. Whetten, The Canal War, pp. 288-289.

95. Ibid., p. 289.

96. Washington Post, 20 Oct. 1973.

97. Hall, Insight, p. 187.

98. Itayim, "Arab Oil," 91.

99. Washington Post, 21 Oct. 1973.

100. Ibid., 22 Oct. 1973 and Whetten, The Canal War, p. 290.

101. Hall, Insight, p. 188.

102. Ibid., pp. 196-202, and Whetten, The Canal War, p. 270.

103. Hall, Insight, p. 218, and Whetten, The Canal War, p. 270.

104.   Ghareeb, "The U.S. Arms Supply to Israel," 114-121.

105.   On the opposition of European states to the American resupply of Israel, see U.S. House of Representatives, United States-Europe Relations and the 1973 Middle East War.   Hearings before the Subcommittees on Europe and on the Near East and South Asia of the Committee on Foreign Affairs, 93 Cong, 1 and 2 Sess, pp. 31-32.

CHAPTER 18

1.   New York Times, 23 Oct. 1973, and Ron Hall, et al., Insight on the Middle East War (London, 1974), pp. 188, 204.

2.   Department of State Bulletin, 12 Nov. 1973.

3.   Hall, Insight, pp. 205-207.

4.   Washington Post, 26 Oct. 1973.

5.   Hall, Insight, p. 212; Fuad Itayim, "Arab Oil--The Political Dimension," Journal of Palestine Studies, III (1974), 95; and Newsweek, 26 Nov. 1973.

6.   Hall, Insight, p. 216.

7.   New York Times, 1-2 Nov. 1973.

8.   Newsweek, 19 Nov. 1973.

9.   New York Times, 9 Nov. 1973.

10.   Ibid., 10 Nov. 1973.

11.   See Itayim, "Arab Oil," 94, and New York Times, 10 Nov. 1973.

12.   New York Times, 12, 13, 14, 15 Nov. 1973.

13.   Newsweek, 3 Dec. 1973.

14.   Ibid., 17 Dec. 1973.

15.   Ibid., 10 Dec. 1973, and New York Times, 27, 28 Nov. 1973.

16.   Newsweek, 10, 17 Dec. 1973.

17.   Ibid., 24 Dec. 1973.

18.   Ibid., 31 Dec. 1973.

19. Ibid., 31 Dec. 1973.

20. New York Times, 3 Jan. 1974.

21. Ibid., 26 Dec. 1973.

22. Ibid., 7, 10 Jan. 1974.

23. Newsweek, 14 Jan. 1974.

24. Ibid., 14 Jan. 1974; Walter J. Levy's article, "World Oil Cooperation or International Chaos," Foreign Affairs, 52 (July 1974) 690-713, makes a strong plea for cooperation among the members of the world community. Also see New York Times, 13 Jan. 1974.

25. Time, 21 Jan. 1974.

26. New York Times, 15 Jan. 1974.

27. Ibid., 19 Jan. 1974.

28. Newsweek, 28 Jan. 1974.

29. Ibid., 11 March 1974.

30. New York Times, 23 Jan. 1974, 1 Feb. 1974.

31. Ibid., 5 Feb. 1974.

32. Ibid., 7 Feb. 1974.

33. Newsweek, 4 Feb. 1974.

34. Time, 11 Feb. 1974.

35. Department of State Bulletin, 4 Mar. 1974.

36. Newsweek, 25 Feb. 1974.

37. Department of State Bulletin, 1 April 1974, and Newsweek, 25 Feb. 1974.

38. Time, 11 March 1974.

39. Ibid., 11 March 1974.

40. Department of State Bulletin, 1 April 1974.

41. Newsweek, 11 March 1974.

42. New York Times, 19 April 1974.

43.   Atlanta Constitution, 30 April 1974.

44.   Ibid., 19, 22, 24 April 1974.

45.   Newsweek, 1, 8, 22 April 1974.

46.   Atlanta Constitution, 21 April 1974.

47.   Ibid., 5 May 1974.

48.   Newsweek, 6 May 1974.

49.   New York Times, 20 May 1974.

50.   Newsweek, 27 May 1974.

51.   New York Times, 1 June 1974.

52.   Newsweek, 17 June 1974.

53.   Department of State Bulletin, 29 Sept. 1975, 466-470.

54.   See U.S. Congress, To Implement the United States Proposal for the Early-Warning System in Sinai. Report of the Committee on International Relations on House Joint Resolution 683, 94
Cong, 1st Sess., and Early Warning System in Sinai. Report from
the Committee on Foreign Relations, U.S. Senate, 94 Cong, 1st
Sess.

CHAPTER 19

1.   On President Nixon's Middle Eastern tour, see Department of State Bulletin, 15 July 1974, 77-122.

2.   See Henry Kissinger's statement in New York Times, 13
Nov. 1973 and Nadav Safran's essay, "The War and the Future of
the Arab-Israeli Conflict," Foreign Affairs, 52 (Jan. 1974), 235.

3.   On the need to maintain an evenhanded policy in the Middle East, see U.S. Congress, The Impact of the October Middle East
War. Hearings before the Subcommittee on the Near East and South
Asia of the Committee on Foreign Affairs House of Representatives.
93rd Cong, 1st Sess, p. 2.

4.   Concerning the rise of Palestinian nationalism and its
relevance to the aspirations of the Arab world, see Don Peretz, ed.,
A Palestine Entity? (Washington 1970) and W. F. Abboushi, The
Angry Arabs (Philadelphia, 1974), p. 250.

5.   On the United States position on the Palestinians and the
PLO, see U.S. Congress, The Middle East, 1974: New Hopes, New
Challenges. Hearings before the Subcommittee on the Near East and

South Asia of the Committee on Foreign Affairs House of Representatives. 93rd Cong, 2nd Session, p. 143, and Department of State
Bulletin, 16 Dec. 1974, 857.

6. On the relationship between a peace settlement and a cut
in Arab oil prices, see U.S. Congress, The Impact of the October
Middle East War, pp. 55, 80-81, and 141; The Middle East, 1974:
New Hopes, New Challenges, pp. 30-31; Newsweek, 30 Sept. 1974;
New York Times, 4 Oct. 1974, 17 Jan. 1975; and J. W. Fulbright,
"The Clear and Present Danger," speech delivered 2 Nov. 1974,
Westminster College, Fulton, Missouri.

7. James D. Richardson, ed., A Compilation of the Messages and Papers of the Presidents (Washington, 1896), I, 221-222.

8. U.S. Congress, The United States Role in Opening the
Suez Canal, Hearing before the Subcommittee on the Near East and
South Asia of the Committee on Foreign Affairs House of Represent-
atives, 93rd Cong, 2nd Sess, p. 46, and the Impact of the October
Middle East War, p. 142.

9. U.S. Congress, The Middle East, 1974: New Hopes, New
Challenges, p. 44.

10. U.S. Congress, The Persian Gulf, 1974: Money, Politics, Arms, and Power. Hearings before the Subcommittee on the
Near East and South Asia of the Committee on Foreign Affairs House
of Representatives, 93rd Cong, 2nd Sess, pp. 121-122, and The Impact of the October Middle East War, p. 141.

11. U.S. Congress, The Middle East, 1974: New Hopes,
New Challenges, p. 90.

12. Ibid., pp. 52, 89, and 134.

13. U.S. Congress, The Persian Gulf, 1974: Money, Politics, Arms, and Power, pp. 1-17.

14. Department of State Bulletin, 31 March 1975, 402-405;
2 Sept. 1974, 335-336; and 16 Sept. 1974, 380-383.

15. On the effects of the oil embargo on the United States
and U.S. dependence on Arab oil, see U.S. Congress, The United
States Oil Shortage and the Arab-Israeli Conflict. Report of a Study
Mission to the Middle East from October 22 to November 3, 1973
pursuant to H. Res. 267, 93rd Cong, 1st Sess.

BIBLIOGRAPHY

PRIMARY SOURCES

I. UNITED STATES

American State Papers: Foreign Relations, 1789-1828. ed. by Lowrie & Clarke (6 vols. Washington, 1833-1859).

Department of State, Bulletin.

Department of State Despatches, Turkey, National Archives.

Department of State Instructions, Turkey, National Archives.

Department of State, Special Missions, National Archives.

Miller, Hunter, ed., Treaties and Other International Acts of the United States of America (8 vols. Washington: GPO, 1933-1948).

United States Treaties and Other International Agreements. (21 vols. Washington: GPO, 1952-1970).

The Diplomatic Correspondence of the United States, September 10, 1783 to March 4, 1789. (7 vols. Washington: 1833-1834).

Department of State, Papers Relating to the Foreign Relations of the United States. (Washington: GPO, 1861-1948).

National Archives, Public Papers of the Presidents of the United States (36 vols. Washington: GPO).

U.S. Congress, Congressional Record.

U.S. Congress, The Debates and Proceedings in the Congress of the United States: Annals of Congress. (Washington: Gales and Seaton, 1834-1856).

U.S. Congress, The United States Oil Shortage and the Arab-Israeli Conflict. Report of a Study Mission to the Middle East from October 22 to November 3, 1973 pursuant to H. Res. 267. 93rd Cong, 1st Session.

U. S. Congress. The United States Role in Opening the Suez Canal. Hearing before the Subcommittee on the Near East and South Asia of the Committee on Foreign Affairs, House of Representatives, 93rd Cong, 2nd Sess.

U. S. Congress, The Impact of the October Middle East War. Hearings before the Subcommittee on the Near East and South Asia of the Committee on Foreign Affairs, House of Representatives, 93rd Cong, 1st Sess.

U. S. Congress, The Middle East, 1974: New Hopes, New Challenges. Hearings before the Subcommittee on the Near East and South Asia of the Committee on Foreign Affairs, House of Representatives, 93rd Cong, 2nd Session.

U. S. Congress, The Persian Gulf, 1974: Money, Politics, Arms, and Power. Hearings before the Subcommittee on the Near East and South Asia of the Committee on Foreign Affairs, House of Representatives, 93rd Cong, 2nd Sess.

U. S. Congress, United States-Europe Relations and the 1973 Middle East War. Hearings before the Subcommittees on Europe and on the Near East and South Asia of the Committee on Foreign Affairs, 93rd Cong, 1st and 2nd Session.

U. S. Congress, Activities of Non-Diplomatic Representatives of Foreign Principals in the United States. Hearing before Committee on Foreign Relations, U. S. Senate, 88th Cong, 1st Sess., Pts. 9-12.

U. S. Congress, To Implement the United States Proposal for the Early-Warning System in Sinai. Report of the Committee on International Relations on House Joint Resolution 683, 94th Cong., 1st Sess.

U. S. Congress, Early Warning System in Sinai. Report from the Committee on Foreign Relations, U. S. Senate, 94th Cong, 1st Sess.

II.   GREAT BRITAIN:

Woodward, E. L. and Butler, Rohan, eds., Documents on British Foreign Policy, 1919-1939. First series, London: H. M. Stationery Office, 1947-1958.

III.   UNITED NATIONS:

General Assembly, Official Records of the Plenary Meetings.

General Assembly. Resolutions Adopted by the General Assembly.

Security Council, Official Records.

United Nations Yearbook.

IV. MISCELLANEOUS:

Adams, Charles Francis, ed., Memoirs of John Quincy Adams.
(Freeport: Books for Library Press, 1969).

Council on Foreign Relations, Documents on American Foreign Relations. (21 Vols. New York, Harper).

Richardson, James D., ed., A Compilation of the Messages and Papers of the Presidents (Washington: Government Printing Office,
1896).

Rutland, Robert A., et al., eds., The Papers of James Madison.
(Chicago: University of Chicago Press, 1973).

MEMOIRS, AUTOBIOGRAPHIES, AND DIARIES:

Acheson, Dean. Present at the Creation: My Years at the State
Department. New York: W. W. Norton Co., 1969.

Byrnes, James F. Speaking Frankly. New York: Harper, 1947.

Child, Richard Washburn. A Diplomat Looks at Europe. New York:
Duffield and Co., 1925.

Churchill, Winston S. The Hinge of Fate. Boston: Houghton Mifflin Co., 1950.

Crum, Bartley C. Behind the Silken Curtain. New York: Simon
and Schuster, 1947.

DeLeon, Edwin. Thirty Years of My Life on Three Continents. 2
vols. London: Ward, Downey, 1890.

Eden, Anthony. Full Circle: The Memoirs of Anthony Eden. Boston: Houghton Mifflin Co., 1960.

_____. The Suez Crisis of 1956. Boston: Beacon Press, 1960.

Einstein, Lewis. A Diplomat Looks Back, ed. by Lawrence E. Gelfand. New Haven, Conn.: Yale University Press, 1968.

Eisenhower, Dwight David. Mandate for Change, 1953-1956: White
House Years. New York: Doubleday, 1963.

_____. Waging Peace, 1956-1961: White House Years. New
York: Doubleday, 1965.

Gates, Caleb Frank. Not to Me Only. Princeton, N. J.: Princeton University Press, 1940.

Grew, Joseph C. Turbulent Era: A Diplomatic Record of Forty Years, 1904-1945. 2 vols. London: Hammond, Hammond, 1953.

Griscom, Lloyd. Diplomatically Speaking: Memoirs of Constantinople and Persia. New York: Literary Guild of America, 1940.

Horton, George. The Blight of Asia. New York: Bobbs-Merrill, 1926.

Hull, Cordell, The Memoirs of Cordell Hull. 2 vols. New York: Macmillan Co., 1948.

Huntington-Wilson, F. M. Memoirs of an Ex-Diplomat. Boston: Bruce Humphries Inc., 1945.

Johnson, Lyndon B. The Vantage Point: Perspectives of the Presidency, 1963-1969. New York: Holt, Rinehart and Winston, 1971.

Kennan, George F. Memoirs, 1925-1950. 2 vols. Boston: Little, Brown, 1967.

Lloyd George, David. Memoirs of the Peace Conference. 2 vols. New Haven, Conn.: Yale University Press, 1939.

McDonald, James G. My Mission in Israel, 1948-1951. New York: Simon and Schuster, 1951.

Millis, Walter, and E. S. Duffield, eds. The Forrestal Diaries. New York: Viking, 1951.

Millspaugh, Arthur C. Americans in Persia. Washington: Brookings Institution, 1946.

_____. The American Task in Persia. New York: Century Co., 1925.

Morgenthau, Henry. Ambassador Morgenthau's Story. New York: Doubleday, 1919.

_____. All in a Lifetime. New York: Doubleday, 1922.

Murphy, Robert. Diplomat Among Warriors. New York: Doubleday, 1944.

Patrick, Mary Mills. A Bosporus Adventure: Istanbul (Constantinople) Women's College, 1871-1924. Stanford, Calif.: Stanford University Press, 1934.

Phillips, William. Ventures in Diplomacy. London: John Murray, 1955.

Porter, David Dixon. Memoir of Commodore David Porter of the
United States Navy. Albany: Munsell, 1875.

Shuster, William M. The Strangling of Persia. New York: Century, 1912.

Straus, Oscar. Under Four Administrations: From Cleveland to
Taft. Boston: Houghton Mifflin, 1922.

Truman, Harry S. Memoirs: Years of Trial and Hope. 2 vols.
New York: Doubleday, 1955.

Warne, William E. Mission for Peace: Point Four in Iran. New
York: Bobbs-Merrill, 1956.

SECONDARY SOURCES--BOOKS

Abboushi, W. F. The Angry Arabs. Philadelphia: Westminster
Press, 1974.

Abu-Lughod, Ibrahim. The Arab-Israeli Confrontation of June 1967:
An Arab Perspective. Evanston, Ill.: Northwestern University
Press, 1970.

_____. The Transformation of Palestine: Essays on the Origin
and Development of the Arab-Israeli Conflict. Evanston, Ill.:
Northwestern University Press, 1971.

_____, and Abu-Laban, Baha, eds. Settler Regimes in Africa
and the Arab World: The Illusion of Endurance. Wilmette, Ill.:
Medina University Press, 1974.

Abu-Jaber, Kamel S. "United States Policy toward the June Conflict," in Ibrahim Abu-Lughod, The Arab-Israeli Confrontation of
of June 1967: An Arab Perspective. Evanston, Ill.: Northwestern
University Press, 1970.

Adams, Michael. Suez and After: Year of Crisis. Boston: Beacon
Press, 1958.

Agwani, Mohammed Shafi. The United States and the Arab World,
1945-1952. Aligarh: Institute of Islamic Studies, 1955.

Allen, Gardner W. Our Navy and the Barbary Corsairs. Hamden,
Conn.: Archon Books, 1905.

Antonius, George. The Arab Awakening: The Story of the Arab National Movement. New York: G. P. Putnams, 1946.

Arakie, Margaret. The Broken Sword of Justice: America, Israel &

the Palestine Tragedy. London: Quartet Books, 1973.

Badeau, John S. American Approach to the Arab World. New York: Harper, 1968.

Bailey, Thomas A. A Diplomatic History of the American People. New York: Appleton-Century-Crofts, 1969.

Barker, A. J. Suez: The Seven Day War. London: Faber and Faber, 1964.

Barnby, H. G. The Prisoners of Algiers: An Account of the Forgotten American-Algerian War, 1785-97. New York: Oxford University Press, 1966.

Barton, James L. Story of Near East Relief, 1915-1930: An Interprepation. New York: Macmillan, 1930.

Beal, John Robinson. John Foster Dulles, 1888-1959. New York: Harper & Bros., 1951.

Beale, Howard K. Theodore Roosevelt and the Rise of America to World Power. Baltimore: Johns Hopkins Press, 1956.

Beard, Charles A. The Idea of National Interest: An Analytical Study in American Foreign Policy. New York: Macmillan, 1934.

Beling, Willard A., ed. The Middle East: Quest for an American Policy. Albany: State University of New York Press, 1974.

Bernstein, Barton J. Politics and Policies of the Truman Administration. Chicago: Quadrangle Books, 1970.

Bierstadt, Edward Hale. The Great Betrayal. New York: R. M. McBridge & Co., 1924.

Bishop, Joseph Bucklin. Theodore Roosevelt and His Time: Shown in His Own Letters. 2 vols. New York: Charles Scribner's Sons, 1920.

Bixler, R. W. The Open Door on the Old Barbary Coast. New York: Pageant Press, 1959.

Blair, Leon Borden. Western Window on the Arab World. Austin: University of Texas Press, 1970.

Booras, Harris John. Hellenic Independence and America's Contribution to the Cause. Rutland: The Tuttle Co., 1934.

Bose, T. C. The Superpowers and the Middle East. New York: Asia Publishing House, 1973.

Broad, Lewis. Anthony Eden: Chronicle of a Career. New York:

Thomas Y. Crowell, 1955.

Bromberger, Serge. Secrets of Suez. London: Sidgwick, 1957.

Bryson, Thomas A. American-Middle Eastern Diplomacy, 1945-1974. St. Charles Mo.: Forum Press, 1975.

_____. Walter George Smith. Washington: Catholic University Press, 1975.

_____. "Woodrow Wilson, the Senate, Public Opinion and the Armenian Mandate Question, 1919-1920," unpublished Ph.D. dissertation, Athens: University of Georgia, 1965.

Buhite, Russell. Patrick J. Hurley and American Foreign Policy. Ithaca, N.Y.: Cornell University Press, 1973.

Burns, James MacGregor. Roosevelt: The Soldier of Freedom, 1940-45. New York: Harcourt Brace Jovanovich, 1970.

Buzanski, Peter. "Admiral Mark L. Bristol and Turkish-American Relations, 1919-1922," unpublished Ph.D. dissertation, Berkeley: University of California, 1960.

Campbell, John C. Defense of the Middle East: Problems of American Diplomacy. New York: Harper, 1960.

Cline, Myrtle A. American Attitude Toward the Greek War of Independence, 1821-1828. Atlanta: Private Printing, 1930.

Cole, Wayne S. An Interpretative History of American Foreign Relations. Homewood, Ill.: Dorsey Press, 1968.

Cook, Ralph Elliott. "The United States and the Armenian Question, 1884-1924." unpublished Ph.D. dissertation, Fletcher School of Law and Diplomacy, 1957.

Crabites, Pierre. Americans in the Egyptian Army. London: George Routledge & Sons, 1938.

Curry, George. James F. Byrnes. New York: Cooper Square Pub. Co., 1965.

Curti, Merle. American Philanthropy Abroad: A History. New Brunswick, N.J.: Rutgers University Press, 1963.

_____. Prelude to Point Four: American Technical Missions Overseas, 1838-1930. Madison: University of Wisconsin Press, 1954.

Dadant, Philip M. "American and Soviet Defense Systems in the Middle East," in Willard A. Beling, ed., The Middle East: Quest for an American Policy. Albany: State University of New York Press, 1973.

Daniel, Robert L. American Philanthropy in the Near East, 1820-1960. Athens: Ohio University Press, 1970.

Davis, John A. The Evasive Peace: A Study in the Zionist/Arab Problem. London: John Murray, 1968.

DeKay, James E. Sketches of Turkey in 1831 and 1832, by an American. New York: Harper, 1833.

DeLeon, Edwin. The Khedive's Egypt. New York: Harper, 1878.

Dennett, Tyler. John Hay: From Poetry to Politics. New York: Dodd, Mead, 1934.

Dennis, Alfred L. P. Adventures in American Diplomacy, 1896-1906. New York: E. P. Dutton, 1928.

DeNovo, John A. American Interests and Policies in the Middle East, 1900-1939. Minneapolis: University of Minnesota Press, 1963.

DeRiencourt, Amaury. The American Empire. New York: Dell, 1968.

Draper, Theodore. Israel and World Politics: Roots of the Third Arab-Israeli War. New York: Viking, 1968.

Drummond, Roscoe, and Gaston Coblentz. Duel at the Brink: John Foster Dulles' Command of American Power. New York: Doubleday, 1960.

Eagleton, Clyde. "The United Nations and the Suez Crisis," in Philip W. Thayer, ed., Tensions in the Middle East. Baltimore: Johns Hopkins Press, 1958.

Earle, Edward Mead. Turkey, the Great Powers and the Baghdad Railway: A Study in Imperialism. New York: Macmillan, 1923.

Eddy, William A. FDR Meets Ibn Saud. New York: American Friends of the Middle East, 1954.

Ellis, Harry B. Challenge in the Middle East: Communist Influence and American Policy. New York: Ronald Press, 1960.

Epstein, Leon D. British Policies in the Suez Crisis. Urbana: University of Illinois Press, 1963.

Esthus, Raymond A. Theodore Roosevelt and the International Rivalries. Waltham: Ginn-Blaisdell, 1970.

Evans, Laurence. United States Policy and the Partition of Turkey, 1914-1924. Baltimore: Johns Hopkins Press, 1965.

Feis, Herbert. Birth of Israel: The Tousled Diplomatic Bed. New

York: Norton, 1969.

_____. Churchill Roosevelt Stalin: The War They Waged and the
Peace They Sought. Princeton, N.J.: Princeton University Press,
1967.

_____. Petroleum and American Foreign Policy. Stanford,
Calif.: Stanford University Press, 1944.

Ferrell, Robert H. George C. Marshall. New York: Cooper
Square Pub. Inc., 1966.

Field, James A., Jr. America and the Mediterranean World, 1776-
1882. Princeton, N.J.: Princeton University Press, 1969.

Finer, Herman. Dulles Over Suez: The Theory and Practice of
His Diplomacy. Chicago: Quadrangle, 1964.

Finnie, David H. Pioneers East: The Early American Experience
in the Middle East. Cambridge, Mass.: Harvard University Press,
1967.

_____. Desert Enterprise: Middle East Oil Industry in Its Local
Environment. Cambridge, Mass.: Harvard University Press, 1958.

Fisher, Carol A. and Fred Krinsky. Middle East in Crisis: A Historical and Documentary Review. Syracuse, N.Y.: Syracuse University Press, 1959.

Fisher, Sydney Nettleton. The Middle East: A History. New York:
Knopf, 1960.

Fleming, D. F. The Cold War and Its Origins. 2 vols. New York:
Doubleday, 1961.

Freeland, Richard M. The Truman Doctrine and the Origins of Mc-
Carthyism: Foreign Policy, Domestic Politics, and Internal Security. New York: Knopf, 1972.

Frye, Richard N. The Near East and the Great Powers. Port
Washington: Kennikat Press, 1951.

Gaddis, John Lewis. The United States and the Origins of the Cold
War, 1941-1947. New York: Columbia University Press, 1972.

Gallagher, Charles F. United States and North Africa: Morocco,
Algiers, Tunisia. Cambridge: Harvard University Press, 1963.

Gallman, Waldemar J. Iraq Under General Nuri. Baltimore: Johns
Hopkins Press, 1964.

Gallup, George H. The Gallup Poll: Public Opinion, 1935-1971.
New York: Random House, 1972.

Gardner, Lloyd C. Architects of Illusion: Men and Ideas in American Foreign Policy, 1941-1949. Chicago: Quadrangle, 1970.

_____. Economic Aspects of New Deal Diplomacy. Madison: University of Wisconsin Press, 1964.

_____. "From Liberation to Containment, 1945-1953" in William Appleman Williams, ed., From Colony to Empire: Essays in the History of American Foreign Relations. New York: John Wiley, 1972.

Gelber, Lionel. America in Britain's Place: The Leadership of the West and Anglo-American Unity. New York: Praeger, 1961.

Gelfand, Lawrence E. The Inquiry: American Preparations for Peace, 1917-1919. New Haven, Conn.: University Press, 1963.

Gerson, Louis. John Foster Dulles. New York: Cooper Square, 1961.

Gibb, George Sweet, and Evelyn H. Knowlton. The Resurgent Years, 1911-1927: History of Standard Oil Company [New Jersey]. New York: Harper, 1956.

Gidney, James B. A Mandate for Armenia. Kent: Kent State University Press, 1967.

Goodhart, A. L. "Some Legal Aspects of the Suez Situation," in Philip W. Thayer, ed., Tensions in the Middle East. Baltimore: Johns Hopkins Press, 1958.

Goold-Adams, Richard. The Time of Power: Reappraisal of John Foster Dulles. London: Weidenfeld & Nicolson, 1962.

Gordon, Leland James. American Relations with Turkey, 1830-1930: An Economic Interpretation. Philadelphia: University of Pennsylvania Press, 1932.

Grabill, Joseph L. Protestant Diplomacy and the Near East: Missionary Influence on American Policy, 1810-1927. Minneapolis: University of Minnesota Press, 1971.

Guhin, Michael A. John Foster Dulles: A Statesman and His Times. New York: Columbia University Press, 1972.

Hall, Luella J. The United States and Morocco, 1776-1956. Metuchen, N.J.: Scarecrow Press, 1971.

Hall, Ron, et al. Insight on the Middle East War. London: André Deutsch, 1974.

Halperin, Samuel. The Political World of American Zionism. Detroit: Wayne State University Press, 1961.

Halpern, Ben. The Idea of a Jewish State. Cambridge, Mass.:
Harvard University Press, 1969.

Harris, George S. Troubled Alliance: Turkish-American Problems
in Historical Perspective, 1945-1971. Stanford, Calif.: Hoover Institution, 1972.

Helmreich, Paul C. From Paris to Sèvres: The Partition of the
Ottoman Empire at the Peace Conference, 1919-1920. Columbus:
Ohio State University Press, 1974.

Hesseltine, William, and Hazel C. Wolf. The Blue and the Gray on
the Nile. Chicago: University of Chicago Press, 1961.

Hinckley, Frank E. American Consular Jurisdiction in the Orient.
Washington: W. H. Lowdermilk & Co., 1906.

Hoopes, Townsend. The Devil and John Foster Dulles. Boston:
Little, Brown, 1973.

Horowitz, David. The Free World Colossus: A Critique of American Foreign Policy in the Cold War. New York: Hill & Wang, 1956.

Hoskins, Halford L. The Middle East: Problem Area in World
Politics. New York: Macmillan, 1957.

Housepian, Marjorie. The Smyrna Affair. New York: Harcourt,
Brace, Jovanovich, 1971.

Hovannisian, Richard G. Armenia on the Road to Independence,
1918. Berkeley: University of California Press, 1969.

_____. The Republic of Armenia, 1918-1919. Berkeley: Univer-
sity of California Press, 1971.

Howard, Harry N. The King-Crane Commission: An Inquiry in the
Middle East. Beirut: Khayats, 1963.

_____. The Partition of Turkey: A Diplomatic History, 1913-
1923. Norman: University of Oklahoma Press, 1931.

_____. Turkey, the Straits and U.S. Policy. Baltimore: Johns
Hopkins Press, 1974.

Howard, Michael, and Robert Hunter. Israel and the Arab World:
The Crisis of 1967. London: Institute for Strategic Studies, 1967.

Hurewitz, J. C. Middle East Dilemmas: The Background of United
States Policy. New York: Harper, 1953.

_____. Middle East Politics: The Military Dimension. New
York: Praeger, 1972.

_____. Soviet-American Rivalry in the Middle East. New York: Praeger, 1969.

_____. The Struggle for Palestine. New York: Greenwood Press, 1968.

Irwin, Ray W. The Diplomatic Relations of the United States with the Barbary Powers, 1776-1816. Chapel Hill: University of North Carolina Press, 1931.

Ismael, Tareq Y. ed. The Middle East in World Politics: A Study in Contemporary International Relations. Syracuse, N.Y.: Syracuse University Press, 1974.

Jabara, Abdeen. "The American Left and the June Conflict," in Ibrahim Abu-Lughod, The Arab Israeli Confrontation of June 1967: An Arab Perspective. Evanston, Ill.: Northwestern University Press, 1970.

Jackh, Ernest. "The Geostrategic Uniqueness of the Middle East," in Ernest Jackh, ed., Background of the Middle East. Ithaca, N.Y.: Cornell University Press, 1952.

Jensen, Merrill. A History of the United States During the Confederation, 1781-1789. New York: Knopf, 1958.

Jones, Joseph Marion. The Fifteen Weeks. New York: Harcourt, Brace and World, 1955.

Joynt, Carey B. "John Foster Dulles and the Suez Crisis," in Gerald N. Grob., ed., Statesmen and Statecraft of the Modern West. Barre, Vt.: Barre Publishers, 1967.

Kaplan, Lawrence S. Colonies into Nation: American Diplomacy, 1763-1801. New York: Macmillan Co., 1972.

Kerr, Malcolm H. The Arab Cold War, 1958-1964: A Study of Ideology in Politics. London: Oxford University Press, 1967.

_____. The Elusive Peace in the Middle East. Albany: State University of New York Press, 1975.

Khadduri, Majid. Republican Iraq. London: Oxford University Press, 1969.

Khouri, Fred J. The Arab-Israeli Dilemma. Syracuse, N.Y.: Syracuse University Press, 1968.

Klay, Andor. Daring Diplomacy: The Case of the First American Ultimatum. Minneapolis: University of Minnesota Press, 1957.

Kirk, George E. The Middle East in the War, 1939-1946. London: Oxford University Press, 1952.

_____ . The Middle East, 1945-50.   London: Oxford University
Press, 1954.

Kolko, Gabriel. The Politics of War: The World and United States
Foreign Policy, 1943-1945. New York: Random House, 1968.

Kolko, Joyce, and Gabriel. The Limits of Power: The World and
United States Foreign Policy, 1945-1954. New York: Harper, 1972.

Lacouture, Jean. Nasser: A Biography. New York: Knopf, 1973.

LaFeber, Walter. America, Russia, and the Cold War, 1945-1966.
New York: John Wiley, 1967.

Lall, Arthur. The UN and the Middle East Crisis, 1967.   New
York: Columbia University Press, 1967.

Laqueur, Walter. The Road to War: The Origin and Aftermath of
the Arab-Israeli Conflict, 1967-68. New York: Penguin, 1968.

_____ . Confrontation: The Middle East and World Politics.
New York: Quadrangle, 1974.

Larrabee, Stephen A. Hellas Observed: The American Experience
of Greece, 1775-1865. New York: New York University Press,
1957.

Lenczowski, George. Middle East in World Affairs. Ithaca, N.Y.:
Cornell University Press, 1956.

_____ . Oil & State in the Middle East. Ithaca, N.Y.: Cornell
University Press, 1960.

_____ . Russia and the West in Iran, 1918-1948. Ithaca, N.Y.:
Cornell University Press, 1949.

_____ . United States Interests in the Middle East. Washington:
American Enterprise Institute for Public Policy Research, 1968.

Lens, Sidney. The Forging of the American Empire from the Revolution to Vietnam: A History of American Imperialism. New York:
Thomas Y. Crowell, 1971.

Lewis, Bernard. The Middle East and the West. Bloomington: Indiana University Press, 1965.

Libby, Ruthven E. "Strategic Military Importance of the Middle
East," in Philip W. Thayer, ed., Tensions in the Middle East. Baltimore: Johns Hopkins Press, 1958.

Lilienthal, Alfred M. The Other Side of the Coin: An American
Perspective of the Arab-Israeli Conflict. New York: Devin-Adair
Co., 1965.

Lohbeck, Don. Patrick J. Hurley. Chicago: Henry Regnery Co.,
1956.

Longrigg, Stephen Hemsley. Oil in the Middle East: Its Discovery
and Development. London: Oxford University Press, 1968.

Love, Kennett. Suez: The Twice Fought War. New York: Mc-
Graw-Hill, 1969.

McDaniel, Robert A. The Shuster Mission and the Persian Constitutional Revolution. Minneapolis: Bibliotheca Islamica, 1974.

McKee, Irving. "Ben Hur" Wallace: The Life of General Lew Wallace. Berkeley: University of California Press, 1947.

McNeill, William Hardy. America, Britain, and Russia: Their Cooperation and Conflict, 1941-1946. New York: Johnson Reprint
Corporation, 1970.

Manuel, Frank E. The Realities of American-Palestine Relations.
Washington: Public Affairs Press, 1949.

Marlowe, John. Arab Nationalism and British Imperialism: A Study
in Power Politics. London: Cresset Press, 1961.

May, Ernest R. Imperial Democracy: The Emergence of America
as a Great Power. New York: Harcourt, Brace and World, 1961.

Meo, Leila. Lebanon, Improbable Nation: A Study in Political
Development. Bloomington: Indiana University Press, 1965.

Mikesell, Raymond F. and Hollis B. Chenery. Arabian Oil: America's Stake in the Middle East. Chapel Hill: University of North
Carolina Press, 1949.

Miller, Merle. Plain Speaking: An Oral Biography of Harry S.
Truman. New York: G. P. Putnam's Sons, 1974.

Mosley, Leonard. Power Play: Oil in the Middle East. New York:
Random House, 1973.

Motter, T. H. Vail. The Persian Corridor and Aid to Russia.
Washington: Government Printing Office, 1952.

Nash, Gerald D. United States Oil Policy, 1890-1964. Pittsburgh:
University of Pittsburgh Press, 1968.

Nevakivi, Jukka. Britain, France, and the Arab Middle East, 1914-
20. London: University of London, 1969.

Nichols, Roy F. Advance Agents of American Destiny. Philadelphia: University of Pennsylvania Press, 1956.

Nicolson, Harold. Curzon: The Last Phase, 1919-1925: A Study in Postwar Diplomacy. New York: Harcourt, Brace, 1939.

Nutting, Anthony. No End of a Lesson: The Story of Suez. New York: Potter Pub. Co., 1967.

Patai, Raphael. The Arab Mind. New York: Charles Scribner's, 1973.

Paullin, Charles Oscar. Diplomatic Negotiations of American Naval Officers, 1778-1883. Baltimore: Johns Hopkins Press, 1912.

Penrose, Stephen B. L., Jr. That They May Have Life: The Story of the American University of Beirut, 1866-1941. New York: Trustees of the American University of Beirut, 1941.

Peretz, Don, et al. A Palestine Entity? Washington: Middle East Institute, 1970.

Perkins, Dexter. A History of the Monroe Doctrine. Boston: Little, Brown, 1941.

Phillips, Clifton Jackson. Protestant America and the Pagan World: The First Half Century of the American Board of Commissioners for Foreign Missions, 1810-1860. Cambridge, Mass.: Harvard University Press, 1969.

Polk, William R. The United States and the Arab World. Cambridge, Mass.: Harvard University Press, 1965.

Porter, David. Constantinople and Its Environs, by an American. 2 vols. New York: Harper, 1835.

Porter, Kirk H., and Donald B. Johnson. National Party Platforms. Urbana: University of Illinois Press, 1956.

Quandt, William B. "Domestic Influences on United States Foreign Policy in the Middle East: The View from Washington," in Willard A. Beling, ed., The Middle East: Quest for an American Policy. Albany: State University of New York Press, 1973.

Ramazani, R. K. Iran's Foreign Policy, 1941-1973. Charlottesville: University of Virginia Press, 1975.

_____. The Persian Gulf: Iran's Role. Charlottesville: University of Virginia Press, 1972.

Reitzel, William. "The Importance of the Mediterranean," in Ernest Jackh, ed., Background in the Middle East. Ithaca, N.Y.: Cornell University Press, 1952.

_____. The Mediterranean: Its Role in America's Foreign Policy. New York: Harcourt-Brace, 1948.

Richardson, John Philip. "The American Military Mission to Armenia," master's thesis, George Washington University, 1964.

Robertson, Terence. Crisis: The Inside Story of the Suez Conspiracy. New York: Atheneum, 1965.

Ross, Frank A., et al. The Near East and American Philanthropy. New York: Columbia University Press, 1929.

Sachar, Howard M. The Emergence of the Middle East, 1914-1924. New York: Knopf, 1969.

_____. Europe Leaves the Middle East, 1936-1954. New York: Knopf, 1972.

Safran, Nadav. From War to War: The Arab-Israeli Confrontation, 1948-1967. New York: Pegasus, 1969.

_____. The United States and Israel. Cambridge, Mass.: Harvard University Press, 1963.

Sarton, George. The Incubation of Western Culture in the Middle East. Washington, 1951.

Sayegh, Kemal S. Oil and Regional Development. New York: Praeger, 1968.

Schuyler, Eugene. American Diplomacy and the Furtherance of Trade. New York: Scribner's, 1886.

Seaburg, Carl, and Stanley Paterson. Merchant Prince of Boston: Colonel T. H. Perkins, 1764-1854. Cambridge, Mass.: Harvard University Press, 1971.

Sheehan, M. K. Iran: Impact of United States Interests and Policies. Brooklyn, N.Y.: Theo. Gaus's Sons, 1968.

Shwadran, Benjamin. The Middle East, Oil, and the Great Powers. New York: Praeger, 1955.

Smelser, Marshall. The Congress Founds the Navy, 1787-1798. South Bend, Ind.: University of Notre Dame Press, 1959.

Smith, Gaddis. American Diplomacy During the Second World War, 1941-1945. New York: John Wiley and Sons, 1966.

_____. Dean Acheson. New York: Cooper Square, 1972.

Smith, Gary V., ed. Zionism: The Dream and the Reality. New York: Barnes and Noble, 1974.

Snetsinger, John. Truman, The Jewish Vote and the Creation of Israel. Stanford, Calif.: Hoover Institution Press, 1974.

Sousa, Nasim. The Capitulatory Regime of Turkey: Its History,
Origins, and Nature. Baltimore: Johns Hopkins Press, 1933.

Speiser, Ephraim. The United States and the Near East. Cambridge, Mass.: Harvard University Press, 1952.

Spielman, William C. The United States in the Middle East: A
Study of American Foreign Policy. New York: Pageant Press,
1959.

Stein, Leonard. The Balfour Declaration. New York: Simon and
Schuster, 1961.

Stevens, Georgianne G. The United States and the Middle East.
Englewood Cliffs, N.J.: Prentice Hall, 1964.

Stevens, Richard P. American Zionism and United States Foreign
Policy. New York: Pageant Press, 1962.

Stocking, George W. Middle East Oil: A Study in Political and
Economic Controversy. Nashville, Tenn.: Vanderbilt University
Press, 1970.

Strausz-Hupé, Robert. "The United States and the Middle East," in
Philip W. Thayer, ed., Tensions in the Middle East. Baltimore:
Johns Hopkins Press, 1958.

Suleiman, Michael W. "America Mass Media and the June Conflict,"
in Ibrahim Abu-Lughod, The Arab-Israeli Confrontation of June 1967:
An Arab Perspective. Evanston, Ill.: Northwestern University
Press, 1970.

Swomley, John M. American Empire: The Political Ethics of
Twentieth Century Conquest. New York: Macmillan, 1970.

Sykes, Christopher. Crossroads to Israel, 1917-1948. Bloomington: Indiana University Press, 1973.

Taylor, Alan, and Richard N. Tetlie, eds. Palestine: A Search for
Truth: Approaches to the Arab-Israeli Conflict. Washington: Public Affairs Press, 1970.

Thayer, Charles W. Diplomat. New York: Harper, 1959.

Thomas, Hugh. Suez. New York: Harper, 1966.

Thomas, Lewis V., and Richard N. Frye. The United States and
Turkey and Iran. Cambridge, Mass.: Harvard University Press,
1951.

Tibawi, A. L. American Interests in Syria, 1800-1901: A Study of
Educational, Literary and Religious Work. New York: Oxford University Press, 1966.

Tillman, Seth. Anglo-American Relations at the Paris Peace Conference of 1919. Princeton, N.J.: Princeton University Press, 1961.

Torrey, Gordon H. Syrian Politics and the Military, 1945-1958. Columbus: Ohio State University Press, 1964.

Trask, Roger. United States Response to Turkish Nationalism and Reform, 1914-1939. Minneapolis: University of Minnesota Press, 1971.

Tully, Andrew. CIA, The Inside Story. (New York: Morrow, 1962).

Turnbull, Archibald D. Commodore David Porter. New York: Century, 1929.

Twitchell, K. S. Saudi Arabia: With an Account of the Development of Its Natural Resources. Princeton, N.J.: Princeton University Press, 1958.

Ulam, Adam B. Expansion and Coexistence: The History of Soviet Policy, 1917-1967. New York: Praeger, 1968.

Utley, Freda. Will the Middle East Go West? Chicago: Regnery, 1957.

Varg, Paul. Open Door Diplomat: The Life of W. W. Rockhill. Urbana: University of Illinois Press, 1952.

Vatikiotis, P. J. Conflict in the Middle East. London: George Allen Unwin, 1971.

Walt, Joseph W., "Saudi Arabia and the Americans, 1928-1951," unpublished Ph.D. dissertation, Northwestern University, 1960.

Weisband, Edward. Turkish Foreign Policy, 1943-1945: Small State Diplomacy and Great Power Politics. Princeton, N.J.: Princeton University Press, 1973.

Welles, Sumner. We Need Not Fail. Boston: Houghton Mifflin Co., 1948.

_____. Where Are We Heading? New York: Harper, 1946.

Westerman, William Linn. "The Armenian Problem and the Disruption of Turkey," in Edward Mandell House and Charles Seymour, eds., What Really Happened at Paris: The Story of the Peace Conference, 1918-19. New York: Scribner's, 1921.

Whetten, Lawrence L. The Canal War: Four-Power Conflict in the Middle East. Cambridge, Mass.: MIT Press, 1974.

Wilmington, Martin W. The Middle East Supply Centre. Albany:
State University of New York Press, 1971.

Wint, Guy, and Peter Calvocoressi. Middle East Crisis. Harmondsworth, England: Penguin, 1957.

Wise, David, and Thomas B. Ross. The Invisible Government.
New York: Random House, 1964.

Wright, L. B., and J. H. McLeod, The First Americans in North
Africa. Princeton, N.J.: Princeton University Press, 1945.

Wright, L. C. United States Policy Toward Egypt, 1830-1914.
New York: Exposition-University Press, 1969.

Wynn, Wilton. Nasser of Egypt: The Search for Dignity. Cambridge, Mass.: Harvard University Press, 1959.

Xydis, Stephen. Greece and the Great Powers, 1944-1947: Prelude
to the Truman Doctrine. Thessaloniki, Greece: Institute for Balkan
Studies, 1963.

Yale, William. The Near East: A Modern History. Ann Arbor:
University of Michigan Press, 1958.

Yeselson, Abraham. United States-Persian Diplomatic Relations,
1883-1921. New Brunswick, N.J.: Rutgers University Press, 1950.

Zinn, Howard, Postwar America, 1945-1971. New York: Bobbs-
Merrill, 1973.

SECONDARY SOURCES--ARTICLES

Adler, Selig, "The Palestine Question in the Wilson Era," Journal
of Jewish Social Studies, X (1948), 303-334.

Akins, James E. "The Oil Crisis: This Time the Wolf Is Here,"
Foreign Affairs, 51 (April 1973), 462-490.

Amuzegar, Jahanigir. "The Oil Story: Facts, Fiction, and Fair
Play," Foreign Affairs, 51 (July 1973), 676-689.

Askew, William C., and J. Fred Rippy. "The United States and
Europe's Strife, 1908-1913," Journal of Politics, 4 (1942), 68-79.

Badeau, John S. "U.S.A. and U.A.R.: A Crisis in Confidence,"
Foreign Affairs, 43 (Jan. 1965), 281-296.

Batal, James. "Truman Chapters on the Middle East," Middle East
Forum, XXXI (Dec. 1956), 11-13 et seq.

Bickerton, Ian J. "President Truman's Recognition of Israel," American Jewish Historical Quarterly, LVIII (Dec. 1968), 173-239.

Brown, Philip Marshall. "The Mandate over Armenia," American Journal of International Law, XIV (1920), 396-97.

Bryson, Thomas A. "Admiral Mark Lambert Bristol: An Open Door Diplomat in Turkey," International Journal of Middle East Studies, 5 (1974), 450-467.

_____. "An American Mandate for Armenia: A Link in British Near Eastern Policy," Armenian Review, XXI (Summer, 1968), 24-41.

_____. "The Armenia-America Society: A Factor in American-Turkish Relations, 1919-1924," Records of the American Catholic Historical Society, 82 (June 1971), 83-105.

_____. "John Sharp Williams: An Advocate for the Armenian Mandate, 1919-1920," Armenian Review, XXVI (autumn, 1973), 23-42.

_____. "Mark Lambert Bristol, U.S. Navy, Admiral-Diplomat: His Influence on the Armenian Mandate Question," Armenian Review, XXI (winter, 1968), 3-22.

_____. "A Note on Near East Relief: Walter George Smith, Cardinal Gibbons and the Question of Discrimination Against Catholics," Muslim World, LXI (1971), 202-209.

_____. "Walter George Smith and the Armenian Question at the Paris Peace Conference, 1919," Records of the American Catholic Historical Society, LXXXI (Mar. 1970), 3-26)

_____. "Walter George Smith and the International Philarmenian League," in Robert Thompson, ed., Recent Studies in Modern Armenian History, Boston: Armenian Heritage Press, 1973.

_____. "William Brown Hodgson's Mission to Egypt, 1834," West Georgia College Studies in the Social Sciences, XI (June 1972), 10-17.

_____. "Woodrow Wilson and the Armenian Mandate: A Reassessment," Armenian Review, XXI (autumn, 1968), 10-28.

Buzanski, Peter M. "The Interallied Investigation of the Greek Invasion of Smyrna, 1919," Historian, XXV (May 1963), 325-43.

Campbell, John C. "The Arab-Israeli Conflict: An American Policy," Foreign Affairs, 49 (Oct. 1970), 51-69.

Cantor, Milton. "Joel Barlow's Mission to Algiers," Historian, XXV (1963), 172-194.

Cottam, Richard W.   "The United States, Iran and the Cold War,"
Iranian Studies, III (winter 1970), 2-22.

Cox, Frederick J.   "American Naval Mission in Egypt," Journal of
Modern History, XXVI (June 1954), 173-178.

Daniel, Robert L.   "The Armenian Question and American-Turkish
Relations, 1914-1927," Mississippi Valley Historical Review, XLVI
(Sept. 1959), 252-275.

_____. "The Friendship of Woodrow Wilson and Cleveland
Dodge," Mid-America, 43 (July 1961), 182-196.

_____. "The United States and the Turkish Republic before
World War II: The Cultural Dimension," Middle East Journal, 21
(winter 1967), 52-63.

Davis, Harold E.   "The Citizenship of Jon Perdicaris," Journal of
Modern History, XIII (1941), 517-526.

DeNovo, John A.   "American Relations with the Middle East: Some
Unfinished Business," in George L. Anderson, Issues and Conflicts,
Lawrence: University of Kansas Press, 1959.

_____. "The Movement for an Aggressive American Oil Policy,
1918-1920," American Historical Review, 61 (July 1956), 854-876.

_____. "Petroleum and the United States Navy before World War
I," Mississippi Valley Historical Review, 41 (March 1955), 641-656.

_____. "A Railroad for Turkey: The Chester Project of 1908-
1913," Business Historical Review, 33 (autumn 1959), 300-329.

_____. "Researching American Relations with the Middle East:
The State of the Art, 1970," 243-264, in Milton O. Gustafson, ed.
The National Archives and Foreign Relations Research (Athens:
Ohio University, 1974).

Doenecke, Justus.   "Iran's Role in Cold War Revisionism," Iranian Studies, V (spring 1972), 96-111.

_____. Revisionists, Oil and Cold War Diplomacy," Iranian
Studies, III (winter 1970), 23-33.

Dougherty, J. E.   "The Aswan Decision in Perspective," Political
Science Quarterly, LXXXIV (1959), 21-45.

Downs, Jacques M.   "American Merchants and the China Opium
Trade," Business History Review, 42 (winter 1968), 418-442.

Earle, Edward Mead.   "American Interest in the Greek Cause, 1821-
27," American Historical Review, XXXIII (Oct. 1927), 44-63.

_____. "American Missions in the Near East," Foreign Affairs, VII (April 1929), 398-417.

_____. "Early American Policy Concerning Ottoman Minorities," Political Science Quarterly, XLII (Sept. 1927), 337-67.

_____. "Egyptian Cotton and the American Civil War," Political Science Quarterly, 41 (1926), 520-545.

_____. "The Turkish Petroleum Company--A Study in Oleaginous Diplomacy," Political Science Quarterly, 39 (1924), 265-277.

Efimenco, N. Marbury. "American Impact Upon Middle East Leadership," Political Science Quarterly, 69 (1954), 202-218.

Field, James A., Jr. "A Scheme in Regard to Cyrenaica," Mississippi Valley Historical Review, 44 (June 1957), 445-68.

Fitzsimons, M. A. "The Suez Crisis and the Containment Policy," Review of Politics, XIX (Oct. 1957), 419-445.

Gardiner, Arthur Z. "Point Four and the Arab World," Middle East Journal, 4 (1950), 296-306.

Ghareeb, Edmund. "The U.S. Arms Supply to Israel During the October War," Journal of Palestine Studies, III (winter 1974), 114-121.

Gidney, James B. "The Middle East: The Last Crusade," West Georgia College Studies in the Social Sciences, IX (June 1970), 16-29.

Grabill, Joseph L. "Missionary Influence on American Relations with the Near East, 1914-1923," Muslim World, LVIII (1968), Part 1, 43-56, and Part 2, 141-54.

Hakim, George. "Point Four and the Middle East," Middle East Journal, 4 (1950), 183-195.

Holden, David. "The Persian Gulf: After the British Raj," Foreign Affairs, 49 (July 1971), 721-735.

Hoskins, Halford L. "Some Aspects of the Security Problem in the Middle East," American Political Science Review, 47 (1953), 188-98.

Hottinger, Arnold. "The Depth of Arab Radicalism" Foreign Affairs, 51 (April 1973), 461-504.

Hourani, Albert. "The Decline of the West in the Middle East," International Affairs, XXIX (Jan. 1953), 22-42 and April 1953), 156-183.

Howard, Harry N. "An American Experiment in Peacemaking: The
King-Crane Commission," Muslim World, XXXII (April 1942), 122-
46.

_____ . "Continuing Trouble in the Turkish Republic," Current
History, 64 (Jan. 1973), 26-29.

_____ . "Jordan in Turmoil," Current History, 63 (Jan. 1972),
14-19.

_____ . "The United States and the Problem of the Turkish
Straits: A Reference Article," Middle East Journal, 1 (Jan. 1947),
59-72.

_____ . "The United States and the Soviet Union in the Middle
East," in Ernest Jackh, Background in the Middle East. Ithaca,
N.Y.: Cornell University Press, 1952.

Huang, T. F. T. "Some International and Legal Aspects of the Suez
Canal Question," American Journal of International Law, LI (1957),
277-307.

Kanet, Roger E. "Soviet-American Relations: A Year of Detente?"
Current History, 63 (Oct. 1972), 156-159.

Khadduri, Majid. "The Problem of Regional Security in the Middle
East: An Appraisal," Middle East Journal, XI (winter 1957), 12-22.

Latourette, Kenneth Scott. "Colonialism and Missions: Progressive
Separation," Journal of Church and State, 7 (autumn 1965), 330-349.

Lebow, Richard Ned. "Woodrow Wilson and the Balfour Declaration," Journal of Modern History, 40 (Dec. 1968), 500-523.

Lenczowski, George. "Arab Radicalism: Problems and Prospects,"
Current History, 60 (Jan. 1971), 32-37.

_____ . "Egypt and the Soviet Exodus," Current History, 64 (Jan.
1973), 13-16.

_____ . "Iraq: Seven Years of Revolution," Current History, 48
(May 1965), 281-289.

_____ . "Tradition and Reform in Saudi Arabia," Current History,
52 (Feb. 1967), 98-104.

Levy, Walter J. "Oil Power," Foreign Affairs, 49 (July 1971),
652-668.

_____ . "World Oil Cooperation or International Chaos," Foreign
Affairs, 52 (July 1974), 690-713.

Lewis, Bernard. "The Great Powers, the Arabs and the Israelis,"

Foreign Affairs, 47 (July 1969), 642-652.

Lewis, Tom T. "Franco-American Relations During the First Moroccan Crisis," *Mid-America,* LV (Jan. 1973), 21-36.

Mallison, W. T., Jr. "The Legal Problems Concerning the Juridical Status and Political Activities of the Zionist Organization/Jewish Agency: A Study in International and United States Law," *William and Mary Law Review,* 9 (spring 1968), 556-629.

_____. "The Zionist-Israel Juridicial Claims to Constitute 'the Jewish People' Nationality Entity and to Confer Membership in It: Appraisal in Public International Law," *George Washington Law Review,* 32 (June 1964), 983-1075.

Morison, S. E. "Forcing the Dardanelles in 1810: With Some Account of the Early Levant Trade of Massachusetts," *New England Quarterly,* I (1928), 208-225.

Nichols, Roy L. "Diplomacy in Barbary," *Pennsylvania Magazine of History and Biography,* LXXIV (Jan. 1950), 113-141.

Nolte, Richard H. "Year of Decision in the Middle East," *Yale Review,* XLVI (winter 1957), 228-244.

Parzen, Herbert. "Brandeis and the Balfour Declaration," *Herzl Yearbook,* V (1963), 309-50.

Plesur, Milton. "The Relations Between the United States and Palestine," *Judaism: A Quarterly Journal of Jewish Life,* III (1954), 469-479.

Polk, William R. "The Nature of Modernization: The Middle East and North Africa," *Foreign Affairs,* 44 (Oct. 1965), 100-110.

Quandt, William B., "United States Policy in the Middle East: Constraints and Choices," in Paul Y. Hammond and Sidney S. Alexander, eds., *Political Dynamics in the Middle East* (New York: American Elsevier Pub. Co., 1972).

Reich, Bernard. "Israel's Quest for Security," *Current History,* 62 (Jan. 1972), 1-5.

_____. "United States Policy in the Middle East," *Current History,* 60 (Jan. 1971), 1-6.

Roosevelt, Kermit. "The Partition of Palestine: A Lesson in Pressure Politics," *Middle East Journal,* II (Jan. 1948), 1-16.

Rubinstein, Albin Z. "The Soviet Union in the Middle East," *Current History,* 63 (Oct. 1972), 165-169.

Rustow, Dankwart A. "Defense of the Near East," *Foreign Affairs,*

XXXIV (Jan. 1956), 271-286.

Sadat, Anwar. "Where Egypt Stands," Foreign Affairs, 51 (Oct. 1972), 114-123.

Safran, Nadav. "The War and the Future of the Arab-Israeli Conflict," Foreign Affairs, 52 (Jan. 1974), 215-236.

Schulz, Ann T. "A Leadership Role for Iran in the Persian Gulf," Current History, 64 (Jan. 1972), 25-30.

Serpell, David R. "American Consular Activities in Egypt, 1849-63," Journal of Modern History, X (Sept. 1939), 344-363.

Simpson, Dwight J. "Israel After Twenty-five Years," Current History, 64 (Jan. 1973), 1-8.

Smolansky, O. M. "Moscow and the Suez Crisis, 1956: A Reappraisal," Political Science Quarterly, 80 (1965), 581-605.

_____. "The Soviet Setback in the Middle East," Current History, 64 (Jan. 1973), 17-20.

Spain, James W. "Middle East Defense: A New Approach," Middle East Journal, VIII (Summer 1954), 251-266.

Stevens, Georgianna G. "Arab Neutralism and Bandung," Middle East Journal, 11 (1957), 139-152.

Tashjian, James H. "The American Military Mission to Armenia," Armenian Review, 1949-1952, Issues 5-17.

Thoman, Roy E. "Iraq and the Persian Gulf Region," Current History, 64 (Jan. 1973), 21-38.

Trask, Roger R. "The Terrible Turk and Turkish-American Relations in the Interwar Period," Historian, XXXIII (Nov. 1970), 40-53.

_____. "Turco-American Reapprochement, 1927-32," in Sidney D. Brown, ed., Studies on Asia (Lincoln: University of Nebraska Press, 1967).

_____. "Unnamed Christianity in Turkey during the Ataturk Era," Moslem World, I, 55 (1965), 66-76; II, 55 (1965), 101-111.

_____. "The United States and Turkish Nationalism: Investments and Technical Aid During the Ataturk Era," Business History Review, 38 (spring 1964), 58-77.

Wilmington, Martin W. "The Middle East Supply Center," Middle East Journal, 6 (1952), 144-166.

Wilson, Evan M. "The Palestine Papers, 1943-1947," Journal of

Palestine Studies, II (summer 1973), 33-54.

Wright, Quincy. "Intervention, 1956," American Journal of International Law, LI (1957), 257-276.

_____. "United States Intervention in Lebanon," American Journal of International Law, LIII (1959), 112-125.

Yale, William. "Ambassador Henry Morgenthau's Special Mission of 1917," World Politics, I (1949), 308-320.

Yost, Charles W. "The Arab-Israeli War, 1967: How It Began," Foreign Affairs, 46 (Jan. 1968), 30.

430   Index